*An Account
of Denmark*

Robert Molesworth

THE THOMAS HOLLIS LIBRARY

David Womersley, General Editor

An Account of Denmark

With *Francogallia* and *Some Considerations for the Promoting of Agriculture and Employing the Poor*

Robert Molesworth

Edited and with an Introduction
by Justin Champion

LIBERTY FUND

Indianapolis

This book is published by Liberty Fund, Inc., a foundation established to encourage study of the ideal of a society of free and responsible individuals.

𒂼𒄄

The cuneiform inscription that serves as our logo and as the design motif for our endpapers is the earliest-known written appearance of the word "freedom" (*amagi*), or "liberty." It is taken from a clay document written about 2300 B.C. in the Sumerian city-state of Lagash.

Frontispiece: The Right Honourable Robert Lord Viscount Molesworth. Mezzotint after Thomas Gibson; print made by Peter Pelham, 1721. © The Trustees of the British Museum. Reproduced by permission.

Printed in the United States of America.

c 10 9 8 7 6 5 4 3 2 1
p 10 9 8 7 6 5 4 3 2 1

Library of Congress Cataloging-in-Publication Data
Molesworth, Robert Molesworth, Viscount, 1656–1725.
[Account of Denmark]
An account of Denmark: with Francogallia and Some considerations for the promoting of agriculture and employing the poor/ Robert Molesworth; edited and with an introduction by Justin Champion.
p. cm.—(The Thomas Hollis library)
First work originally published in London in 1694; 2nd work originally published under title: Franco-Gallia, or, An account of the ancient free state of France, and most other parts of Europe, before the loss of their liberties / written originally in Latin by Francis Hotoman, in 1574, and translated by Robert Molesworth in 1711; 3rd work originally published in Dublin, 1723.
Includes bibliographical references and index.
ISBN 978-0-86597-803-4 (hc: alk. paper)—ISBN 978-0-86597-804-1 (pbk.: alk. paper)
1. Denmark—Politics and government—Early works to 1800. 2. Denmark—History—Christian V, 1670–1699. 3. France—Politics and government—Early works to 1800. 4. Constitutional history—France—Early works to 1800. 5. Agriculture—Ireland—Early works to 1800. 6. Poor—Ireland—Early works to 1800. 7. Representative government and representation—Early works to 1800. I. Champion, Justin. II. Hotman, François, 1524–1590. Franco-Gallia. English. III. Molesworth, Robert Molesworth, Viscount, 1656–1725. Some considerations for the promoting of agriculture and employing the poor. IV. Title.
DL195.3.M65 2011
948.9′03—dc22   2010037546

LIBERTY FUND, INC.
8335 Allison Pointe Trail, Suite 300
Indianapolis, Indiana 46250-1684

CONTENTS

THE THOMAS HOLLIS LIBRARY

Thomas Hollis (1720–74) was an eighteenth-century Englishman who devoted his energies, his fortune, and his life to the cause of liberty. Hollis was trained for a business career, but a series of inheritances allowed him to pursue instead a career of public service. He believed that citizenship demanded activity and that it was incumbent on citizens to put themselves in a position, by reflection and reading, in which they could hold their governments to account. To that end for many years he distributed books that he believed explained the nature of liberty and revealed how liberty might best be defended and promoted.

A particular beneficiary of Hollis's generosity was Harvard College. In the years preceding the Declaration of Independence, Hollis was assiduous in sending over to America boxes of books, many of which he had had specially printed and bound, to encourage the colonists in their struggle against Great Britain. At the same time, he took pains to explain the colonists' grievances and concerns to his fellow Englishmen.

The Thomas Hollis Library makes freshly available a selection of titles that, because of their intellectual power, or the influence they exerted on the public life of their own time, or the distinctiveness of their approach to the topic of liberty, constitute the cream of the books distributed by Hollis. Many of these works have been either out of print since the eighteenth century or available only in very expensive and scarce editions. The highest standards of scholarship and production ensure that these classic texts can be as salutary and influential today as they were two hundred and fifty years ago.

David Womersley

INTRODUCTION

Robert Molesworth and Gothic Liberty

Robert Molesworth (1656–1725) famously diagnosed the causes of a disordered commonwealth in the much reprinted and translated *An Account of Denmark* (1694).[1] His works connected the three ages of revolution between 1649 and 1776.[2] According to his insights, manners and customs were shaped by the experience of the institutions and laws of a nation: liberty was cultivated by the land. Through his writing, his parliamentary career, and his stewardship of his own country estates in England and Ireland, Molesworth embodied republican ideals of the industrious and independent gentleman, stalwart in defense of public liberty, hostile to tyranny, yet dynamic in nurturing improvement.

A consistent defender of "civil rights," Molesworth conceived his political career as defending the continuing liberty first manifest in the "ancient free state." He hoped "that my friends, relations and children, with their posterity, will inherit their share of this inestimable blessing, and that I have contributed my part to it."[3] A defense of this vision was the

1. See the list of editions detailed in Bibliographical Descriptions, pp. xliii–xlviii.
2. See the arguments of J. G. A. Pocock (ed.), *Three British Revolutions: 1641, 1688, 1776* (Princeton: Princeton University Press, 1980).
3. Molesworth, "Preface to the Reader," *Francogallia* (1711), p. 173.

consistent pattern of his post-1689 life. The edition of the radical Calvinist writer François Hotman's *Francogallia* (1574) executed in 1705, first published in 1711 and republished in 1721, is testimony to this durability of political commitment and indeed to Molesworth's political imagination in reconfiguring Hotman for an eighteenth-century readership.

John Cannon has dismissed Molesworth's legacy as one of "bookish radicals with antiquarian tastes" whose "scale of operations was small, their impact on important politicians slight, and their influence on the public at large negligible."[4] This volume aims to provide evidence to the contrary.

Unlike many modern historians, Molesworth perceived no discontinuity between the commonwealth ideologies of the 1640s and the 1700s: the core principle of this ideology was that "the Good of the Whole is taken care of by the Whole."[5] Importantly, this made the question of whether a monarchy existed constitutionally irrelevant; as he put it, "the having a King or Queen at the Head of it, alters not the Case."[6] Such a political community, committed to universal liberty, and independent of religious confession, would encourage each to use their "Body, Estate, and Understanding, for the publick Good."[7] The end of such a community was to provide the grounding for improvement so that each could "securely and peaceably enjoy Property and Liberty both of Mind and Body."[8] By such provision both individuals and the entire community benefited: as he clarified, "the thriving of any one single Person by honest Means, is the thriving of the Commonwealth wherein he resides."[9] Molesworth's conception of the purpose of political society was to enable a flourishing and industrious civic life.

Molesworth's political reputation as "the patriot brave and sage" was shaped by the reception and afterlife of his first and most infamous work, *An account of Denmark as it was in the year 1692* (1694), a republi-

---

4. J. Cannon, *Parliamentary Reform 1640–1832* (Cambridge: Cambridge University Press, 1973), p. 45.
5. Molesworth, "Translator's Preface," *Francogallia* (1721), p. 175.
6. Ibid., p. 175.
7. Ibid., p. 179.
8. Ibid.
9. Ibid.

can counterblast to modern tyranny.[10] Combined with his defense of the Glorious Revolution of 1689, his translation of François Hotman's *Francogallia* (1574), and the evidence of a parliamentary career (in England and Ireland) that spanned three decades, Molesworth has been recognized as the last of the "Real Whigs." Understood through the historiographical prism of Caroline Robbins's *The Eighteenth-Century Commonwealthman*, Molesworth and his friends exercised a powerful influence over the "Republican fringe" of eighteenth-century Whiggism. It is worth citing her conclusions at length:

> The Whiggish malcontents or Commonwealthmen in varying ways provided a deterrent to complacency, and reminders of the need for improvement and the continual adaptation of even good governments to economic and political changes. . . . In an age when Englishmen stressed the sovereignty, not of a divinely appointed king but of a triumphant parliament, the Real Whigs reminded them of the rights of electors and of the unenfranchised, of the virtues of rotation in office and of the necessity of constant vigilance against the corruptions of power whether wielded by king, ministers or estates. Molesworth and his friends admonished their countrymen about present dangers. They called attention to the lessons of history and the possibilities of the future.[11]

This account of the powerful and persisting legacy of Molesworth's republican critique of monarchy and public power is worth reassessing in the light of more contemporary historical writing, which characterizes the eighteenth century as an age of ancien régime institutions and cultural values.

The rallying call of what Thomas Hollis admiringly referred to as Molesworth's "golden prefaces" continued, decades later, to exercise an enchanting authority over oppositional ideologies, most notably mobiliz-

---

10. See the black-framed commemoration, M.B., *An elegy on the universally lamented death of the Right honourable Robert Lord Vis. Molesworth* (1725); see also M. Browne, *The throne of justice; a pindaric ode; humbly dedicated to the Right Honorable the Lord Viscount Molesworth* (London, 1721).

11. Caroline Robbins, *The Eighteenth-Century Commonwealthman* (Cambridge, Mass.: Harvard University Press, 1959), p. 133.

ing support around John Wilkes in the 1760s and those defending colonial independence in the 1770s.[12] The longer works, which presented a neo-Tacitean account of the mechanics of modern tyranny, meshed with the writings of Trenchard and Gordon to provide a standard source for the analysis of political corruption. Unlike Locke, Molesworth provided insight into processes of corruption rather than simply a set of prescriptive juristic values. In the *Account of Denmark* especially, Molesworth established how tyranny worked, identifying the contaminating ideologies and institutions. *De jure divino* claims to authority—the "designs of priestcraft"—especially from the Church, lay at the root of all perfidy.[13]

Molesworth's works, reprinted throughout the eighteenth century, were read in the British Islands, continental Europe, and North America—where Benjamin Franklin, Thomas Jefferson, John Adams, James Madison, and James Logan all owned copies. The *Elegy* printed upon his death celebrated Molesworth's deeds, not just as a defender of the Revolution but as "the labourers friend." Just as his political and diplomatic acts saved the kingdom from "a proud oppressing slave," so his improving economics "found work for one hundred-thousand hands."[14]

The Life

For Molesworth, associated as he was with many of the leading political figures of the period, his political career promised more than it achieved. Concerned with principle as much as place, Molesworth was never cautious about advancing either his own opinions or abilities, or (later) those of his sons, to the ministers and even kings of the day.

Outspoken against political and religious corruption, Molesworth was rewarded with a measure of recognition after 1714 by the Hanoverian regime, only (as he saw it) to be thrust into opposition by corrupt men after the debacle of the South Sea Bubble. It is a measure of his charisma

12. The phrase is used in annotations by Hollis on the initial blank page of Mary Monck's *Marinda: Poems and Translations upon several occasions* (1716) [Harvard call mark *EC75.H.7267.Zz716m].

13. Robbins, *Eighteenth-Century Commonwealthman*, p. 95.

14. M.B., *Elegy on the universally lamented*.

and vitality of commitment that as a man in his late sixties he was considered by others, and indeed considered himself, a suitable candidate for contesting the parliamentary seat of Westminster in 1722.

Molesworth was not a lone commonwealthman but gathered a circle of like-minded men into his milieu. The most notorious of these was John Toland, with whom he had been acquainted since the early 1700s.[15] Like many of his relationships, this connection, although driven primarily by political ambition, also had literary dimensions. While Molesworth hoped to persuade his friend to collaborate on a "history of the late wars," Toland had certainy seen a now lost work of Molesworth's resembling "so nearly Cicero's *de respublica*."[16]

Molesworth moved freely in circles of political influence and sociability in Dublin, London, and Yorkshire. His surviving correspondence with men like Shaftesbury, Godolphin, and William King allows a detailed reconstruction of this political life. Molesworth's correspondence also gives an intimate and at times touching account of his family life and political connections.[17] His involvement with diplomatic and political circles is manifest, while his continual disappointment at the conduct of leading ministers, the missed opportunities for personal advancement, and the cost of promoting himself and his sons are persistent themes. At times all these themes merged, as he noted in November 1695: "My election, if I carry it, will cost me sauce, so that we must endeavour to make it up by good husbandry."[18]

Insight into his self-esteem and political commitments is unparalleled. As he wrote to Mrs. Molesworth in September 1712, he managed to combine a reflection on the death of his friend Godolphin with remarks about his own continual disappointment not to be called to great office: "My dear Lord Godolphin is dead! The greatest man in the whole world for honesty, capacity, courage, friendship, generosity, is gone: my best friend

15. The manuscript letters are in British Library Additional Mss 4465, Collection of Letters and Papers of John Toland, folios 19, 21, 23, 27, 29, 36, 37.

16. J. Toland, *Collections* (1726), vol. 2, pp. 461, 487, 491.

17. Historical Manuscripts Commission, *Report on Manuscripts in Various Collections*, vol. 8 (Hereford, 1913) [hereafter *HMC*], p. 319.

18. *HMC*, p. 217.

is gone! As if my friendship were fatal to all that ever take it up for me. So now there is another great article to be added to the misfortunes of my family this year, which indeed are insupportable. This great patriot could not survive the liberties of his country, whilst I like a wretch, am like to live a slave, and have reared up children to no better an end."[19]

His letters deliver (among many other topics of the day) commentaries on the Peace of 1711, the South Sea Bubble, the conduct of the High Church faction in Convocation, and, interestingly, drafts of his position in regard to the issue of Irish independency in 1719.[20] Molesworth's persistent parliamentary defense of liberty and the Hanoverian succession was associated with a formal political thought premised on the vindication of liberty and a profoundly anticlerical commitment to religious toleration. It shows that Molesworth was a man driven not just by political commitments and opportunities for agricultural improvement but also by the life of the mind. Although his collaborative reading with Toland is evidence enough of this, his archive also contains glimpses of a broader intellectual culture that saw Molesworth at the center of a community involved in the circulation of scribal works.[21]

After Toland's death, when Molesworth withdrew from the mainstream of national politics, he became the focus of another circle of younger thinkers and writers. Unfortunately, no records of Molesworth's library or book purchases survive, but there is some evidence to suggest that Molesworth encouraged reading and learning in his own household. His daughter Lettice noted that her child "Little Missy" was learning to spell as a precondition for reading: "I take all possible care of her eyes and hold her books as you desired."[22]

That Molesworth had encouraged his daughters as well as sons into commerce with books and learning is clear from the life and work of his daughter Mary Monck (1677–1715), whose poems were posthumously published in 1716 and edited by her father. *Marinda: Poems and transla-*

19. Ibid., p. 259.
20. Ibid., pp. 252, 283–84, 287, 312.
21. Ibid., pp. 258–59.
22. Ibid., p. 272, October 1717, Lettice Molesworth to her mother, Lady Molesworth.

tions upon several occasions [by Mary Monck] was published in London by Jacob Tonson. The work was dedicated to Caroline, Princess of Wales, and included a long preface written by Molesworth underscoring his commitment to the education of women. This in itself is a significant elaboration of the position developed by Toland in his *Letters to Serena* (1704), dedicated to the Queen of Prussia. Molesworth made this connection explicit when he applauded Caroline's "frequent and intimate conversation with that incomparable princess, the late Electress Sophia, and your indefatigable Reading the best books in all the modern languages."[23]

Molesworth presented his deceased daughter's work to the new court as a product worthy of public emulation for its liberty, honor, and virtue. Mary's poems were the result of her reading in a "good library." Spending her leisure hours reading, this gentlewoman had acquired several languages and "the good morals and principles contain'd in those books, so as to put them in practice." Some of Mary's work was already in scribal circulation through the agency of the young Lady Mary Wortley Montagu, but this impressive volume (with parallel pages of the original text and an English translation) broadcast her learning to a wider audience, and, most important, was framed within the political languages of liberty and what Molesworth called "the Good Old English Customs."

The importance of good reading and a virtuous education in the principles of liberty and true religion (rather than bigotry and superstition) underlay much of Molesworth's political commitment to the reform of the universities after 1716. This commitment took an even more academic turn in late 1722, when Molesworth became involved in the affairs of the University of Glasgow, where he had been appointed Rector by popular assent of a clique of radical students. One correspondent, William Wishart, writing in October 1713, applauded Molesworth for his role in "the dawnings of a revival of ancient virtue and the love of true liberty."[24] Holding up the model of Molesworth's preface to the *Account of Denmark*, which distinguished the educational principles of philosophy and priestcraft, Wishart bewailed the fact that "the abettors of savage zeal, fierce

23. M. Monck, *Marinda: Poems and translations upon several occasions* (1716), pp. 10–11.

24. *HMC*, p. 347.

bigotry and dire superstition have the advantages of those corrupt passions and inveterate prejudices of men's minds to favour their designs."[25]

The anticlericalism of this correspondence was profound: in a later letter George Turnbull condemned the "proud domineering pedantic priests, whose interest it is to train up the youth in a profound veneration to their sensible metaphysical creeds and catechisms."[26] Such tuition was not only bewildering but was also "admirably fitted . . . indeed to enslave young understandings and to beget an early antipathy against all free thought."[27] Both Wishart and James Arbuckle acknowledged that they had read Molesworth's work on Denmark and "Cato's letters," but they also made inquiry about suitable further reading.[28]

Molesworth not only recommended books but even sent copies of his own works. As George Turnbull wrote, "There is nothing I would be prouder of than to have your works in my library *ex dono* the worthy author."[29] Molesworth offered detailed directions toward further reading. William Wishart in passing his thanks to the older man explained what he had done with his "excellent instructions." He started by reading Buchanan's *De jure regni apud Scotos,* which gave him excellent notions "of the nature and design of government and the just boundaries of it," describing the beautiful lineaments of a good king and the ghastly picture of a tyrant. This was followed by reading Machiavelli on Livy, "by which I have received a great deal of light into the true principles of politics." The final books recommended by Molesworth were Harrington's works (edited by Toland, of course) and Confucius's morals, which the student had only "dipped into."[30]

Led by Molesworth's reading lists, these young men gathered as a literary club to discourse "upon matters of learning for their mutual improvement." The club attracted a reputation for heterodoxy, and its members were vilified as "a set of Latitudinarians, Free-thinkers, Non-subscribers,

25. Ibid., p. 349.
26. Ibid., p. 352.
27. Ibid.
28. Ibid., pp. 348, 351, 354–55.
29. Ibid., pp. 360–61, May 1723.
30. Ibid., pp. 366–67, November 1723.

and Bangorians, and in a word, Enemies to the jurisdictions, powers, and the divine authority of the clergy."[31]

The Ideas

There is little doubt that Molesworth, who had Toland design electoral propaganda representing himself as Cato, was a key figure in preserving the republican tradition into the eighteenth century (as well as founding a short-lived dynasty of Whig politicians). Ample testimony to this reputation is evident in Thomas Hollis's admiration for the Irishman's life and works. As Hollis recorded, he regarded Molesworth as the author who most neatly captured "My Faith." Indeed, Hollis was very active in disseminating Molesworth's writings (which were included in his list of "canonical books"). Blackburne recorded (in his edition of the *Memoirs of Thomas Hollis*) that Hollis had given away twenty copies of the *Account of Denmark*.[32] Hollis placed a high value on Molesworth's contributions to the republican tradition, noting him as one of the "last of the English."

This admiration took a variety of forms. The most public was the reprinting and distribution of Molesworth's works, but Hollis also commissioned an engraved portrait of Molesworth from Thomas Snelling. A more intimate commemoration can be seen in the "invisible pantheon" inscribed into the landscape at Dorset. As Patrick Eyres has explained, a key signal of Hollis's admiration for Molesworth's contributions is embodied in his naming the highest fields on the downland ridge above his Urles farm after him (and his political intimate, Shaftesbury). So Molesworth was not only central to the Whig canon but also stands at the apex of Hollis's Dorset pantheon.[33]

Hollis personally owned two volumes of Molesworth's works and related pieces, which although evidently specially bound in red morocco,

31. See M. A. Stewart, "John Smith and the Molesworth Circle." *Eighteenth-Century Ireland* 2 (1987), pp. 89–102, at pp. 95–96.

32. F. Blackburne, *Memoirs of Thomas Hollis* (1780), vol. 1, p. 235.

33. See P. Eyres, ed., "The Invisible Pantheon: The plan of Thomas Hollis as Inscribed at Stowe and in Dorset." *New Arcadian Journal* 55/56 (2003), pp. 45–120, at p. 86.

are not decorated with any of his commonplace characteristic symbols of liberty embossed in gilt on the spine or covers.[34] As many have noted, Hollis typically annotated his volumes with a record of his intellectual dispositions. So it was with copies of Molesworth's works. On the initial blank leaves of both volumes, there are scribal notes made by Hollis consisting of a quotation of six lines from the poet Mark Akenside's *Odes* and on the following blank page: "The Preface to the Account of Denmark, and the Translator's Preface to the Franco-Gallia, are justly esteemed two of the most manly, & noble Compositions, in their kind, in the English Language."

In volume 2 of these works (which includes a copy of the 1721 printing of Hotman's *Francogallia*), Hollis has written on the title page "A most curious valuable Treatise." Above "The Translator's Preface" he commented, "Observe this Preface. The Translator's preface to the Franco-gallia, and the preface to the Acc. of Denmark are two of the NOBLEST prefaces in the English language."[35] These "Golden prefaces" were to remain a staple of the eighteenth-century-commonwealth outlook in Europe and North America.[36]

The high-water mark of Molesworth's reputation, prompted especially by the reception of the *Account of Denmark,* was achieved in the second half of the eighteenth century. On this subject he was, as Aylmer has noted, "much the most controversial writer of the whole century."[37] Molesworth had inside knowledge of the Danish context, having been chosen by William III in 1689 as envoy to counter Louis XIV's influence at that court. More specifically, his task was to organize the supply

34. Harvard Houghton Library, call mark Typ 705.38.579, vol. 1 and vol. 2. I owe these references to the kindness of David Womersley.

35. *Franco-Gallia* (1721), Harvard Houghton Library, call mark *EC75.H7267. Zz721h (A). Similar notes are reproduced in *Account of Denmark* (1738), Houghton Library, *EC75.H7267.Zz738m. Again, I am very grateful to David Womersley for providing transcripts of this material.

36. See Trevor Colbourn, *The Lamp of Experience: Whig History and the Intellectual Origins of the American Revolution* (Chapel Hill: University of North Carolina Press, 1965; repr., Indianapolis: Liberty Fund, 1998).

37. G. E. Aylmer, "English Perceptions," in *Europe and Scandinavia: Aspects of Integration in the Seventeenth Century,* ed. G. Rystad (Lund: Esselte Studium, 1983), pp. 181–99, at p. 190.

of Danish troops for William's campaigns. The difficulty of arranging the exchange of subsidy for arms—and the deceitful behavior of the French faction—set the tone for Molesworth's hostility to the Danish monarchy.[38] Molesworth, a convinced follower of Sidney's anticourt disposition, clearly held no deference for Danish regality, as William King, a hostile source, reported. Molesworth broke protocols of access and indeed poached the Danish king's hares without remorse. As one hostile account noted, "These Actions being represented to the King, his Majesty was extreamly offended at them, and showed it by the cold Reception the Envoy afterwards met with at Court."[39] There was little surprise then that Molesworth, declared *persona non grata*, took pleasure in reproducing Sidney's notorious annotation of the ambassadorial commonplace book: *manus haec, inimica tyrannis ense petit placidam sub libertate quietem.*[40]

Molesworth's account of the constitutional revolution of the *lex regia* in Denmark of 1660 (which saw Gothic liberty displaced by a formal legal hereditary absolutism) remained dominant for a century. His bold question, "How did the Danes lose their freedom?" was a persistently urgent one not only for those contemporaries in the British Isles, but for Frenchmen living under Louis XIV, and later for Middlesex citizens and Americans living under George III.

There is little doubt that Molesworth was a key player in the republican refurbishment of Whig ideology after 1689. As an active diplomat and politician in Westminster and Dublin, he both engaged in practical politics and developed an ideological account of republican traditions adapted to present circumstances. He was the backbone of the "true," "old," and "real" Whiggism, which as M. A. Goldie has put it, "remained consistently committed to a fundamental redistribution of constitutional power."[41] Molesworth's works—both the *Account of Denmark* and his edi-

---

38. M. Lane, "The Relations Between England and the Northern Powers, 1689–1697. Part 1. Denmark." *Transactions of the Royal Historical Society* 5 (1911), pp. 157–91, at p. 161.

39. William King, *Animadversions on a pretended account of Denmark* (1694), preface, pp. 10–11.

40. "This hand, an enemy to tyrants, seeks with the sword calm peace in freedom."

41. M. A. Goldie, "The Roots of True Whiggism 1688–94." *History of Political Thought* 1 (1980): 197.

tion of *Francogallia*—combined to provide eighteenth-century British, European, and North American audiences with a robust and authoritative account of the institutional and historical origins of liberty in the West.

Building on traditions that drew from Tacitus's *Germania* and a variety of ancient constitutionalisms, Molesworth provided a comparative account of both the flourishing and the corruption of political liberty. The historical cast of the ancient freedoms of the Franks recorded in the edition of Hotman was balanced by the analysis of a contemporary sociology of liberty in the Danish example. Molesworth's project was not naively nostalgic, but sought to establish the existence of living traditions in modern institutions and to nurture such traditions where they already existed. As he explained, in translating the account of the "ancient free state" of Europe, he desired to instruct "the only Possessors of true Liberty in the World, what Right and Title they have to that Liberty."[42]

Many historians have engaged with the political uses of the past in the early modern period. Accounts of the complex historical relationships between the ancient constitution, the feudal law, the so-called Gothic bequest, and the Norman Conquest, all had contested consequences for contemporary political society.[43] As J. G. A. Pocock has underscored, "to understand the role of historical argument after 1688–89, we must understand that the Gothic liberties and the Norman Yoke, as well as the ancient constitution and the feudal law, persisted into the coming century."[44] Although not explored by Pocock, Molesworth's writings were the starting point for the continuation and repositioning of this earlier discourse. His encounter with the Gothic past operated in a more profound way than simply the invocation of perdurable historical precedent. Far from declining as a way of engaging with the present, the events of the Glorious Revolution of 1688–89, and the 1701 Act of Settlement, prompted a renegotiation of past and present. These "Gothic" claims—articulated powerfully by writers like Nathaniel Bacon and Algernon Sidney—were

42. "Translator's Preface," *Francogallia*, p. 167.
43. See R. J. Smith, *The Gothic Bequest: Medieval Institutions in British Thought, 1688–1863* (Cambridge: Cambridge University Press, 1987).
44. J. G. A. Pocock, *The Ancient Constitution and the Feudal Law* (Cambridge: Cambridge University Press, 1957, repr. 1987), p. 361.

distinct from the immemorialism of legal mindsets articulated earlier in the seventeenth century, which proclaimed the precedence of common law. A core value, and one fundamental to Molesworth's account, was that any crown was held conditionally by consent of the people. Molesworth's decision to redeploy the Gothic model described in *Francogallia* for eighteenth-century readers meant that those who encountered the text had to establish for themselves the pertinence of sixteenth-century arguments for their own contemporary contexts.[45]

The sixteenth and seventeenth centuries saw very different (and competing) historical constructions of these "Gothic" traditions. Some recovered fundamental constitutions; others explored the history of the elective crown in Saxon history. Historical inquiries into the nature of the Norman Conquest, into the origins and authority of Parliament (or more specifically into the rights and privileges of the Commons), were frequently influenced by accounts of these continental "Gothic" experiences. Indeed, the permeability of this pan-European constitution implied that nationally specific experience was potentially comprehended from these broader traditions. Molesworth's writings are a classic expression of this. In the *Account* he delivered an analysis of Danish tyranny; in his edition of Hotman he presented the glories of Frankish liberty. Both of these works were regarded as having specific pertinence to the contemporary British experience, and British readers were expected to make sense of these nonindigenous traditions and apply them to their own circumstances.

The strength of Molesworth's writing was that, as Colin Kidd has noted, it delivered a "robust science of society," which resonated with a variety of powerful anti-absolutist discourses exploring the ethnic and institutional dimensions of liberty. After Molesworth, "in France as well as England, Denmark had become a byword for modern despotism."[46] More important, Molesworth's *Account* delivered a method as well as a mes-

45. See J. W. Allen, *A History of Political Thought in the Sixteenth Century* (New York: Dial, 1928), p. 310, who makes the same point about Hotman's original readers.

46. C. Kidd, "Northern Antiquity: The Ethnology of Liberty in Eighteenth-Century Europe," in *Northern Antiquities and National Identities,* ed. K. Haakonssen and H. Horstboll ([Copenhagen]: Royal Danish Academy, 2008), text pp. 19–40 at p. 29 and notes pp. 307–11.

sage. As emphasized in his preface, the examination of a "constitution" (whether physical or political) was a matter of natural observation. By observational experience, gathered from the rational study of history or derived from traveling, it was possible to know "experimentally" the causes of the decay of liberty and health.

This empirical dimension to Molesworth's work was recognized by contemporaries—indeed, extracts and abridgements from the *Account* were included in collections of travel and ethnographic writings in the 1740s and 1760s. A member of the Royal Society, Molesworth was adept at reading the political consequences of cultural practices, as his collaborative annotation with Toland of Martin Martin's *Western Isles* demonstrated.[47] Core to this method was the principle of a good education calculated to liberate the mind from dependence on "slavish opinion." As Molesworth insisted, "good learning as well as travel is a great antidote against the plague of tyranny." Here his polemic was directed against even the Protestant churchmen of his time who, in their stranglehold on the universities, were perceived as the main corruptors of the "public spirit." For Molesworth, since tyranny began in the mind, the principles of liberty and the free state needed to be promoted by a philosophical education. The monkish bigotry of the pulpit taught only "servile opinions" in place of the principles of rational liberty.

Whig political thought in Molesworth's time was a complex mixture of contract, resistance, and ancient constitution—in effect a blend of history and theory. A common assumption underpinning this complexity was that liberty had premodern origins: "I conceive the original of the subject's libertie was by those our forefathers brought out of Germany."[48] For many, the Saxon origin of such Gothic liberty was "a matter of fact"; for opponents of such historical assumptions like the Tory Brady, this was "meer Romance."[49] The source most commonly associated with this

47. J. A. I. Champion, "Enlightened Erudition and the Politics of Reading in John Toland's Circle." *Historical Journal* 49 (2006), pp. 111–41; M. Brown, "Francis Hutcheson and the Molesworth Connection." *Eighteenth-Century Ireland* 14 (1999), pp. 62–76.

48. J. Rudolph, *Revolution by Degrees: James Tyrrell and Whig Political Thought in the Late Seventeenth Century* (Basingstoke: Palgrave Macmillan, 2002), p. 71.

49. Rudolph, *Revolution by Degrees*, p. 71.

account was Tacitus's *Germania,* which represented a primitive Gothic honor and simplicity against a vision of Roman urban luxury and moral torpor. As one commentator noted in 1689, "some have sent us to Tacitus and as far as Germany to learn our English Constitution." The assumption promulgated by Molesworth was neatly summarized and shared even by court Whig John Oldmixon in 1724: "no nation has preserv'd their Gothic constitution better than the English."[50] Written in the 1690s and 1700s in the context of the Hanoverian succession, Molesworth's defense of an *anglia libera,* prompted by a Tacitean reading of Frankish liberty, provided a British readership with a non-Roman and anti-Gallic source of constitutional legitimacy.[51]

The political context for Molesworth's contributions was not simply domestic but European: internally the war against popery and arbitrary power in the guise of Tory Jacobitism was rendered more complex by the threat of Louis XIV's foreign policy. The fragility of the Revolution settlement and, especially after 1700, the insecurity of the succession of the Hanoverian line meant that Molesworth's polemic against Danish absolutism was a stalking horse for the indictment of latent tyranny at home and practical despotism abroad. The lamentation for the loss of Danish freedom was tuned to English, French, and Dutch ears. Great attention was paid to the preparation of the many French editions of the *Account.* The inclusion of maps and emblematic frontispieces representing Danish liberty is evidence of this concern to ensure an engaged readership. Later French editions also included useful indices drawing the attention of the reader to significant themes: for example, "Absolus. Les Princes n'ont pû acquerir legitiment le droit d'être absolus"; "Governement Anglois, trop parfait pour recevoir aucun amendement"; and "Prêtres, ont beaucoup

50. Samuel Kliger, *The Goths in England* (Cambridge: Harvard University Press, 1952), pp. 112, 202.

51. D. R. Kelley, "*Tacitus Noster:* The *Germania* in the Renaissance and Reformation," and H. D. Weinbrot, "Some Uses of Tacitus in Eighteenth-Century Britain," in *Tacitus and the Tacitean Tradition,* ed. T. J. Luce (Princeton: Princeton University Press, 1993), at pp. 169, 178; W. Bennario, "Gordon's Tacitus." *The Classical Journal* 2 (1976–77), pp. 107–14. For an account of the context see J. Scott, *Commonwealth Principles: Republican Writing of the English Revolution* (Cambridge: Cambridge University Press, 2004), pp. 192–99.

contribué à render le gouvernement de la Russie et de la Muscovie tyran-nique"; "Les païsans de la Zelande y sont aussi esclaves que les negres dans les Barbades."[52] It is clear that the Huguenot diaspora of the 1690s would have valued the anti-absolutist thrust of the *Account;* what is more signifi-cant is that twenty years after its initial publication (alongside the edition of *Francogallia*) French audiences found it a useful resource for engaging with the Ludovicean regime.[53] Certainly in the decade of 1710 the recep-tion of the two works connected with the *nobilaire* and *parlementaire* resis-tance in France especially associated with the so-called Burgundian circle coordinated by Boulainvilliers. The nature of the Gothic constitution de-scribed in Hotman's work and the *Account* set some of the key terms of political debate.[54] The Francogallian constitution with its emphasis on the role of an ancient and virtuous aristocracy was a useful polemical weapon against Louis XIV's conception of monarchy.[55]

Indeed, the French reception of Molesworth's project was a contrib-uting element to the complex diplomatic politics surrounding the peace settlement of the War of the Spanish Succession, between 1709 and 1712. Contributing to the paper war around the so-called renunciation crisis (which demanded the recall of the Estates-General to formally register Philip of Spain's renunciation of the French throne), civil history was pitched as a challenge to Ludovicean absolutism. Very much like Moles-worth, Boulainvilliers exploited historical writing to deliver a narrative of the past that showed an unhallowed conspiracy of Gaulish bishops and Merovingian kings subverting Frankish liberty. Ambitious clergy, credu-lous laymen, and despotic kings are recurring themes of both English and French commonwealth historical writing. Dynastic privilege was dis-

52. *Etat present* (1715), Beinecke Library, Yale University, New Haven, Conn., call mark Edas692Mhf.

53. See Guy H. Dodge, *The Political Theory of the Huguenots of the Dispersion* (New York: Columbia University Press, 1947), especially pp. 151–54.

54. H. M. Baird, "Hotman and the '*Francogallia*,'" *American Historical Review* 1 (1896), pp. 609–30, at pp. 622–23.

55. See F. Ford, *Robe and Sword: The Regrouping of the French Aristocracy After Louis XIV* (Cambridge: Harvard University Press, 1966); W. Doyle, "Was There an Aristocratic Reaction in Pre-Revolutionary France." *Past and Present* 57 (1972), pp. 97–122; J. H. Shennan, "The Political Role of the Parlement of Paris Under Cardi-nal Fleury." *English Historical Review* 81 (1966), pp. 520–42.

missed as an "absurd fact": constitutional form, which promoted the involvement of aristocratic virtue over hereditary principle, was commonly applauded.[56]

Much later in the 1780s, Molesworth's polemic account of the history of Danish tyranny was redeployed for revolutionary French audiences in a short extract of chapters 7 and 8. The brief prefatory comments of this pamphlet remark, "Ce livre n'a point été fait pour les circonstances présentes; il est dans toutes les Bibliothèques; J'en ai tiré deux chapitres, dont la lecture m'a fait frémir."[57] The point of reproducing the text was to indict the role of the Church as an agent of despotism. Despite the existence of a good constitution, the Church had turned the Danes into slaves: "cette Révolution fut opérée par le dévoument hypocrite des prêtres; par la colère aveugle des communes, par l'imprudent obstination des nobles."[58] The afterlife of Molesworth's writing was persistent.

Molesworth not only defended the value of liberty but also undertook a philosophical and historical inquiry into the conditions for its preservation and corruption. In effect he extended the project of Machiavelli's commentaries on Livy into the circumstance of more modern and contemporary societies. Despite the work of Nathaniel Bacon and Algernon Sidney, in the absence of an account of a specifically Britto-Gallian past (George Buchanan's history of Scottish liberty and Hotman's French version provided prescriptive models), Molesworth produced material for the politi-

---

56. R. Briggs, "From the German Forests to Civil Society: The Frankish Myth and the Ancient Constitution in France," in *Civil Histories: Essays Presented to Sir Keith Thomas,* ed. Peter Burke, Brian Harrison, and Paul Slack (Oxford: Oxford University Press, 2000), pp. 231–50, at p. 233; H. A. Ellis, *Boulainvilliers and the French Monarchy: Aristocratic Politics in Early Eighteenth-Century France* (Ithaca: Cornell University Press, 1988), pp. 13, 85; J. Klaits, *Printed Propaganda Under Louis XIV: Absolute Monarchy and Public Opinion* (Princeton: Princeton University Press, 1977); P. K. Leffler, "French Historians and the Challenge to Louis XIV's Absolutism." *French Historical Studies* 14 (1985), pp. 1–22.

57. "This book was not made for the present circumstances; it is in all the libraries; I have drawn from it two chapters, the reading of which causes me to tremble."

58. "This revolution was brought about by the hypocritical self-sacrifice of the priests; by the blind anger of the people; by the reckless stubbornness of the nobility." *Extrait d'un livre intitulé: État du royaume de Dannemarck, tel qu'il étoit en 1692 . . . Traduit de l'Anglois suivant la troisième edition de Londres* (Amsterdam: Adrian Braakman, 1695 [1790]), p. 3.

cal imagination of British audiences.[59] He provided, however, not simply an ancient constitution for implementation but a broader sociological inquiry into the origins and fortunes of liberty, which readers might refine and apply to contemporary circumstances. The evidence of Molesworth's political writings and their afterlife also allows us to glimpse how traditions of thinking about liberty developed between the sixteenth and eighteenth centuries. Molesworth's edition of *Francogallia* acted as a conduit for repositioning the resistance theory of the French wars of religion into a form digestible and pertinent to the age of revolutions. With this "contagion of liberty," works written as *livres de circonstance,* in order to legitimate specific acts of resistance against religious tyranny, were transformed into volumes encouraging ideological opposition to corruptions in contemporary political societies. Readers of *Francogallia* in the 1570s might have been embarked on raising arms against the French or Spanish monarchy, whereas readers of the English editions in the 1710s or 1760s read more to validate public political principles shared by large numbers of other like-minded readerships.[60] Recommendations to read the works in newspapers and advertisements significantly broadened their readerships and enhanced the possibilities of their enjoying practical political consequences.

Molesworth's writings provide ample material for an answer to J. W. Gough's very pertinent question, "How did political liberty in the eighteenth century depend on what had happened in ancient France?"[61] Molesworth mobilized historical erudition for public debate. Working with earlier discourses he searched for what was regarded as a set of historically intelligible fundamental principles. By combining Hotman's *gaulois* constitution with Tacitus's Germanist traditions, he claimed to have identified extant institutions and processes that instantiated principles of liberty. He also identified those agencies (beliefs and institu-

---

59. On Buchanan see H. Trevor-Roper, *The Invention of Scotland: Myth and History* (New Haven: Yale University Press, 2008), pp. 3–74.

60. For one study of such an afterlife see Bernard Bailyn, *The Ideological Origins of the American Revolution* (Cambridge: Harvard University Press, 1967).

61. J. W. Gough, "James Tyrrell, Whig Historian and Friend of John Locke." *The Historical Journal* 19 (1976), pp. 581–610, at p. 588.

tions) that corrupted freedom. The point of the combination of the edition of *Francogallia* and the analysis of the Danish case was to establish how historically contingent these traditions of freedom were. By drawing from the final chapter of the 1576 version of *Francogallia* (not reproduced in Molesworth's editions) on superstition, Molesworth significantly contributed to the identification of the corrupting role of clerical institutions.

Scattered throughout Molesworth's correspondence are barbed comments about the popery and tyranny of the High Church. Even men like the Low Church polemicist Benjamin Hoadly were dismissed as traitors when they accepted preferment over principle.[62] This is not to say that Molesworth was irreligious: he left money in his will to build a church at Philipstown; in 1704 he instructed his wife not to forget to "enter the children's ages in the great bible at Breckdenston."[63] Even late in his life he took a lively concern in the selection of curates: his son dismissed one candidate with the comment that "when he finds himself armed with credentials from Heaven and the Ecclesiastical Authority on earth to back them, it would be very extraordinary if he grew more modest."[64]

Throughout his political career in London and Dublin, Molesworth had opposed intolerance and ecclesiastical tyranny. This had led him to support attempts to strengthen the legal basis of liberty of conscience. But it had also led him into direct conflict with the political institution of the Church in Ireland in 1713 when he suffered deprivation of his privy council seat for accusing the High Church clergy of turning "the world upside down."[65] As a consequence Molesworth was regarded as being in "odious colours" for his "intolerable profanation of the Holy Scriptures."[66]

A friend of freethinking and heterodox men like Toland, Matthew Tindal, and Anthony Collins, Molesworth was explicit in regarding all clerical claims to political authority as "popery" and priestcraft. According to Molesworth, churchmen, even of Protestant varieties, exploited their

---

62. *HMC*, p. 324, September 1721.
63. Ibid., p. 229.
64. Ibid., p. 327.
65. See *Mr. Molesworth's Preface. With Historical and Political Remarks* (1713).
66. N. Tindal, *The continuation of Mr. Rapin de Thoyras's History of England, from the revolution to the accession of King George II* (1751), p. 331.

authority in education to create servile prejudice and their own advancement—intolerance, persecution, and mental dependence lay at the root of tyranny. Citing the case that the Protestant Calvin had burned Servetus at Geneva, he confirmed "whosoever is against *Liberty of Mind*, is, in effect, against *Liberty of Body* too." All *de jure divino* claims, such as "Monarchy, Episcopacy, Synods, Tythes, the Hereditary Succession to the Crown," were improper and unacceptable to "real Whigs."[67] Indeed, as Molesworth took delight in reinforcing, Whiggism was constrained to no particular religious confession—Jews, Turks, even "Papists," might be "great lovers of the constitution and liberty." Toleration should be extended to "Pagans, Turks, Jews, Papists, Quakers, Socinians, Presbyterians, or others" because, Molesworth insisted, bigotry was the "very Bane of human Society, and the Offspring of Interest and Ignorance, which has occasion'd most of the great Mischiefs that have afflicted Mankind."[68] Religious tyranny created a dependent mind and by consequence a more effective political slavery: true commonwealth liberty lay in the freedom of reason and a good constitution.

Molesworth's writings transformed the resistance theory of the previous century into an ideology of vigilance against the latent possibilities of contemporary despotism. This account of commonwealth ideology did not categorically oppose either monarchy or the modern and developing institutional forms of the state and society; however, it warned its readers to remain alert to the preconditions of tyranny in cultural, political, and economic forms.

The History and Reception of the Texts

An Account of Denmark was recorded in the Stationer's Register on December 16, 1693, to publisher Timothy Goodwin. Subsequently, Daniel Poplar was threatened with prosecution for licensing the work. David Hayton has discovered evidence that throws important light on the scribal circulation of the text in the winter of 1693. John Stanley noted in correspondence with Robert Harley (at that time the driving force of the Country

---

67. "Translator's Preface," *Francogallia*, p. 177, p. 179.
68. Ibid., p. 177.

interest) that he possessed a copy of the work to which Molesworth was keen to restrict access. "Importuned by some of his friends," Molesworth judged that it was best to coordinate publication with the new Parliamentary session in early October.[69]

After publication, although the *Account* was admired by many Whigs, the reputation of the work was tarnished by the king of Denmark's formal complaint to the Privy Council.[70] Nevertheless (or perhaps because of this), demand was such that Goodwin, his first edition possibly selling some one thousand per week, produced a third edition in March 1694. A second "foxed" edition was also produced by unknown persons. It is estimated that some six thousand copies were sold at this early stage. Continental editions followed almost immediately, with Dutch clandestine versions in French produced under the imprints (fictitious and not) of Pieter Rabus, Adrian Braakman, and Pierre Marteau. Certainly the work remained available for purchase. The exiled Thomas Johnson in the bookshop familiarly named the Libraire Anglois, Pooten in the Hague, offered copies in the 1700s alongside other classics of the Whig and republican canon such as Buchanan, Ludlow, Spinoza, Locke, Tyrrell, and Sidney. The work was a best-seller, outperforming contemporary works by Locke and others and receiving reviews in English and continental literary journals such as *Journal de Hambourg* (1695) and *Histoire des ouvrages des scavans* (1694). A fragment of the preface was also published in 1713.[71] As the Bibliographical Descriptions indicate, the work reached some twenty-two editions in the eighteenth century. Records of book ownership suggest it was widely owned in the British Isles and North America.

The semiofficial response of the Danish government was coordinated by Skeel from April 1694. The complaint that William III should have the book burned and the author executed met with a frosty response: "That I cannot do but, if you please, I will tell him what you say, and he shall

69. For this account see D. Hayton, "The Personal and Political Contexts of Robert Molesworth's *Account of Denmark*," in *Northern Antiquities and National Identities*, ed. K. Haakonssen and H. Horstboll ([Copenhagen]: Royal Danish Academy, 2008), pp. 41–67, at pp. 56–57.

70. R. Astbury, "The Renewal of the Licensing Act in 1693 and Its Lapse in 1695," *The Library* 32 (1978), pp. 296–322, at p. 298.

71. See *Mr. Molesworth's Preface. With Historical and Political Remarks* (1713).

put it into the next edition of his book."[72] A number of profoundly hostile English-language works, notably William King's *Animadversions on a pretended account of Denmark* (1694), disputed Molesworth's reports of "habitual slavery" as "due obedience to supreme powers."[73] Evidence of the capacity of the work to provoke debate is confirmed by the fact that it was later cited in the House of Commons by a member of Parliament critical of William III's use of the veto.[74]

Molesworth completed his translation of Hotman's *Francogallia* sometime in 1705; it was first published in 1711 by Timothy Goodwin, without the original editorial preface, which was regarded as too incendiary for the times. Subsequently, the complete edition was published in 1721 by another publisher, Edward Valentine, this time with additional material from Pierre Bayle's biographical account of Hotman. The preface—later known under the title *The Principles of a Real Whig*—became a clarion call for the commonwealth tradition in the eighteenth century. Editions of both the *Account* and *Francogallia* were available throughout the century. Booksellers' advertisements in newspapers indicate that the two volumes were usually sold for common *binding*, or for binding together in one volume. (The publication of new editions of the *Account* prompted notice of the translation of Hotman's French work, as the flurry of monthly ads in the *London Evening Post* between January 1758 and 1761 indicates.)

Evidence of the persisting relevance of the edition can be found in an item in the *Gazetteer and London Daily Advertiser* of March 13, 1764, responding to defenses of royal prerogative; the author of that "ill designed piece is either a madman, or an arrant Tory, i.e., a villain willingly ready to metamorphose himself into a low petty fawning cur to any ignorant weak king, as soon as such a one shall sit on the throne." Extracting passages from chapter 15 of *Francogallia*, which suggested monarchs were secondary to the "whole politic body," the article continued to recommend

---

72. P. Ries, "Robert Molesworth's *Account of Denmark:* A Study in the Art of Political Publishing and Bookselling in England and on the Continent Before 1700." *Scandinavica* 7 (1968), pp. 108–25; E. Seaton, *Literary Relations of England and Scandinavia in the Seventeenth Century* (Oxford: Clarendon, 1935), p. 134.

73. King, *Animadversions*, pp. 90–91.

74. Hayton, "The Personal and Political Contexts," p. 316.

"the serious reading not only of the *Francogallia,* but also of the other most valuable performances of that rare patriot, the real nobleman, Lord Molesworth." Men like him, "the immortal Whigs," had begun and completed "the preservation and defence of the natural and social rights of Great Britain," which were a durable model of how to engage with "tyrannical oppression."[75] Newspaper comments in 1788 and 1793 reinforced this persisting afterlife in commending the lessons of *Francogallia* to the cause of "publick liberty" in France.[76]

The edition of Hotman's work was translated from a combination of the first edition and the 1576 Latin edition. Between the publication of the 1705 and 1721 editions, Molesworth included supplementary material from the original (chapter 19, "concerning the most important affairs of religion").[77] This latter edition saw the expansion of the "preface" from one that made brief remarks about the defense of liberty to the full-blown articulation of "real Whig" ideology.

Indeed, in the interval between the two versions the precise context for the work altered considerably. The 1711 edition had been published under the rule of a queen (which accounts for the judicious remarks made by Molesworth, who was critical of Hotman's hostile tone in the chapter concerning the rule of queens). The book was also made public at a time when Louis XIV's military power threatened the security of the Protestant succession (it may well have been calculated to appeal to audiences involved in the complex diplomatic context of the end of the War of the Spanish Succession).

Molesworth also included (in both editions) a biographical portrait of Hotman drawn almost exclusively from Pierre Bayle's *Historical Dictionary.* This account reworked the complex ballet between main text and footnotes in Bayle's original into a seamless celebration of Hotman's dedication to the principles of constitutional liberty and erudition. Interest-

75. *The Gazetteer and London Daily Advertiser* of March 13, 1764, no. 10,918.
76. See items in *The Whitehall Evening Post,* October 11, 1788; *The Morning Chronicle,* February 8, 1793; *The St. James Chronicle,* September 3, 1793.
77. François Hotman, *Francogallia,* ed. Ralph E. Giesey; trans. J. M. H. Salmon, Edition "b" (Cambridge: Cambridge University Press, 1972). Hereafter abbreviated as "GS *Franc.*"

ingly, Molesworth decided to exclude the material Bayle composed related to Hotman's theological commitments, preferring to represent his contributions as predominantly civil in idiom.

While complete editions of *Francogallia* were subsequently republished after 1738, the afterlife of the preface to the volume was even more complex. Large fragments were published in John Ker's memoirs.[78] A full transcription was included in the Wilkesite monthly pamphlet *The Political Register*, produced by John Almon (later successfully prosecuted for publishing Junius's letters) in April 1768. The issue was subsequently reprinted in collected volumes of the same work. Almon, under the sobriquet "an independent Whig," was later to publish works by Paine, Wilkes, and others. Indeed, it seems likely that he also published an unacknowledged history of Denmark based on Molesworth's work. A list of books and pamphlets printed in 1768 notes "this day are published" *An Account of Denmark. Antient and Modern,* which was meant to contain "its history from Swain the first Christian King to the present time." Ornamented with a print of the contemporary king and queen, it was priced at "3s. sewed."[79] Demand was such that John Almon certainly produced a new printing of *Francogallia* in the winter of 1771–72.[80]

Even more significantly, an edition of the preface was produced by the "real Whig" London Association in 1775 (sold at 3d each or fifty copies for 8 shillings), dedicated to the "protesting peers, the uncorrupted minority in the House of Commons, the patriotic Freeholders of Middlesex." Indeed the preface was suitable for "every true, free Englishman, in the British Empire, who is willing and ready to maintain a steady opposition to the introduction of Popery and Slavery into these realms."[81] Thomas Hollis had displayed sympathy for American attempts to preserve the

78. John Ker, *Memoirs and secret negotiations,* part III (1726), pp. 191–217.

79. See R. Rea, "The Impact of Party Journalism in the *Political Register." The Historian* 17 (1954), pp. 1–17.

80. See *London Evening Post,* January 17, 1758; November 14, 28; December 8, 26, 1758; January 16, 1759; and further in March, April, and September 1759. Almon's advertisement is ibid., December 5, 1771, issue 6852.

81. Page 24 indicates that "in a few Days will be published, elegantly printed, Hotman's *Francogallia,* translated by the late Lord Molesworth" by J. Williams at no. 39 Fleet Street.

traditions of English liberty and indeed circulated copies of works like James Otis's *Rights of the British colonists asserted and proved*. Closely allied with Wilkes and printers like Almon, groups of like-minded common-wealthmen gathered in London clubs like the Honest Whigs, the Bill of Rights Society, and the Constitutional Society to mobilize civic support for America among the common councilmen and aldermen.

Published in the early autumn of 1775, Molesworth's preface was offered to a new readership as a radical defense of the revolutionary military resistance of the colonies at Lexington and Concord against arbitrary power. The London Association, formed in the summer of 1775 at the Globe Tavern from a group of the capital's more radical tradesmen and artisans, was, as a hostile contemporary noted, "principally intended to recommend and abett in this country the Rebellion which now exists in America."[82] Produced by men with connections to both John Wilkes and Thomas Hollis, the publication explicitly connected the traditions of 1689 with the political values inscribed in Molesworth's preface: promotion of a frequent and independent parliament, regulations against bribery and corrupt office holding, pro-trade taxation policy, anti–standing army, and pro–citizen militia. The 1775 republication chimed with the ambitions of the colonies in promoting "Constitutional Freedom and National Happiness." As the London Association's attached circular letter made clear, "arbitrary" behavior by ministers had "*openly violated* and endeavoured to *subvert* our excellent *constitution*." The ambition was to encourage similar associations for "reciprocal communication." To this end the London Association in partnership with the bookseller John Williams, and following Hollis's model, offered a range of other works, "[including] in a few days will be published, elegantly printed, HOTOMAN's FRANCO-GALLIA, translated by the late Lord Molesworth." On this list were many works of Wilkes and others defending popular rights of petitioning, popular sovereignty, and civic freedom.[83] The London Association also

---

82. J. Sainsbury, "The Pro-Americans of London, 1769 to 1782." *William and Mary Quarterly* 35 (1978), pp. 423–54, at p. 436.

83. This included the reprinting of works by John Somers defending the revolution of 1689 (1710) and more contemporary titles like *A guide to the knowledge of the Rights and Privileges of Englishmen* (1757).

sponsored the colonialists' *Declaration . . . setting forth the causes and neces-*
sity of taking up Arms (1775) "for the noble purpose of opposing the Inroads
of Tyranny."[84]

The London Association used the newspapers to promote an ideology
based almost exclusively on Molesworth's preface. The September 14 edition of the *London Evening News,* noting the forthcoming publication of
Molesworth's preface, recommended it to the "public" as encapsulating
"those genuine principles of a real Whig which actuate the London Association, and are the solid groundwork of all their resolutions." Reading
Molesworth would restore the constitution and "save a sinking nation." To
complement this invocation of the real Whig legacy, the London Association had duplicate copies published of an account of the reading habits of
a Whig Shrewsbury brass-metal worker of the 1730s. As it described how
the unnamed worthy, persecuted by Tories, found solace and "rapture" in
frequent reading of Molesworth's works, the distinction between those
who approved of encroachments on the constitution and those who maintained the "people's prerogative" was ever persistent. The nomenclature of
Cavaliers and Roundheads, High Church and Low, Court and Country
was more generally recorded as Whig and Tory. Too many were deluded
by "a numerous herd of prostitute writers" into an unthinking dependency,
but underneath, "the majority of people are naturally OLD WHIGS."
Now was the time to abandon neutrality by reading Molesworth's preface.
As the item concluded, "*I wish every man in the nation* would *condescend* to
read it."[85]

Evidence that Molesworth was a sensitive and thoughtful witness of
contemporary society is found in the economic reflections and recommendations of the final text included in this collection: *Some considerations
for the promoting of agriculture, and employing the poor,* published in Dublin in 1723. Surviving correspondence reveals Molesworth to have been a

---

84. J. Sainsbury, *Disaffected Patriots. London Supporters of Revolutionary America
1769–1782* (Gloucester, 1987), pp. 106–13.

85. *The Craftsman or Say's Weekly Journal,* September 30, 1775; see also *The Gazetteer or New Daily Advertiser,* September 26, 1775. Signed by "An Old English Merchant. G.I.L.H." The first iteration also noted where Molesworth's "preface" might
be purchased and its price.

keen observer of natural and agricultural life. His letters are littered with repeated discussions of a variety of agricultural matters: the stocking of fishponds was evidently a particular interest.[86] The arguments developed in the *Considerations* drew from his skill and abilities in the world of estate management and domestic economy. He turned this practical experience into a thoughtful discussion of the role the state could assume in developing a more productive economy and social policy. As with the *Account of Denmark,* Molesworth understood that there was a connection between material circumstances, public institutions, and political values.

Undertaking a comparative analysis of landownership, leases, and tithing practices in Ireland and England, Molesworth turned his own experience of managing estates into an instrument for the cultivation of a better civic community. Following Harringtonian commonplaces, Molesworth emphasized the role of landownership as the platform for virtuous public service. A prerequisite for membership in the House of Commons should be the possession of "Estates in the Kingdom." Such properties should not be "fleeting ones, which may be sent beyond Sea by Bills of Exchange by every Pacquet-Boat, but fix'd and permanent." Those merchants, bankers, and "money'd men" ambitious of senatorial position "should have also a competent, visible Land Estate." Disagreeing with the contemporary argument that moneyed status was preferable to having estates encumbered with debts and mortgages, he suggested that those with estates would have the same interest as the rest of the country when it came to "publick Taxes, Gains and Losses."[87]

Despite this apparent conservatism, Molesworth's broader vision of economic life was active. He was, for example, in favor of a general naturalization as a device to increase the population and stimulate trade. Expanding the number of workmen in any town would enable the community to thrive. As a consequence, "the greater will be the Demand of the Manufacture, and the Vent to foreign Parts, and the quicker Circulation of the *Coin*."[88] Decrying the restrictive practices of many town corporations where commerce was entangled in complex bylaws, Molesworth

86. *HMC,* p. 220, p. 275.
87. Molesworth, "Translator's Preface," *Francogallia,* p. 181.
88. Ibid., p. 183.

argued that new unincorporated villages were "more liberal" in their regulatory structures and by consequence deserved parliamentary representation. Such "better peopled" (i.e., more populous) and "more industrious" places were preferable to wastes and deserts like Old Sarum.[89]

Benefiting "the public" was the criterion for economic and fiscal policy. Potentially, "Parliamentary Credit" could promote "all publick Buildings and Highways, the making all Rivers Navigable that are capable of it, employing the Poor, suppressing Idlers, restraining Monopolies upon Trade, maintaining the liberty of the Press, the just paying and encouraging of all in the publick Service."[90] Far from decrying the burdens of taxation to support such government initiatives (especially in the costly business of continental war), Molesworth insisted that "no true Englishman will grudge to pay Taxes whilst he has a Penny in his Purse." Since the cost of government was managed in a frugal manner, a citizen who "sees the Publick Money well laid out for the great Ends for which 'tis given" would contribute according to his abilities.[91] Notwithstanding Molesworth's commitment to the virtues of landed property and its political culture, he was appreciative of the possibilities of an industrious nation.

Molesworth's extensive correspondence reveals a predisposition to value the political function of a landed aristocracy combined with an appreciation of the contributions of commerce and industry. Molesworth spent most of his life in pursuit of financial security for his extensive family. His hope that government office would bring with it secure income was repeatedly disappointed. His sons feared that their interest was compromised by the fierce paternal reputation for "true noble Roman courage that neither rewards nor threatenings can change."[92] This pursuit of security and independence ironically drove Molesworth into an unwise decision to invest in South Sea stock, which resulted only in further debt. A frugal man (drawing only £25 per month "for all expenses relating to myself in England"), he regretted the folly of his speculative investment in South Sea stock. The £2000 he invested was borrowed in the vain hope

89. Ibid., p. 184.
90. Ibid., p. 189.
91. Ibid., p. 190.
92. *HMC*, pp. 287, 288–89.

that the stock would "further rise, and in order to cheat some other buyer, fancying that it would not die in my hands."[93] That the price fell two days after he had purchased the stock, as he lamented, served him right. Molesworth's daughter had dabbled, too, in the hope of securing a fortune to relieve her family from uncomfortable dependence on the court. The prospect of "imaginary riches" had tempted, it seems, many in the Molesworth connection.[94]

The best remedy for the current crisis was "improvement" of trade. Daniel Poultney put it most succinctly when he insisted that "we must put a stop to all sort of gaming in stocks, encourage trade and manufacture, industry and frugality."[95] Molesworth's management of his own domestic economy reflected these values. The "sheet anchor" was his Irish estate, where he and his wife had undertaken virtuous "projects in good husbandry."[96] Late in life he wrote in some considerable pique against the charge that he had been extravagant in matters of estate improvement in Yorkshire. The rumor that thousands of pounds had been spent was spread about by "envious fools." As he explained, "I never exceed above 150*l.* per annum, whatever you may hear to the contrary." He admitted he had spent a considerable amount on digging a canal, but that had profited him by £300. He continued, "There is neither bench, statue, fountain of stone, stairs, urn or flower-pot here as yet, so that you may judge that mere grass, trees and hedges cannot cost much."[97] The evidence of his correspondence with his wife, sons, and daughters suggests that Molesworth was a landowner with a keen eye to opportunity and development of his agrarian resources. This is supported by Finola O'Kane's brilliant study of his architectural and gardening projects, which were underpinned by his enduring concern with the rental potential of the estates in Yorkshire and Ireland.[98] The decision to adjust the nature of property titles from freehold to twenty-one-year leases marked (according to his son) "a

93. Ibid., pp. 296, 301–3.
94. Ibid., pp. 312–13, 350–51.
95. Ibid., p. 286.
96. Ibid., p. 350.
97. Ibid., p. 357.
98. F. O'Kane, *Landscape Design in Eighteenth-Century Ireland* (Cork, Ireland: Cork University Press, 2005).

way of improvement, which it never was before." In the same instance, he encouraged the trade in Philipstown by collaboration with two "master manufacturers" (who happened, much to the disgust of the local cleric, to be Quakers). One of these, John Pym, employed the poor to spin his wool "to the great satisfaction of all the country and increase of the market."[99] Even toward the end of his life, Molesworth had a vision for how estate improvement could pay off the family's debts: "the selling of woods, the setting out of St. Patrick's well land, the Alnage revenue, and the improvement of Philipstown and Swords are groundworks to raise a new estate from."[100]

Attentiveness to the potential of new rentals was matched by meticulous attention to detail over the rights and privileges of his estates. Neighbors who threatened to enclose his land, tenants who took advantage of mowing allowances, and people who exploited short-term rental rates for their private advantage and at damage to the integrity of the land, were all dealt with in no uncertain terms in order, as Molesworth put it, to "vindicate our right."[101] This dedication to the integrity of the estates was not simple personal advantage. Good management of tenancies (set at a reasonable price) benefited both landlord and tenant: severe measures had beneficial effects. Replacement of "unimproving idle people" by "better tenants" made the land more productive. Molesworth did not take the fixing of his rents lightly. Having researched the historical fluctuation of costs over four decades, he was aware of the range of options. He was also profoundly aware that his relationship with individual tenants necessarily involved their dependence on him. In one instance Molesworth was explicit in this regard. He was, he explained to his wife, quite against giving his "tenants at will" parchment copies of their leases: "they are so already at their own will, and it is but just they should be so at ours." The point in refusing a material copy of the leases was not to turn out or raise the rents upon good tenants, but to "keep them in awe and hinder them from destroying our estate." Here is an insight into the forms of dependence

99. *HMC*, p. 369.
100. Ibid., p. 370.
101. Ibid., pp. 230-31.

that Harrington theorized in his account of empire following the balance of property.[102]

Molesworth, too, theorized his experience and applied its lessons to the decay of gentlemanly cultivation in Ireland. Echoing both Cicero and Harrington, he stated that it was fundamental to his convictions that "*Agriculture* is not only a Science, but the most useful one to Mankind."[103] The ablest statesmen, philosophers, and poets had devoted considerable effort to elucidating the best principles of agricultural practice, "knowing it to be that whereon the Life and well-being of the Community depends."[104] Fundamental to his project was the need for honest and "improving" tenants who would enable the gentry to undertake two sorts of cultivation: of the soil and of their minds. Good tenants would allow gentlemen the leisure to improve their "natural Parts" by reading; the counterexample was the experience of the Irish gentry who were forced (in order to avoid the destruction of their estates by bad tenants) to "manage their own Lands, and turn their own Husband-men." Such low employment and mean company meant that the gentry "degenerate by degrees; the best Education of many of their Sons, reaching no higher, than to know how to make the most of a Piece of Land." As Molesworth made very explicit, this relationship with the land was no training ground for republican virtue. Understanding "the Business of Parliament, the Duty owing to ones Country, and the Value of Publick Liberty" was not cultivated "under such a cramp'd, and low Education." Such gentry would become "narrow Spirited, covetous and ungenteel."[105]

One remedy was to create "schools for husbandry" in each county to teach the best principles of agricultural conduct and good manners. Thriving and industrious farmers would produce more food and thereby alleviate the poverty of the nation. Reform of agricultural practices that had been distorted by religious sentiment (in particular by tithes and saints' days) would create further benefit. Such scarcely disguised anticlericalism

---

102. *HMC*, pp. 239, 241, 249, 250.
103. Molesworth, *Some Considerations for the Promoting of Agriculture and Employing the Poor*, p. 332.
104. Ibid.
105. Ibid., p. 344.

was mixed with economic principle when Molesworth declared, "I wish all the Saints Days were let slip, with all my Heart, and that People might be left at liberty to keep open Shop, plow, sow, reap and follow their lawful Trades on those Days; they would serve God better, and their Country and private Families, than now they do."[106]

Molesworth, then, had an intimate understanding of the politics and economics of his relationship with the land, his tenants, and the status they conferred. He did, upon occasion, even turn his hand to the plough (something no self-respecting Roman senator would have considered). He was able to calculate the potential financial benefits of renegotiating rentals, but also to consider mortgaging his lands for ready cash in order to ensure that his son's embassy in Turin was a success.

Molesworth was a man who certainly took enormous delight and pride in the application of *opificio* to his estates: the correspondence is teeming with references to specific arboreal projects, agrarian developments, and piscatorial undertakings. He was clearly an expert across a range of horticultural and natural knowledge, and the pride he took in improvement is evident in his remarks about developments on the Yorkshire estate of Edlington: "all the coarse, rough, unimproved land is taken in and under fine grass of tillage, a deal of new closes and hedging and building, and repairs, and planting the town street full of new industrious tenants, the commons taken in and turned to the best profitable land."[107] Here the language of improvement, industry, and profit illustrates the core values of a republican understanding of the function of landed property. Constantly anxious about the need for money to support his sons in their careers, Molesworth bemoaned that "all our care and industry cannot set us at ease in the world." Despite these moments of despair, he continued, if somewhat compulsively, to plan improvements that would secure and advance the common benefit.[108]

Justin Champion

106. Ibid., p. 349.
107. *HMC*, pp. 221, 257, 261.
108. Ibid., pp. 248, 283.

EDITORIAL APPARATUS

The edition of the *Account of Denmark* reproduced here is a collated text from the first four English-language editions (1694–1738) identified below in Bibliographical Descriptions as items 1–3 and 5 under the heading "English Editions." The copy text is the third edition of 1694 (item 3), which is the final textual state to be corrected and acknowledged by the author.

Subsequent eighteenth-century editions indicate some very minor typographical and orthographical revisions but no significant addition or excision of the text. A comparison with the early French-language editions has also been made and has established little significant deviation. The later eighteenth-century European reception and the subsequent abridged and extracted editions of the work in French, although worthy of further attention, exceed the ambitions of this volume.

A commentary on the preface to the *Account* was published in 1713.

The editions of Hotman's *Francogallia* (1711; 1721, reprinted in 1738), including the prefatory material later known as *The Principles of a Real Whig* (composed 1705; published 1721; extracted and reproduced in variants in 1726, 1768, and 1775) have been collated. The only notable difference between the first and second editions was the inclusion in the later volume of chapter 19, "Of the authority of the assembly of states concerning the most important affairs of religion." A number of reasons may account for this: the most likely is that Molesworth had seen the later

xli

edition and subsequently updated his own edition. Giesey and Salmon[1] note that the 1711 version was based on the 1574 Latin original, whereas the expanded 1721 edition clearly borrowed material from the 1576 Latin edition (specifically passages from chapter 18 that were not present in the original version).

The preface to *Francogallia,* later reprinted as a separate pamphlet, *The Principles of a Real Whig,* is one of the key texts of eighteenth-century commonwealth ideology. Its analysis of the variants of "true Whiggism" has also become a standard historiographical tool for understanding the influential accounts found in Pocock, Kenyon, and Bailyn. The distinction between a Whiggism of principle or place, between radical and self-interested milieux, still drives accounts of the political history of the relationship between power and liberty in the eighteenth century.

Molesworth's translation is an interesting one. Comparison with the modern Cambridge edition suggests that he worked hard to make the prose connect with early-eighteenth-century Anglophone readers, thus enabling the "we" of Hotman's original text to become the "we" of his audience. One clear trait is his emphasis on languages of community, the public, and liberty: for example, unlike the Cambridge edition, Molesworth commonly translated *libertas* as "publick liberty" rather than simply "liberty"; elsewhere, phrases like *publico consilio* became "universal consent" rather than "public consent" (GS *Franc.,* pp. 234–35; 1721 edition, p. 44); a preference for translating *abdicare* as "abdicate" rather than "resign" and *populi comitia* as "public council" or "public convention" (rather than "assembly of the people") also exposes contemporary concerns. Likewise, the vocabulary of "king," "nobles," and "commons"—or even more appropriately "representatives of the commons"—anchored the reception in the language of eighteenth-century Britain.

---

1. See note 77 in the Introduction.

BIBLIOGRAPHICAL DESCRIPTIONS
Editions, Translations, and Extracts, 1694–1789

English Editions

1. *An account of Denmark, as it was in the year 1692.* (London, 1694). [52], 271, [1] p. 8°; see also *An account of Denmark, as it was in the year MDCXCII.* (London: Printed in the year 1694). [24], 172 p.; 12°. Wing M2382A (Donald Wing, *Short-Title Catalogue of Books Printed in England, Scotland, Ireland, Wales and British America, and of English Books Printed in Other Countries, 1641–1700.* 2nd ed., rev. 4 vols. New York: Modern Language Association, 1972–98. Covers all extant books, pamphlets, and broadsides printed in English between 1641 and 1700).

2. *An account of Denmark, as it was in the year 1692.* (London: Printed in the year 1694). 26 p. l., 271 p.; 20 cm. Notes: Errata corrected, no list on p. 271. Title-page, list of contents, and some pages of the preface from the same typesetting. Wing M2382A.

3. *An account of Denmark, as it was in the year 1692.* 3rd edition corrected. (London: For T. Goodwin, 1694). [40], 120, 119–246 p.; 8°. Wing M2383.

4. *Mr. Molesworth's preface. With Historical and Political remarks. To which is added, A True State of his Case, with respect to the Irish Convocation; their Com-*

plaint, and the Proceeding of the House of Lords upon it; As also His own Justifi-cation. (London: Printed, and sold by J. Roberts at the Oxford Arms in War-wick Lane, 1713). [2], 38 p.; 8°.

5. *An account of Denmark: as it was in the year 1692.* The fourth edition, carefully revised. (London: Printed for Tho. Longman, 1738). [8], xxiii, [1] 432 p.; 8°.

6. *Navigantium atque itinerantium bibliotheca. Or, a complete collection of voyages and travels. Consisting of above six hundred of the most authentic writers, beginning with Hackluit, Purchass, &c. in English; . . . To which is prefixed a copious intro-duction, . . . Originally published in two volumes in folio, by John Harris, . . . Now carefully revised, with large additions, . . .* (London: Printed for T. Woodward, A. Ward, S. Birt, D. Browne, T. Longman, 1744-48). Republication of 1705 work by John Harris. Volume 2, pp. 503-8, reproduces extracts from the *Account.*

7. *An account of Denmark, as it was in the year 1692 By the Right Honourable Robert Lord Viscount Molesworth.* The fifth edition. (Glasgow: Printed by R. Urie and Company, 1745). [4], xxvii, [1], 190 p.; 8°.

7a. *An account of Denmark, as it was in the year 1692. By the Right Honour-able Robert Lord Viscount Molesworth.* The sixth edition. (Glasgow: Printed by R. Urie, 1752). xxxii, [2], 188 p.; 12°.

8. *Franco-Gallia: or, an account of the ancient free state of France, and most other parts of Europe, before the loss of their liberties. Written originally in Latin by . . . Francis Hotoman, in the year 1574.* (London: Printed for Tim. Goodwin, 1711). [4], vi, [6], 10, vi, 144 p.; 8°.

9. *Franco-Gallia: or, an account of the ancient free state of France, and most other parts of Europe, before the loss of their liberties. Written originally in Latin by . . . Francis Hotoman, in the year 1574.* (London: Printed for Edward Valentine, 1721). "The second edition, with additions, and a new preface by the trans-lator." [6], xxxvi, [6], 10, vi, 148, [6] p.; 8°.

9a. *Franco-Gallia: or, an account of the ancient free state of France, and most other parts of Europe, before the loss of their liberties. Written originally in Latin by the famous civilian Francis Hotoman, in the year 1574. And translated into English by the author of the Account of Denmark.* "The second edition, with additions, and a new preface by the translator." (London: Printed for T. Longman, 1738). [6], xxxvi, [6], 148, [4], p.; 8°.

10. *The principles of a Real Whig* in John Ker, *The memoirs and secret negotiations of John Ker, of Kersland, Esq; Part IIId and last. To which is added, A Copy of the Information exhibited by the Attorney-General against the First Part of these Memoirs. Published by his express direction.* (London: Printed in the Year 1726 [1727]), pp. 191–217.

11. *The principles of a real whig; contained in a preface to the famous Hotoman's Franco-Gallia, Written by the late Lord-Viscount Molesworth*, item XIII, April 1768, in John Almon (ed.), *The Political Register* (1768), vol. 2, pp. 281–96.

12. Extracts from the *Account* were published in *The world displayed; or, a curious collection of voyages and travels, selected from the writers of all nations. In which the conjectures and interpolations of several vain editors and translators are expunged, . . . Illustrated and embellished with a variety of maps and prints.* (London: Printed for J. Newbery, 1759–61). Volume 20 (published in 1761), pp. 54–73. This project compiled by Christopher Smart, Oliver Goldsmith, and Samuel Johnson extracted material from Molesworth's volumes but "omitted . . . whatever appears to be dictated by partiality." The work was reprinted a number of times, reaching a third edition by 1778.

13. *The principles of a real whig; contained in a preface to the famous Hotoman's Franco-Gallia, Written by the late Lord-Viscount Molesworth; and now reprinted at the request of the London Association.* "To which are added, their resolutions, and circular letter." (London: Printed for J. Williams, 1775). 26 p.

14. *Some considerations for the promoting of agriculture, and employing the poor.* (Dublin: Printed by George Grierson, 1723). [2], iii, [1], 44 p.; 8°.

European Editions[1]

1. *Etat present de Danemarc: par lequel on voit le fort, & le foible de cette couronne, avec des remarques très utiles, sur son gouvernement despotique, & la con-*

---

duite qu'elle tient aujourd'hui . . . traduit de l'anglois. (A Londres, Chez Thomas Fuller, 1694). 32 p. l., 264 p.; 14 cm. Wing 2383aA.

2. *De Vrye Staats-Regering, Geschetst in een Beschrijvinge van Denemarken, Zoo als 't was in den jare 1692.* (Te Rotterdam: Pieter van der Slaart, 1694). With additional "To the reader" and poems signed by the Dutch journalist Pieter Rabus (1660–1702). 8°.

3. *Mémoires de M. Molesworth, envoié de Sa Majesté britannique à la cour de Danemarc, l'an 1692.* (Nancy: Chez l'imprimeur, 1694). 2 p. l., 412 p.; 16 cm. Wing M2383aA.

4. *Mémoires de M. Molesworth, envoié de Sa Majesté britannique à la cour de Danemarc, l'an 1692.* (Nancy: Chez l'imprimeur, 1695).

5. *État du Royaume de Danemark, tel qu'il étoit en 1692, etc. Traduit de l'Anglois suivant la troisième édition de Londres.* (Amsterdam: Adrian Braakman, Marchand Libraire dans le Beursstraat, prés le Dam à L'enseigne de la Ville d'Amsterdam, 1695). 303 p.; 12°.

6. *Dännemarks gegenwärtiger Staat, unter der numehro [sic] souverainen Regierung Christiani V . . . / erstlich in Englisch und Frantzösisch, nachgehends in Holländisch, nunmehro aber wegen dessen unvergleichlicher Curiosität auch in unsre teutsche Mutter-Sprache, den Geschicht- und Staats-Liebhabenden zum besten übersetzet.* (Cölln: Bey Pieter Marteau, 1695). 158 p. 16 × 20 cm. Reprinted 1720.

7. *Extrait d'un livre intitulé: État du royaume de Dannemarck, tel qu'il étoit en 1692 . . . Traduit de l'Anglois suivant la troisième édition de Londres.* (Amsterdam: Adrian Braakman, 1695). 62 p.; 8°. The British Library copy of this work [F.579 (5)] is bound with a number of other French pamphlets from the 1780s and 1790s. It extracts chapters 7 and 8 of the original (chapter 7, pp. 1–42; chapter 8, pp. 43–62). The point of reproducing the text was to underscore the role of the Church as an agent of despotism. Despite a good constitution, the Church had turned the Danes into slaves: "cette Révolution fut opérée par le dévoument hypocrite des pretres; par la colère aveugle des communes, par l'imprudent obstination des nobles."

7a. *Extrait d'un livre intitulé État du royaume de Dannemarck, tel qu'il étoit en 1692 . . . Traduit de l'anglois, suivant la troisième edition de Londres.* (A Amsterdam, chez Adrian Braakman, 1695). 62 p.; translation of chapters 7 and 8 of the *Account of Denmark, as it was in the year 1692.* Republished in 1789, see Horace E. Hayden, *French Revolutionary Pamphlets* (New York: New York Public Library, 1945).

8. *Etat du royaume de Danemark, tel qu'il étoit l'an 1692 Suivant la troisième édition de Londres.* (Amsterdam, 1695). [6], 412, [24] p. (pp. [1]-[2].) [1] leaf of plates; 8°.

9. *Memoires de Mr. Molesworth: dans lesquels on voit l'état du royaume de Danemark, tel qu'il étoit l'an 1692. Derniere édition, augmentée d'un indice tres necessaire.* (A Paris, Chez la veuve Mabre Cramoisy, 1697). [5], 412, [24] p.; [1] p. [436]; 8°. Includes index.

10. *Dännemarks gegenwärtiger Staat, unter der numehro [sic] souverainen Regierung Christiani V . . . / erstlich in Englisch und Frantzösisch, nachgehends in Holländisch, nunmehro aber wegen dessen unvergleichlicher Curiosität auch in unsre teutsche Mutter-Sprache, den Geschicht- und Staats-Liebhabenden zum besten übersetzet.* (Cölln: Bey Pieter Marteau, 1697).

11. *Mémoires de Mr. Molesworth: dans lesquels on voit l'état du Royaume de Danemark. Nouvelle édition, etc.* (Paris, 1705). 412 p.; 8°.

12. *Memoires de Mr. Molesworth: dans lequel on voit l'état du royaume de Danemark. Nouvelle édition, augmentée d'un indice très necessaire.* (A Paris, Chez la veuve de Mabre Cramoisy, 1705). [4], 412, [24] p.; 8°.

13. *Etat present du royaume de Danemarc: par lequel on voit le fort, & le foible de cette couronne, avec des remarques très-utiles, sur son gouvernement despotique, & la conduite qu'elle tient aujourd'hui.* (A Paris, Chez la veuve Mabre Cramoisy, 1714). 2 p. l., 412 p., 12 l.; front. 8°.

14. *Etat present du royaume de Danemarc: par lequel on voit le fort, & le foible de cette couronne, avec des remarques très-utiles, sur son gouvernement despotique,*

& la conduite qu'elle tient aujourd'hui. (Paris: Chez la veuve Mabre Cramoisy, 1715). 3 p. l., 412, [23] p.; 8°.

15. *État present de Danemarc . . . : Trad. de l'Anglois* (Amsterdam: Jean Baptiste Desroches de Parthenay, 1732).

16. *Berättelse, huruledes konunga riket Dannemark ifrån et fritt wal-rike blifwit inom fyra dagar förwandlat til et ärfteligit enwäldigt rike, på riks dagen i Köpenhamn år 1660.* (Stockholm: Nordström Wennberg, 1771).

TEXTUAL POLICY

The intention has been to produce an edition of Molesworth's major political writings that is accurate yet easily accessible to modern readers. The text has been modernized only in minor respects. Capitalization has generally been retained according to the original printed editions. Significant adjustment has been made to typographical layout: section titles, running heads, catchwords, and original pagination have been retained only where judged significant for authorial meaning or contemporary readings.

For the *Account,* which went into six editions—three published during Molesworth's life—I have taken the third corrected edition as the copy text. The 1738 edition (owned by Thomas Hollis) was also collated, and some corrections of punctuation and spelling have been silently adopted from this edition (most commonly the replacement of a semicolon with a full stop).

Italics

In the original printed editions of the *Account* and *Francogallia,* italics were used for proper names, foreign language phrases, and terms under discussion, such as "Cologne" or "publick." Quotations and paraphrases from other works were sometimes given in italics: the present edition abandons this practice in favor of using quotation marks where possible for citations. Italics for proper names and place names have been preserved where significant.

Spelling and Footnotes

This edition has preserved the irregular orthography of Molesworth's day, including that of proper names and place names, except where there are clear mistakes (and these have been silently corrected). Spellings in old style have been retained: for example, *chuse, compleat, shew, publick* (and other *–ck* endings); similarly, words with contracted *–ed* endings have been retained, but those like *rendred* have silently become "rendered."

Other silent adjustments to spelling and grammar have been made for clarity's sake: for example, square brackets denote the inclusion of footnotes and words not in the original. Latin phrases have been reproduced as in the original (also italicized).

In this edition of *Francogallia* all instances of "Capevingian" have been replaced with the more modern "Capetian," and "Carlovingian" with "Carolingian."

Unless stated otherwise, all translations are by the editor.

LIST OF SOURCES

Where possible, all sources used by Molesworth in the *Account of Denmark* have been identified in appropriate footnotes. In Molesworth's edition of Hotman's *Francogallia,* he meticulously reproduced, generally in the main body of the text, references from the original editions that he had consulted (the 1576 Latin and French versions rather than the 1574 edition). The present edition has preserved this aspect of the translation. As Giesey and Salmon establish in their parallel Latin and English edition, Hotman identified his citations by italics (although not all such passages were direct quotations, sometimes being condensed or partially adjusted). The modern Cambridge University Press edition supplies precise pagination in accessible editions for these original sources. Readers who wish to explore the erudition at play in the work should consult the 1972 apparatus.

This Liberty Fund edition includes footnotes to identify sources where either Hotman or Molesworth failed to give a bibliographical reference. In general, references to classical sources will give author, title, book, and chapter or paragraph in standard style. A full and precise reference can be gathered from consulting Giesey and Salmon's edition. A selected account of sources available to Hotman and Molesworth has been included in Appendix 1 for cross-reference to available sixteenth- and seventeenth-century printed editions. Because the most commonly used editions for reference purposes are the volumes from the Loeb Classical Library, citation to these volumes will simply be "Loeb" and the appropriate page number, or the volume and page number of a specific author's work. Thus Suetonius, *Caesar* 25 (Loeb 1:32) is Loeb's *Suetonius,* vol. 1, p. 32. Full references to cited classical sources are listed in the section "Loeb Classical Library" in Appendix 1.

FURTHER READING

Bond, William Henry. *Thomas Hollis of Lincoln's Inn: A Whig and His Books.* Sandars Lectures in Bibliography. Cambridge: Cambridge University Press, 1990.

Brown, Michael. "Francis Hutcheson and the Molesworth Connection." *Eighteenth-century Ireland: Iris an dá chultúr* 14 (1999): 62–76.

Champion, Justin. *Republican Learning: John Toland and the Crisis of Christian Culture, 1696–1722.* Manchester: Manchester University Press, 2003.

———. "Enlightened Erudition and the Politics of Reading in John Toland's Circle." *Historical Journal* 49 (2006): 111–41.

Ellis, Harold A. "Genealogy, History, and Aristocratic Reaction in Early 18th Century France: The Case of Henri de Boulainvilliers." *Journal of Modern History* 58 (1986): 414–51.

———. *Boulainvilliers and the French Monarchy: Aristocratic Politics in Early Eighteenth-Century France.* Ithaca: Cornell University Press, 1988.

Goldie, Mark. "The Revolution of 1689 and the Structure of Political Argument: An Essay and an Annotated Bibliography of Pamphlets on the Allegiance Controversy." *Bulletin of Research in the Humanities* 83 (1980): 473–564.

———. "The Roots of True Whiggism 1688–94." *History of Political Thought* 1 (1980): 195–236.

———. "The English System of Liberty." In *The Cambridge History of Eighteenth-Century Political Thought,* edited by Mark Goldie and Robert

Wokler, 40–78. The Cambridge History of Political Thought series. Cambridge: Cambridge University Press, 2006.

Hayton, D. W. "The Personal and Political Contexts of Robert Molesworth's *Account of Denmark*." In *Northern Antiquities and National Identities: Perceptions of Denmark and the North in the Eighteenth Century*, edited by K. Haakonssen and H. Horstboll, 41–67 (text) and 311–16 (notes). [Copenhagen]: The Royal Danish Academy of Sciences and Letters, 2008.

Hotman, François. *Francogallia*. Edited by Ralph E. Giesey. Translated by J. M. H. Salmon. Cambridge: Cambridge University Press, 1972.

Kelley, Donald R. *François Hotman: A Revolutionary's Ordeal*. Princeton: Princeton University Press, 1973.

Kenyon, J. P. *Revolution Principles: The Politics of Party, 1689–1720*. Cambridge: Cambridge University Press, 1977.

Kidd, C. "Northern Antiquity: The Ethnology of Liberty in Eighteenth Century Europe." In *Northern Antiquities and National Identities: Perceptions of Denmark and the North in the Eighteenth Century*, edited by K. Haakonssen and H. Horstboll, 19–40 (text) and 307–11 (notes). [Copenhagen]: The Royal Danish Academy of Sciences and Letters, 2008.

Klaits, Joseph. *Absolute Monarchy and Public Opinion: Printed Propaganda Under Louis XIV*. Princeton: Princeton University Press, 1976.

Marshall, Peter. "Thomas Hollis (1720–74): The Bibliophile as Libertarian." *Bulletin of the John Rylands University Library of Manchester* 66 (1984): 246–63.

O'Kane, Finola. *Landscape Design in Eighteenth Century Ireland*. Cork: Cork University Press, 2005.

Olden-Jorgensen, S. "Robert Molesworth's *Account of Denmark:* A Political Scandal and Its Literary Aftermath." In *Northern Antiquities and National Identities: Perceptions of Denmark and the North in the Eighteenth Century*, edited by K. Haakonssen and H. Horstboll, 68–87. [Copenhagen]: The Royal Danish Academy of Sciences and Letters, 2008.

Patterson, Annabel. *Early Modern Liberalism*. Cambridge: Cambridge University Press, 1997.

———. *Nobody's Perfect: A New Whig Interpretation of History*. New Haven: Yale University Press, 2002.

Pocock, J. G. A. *The Ancient Constitution and the Feudal Law: A Study of English Historical Thought in the Seventeenth Century*. Cambridge: Cambridge University Press, 1957. Reissued 1987.

———. *Virtue, Commerce and History: Essays on Political Thought and His-*

tory, Chiefly in the Eighteenth Century. Cambridge: Cambridge University Press, 1985.

Pocock, J. G. A., ed. *The Varieties of British Political Thought, 1500–1800*. With the assistance of Gordon J. Schochet and Lois G. Schwoerer. Cambridge: Cambridge University Press, 1993.

Robbins, Caroline. "Library of Liberty: Assembled for Harvard College by Thomas Hollis of Lincoln's Inn." *Harvard Library Bulletin* 5 (1951): 5–23, 181–96.

———. *The Eighteenth-Century Commonwealthman: Studies in the Transmission, Development and Circumstance of English Liberal Thought from the Restoration of Charles II Until the War with the Thirteen Colonies*. Cambridge, Mass., and London: Harvard University Press, 1959. Reprint, Indianapolis: Liberty Fund, 2004.

———. "The Strenuous Whig, Thomas Hollis of Lincoln's Inn." *William and Mary Quarterly* 7 (1950): 406–53.

———. "Thomas Brand Hollis, 1719–1804, English Admirer of Franklin and Intimate of John Adams." *Proceedings of the American Philosophical Society* 97 (1953): 239–47.

Rudolph, Julia. *Revolution by Degrees: James Tyrrell and Whig Political Thought in the Late Seventeenth Century*. Basingstoke: Palgrave Macmillan, 2002.

Salmon, J. H. M. *The French Religious Wars in English Political Thought*. Oxford: Clarendon Press, 1959.

Scott, Jonathan. *Commonwealth Principles: Republican Writing of the English Revolution*. Cambridge: Cambridge University Press, 2004.

Stewart, M. A. "John Smith and the Molesworth Circle." *Eighteenth-Century Ireland: Iris an dá chultúr* 2 (1987): 89–102.

Worden, Blair. "Republicanism and the Restoration, 1660–1683." In *Republicanism, Liberty, and Commercial Society, 1649–1776*, edited by David Wootton, 139–93. Stanford: Stanford University Press, 1994.

———. "The Revolution of 1688–1689 and the English Republican Tradition." In *The Anglo-Dutch Moment: Essays on the Glorious Revolution and Its World Impact*, edited by Jonathan Israel, 241–77. Cambridge: Cambridge University Press, 1991.

———. *Roundhead Reputations: The English Civil War and the Passions of Posterity*. London: Penguin, 2002.

———. "Whig History and Puritan Politics: The Memoirs of Edmund Ludlow Revisited." *Historical Research* 75 (2002): 209–37.

ACKNOWLEDGMENTS

I am very grateful to David Hayton, Blair Worden, and David Womersley for their direct help and advice in the preparation of this edition, both for pointing me toward items I certainly would have missed and for general and specific comment. I am also exceptionally grateful to Rachel Hammersley, who very generously allowed me to read a draft of her important monograph *The English Republican Tradition and Eighteenth-Century France* (Manchester University Press, 2010), which explores in much more detail the broader influence of the English commonwealth tradition. Patrick Eyres offered wise advice and copies of key articles. My colleagues at Royal Holloway, Sandra Cavallo and Hannes Kleinicke, gave very helpful assistance with some of the Italian and Latin sources. Polly Bull assisted with a forensic eye in the preparation of the source texts and bibliographies.

An Account
of Denmark

AN

ACCOUNT

OF

Denmark

AS

It was in the Year 1692.

*Pauci prudentiâ, honesta ab deteri-
oribus, utilia ab noxiis discernunt;
plures aliorum eventis docentur.*
Tacitus, lib. 4 Ann.[1]

Vincit amor patriae.
Virgil, *Aeneid.*[2]

The Third Edition Corrected.

LONDON:
Printed for Timothy Goodwin, at
the Queen's Head against St. Dunstan's
Church in Fleetstreet. 1694.

[1.] "Few men distinguish right and wrong, the expedient and the disastrous, by native intelligence; the majority are schooled by the experience of others." Tacitus *Annals*, bk. 4, chap. 33 (Loeb 4:57).

[2.] "The love of country will be victorious." Virgil *Aeneid* 6, 823.

THE CONTENTS

THE PREFACE

Health and Liberty are without dispute the greatest natural Blessings Mankind is capable of enjoying; I say natural, because the contrary states are purely accidental, and arise from Nature debauched, depraved or enforced. Yet these Blessings are seldom sufficiently valued whilst enjoy'd; like the daily advantages of the Sun and Air, they seem scarce regarded because so common, by those that are in possession of them.

But as an Italian that passes a Winter in Groenland, will soon be convinc'd through his want of the kind Influences of that glorious Planet, how much Misery he endures, in comparison of those who dwell in his Native Country, so he that knows by Experience the trouble of a languishing Sickness, or the loss of his Liberty, will presently begin to have a right esteem of that which formerly he scarce thought worth his notice.

This Experience is either what a Man learns by that which befalls himself, or by making Observations on the condition of other People. The first is the common guide to the generality of Mankind, who are not apt to look beyond themselves, unless with St. Thomas they feel as well as see, they will not believe. Thus in the instance of bodily Health, we find those that have been always accustom'd to it, have scarce any Notion of the Misery of the contrary state, and therefore are careless in shunning those Excesses which might bring Diseases upon them; the sad Examples seen every day of miserable sick Debauchées, being not sufficient to deter others from lewdness. But the second sort of Experience is the Instructress of wise Men: For the Prudent will not fail to benefit themselves by the Accidents that befall others, both in their *Health* and *Liberty*, by avoiding the occasions of them: And this is one of the great Advantages of Society, that not only the Assistance, but even the Misfortunes of others, may be of use to us.

Want of *Liberty* is a Disease in any Society or Body Politick, like want of Health in a particular Person; and as the best way to understand the nature of any Distemper aright, is to consider it in several Patients, since the same Disease may proceed from different causes, so the disorders in Society are best perceived by observing the Nature and Effects of them in our several Neighbours: Wherefore Travel seems as necessary to one who desires to be useful to his Country, as practising upon other Mens Distempers is to make an able Physician. For although a Man may see too frequently the Misery of such as are depriv'd of Health without quitting his own Country, yet (thanks to Providence) he must go out of these Kingdoms who would know experimentally the want of *Publick Liberty.* He that Travels into a Climate infected with this Disease (and he can find few that are not) does not only see, but in some measure feel the Grievances occasioned by it in the several Inconveniencies of living, in some proportion with the Natives; so as to relish better upon his return (which we suppose depends upon his choice) the freedom and ease of his own home Constitution; and may make good use of this Experience without having paid too dear for it. But a Man cannot transmigrate himself for a while into a distemper'd Body as he may Travel into an Enslaved Country, with equal facility of getting rid of each of them again.

Thus 'tis a great, yet rare advantage to learn rightly how to prize *Health* without the expense of being Sick, but one may easily and cheaply grow sensible of the true value of *Liberty* by Travelling into such Countries for a Season as do not enjoy it.

And this can be done by no Nation in the World so commodiously as the English: The affluence of their Fortunes and Easiness in their private Affairs are evidently greater than those of other People of Europe; so that generally speaking, none are in a condition to spend more freely, or may propose to reap greater benefit by Travel, and yet none have practised it less.

In other Countries some Princes and Men of the first quality may have Purses strong enough to bear the expense, but few of the middling sort venture upon it; and those are commonly either Military Men, who have other designs in view than the knowledge of the World; or the Unfortunate, who chuse it as a diversion or a refuge, and who have their Heads too full of their own Miseries, to be at leisure to make their Observations on others. And besides, we often see the like Arbitrary Practices at home (they having been always train'd up in Servitude) do so far vitiate their Reason, as to put them out of a capacity of judging aright; for 'tis not only possible, but very usual, that People may be so season'd to and hardened in *Slavery,* as not only to have lost the very Taste of *Liberty,* but even to love the contrary State: as Men over-run with the Spleen take pleasure in their Distemper.

But in England there are very many Gentlemen, whose Estates will afford them either to travel in Person, or to send abroad such of their Sons for four or five Years as have the most solid Judgments, in which time they may acquire such Manners, and make such Observations as shall render them useful to their Country; and thereby advance their private Fortunes, more than what is saved by keeping them at home would amount to.

The Method which has been generally follow'd by us in sending young Gentlemen to Travel can hardly answer any of these ends: on the contrary it has hitherto been so mischievous, that 'tis well travelling has been so little in fashion. We send them abroad Children, and bring them home great Boys, and the returns they make for the Expenses laid out by their Parents, are suitable to their Age. That of the Languages is the very best, but the most common is an affected Foppishness, or a filthy Disease, for which they sometimes exchange their Religion: Besides, the Pageantry, Luxury, and Licentiousness of the more Arbitrary Courts have bribed them into an Opinion of that very Form of Government: Like Idiots, who part with their Bread for a glittering piece of Tinsel, they prefer gilded *Slavery* to coarse domestick *Liberty,* and exclaim against their old fashion'd Country-men, who will not reform their Constitution according to the new foreign Mode. But the Travelling recommended here is that of

Men, who set out so well stock'd with the Knowledge of their own Country, as to be able to compare it with others, whereby they may both supply it where they find it wanting, and set a true value on it where it excels. With this help such Travellers could not fail of becoming serviceable to the Publick, in contributing daily towards the bettering of our Constitution, though without doubt it be already one of the best in the World.

For it were as fond to imagine we need not go abroad, and learn of others, because we have perhaps better Laws and Customs already than Foreigners, as it were not to Trade abroad, because we dwell in one of the plentifullest Parts of the World. But as our Merchants bring every day from barren Countries many useful things, which our own good one does not produce; so if the same care were taken to supply us with exact Accounts of the Constitutions, Manners, and Condition of other Nations, we might without doubt find out many things for our purpose, which now our mere Ignorance keeps us from being sensible that we want. The Athenians, Spartans, and Romans did not think themselves too wise to follow this Method, they were at great Expense to procure the Laws of other Nations, thereby to improve their own: and we know they throve by it, since few Governments are so ill constituted, as not to have some good Customs. We find admirable Regulations in Denmark, and we read of others among the Savage Americans fit to serve for Models to the most civilized Europeans.

But although the Constitution of our Government were too perfect already to receive any Improvement, yet the best Methods conducing to the peaceable Conservation of its present Form, are well worth every Englishman's enquiry; neither are these so easily to be found in this Age, which were judged so difficult, (if not altogether impracticable) by the greatest of Politicians in his time.[3] 'Tis true, the Wisdom of our Ancestors, or their good Fortune, has hitherto made these our Kingdoms an Excep-

---

[3.] There is a marginal note here from Tacitus, *Annals,* bk. 4, chap. 33 (Loeb 4:57): "Cunctas Nationes & Urbes populus aut primores aut singuli regunt; delecta ex his, & constituta Reipublicae forma, laudari, facilus quam evenire, vel si evenit haud diuturna esse potest." Translation: "The people, or chiefs, or individuals, govern all nations and cities; and the constituted form of a commonwealth chosen from them is more easily praised than practiced; or if it be so (constituted) it cannot long exist."

tion to his general Maxim; yet we all know how many grievous Tempests (which as often threatened Shipwrack) this Vessel of our Commonwealth has undergone. The perpetual Contests between the Kings and the People (whilst those endeavour'd to acquire a greater Power than was legally due, and these to preserve or recover their just Liberties) have been the contending Billows that have kept it afloat; so that all we pretended to by the late Revolution (bought with so great Expense, yet not too dearly paid for) was to be as we were, and that every one should have his own again; the effecting of which may be called a piece of good Luck, and that's the best can be said of it. But must frequent Blood-lettings be indispensibly necessary to preserve our Constitution? Is it not possible for us to render vain and untrue that Sarcasm of Foreigners, who object to us that our English Kings have either too little Power, or too much, and that therefore we must expect no settled or lasting Peace? Shall we for ever retain the ill Character they give us of the most mutable and inconstant Nation of the World? Which however we do not deserve, no more than England does that of *Regnum Diabolorum*,[4] so common in unconsidering Foreigners Mouths? Methinks a Method to preserve our Commonwealth in its legal State of Freedom, without the necessity of a Civil War once or twice every Age, were a benefit worth searching for, though we went to the furthest Corners of the World in quest of it.

Besides the Knowledge of the present State of our Neighbour Nations (which is best acquired by Travel) is more incumbent on the Gentlemen of England than any others; since they make so considerable a part of our Government in Parliament, where foreign Business comes frequently under Consideration, and at present more than ever.

'Tis none of the smallest Advantages which his Majesty has procured us by his accession to the Crown, that we make a greater Figure in the World than formerly; we have more foreign Alliances, are become the Head of more than a Protestant League, and have a right to intermeddle in the Affairs of Europe, beyond what we ever pretended to in any of the preceding Reigns: For 'tis a true, though but a Melancholy Reflexion, that our late Kings half undid us, and bred us up as narrow spirited as they

[4.] "Kingdom of devils."

could, made us consider our selves as proscribed from the World; in every sense *toto divisos orbe Britannos.*[5] And indeed they had withdrawn us from the World so long till the World had almost overlooked us; we seldom were permitted to cast an Eye farther than France or Holland, and then too we were carefully watched: But at present Matters are otherwise; we have a Prince that has raised us to our natural Station, the Eyes of most parts of the World are now upon us, and take their Measures from our Councels: We find every day occasion to inform our selves of the Strength and Interests of the several Princes of Europe. And perhaps one great reason why we live up no better to the mighty Post we are advanced to, nor maintain our Character in it with great Reputation, is because our Education has been below it, and we have been too much lock'd up at home, when we should have been acquainting our selves with the Affairs of the World abroad.

We have lately bought the Experience of this Truth too dear, not to be now sensible of it. 'Tis not very long ago since nothing was more generally believed (even by Men of the best sense) than that the Power of England was so unquestionably establish'd at Sea, that no Force could possibly shake it, that the English Valour and Manner of Fighting was so far beyond all others, that nothing was more desirable than a French War. Should any one have been so regardless of his Reputation, as at that time to have represented the French an overmatch for the united Forces of England and Holland; or have said that we should live to see our selves insulted on our own Coasts, and our Trade indanger'd by them, that we should be in Apprehensions every Year of an Invasion and a French Conquest; such a venturesome Man must have expected to have pass'd for a very Traveller, or at best for an ill-natur'd or unthinking Person, who little consider'd what the irresistible Force of an English Arm was; But our late Experience has reclaim'd us from these Mistakes; our Fathers and Grandfathers told us indeed these things when they were true, when our Yeomanry and Commonalty were every day exercised in drawing the Longbow and handling the Brown-bill, with other Weapons then in use, wherein we excell'd all the World; but we have liv'd upon the Credit of

[5.] From Virgil, *Eclogues*, 1.67: "to the Britons, cut off from the whole world."

those Times too long, and superciliously neglected our formidable Neighbour and Enemy, whilst he was improving his Strength, and we through the Encouragement, and by design of our late Rulers were enervating our own.

The *Ecclesiasticks* of most Religions, who are allow'd to understand and prosecute their own Interests best of any People, though they be generally Persons whose Function obliges them to a sedentary and studious Course of Life, have not omitted to draw such Advantages from Travel as conduce to their Honour and Profit. These Men, whose conversing with Books makes them know more than others, have yet found their Account in sending some of the most judicious of their Members and Fraternities to fetch home Knowledge and Experience from the remotest parts of the World. The College *De propaganda fide* was establish'd under pretence indeed of serving Religion, but we know the Founders of it are no farther slaves to Religion than 'twill be serviceable to them, neither was it so much through zeal for Conversions, as to increase their Revenues, and learn Foreign Policies in Church and State Affairs. The Jesuits have brought several Maxims, as well as Sums, from as far off as China and Japan, thereby improving their Knowledge, so as to outwit their Friends at home, and by following their Example in this, I am sure we can run no hazard, at least of passing for Fools. These Men (whose firm adherence to the most exquisite Tyranny is manifest by their indefatigable endeavours in behalf of the French King's Interests, as formerly of the House of Austria's, whilst it was in its height) have by these Arts ingrossed to themselves the Education of the Youth in all Popish Countries. The Lutheran Priests (who have an entire dependence on their Kings and Princes) are intrusted with the like in those Countries which observe the Confession of Augsburg. They also send abroad some of their hopefullest young Students, several of which may be met with at Oxford, Cambridge, and Paris: The use they make of Travel being not only to improve their Knowledge in Sciences, but to learn fit Methods to please their Sovereigns at the expense of the People's Liberties. Now in former Ages, whilst the *Ecclesiasticks* were both ignorant and scandalously wicked, they were not esteemed by the Laity, and consequently had not so much power to do mischief: But since that through a Reformation of Manners, and Knowledge of the World, they have recover'd credit, and that the restored Learning of Europe is principally lodg'd among them, they have gained a much greater influence both on the Opinions and Practices of their Disciples, and promoted a pernicious Doctrine with all the success they themselves could desire. But the same Travel will afford the best Antidote for this Poison, and teach a Gentleman, who makes right use of it, by what steps *Slavery* has within these last 200 Years crept upon Europe, most of the Protestant, as well as Popish Countries having in a manner quite lost the precious Jewel, *Liberty*. This cannot be attributed to any more probable cause than the enslaving the Spirits of the People, as a preparative to that of their Bodies; for since those Foreign Princes think it their Interest that Subjects should obey without Reserve, and all Priests, who depend upon the Prince, are for their own sakes obliged to promote what he esteems his Interest; 'tis plain, the Education of Youth, on which is laid the very Foundation Stones of the publick Liberty, has been of late years committed to the sole management of such as make it their business to undermine it; and must needs do so, unless they will be false to their Fortunes, and make the Character of *Priest* give place to that of true *Patriot*.

'Tis confest that in their Schools and Universities, excellent Rules for attaining Languages and Sciences are made use of with greater success than any heretofore: Those Youths especially, who have been bred among the Jesuits, are justly remarked to excel others of equal Parts instructed elsewhere: But still this is only a training up in the knowledge of Words and Languages, whereof there is seldom any occasion, as if the Pupils were intended to be made School-masters; whilst the weightier Matters of true Learning, whereof one has occasion every hour; such as good Principles, Morals, the improvement of Reason, the love of Justice, the value of Liberty, the duty owing to one's Country and the Laws, are either quite omitted, or slightly passed over. Indeed they forget not to recommend frequently to them what they call the *Queen of all Virtues*, viz. *Submission* to Superiors, and an entire blind *Obedience* to Authority, without instructing them in the due measures of it, rather teaching them that 'tis without all bounds: Thus the Spirits of Men are from the beginning inured to Subjection, and deprived of the right Notion of a generous and legal Freedom, which few among them (so hardly are the prejudices of

Education shaken off) grow sensible of, till they become of some Age and Maturity, or have unlearn'd by good Company and Travel those dangerous passive Doctrines they suck'd in at the Schools and Universities. But most have the Misfortune to carry these slavish Opinions with them to their Graves.

Had these Countries, whilst they were free, committed the Government of their Youth to *Philosophers* instead of *Priests*, they had in all probability preserv'd themselves from the Yoak of Bondage to this day, whereas now they not only endure it, but approve of it likewise: *tantum relligio potuit.*[6]

The Greeks and Romans instituted their Academies to quite another purpose, the whole Education of their Youth tended to make them as useful to the Society they lived in as possible. There they were train'd up to Exercise and Labour, to accustom them to an active Life: No Vice was more infamous than Sloth, nor any Man more contemptible than him that was too lazy to do all the Good he could; the Lectures of their Philosophers served to quicken them up to this. They recommended above all things the Duty to their Country, the preservation of the Laws and the publick Liberty; subservient to which they preach'd up Moral Virtues, such as Fortitude, Temperance, Justice, a contempt of Death, etc. Sometimes they made use of pious Cheats, as Elysian Fields, and an Assurance of Future Happiness, if they died in the Cause of their Country; and even deceived their Hearers into Greatness: Hence proceeded all those Noble Characters wherewith their Histories are so stock'd: Hence it was that their *Philosophers* were deservedly look'd upon as Supports of the State, they had their dependence wholly upon it; and as they could have no Interest distinct from it, they laid out themselves towards the advancing and promoting the good of it, insomuch that we find the very good Fortune of their *Commonwealths* often lasted no longer than they did. The managers of our modern Education have not been quite so publick Spirited, for it has been, as I have shewn, for the most part in the hands of Men who have a distinct Interest from the publick; therefore 'tis not to

[6.] A fragment of Lucretius [*de rerum natura*, 1. 101] commonly cited by Montaigne, translated as "so great are the evils Religion has encouraged." Sometimes *religio* is translated as "superstition." The 1738 edition includes an exclamation mark.

be wondered at, if like the rest of the World, they have been byassed by it, and directed their principal Designs towards the advancing their own Fortunes.

Good Learning as well as Travel is a great Antidote against the Plague of *Tyranny*. The Books that are left us of the Ancients (from whence, as from Fountains, we draw all that we are now Masters of) are full of Doctrines, Sentences, and Examples exhorting to the Conservation or Recovery of the publick Liberty, which was once valued above Life. The Heroes there celebrated are for the most part such as had destroyed or expelled *Tyrants;* and though *Brutus* be generally declaimed against by modern School-boys, he was then esteemed the true Pattern and Model of exact Virtue. Such was *Cato* of *Utica,* with others of like stamp. The more any person is conversant with good Books, the more shall he find the practices of these Great Men in this particular founded upon Reason, Justice, and Truth; and unanimously approv'd of by most of the succeeding Wise-men which the World has produc'd.

But instead of Books which inform the Judgment, those are commonly read in the Schools abroad, wherein an Elegancy of Latin and Greek Style is more sought after than the matter contained in them: So that such as treat a little boldly of publick Liberty occur to the reading of few, and those grown Men, rather through Chance or their Curiosity, than the recommendation of their Instructors.

'Twas not to learn Foreign Languages that the Graecian and Roman Youths went for so long together to the Academies and Lectures of their *Philosophers.* 'Twas not then, as now with us, when the Character of a Scholar is to be Skilled in Words; when one who is well versed in the dark Terms and Subtilties of the Schools passes for a profound Philosopher, by which we seem so far to have perverted the Notion of Learning, that a Man may be reputed a most extraordinary Scholar, and at the same time be the most useless Thing in the World; much less was it to learn their own Mother Tongues, the Greek and Latin, which we hunt after so eagerly for many Years together, (not as being the Vehicles of good Sense, but as if they had some intrinsick Virtue). 'Twas to learn how and when to speak pertinently, how to act like a Man to subdue the Passions, to be publick Spirited, to despise Death, Torments, and Reproach, Riches and the

Smiles of Princes, as well as their Frowns, if they stood between them and their Duty. This manner of Education produced Men of another stamp than appears now upon the Theatre of the World; such as we are scarce worthy to mention, and must never hope to imitate, till the like manner of Institution grows again into Reputation; which in Enslaved Countries 'tis never likely to do, as long as the *Ecclesiasticks,* who have an opposite Interest, keep not only the Education of Youth, but the Consciences of old Men in their Hands.

To serve by-ends, and because Priests thought they should find their own account in it, they calculated those unintelligible Doctrines of *Passive Obedience* and *Jus Divinum;* that the People ought to pay an absolute Obedience to a limited Government; fall down and worship the work of their own Hands, as if it dropt from Heaven; together with other as profitable Doctrines, which no doubt many are by this time ashamed of, tho' they think it below them to condescend so far as to confess themselves to have been in the wrong. For this Notion of *Jus Divinum* of Kings and Princes was never known in these Northern Parts of the World till these latter Ages of *Slavery:* Even in the Eastern Countries, though they adore their Kings as Gods, yet they never fancied they received their Right to Reign immediately from Heaven. The single Example in Scripture so much insisted on, viz. the Reign of Saul over the Jews, and Samuel's Description of what a King would be, not what he lawfully might be; proves either nothing at all, or the contrary to what some would have it; for besides that there are many Relations of Fact in the Old Testament, not condemned there, which it would not be only inconvenient, but sinful for us to imitate: Whoever peruses the whole Story of Saul and his Successor, will therein find more substantial Arguments against the *Jus Divinum* and *Non Resistance,* than for it: But we shall leave this, both as being too large an Argument for the compass of a Preface, and as being already fully handled by more able Pens.

All Europe was in a manner a free Country till very lately insomuch that the Europeans were, and still are, distinguish'd in the Eastern Parts of the World by the name of Franks. In the beginning small Territories, or Congregations of People, chose valiant and wise Men to be their Captains or Judges, and as often Deposed them upon Mis-management.

These Captains (doing their Duty well and faithfully) were the Originals of all our Kings and Princes, which at first, and for a long time were every where *Elective*. According to their own Warlike Temper, or that of the People which they govern'd, they (upon the Score of Revenge, Ambition, or being over-thronged with Multitudes at home) encroached upon their Neighbours; till from petty Principalities their Countries waxed to mighty Kingdoms. Spain alone consisting of twelve or thirteen till t'other day, and one part of our Island of no less than seven: Each of these was at first made through an Union of many petty Lordships. Italy from several small Commonwealths was at length swallowed up by the Emperors, Popes, Kings of Spain, Dukes of Florence, and other lesser Tyrants. Yet 'tis to be remark'd that the ancient State of Europe is best preserved in Italy even to this day, notwithstanding the Encroachments which have been there made on the *People's Liberties;* of which one Reason may be, that the *Republicks,* which are more in number and quality in that Spot of Ground than in all Europe besides, keep their *Ecclesiasticks* within their due bounds, and make use of that natural Wit which Providence and a happy Climate has given them, to curb those, who if they had Power would curb all the World.

Every one ought to know how great the Rights of the People were very lately in the *Elective* Kingdoms of Sweden and Denmark; how Germany was freer than any other part of Europe, till at length 'twas Lorded by Captains, who (in process of time grew Princes and Electors) and by Bishops with Temporal Authority, who may thank Charles the Great (a very bigotted Prince) for their double Sword of Flesh and Spirit.

If it be objected, that Princes have acquired a Right to be absolute and arbitrary where the Subjects have given up their *Liberties,* there are some in the World who venture to answer, That no People in their right Wits, (that is) not guided by Fear or Tumult, can be supposed to confer an absolute Dominion, or to give away the Freedom of themselves and their Posterity for all Generations; that such a Donation ought to be esteemed of no greater validity than the Gift of an Estate by a Child or a Madman from his lawful Successor; that the People can no more part with their legal *Liberties,* than Kings can alienate their Crowns: That nothing which even the Representative Body of the People does, which shall afterwards tend to the detriment of the Universality can then be obligatory, because many things good and profitable at the time of making those Laws may be the quite contrary afterwards, and as soon as any Law grows apparently mischievous to the whole Body that made it, or their Successors, it ought by them to be repealed, and would certainly be so in Countries where frequent free Assemblies of the States are in use. That if these Assemblies be hindered, or corrupted by sinister Practices, the obliging quality of such a Law determines of it self through its own nature, it being supposed that the true Representatives of the People would have annull'd it, had they been permitted to meet and act freely: That the Acts of one general Parliament, though a free one, are not perpetually obliging, since that as well as particular Persons is liable to mistakes; but the Acts of an eternal Succession of Parliaments, who make, confirm, change, or repeal Laws at their pleasure.

These are hard Sayings in the Opinion of many; but thus much we are sure of, whoever goes about to destroy or diminish the Right of the People in the disposal of the Crown, at the same time subverts their Majesty's Title to it. 'Tis therefore seasonable now or never to assert both; notwithstanding the prevarication of those who dare act under and receive benefit by this Revolution which they contributed nothing to, but which the People through God's Assistance procured for themselves; yet will not dive into the Merits of the Cause, nor own the Lawfulness of the Fact; but either cautiously avoid the Argument, or if it comes cross their way, mumble it as tenderly as the *Ass* did the *Thistle,* which caused the Philosopher to laugh, who never did it in his Life but that once; so this manner of Behaviour would move both the Laughter and Indignation of all understanding Persons, Lovers of their Countries *legal Liberties,* for none are forced to fall under greater Absurdities, or to make more terrible Blunders in Divinity, Politicks, and good Sense, than such as would fain reconcile present Interest to their old beloved Maxims: *res est ridicula & nimis jocosa.*[7] But Heaven be praised, the Nation is almost freed from the gross Error of that *slavish Doctrine,* in spite of the Endeavours of such as

---

[7.] Catullus, *The Carmina of Caius Valerius Catullus* 56, "To Cato." The phrase translates as "the thing is ridiculous, and laughable beyond measure."

would keep it alive, like hot Embers cover'd over with Ashes, ready to be blown up again into a flame upon the first occasion.

In Russia and Muscovy the Government is as Tyrannical as in any of the more *Eastern Monarchies*. The *Priests* there have very much contributed both to make and keep it so. To the end that the People may be kept in the requisite Temper of Obedience, none are permitted to Travel upon pain of Death, except such as have special License, which are exceeding few; neither are any Gentlemen of those Countries to be met with abroad, but publick Ministers and their Retinue: The Cause of this severe Prohibition is, lest such Travellers should see the Liberty of other Nations, and be tempted to covet the like for themselves at home, which might occasion Innovations in the State. The same reason which induces Tyrants to prohibit Travelling, should encourage the People of free Countries to practice it, in order to learn the Methods of preserving that which once lost is very difficultly recover'd; for *Tyranny* usually steals upon a State by degrees, and is (as a wise Man said) like a hectick Fever, which at first is easie to be cured, but hardly can be known; after 'tis thoroughly known it becomes almost incurable. Now travel best of all other Methods discovers (at least expense) the Symptoms of this pernicious Disease, as well as its dismal Effects when grown to a head; and 'tis certainly of greater Importance to understand how to preserve a sound Constitution, than how to repair a crazed one, though this also be a beneficial piece of Knowledge.

In our own *Universities*, which are without controversy the best in the World, whether we consider their Revenues, their Buildings, or their Learning, there are travelling Fellowships establish'd; which in a Country where the *Clergy's* Interest is not distinct from that of the *Laity*, is so far from being prejudicial to the legal Liberties of the People, that it tends to the Conservation of them; for such worthy Men as are employ'd abroad, may bring home generous Notions of Liberty, and make admirable Remarks on the contrary State; which being inculcated from the Pulpit, and enforced by the learned Arguments of able Divines, must needs overthrow those servile Opinions, which of late have been too much back'd by God's *Authority*, almost to the ruin of a *Free People*.

I do not hereby mean to reflect on the Order which generally has the government of our Youth; we have had the Experience of many among them who have given proof of a freer Education and useful Learning: And without question the chief Posts of the Gown of both kinds were never better fill'd than at present. I only lament the ill Contrivance of their Constitution, for while Interest draws one way, and Honesty another, when a Man may make his Fortune by forgetting his Duty to his Country, but shall always stick at Mark while he serves it; 'tis scarcely to be hoped Men should hold out against such Temptations, unless they be more gifted with Honesty than the generality of Mankind are. And since they continue still upon the same bottom, it must be expected the same, or other as mischievous Doctrines will every day be broach'd: whereas if they were once set upon the same foot the Philosophers of old were, if Honesty and the Duty to their Country were made their private Interest, and the way to thrive; we should soon see them shift hands, and the Spirit of those *Philosophers* revive again in them.

The Constitution of our *Universities*, as to Learning, seems as unfortunately regulated as it is to Politicks. We receive the directions of our Studies there, from Statutes made by those who understood nothing of the Matter, who had a quite different Notion and Taste of Learning from what the World has at present: It seems as ridiculous to take Patterns for the gentile Learning of this Age from the old fashion'd Learning of the Times wherein the University Statutes were compiled, as it would be for one who would appear well dress'd at Court, to make his Cloaths after the Mode in Henry the VIII's day: But 'tis of infinitely worse consequence; for the Prejudices and wrong Notions, the stiffness and positiveness in Opinion, the litigiousness and wrangling, all which the old Philosophy breeds, besides the narrow Spiritedness, and not enduring of Contradiction, which are generally contracted by a Monastick Life, require a great deal of time to get rid of, and until they be filed off by Conversation in the World abroad, a Man's Learning does but render him more useless and unfit for Society.

I dare appeal to common Experience, whether those excellent Men that of late Years have been preferred in our Church (than which Set of Divines England scarce ever knew a better) be not for the most part such as have been very conversant with the World; and if they have not all travell'd out of this Kingdom, have at least spent the best part of their days in this Epitome of the World, the City of London, where they have learnt Christian Liberty as well as other Christian Virtues. The great difference between these and others of narrow *Opiniastre* Tempers caus'd by their Monk-like Education is discernable by every Body, and puts it out of all doubt, that such who have seen most, of what Profession soever they be, prove the most honest and virtuous Men, and fittest for Humane Society: these embrace better Notions relating to the Publick, weigh Opinions before they adhere to them, have a larger Stock of Charity, a clearer Manner of distinguishing between Just and Unjust, understand better the Laws of our own Land, as well as the Privileges and Frailties of Human Nature; And all this in a degree far excelling the most zealous learned religious Person who has been brought up in his Cell, and is therefore what we call a *Bigot,* stiff in an Opinion, merely because he has been used to it, and is ashamed to be thought capable of being deceived.

Lawyers, whose manner of Breeding is much abroad in the World, and who are used to promiscuous Conversation, have been observed in most places to be great Favourers of *Liberty,* because their knowledge of ancient Practice, and the just Title which the People have to their Privileges (which they meet with every where in their course of Reading) makes them less scrupulous of committing what some Divines miscall a Sin in those that endeavour to preserve or recover them; the Oversights of some few Gentlemen of this honourable Profession are therefore the less excusable; for I must confess, among other things, that Motto, *A Deo Rex, à Rege Lex,*[8] wherein the Divine Right of the impious Will of a Tyrant is as strongly asserted as could be in the compass of a Ring, has occasioned frequent Reflections, not much in favour of those that made use of it.

Thus I have touch'd upon the Manner of Education necessary to the beginning and finishing a Gentleman, who is to be useful to his Country, which I suppose ought to be the principal end of it. And I can't but believe, if in our Schools our Youth were bred up to understand the Meaning of the Authors they are made to read, as well as the Syntax of the Words.

[8.] A favorite motto of James I: "The King is from God, the law from the King." See E. Kantarowitz, *The King's Two Bodies* (Princeton, 1957), p. 415. The 1738 edition has a margin note that reads, "In January 1683, 35 Car. II there was a call of sixteen sargeants at law, who gave rings with this motto."

If there were as much care taken to inculcate the good Maxims, and recommend the noble Characters the old Historians are so full of, as there is
to hammer into their Heads the true Grammar of them, and the fineness
of the Phrase: If in our *Universities* a proportionable Care were taken to
furnish them with noble and generous Learning: If after this they were
duly informed in the Laws and Affairs of their own Country, trained up in
good Conversation and useful Knowledge at home, and then sent abroad
when their Heads began to be well settled, when the heat of Youth was
worn off, and their Judgments ripe enough to make Observation: I say, I
cannot but believe that with this manner of Institution a very moderate
Understanding might do wonders, and the coming home fully instructed
in the Constitutions of other Governments, would make a Man but the
more resolute to maintain his own.

For the advantage of a free Government above its contrary needs no
other help to make it appear, than only to be exposed to a considerate
View with it: The difference may be seen written in the very Faces of
the several People, as well as in their manner of Living; and when we
find nothing but Misery in the fruitfullest Countries subject to Arbitrary
Power, but always a Face of plenty and Chearfulness in Countries naturally unfruitful, which have preserv'd their Liberties, there is no further
room left for Argument, and one cannot be long in determining which
is most eligible. This Observation is so obvious that 'tis hard for any that
Travels not to make it; therefore 'tis a sufficient reason why all our Gentry
should go abroad. An English Man should be shewn the Misery of the
enslaved Parts of the World, to make him in Love with the Happiness of
his own Country; as the Spartans exposed their drunken Servants to their
Children, to make them in love with Sobriety.

But the more polish'd and delicious Countries of France, Spain, or
Italy, are not the places where this Observation may be made to great-
est advantage; the Manner of Living, Goodness of the Air and Diet, the
Magnificence of the Buildings, Pleasantness of the Gardens, pompous
Equipage of some great Persons, dazzle the Eyes of most Travellers, and
cast a disguise upon the Slavery of those Parts; and as they render this
Evil more supportable to the Natives, so they almost quite hide it from the
view of a Cursory Traveller, amusing him too much from considering the

Calamities which accompany so much Splendour, and so many Natural Blessings: or from reflecting how much more happy the Condition of the People would be with better usage. But in the Northern Kingdoms and Provinces there appears little or nothing to divert the Mind from contemplating Slavery in its own Colours, without any of its Ornaments. And since, for that reason, few of our Gentlemen find temptation enough to Travel into those Parts, and we have hardly any tolerable Relation of them extant, though we have frequent occasions of being concerned with them, I thought it might be of use to publish the following *Account* of *Denmark,* which I took care to be informed of upon the place with the greatest Exactness possible, and have related fairly and impartially, which may save the Curious the labour and expense of that Voyage.

That Kingdom has often had the Misfortune to be govern'd by French Counsels. At the time when Mr. Algernon Sydney was Ambassador at that Court, Monsieur Terlon, the French Ambassador, had the Confidence to tear out of the Book of Motto's in the King's Library, this Verse, which Mr. Sydney (according to the liberty allowed to all noble Strangers) had written in it: *manus haec inimica tyrannis Ense petit placidam sub libertate quietem.*[9] Though Monsieur Terlon understood not a word of Latin, he was told by others the Meaning of that Sentence, which he considered as a Libel upon the French Government, and upon such as was then a setting up in Denmark by French Assistance, or Example.

To conclude; A considering English Traveller will find by experience, that at present nothing is so generally studied by the Sovereign Princes of the World, as the Arts of War, and the keeping of their own Countries in the desired Subjection. The Arts of Peace, whereby the Encrease and Prosperity of their Subjects might be promoted, being either intirely neglected or faintly prosecuted; he will further be convinced what great reason he has to bless Providence for his being born, and continuing yet a Freeman: He will find that the securing this inestimable Blessing to himself, and transmitting it to late Posterity, is a Duty he owes to his Country; the right performance of which does in a great measure depend upon

[9.] "This hand an enemy to tyrants seeks with the sword calm peace in freedom." This became the motto of the state of Massachusetts.

a good Education of our Youth, and the Preservation of our Constitution upon its true and natural Basis, The *Original Contract.* All other Foundations being false, nonsensical, and rotten; derogatory to the present Government, and absolutely destructive to the legal Liberties of the English Nation. *Salus populi suprema lex esto.*[10]

[10.] "The safety of the people is the supreme law."

CHAPTER I

Of the Territories belonging to the King of Denmark, and their Situation

If we consider the Extent of the King of Denmark's Dominions, he may with Justice be reckoned among the greatest Princes of Europe; but if we have regard to the importance and value of them, he may be put in Balance with the King of Portugal, and possibly be found lighter.

His Style is King of Denmark and Norway, of the Goths and Vandals, Duke of Sleswick and Holstein, Stormar, and Ditmarsh; Earl in Oldenburg and Delmenhorst; all which Countries he actually possesses either in whole or in part: so that except that of the Goths and Vandals, which Title both he and the King of Sweden use, and which the Crown of Denmark has retained ever since it was Master of Sweden (as we in England do that of France) all the rest are substantial and not empty Titles.

My design is to acquaint you with the present State of these Countries, and to offer nothing but what I have either Collected from sensible grave Persons, or what my own Knowledge and Experience has confirm'd to be Truth.

Since the late Wars between that famous Captain Charles Gustavus of Sweden, and Frederic the Third, which ended in a Peace *Anno* 1660 Denmark has been forced to sit down with the loss of all its Territories which lay on the other side of the Baltick Sea; Schonen, Halland, and Bleking remaining to the Swedes, notwithstanding frequent Struggles to recover them. These three (especially Schonen) were the best Provinces belonging to Denmark, and therefore are still looked upon with a very envious Eye by the Danes: And for this very reason 'tis reported, that the Windows of Cronenburgh Castle, whose Prospect lay towards Schonen, were wall'd up, that so hateful an Object might not cause continual heart-burnings.

Denmark therefore, as it is thus clipp'd, is at present bounded on all sides with the Sea, except one small Neck of Land, where it joins to Holstein; the German Ocean washes it on the West and North-west; the entrance into the Baltick, called the Categate on the North, and North-East; the Baltick on the East; and the River Eyder on the South; which having its source very near the East Sea, takes his course Westward, and falls into the Ocean at Toningen, a strong Town of the Duke of Holstein Gottorp's: So that if a Channel were made of about three Danish Miles from that River to Kiel, 'twould be a perfect Island. I include in this Account the Dutchy of Sleswick as part of Denmark, but not the Dutchy of Holstein; because the former was a Fief of that Crown, the latter of the Empire.

All Denmark therefore comprehending its Islands, as I have thus bounded it, lies in length between the degrees of $54^{gr.}\ 45^{min.}$ and $58^{gr.}\ 15^{min.}$ North Latitude, the breadth not being proportionable; and may at a large Computation be reckoned to amount to the bigness of two thirds of the Kingdom of Ireland.

Norway, which lies North from Denmark, and is separated from it by that Sea which is usually called the Categate, is a vast and barren Country, full of Mountains and Fir trees; it reaches from 59 to 71 degrees of North Latitude; but is very narrow in respect to its length. It is bounded on the West and North by the Ocean, on the East by Sweden and the Territories belonging to it; on the South by the Sea lying between it and Denmark. The Sea is so deep about it, that there is no Anchorage for Ships; and therefore its Coasts are accounted the most dangerous of any in Europe to run with in the Night, or in a Storm; on which if you chance to be driven, there is no scaping, the Shoar being all along high Rocks, at the very foot of which one may find 200 Fathom Water.

Holstein, which includes Ditmarsh and Stormar, is bounded by the Dutchy of Sleswick on the North, the Dutchy of Saxe Lawenburg on the South-East, the River Elbe on the South-West, the rest of it is washed by the Ocean and Baltick Sea. It lies between the 54th and 55th degrees of North Latitude.

Oldenburg and Delmenhorst are two Counties in Germany that lye together, detached from all the rest of the King of Denmark's Countries; the two Rivers, Elb and Weser, and the Dutchy of Bremen, interposing between them and Holstein. They are bounded on the North-East by the Weser, on the West by East-Friesland and the County of Embden, on the South by part of the Bishoprick of Munster. They are a small Territory of about 35 English Miles in Diameter; the middle of which is in the Latitude of 53 degrees and a half.

The rest of the King of Denmark's Territories not mentioned in the enumeration of his Titles, are the Islands of Feroe, and Iceland in the Northern Ocean. St. Thomas, one of the Caribbee Islands in the West-Indies. A Fort upon the Coast of Guinea, call'd Christiansburg; and another in the East-Indies, call'd Tranquebar. He has likewise a Toll at El-fleet upon the River Weser.

Thus much may serve in general touching the Dominions of that King, which have this great inconveniency, that they are mightily disjoined and separated from each other; it being certain, that a State which is confined by many Principalities is weak, exposed to many dangers, and requires a more than ordinary Expense, as well as Prudence, to preserve it entire: And it is to this principally that the Conquests which the Swedes have gained upon them may be ascribed.

CHAPTER II

Of Denmark in particular, and the Island of Zealand

This being the most considerable, and in value four parts in five of all the Territories belonging to the Crown of Denmark, I shall give a more particular account of it than of the rest. Others, I know, have given us the Genealogies and Succession of its Kings, ancient Names, Inhabitants, Conquests, etc. my business is only to inform how it stands at this day, and to enter no further into the former History, or the Geography of the Country, than is necessary to the understanding the present State of it.

Denmark then, properly so called, consists of many Islands in the Baltick Sea, and of that part of the Continent which is now called Jutland: The Dutchy of Sleswick, which I reckoned in the former Chapter as part of it, shall be treated of by it self, because it is divided between the King and the Duke of Holstein Gottorp; whereas these above-mentioned are wholly the King's. Jutland is the biggest and most fertile Country, but the Islands are more considerable in regard of their Situation, especially Zealand; because Copenhagen, the Chief City of Denmark, is seated in it, and the famous passage of the Sound is bordered by its Shoar, where, on the narrowest part the Town of Elsinor stands: wherefore I shall begin with a description of them, and first of Zealand.

It is almost of a Circular Figure, and contains about 180 English Miles in Circumference; I cannot commend its Fertility, there being no Bread corn growing in any part of it except Rye, which indeed is in good quantity, and whereof most of their Bread is made. There are few Meadows in it, and yet there is no want of good Hay: Most of their Grass, which is short and sweet, grows by the sides of their Corn Fields, or in some scattered spots of Marish Grounds. It has no Rivers, nor above half a score Brooks that are able to turn a Mill; to supply this, there is a great number of fine Lakes sufficiently stored with Fish. The Air is but indifferent, especially in and near Copenhagen; which is occasioned by the frequent Fogs and low Situation; yet Colds of the Lungs are very rare here; this I attribute to the pureness of their firing, which is Beechwood, the only sort of Timber trees which abound in this Island. About one fourth part of it is Forest, lying open for the King's Hunting and his Game, such as Staggs, Wild-Boars, Roe-Bucks, etc. these are such Sacred things that no Body dares touch them, though they find them in whole Herds destroying their Corn, to the infinite yearly damage of the poor Peasants.

The Face of the Land is pleasant in many places, abounding with little Hills, Woods and Lakes in a very agreeable diversity. For Sea-Ports, that most excellent one belonging to Copenhagen must make amends for the want of them, not only in this, but many other of the Islands; there being few others, that I know of, capable of harbouring a Vessel of 200 Tuns.

Neither is this a sensible want, because there are no Commodities in this Island for Exportation: In good years, that is, wet ones (for the Soil being altogether Sandy, requires frequent Rains, even thus far North) there may be some overplus of Rye; and I have been told, that about forty years ago, ten or twelve Dutch Flyboats found yearly their Lading at Kiog, a pretty flourishing Town at that time, within twenty English Miles of Copenhagen; but of late they seem to be well satisfied if the Product of the Isle maintains in this sort of Grain the Inhabitants of it: Not that the numbers of these are increased, but Husbandry is not so much encouraged now as when the Taxes of the poor Country People were less frequent and grievous.

The Cattle here are generally small and lean; kept within doors seven or eight Months in the Year; where their Feeding is partly Hay, partly Brewers Grains, Roots, Weeds, and such Trash as their Owners can provide for them. In Summer time their Beef is sweet and juicy; but Wether Mutton was a rare thing till of late; nor is it common now, they being not used to Geld their Sheep; and therefore 'twas usually eaten while it was Lamb.

The feeding of the Commonalty generally throughout all Denmark is very mean; the Burgers and Citizens sustaining themselves with Rye-bread, Salt-flesh, Stock-fish, Bacon, and very bad Cheese; insomuch that the Inspectors of our Markets in England, who use to destroy or send to the Prisons all such Victuals as are not judged wholsom, would (if they found them no better provided than at Copenhagen) go near to empty the Markets, and leave little to either Buyer or Seller. The Peasants live on Roots, white Meats, and Rye-bread; seldom tasting fresh Fish, and scarce ever Flesh, unless on some extraordinary Festivals, as on St. Martin's Eve, when each Family in Denmark, without fail, makes merry with a roasted Goose at Supper.

Here, and in all Denmark, are but two Seasons of the Year, Winter and Summer; those two other more agreeable ones of Spring and Autumn not being commonly known; the Spring never, and the Autumn seldom; you immediately leap from extremity of Heat to extremity of Cold; and so on the contrary, when Winter is over, from Cold to Heat. During the three Months of June, July, and August, the Heat is much more intense than in England, and very sultry in the Nights, but 'tis a gloomy Heat, and People generally perceive some interposition of thick Vapours between them and the Sun. In Copenhagen, during these three Months, they are constantly troubled with the Plague of Flies, which they endeavour to destroy by a poisoned Water; upon the laying of which in their Kitchins and Chambers, I have seen whole Bushels of dead Flies swept together in one Room.

The Baltick Sea near this City is very ill stored with good Fish; neither did I ever know any Sea-Town of that Consequence worse served with it: Whether it be that the Sea wants its requisite saltiness, (being rather to be esteemed brackish than salt) or that the People are not industrious enough to take them; but I rather believe the former.

The principal things of this Island, and indeed of all Denmark, are the

City of Copenhagen, and the Passage of the Sound. I will begin with the City, the rather because when I have done with that I have little more to say of any other in the King of Denmark's Dominions; there being no other belonging to him much better than our Town of St. Albans.

Copenhagen is no ancient City, nor a very large one; it approaches in bigness nearest to Bristol of any of our English Cities; but it increases in Buildings every day, notwithstanding the many discouragements it lies under. The Fortifications of it enclose a great deal more Ground than is built upon; and many small Buildings, which upon a further increase of its Riches, will be pulled down. Its Situation for Trade is one of the best in the World, because of the excellency of its Port; so that without doubt, were Copenhagen a free City, it would be the Mart and Staple of all the Traffick of the Baltick. This Port is inclosed by the Bulwarks of the Town, the entrance into it being so narrow, that but one Ship can pass at a time; which entrance is every Night shut up with a strong Boom; the Citadel on one side, and a good Block-house well furnished with Cannon on the other, Commands the Mouth of it. Within this Haven rides the Navy Royal, every Ship having his place assigned to it; a wooden Gallery ranges round the whole Inclosure where the Fleet lies, laid over the Water in such manner, that all the Ships may be viewed near at hand as easily and commodiously as if they lay on dry Land. This Harbour is capacious enough to hold 500 Sail, where neither Wind nor Enemies can do them the least mischief. The Road without is very good and safe; being fenced from the Sea by a large Sand Bank, on the Points of which float always a couple of Buoys to direct all Ships that come in or go out. Here are no Tides to fear, but always a sufficient depth of Water. Sometimes indeed, according as the Winds blow in or out of the Baltick, there sets a Current; but 'tis not frequent, nor dangerous. To conclude, this Port may justly be reckoned in all respects one of the best in the whole World.

The Town is strong, being situated in a flat Marish Soil, not commanded by any height; the Air is bad by reason of the stink of the Channels which are cut through it. The Works of it are only of Earth and Sodds, yet raised according to the Rules of Modern Fortification, and in tolerable good Repair. The Buildings both in this City and elsewhere, are generally very mean, being Cagework, and having the Intervals between the Timbers filled up with Brick. 'Tis observable, that all the good Publick Build-ings in it, such as the Change, Arsenal, Round-Steeple, etc. were built by King Christian the Fourth, the present King's Grandfather, and a very brave, though not a Fortunate Prince; who did more with less Revenues than all the succeeding Princes; the Monarchy being at that time neither Hereditary nor Absolute. He used often to say, "That he knew the Purses of his Subjects would be always open for his and the Kingdoms just Occa-sions; and that he had rather they were his Cash-keepers than a High-Treasurer, who might abuse him." Although the principal Decorations of this Town are owing to him, yet he either forgot or delay'd the Building of a Palace for himself and his Successors, and no Body has undertaken it since; though certainly in no Kingdom is there greater occasion; this King's House of Residence being for Situation, Meanness, and Inconve-nience the worst in the World; and as singular for badness as the Port is for goodness. Several of the Noblemen, as his High Excellency Guldenlieu, the great Admiral Juel, with others, being infinitely better lodged than the whole Royal Family: Yet to make amends for this, his Majesty has near him an excellent Stable of Horses; and handsome large Gardens, with a good Garden-House, called Rosenburg, some distance from the Palace, at the other end of the Town.

CHAPTER III

Of the Sound

This Passage or Streight called the Sound, or Ore-sound, which has so great a Reputation in these Northern Parts of the World, lies between this Island of Zealand and the firm Land of Schonen. On Denmark side, where it is narrowest, stands the Town of Elsinore, and the strong Fortress of Cronenburg; near which is a tolerable good Road for Ships. On Sweden side is the Town of Helsinburg with a demolished Castle, whereof only one old Tower remains, sufficient to hold half a dozen great Guns to repay the Salutes of Men of War which pass through.

Betwixt these two do pass and repass all Vessels that Trade into the Baltick; so that next that of Gibraltar, one may justly reckon this Streight the most important and frequented of any in Europe. The loss of Schonen, though it was considerable in regard of the largeness and fruitfulness of the Province, yet it was more so in respect to the Dominion of this great Passage; for although the Danes, by the Treaty of Peace, have expressly retained their Title to it, and receive Toll from all Ships that pass except Swedes, yet they do not esteem the Security of that Title so firm as they would wish; for being not Masters of the Land on both sides, they may have the Right, but not the Power to assert it upon occasion, and seem only to enjoy it at present according to their good Behaviour; their stronger Neighbour the Swede being able to make use of the first Opportunity given him to their Prejudice.

This Toll, being very considerable, and of late years occasioning many Disputes which are not yet determined, I thought it might not be amiss to set down in this place, what I have learnt of the Original and Nature of it, after having made as strict Enquiry as was possible from the most ancient, and most understanding Persons I could meet with.

The most rational Account then is, That it was at first laid by the Consent of the Traders into the Baltick, who were willing to allow a small matter for each Ship that passed, towards the maintaining of Lights on certain places of that Coast, for the better direction of Sailors in dark Nights: Hereupon this Passage of the Sound became the most practised; that other of the Great Belt being in a little time quite neglected; as well because of the great Conveniency of those Lights to the Shipping that passed in and out of the East-Sea, as because of an Agreement made that no Ships should pass the other way, to the end that all might pay their shares; it being unreasonable that such Ships should have the benefit of those Lights in dark or stormy Winter Nights, who avoided paying towards the maintaining of those Fires, by passing another way. Besides, if this manner of avoiding the Payment had been allowed, the Revenue would have been so insignificant, considering the small Sum which each Ship was to pay, that the Lights could not have been maintained by it; and the Danes were not willing to be at the Charge solely for the use and benefit of their own Trading Ships, in regard they were Masters of so few as made it not worth their while; the Lubeckers, Dantzickers, and Merchants of other Hanse Towns, being the greatest Traders at that time in the Northern Parts of Europe, by which they arrived to a great height of Power and Riches.

But there being no fixed Rule or Treaty whereby to be governed with regard to the different Bulk of the Ships belonging to so many several Nations, the Danes began in process of time to grow Arbitrary, and exacted more or less Sums, according to the strength or weakness of those they had to deal with, or according to their Friendship or Discontent with those Princes and States to whom the several Ships belonged: Therefore the Emperor Charles the Fifth, to ascertain this Toll, concluded a Treaty with the King of Denmark, which was signed at Spire on the Rhine, and was in behalf of his Subjects of the Seventeen Provinces of the Low Countries, who had great Traffick in the Baltick; and agreed that as a Toll-Custom in the Sound, every Ship of 200 Tuns and under, should pay two Rose Nobles at its Entrance or Return from the Baltick, and every Ship above 200 Tuns three Rose Nobles.

This Agreement remained in force till such time as the United Provinces shook off the Spanish Yoak, and then the Danes taking the advantage of those Wars, raised their Toll to an extravagant height, the troublesome Times not affording leisure to the Dutch to mind the redressing of such a Mischief.

However, about the Year 1600 they joined themselves with the City of Lubeck, in opposition to such an exorbitant Toll as was taken from both of them; so that from thenceforth the Dutch paid more or less, according as Fortune was favourable or adverse to them, but generally little.

Anno 1647 the first Treaty was made between Denmark and the United Provinces (as Sovereigns) for this Toll; and they were obliged to pay a certain Sum for each Ship; this Treaty was to last Forty years; after the expiration of which, if in the mean time no new Treaty were made, that of Spire was to be in force.

This Treaty of 1647 expired 1687; and the Danes agreed to make an interim Treaty, till such time as the many Differences between them and the Hollanders in this and other Matters could be adjusted at leisure, and concluded in a more lasting and solemn one.

This interim Treaty, which was but for Four years, expired in the Year 1691; so that no new Treaty being made and finished during that time, it is evident that only the ancient Treaty of Spire remains in force, and no other.

The English Treaties with Denmark are grounded on those between the Dutch and that Kingdom, and have reference to them; with a Covenant that we shall be treated *tanquam gens amicissima;*[11] excepting always Sweden, whose Ships pay no Toll at all.

[11.] Diplomatic term for "privileged nation status."

So that at present both the English and Dutch have occasion for new Treaties with Denmark in this and other Affairs of Trade, unless it be agreed by all Parties that the Treaty of Spire shall for so much remain in vigour hereafter.

From this short History of the Original of this Imposition it appears, how slightly grounded the King of Denmark's Title is to this Right of exacting the Toll of the Sound; which from an easie Contribution which Merchants chose to pay for their own Convenience, and whereof the King of Denmark was only Treasurer or Trustee, to see it fairly laid out for the common use, is grown to be a heavy Imposition upon Trade, as well as a kind of servile acknowledgment of his Sovereignty of those Seas; and is purely owing to his taking an Advantage of the Difficulties of the Hollanders during their Wars with Spain, and the Connivance of King James the First in prejudice of the English; who favoured the Danes upon account of his Marriage to a Daughter of that Crown; upon whose two Examples all the lesser States were forced to submit. Nor can it be conceived how it could be otherwise brought about; since it is very well known, that the Passage of the Sound is not the only one to the Baltick Sea, there being two others called the Greater and Lesser Belts; and that of the Greater Belt so commodious and large, that during the late Wars the whole Dutch Fleet chose to pass through it, and continue in it for four or five Months together; and the Danish Strength at Sea never appeared yet so formidable as to be able to oblige the English and Dutch to choose, which Passage it pleased: Besides, the breadth of the Sound in the narrowest part is four English Miles over; and every where of a sufficient depth; so that his Castles could not Command the Channel when he was Master of both sides; much less now that he has but one. So that it is plain, this pretended Sovereignty is very precarious, being partly founded on a Breach of Trust, as well as the Carelessness of some of the Princes concerned in it, to the great Injury of Trade: And the Spaniards may, with as much right, lay claim to the Sovereignty of the Streights of Gibralter, where there is but one Passage; or the Swede, who is now Master of one of the Castles on the Sound, demand another Toll of all Ships, since both are better able to support their Claims.

For the further clearing of this Point, and to shew how it agrees with the Account I have already given, I have thought fit to insert in this place the Copy of a Letter from a very understanding Person, March 31. 1691.

Sir,

The Duties or Customs in the Sound were of old times no more than a Rose Noble for each Ship, Loading included; but within these hundred Years, some say since King James of Scotland came to the Crown of England, and winked at it, the Kings of Denmark having the Lands on both sides the Passage, began to impose Taxes on the Merchandize, and raise higher those which were formerly on the Ships; which the Lubeckers, who were then powerful, refused to pay.

Anno 1640 the King caused a Book of Rates to be printed, whereof I have one, according to which a Ship of 100 Lasts, or 200 Tuns, (which is the same thing), did pay as followeth: For 100 Last of Salt to the East 300 Rix Dollars; for the Ship and petty Charges on the Salt 34 Rix Dollars, 24 Stivers; and for 100 Last of Rye from the East 150 R.D. for Ship and petty Charges, as above, 34 R.D. 24 Stivers. So that the Charges of a Ship of this Burden, with its Lading forward and backward was 519 Rix Dollars.

Hereupon the Hollanders made an Alliance with the Swedes, who Anno 1643 by the way of Germany invaded Denmark, and the Dutch lent them Ships; then the King Prints another Book of Rates more favourable, demanding for 100 Last of Spanish Salt 100 Rix Dollars, for 100 Last of Rye 75 R.D. Ships Charges in and out, as above, 69 R.D. the whole amounting to 244 R.D. But this was neither done time enough, nor the Rates lowered enough. The Hollanders, by their Treaty with Denmark of 1646 or thereabouts, brought them thus, The 100 Last of Salt to 50 Rix Dollars, 100 Last of Rye to 50 R.D. Ships, and other petty Charges, nothing: in all for each Ship 100 Rix Dollars. And by reason of this untimely heightening of their Customs it is, that the Kings of Denmark have lost so many Territories to the Swedes.

But to Answer your Demand more fully, it was in those days, that is, about the Year 1640, that the Customs of the Ore-Sound yielded per Annum from 240,000 Rix Dollars to 300,000 R.D. But since 1645 they have not at any time render'd above 150,000 R.D. nor ever so much, except in time of War with the Swedes, when all did pay without Exemption. During the last War, I remember it yielded but 143,000 Rix Dollars; but before that War, and since (the Swedish Ships freeing all Goods that are carried in them, and the Swedish Goods in Foreign Ships being also free by Treaty) it has not yielded above 80,000 Rix Dollars per Annum; and the last Year past it did not reach to full 70,000 Rix Dollars.

The Court of Denmark is not to be blamed therefore for being wonderful jealous of any Infraction of this their pretended Sovereignty, as People are most careful and suspicious in behalf of an Estate wherein their Title is weak, it being so much the Interest not only of the English and Dutch, but also of the Swede, to have it set right, both to encourage Trade to his own Country, and to lessen the Revenue of his Neighbour; neither can it be said, that the English and Dutch did ever entirely yield the Point; for though they agreed to pay a small Toll on Merchandize, yet no manner of searching or stopping is to be allowed, or has ever been. The Danes are now obliged to take the Master of the Vessel's word for the quality and quantity of the Lading; and thought it prudence never to press this Point further, least we should grow angry, and make too narrow an Inspection both into their Original Right, and into their Ability to maintain it: For whilst we and the Dutch are content to pay this Toll, all the other petty Princes and States do it without Murmur, but if we once broke the Chain, they would shake off their part of it likewise.

CHAPTER IV

Of the other Islands, and Jutland

The most considerable Islands next to that of Zealand, are, Funen or Fionia, Laland, Langland, Falstria, Mune, Samsoe, Arroe, Bornholm, and Amack; there are besides many other small ones of less note.

Funen is second to Zealand, whether its bigness or the goodness of its Soil be considered; it has plenty of Corn, Hogs, Lakes, and Woods; the chief Town of it is Odensee, a well-seated, and formerly a flourishing little City, but at present much fallen to decay. This Island produces nothing for the Merchant to export, except some few Horses, the Inhabitants usually consuming their own Commodities. This is a principal Government, called a Stifts Ampt. The present Governor is Mr. Winterfelt.

Laland is a small, but plentiful Island, producing all sorts of Corn in abundance, and particularly Wheat, wherewith it supplies the City of Copenhagen, and all other parts of Denmark, where it is a rarity. The Hollanders buy yearly, and ship off great quantities of Corn from hence. This likewise is a Stifts Ampt, having several of the lesser Islands under its Jurisdiction. The Governor of it is Mr. Geugh, who formerly had a Publick Character, and resided a long time in England.

Falstria, Langland, and Mune are fertile Islands; the two first Export yearly some Corn. Arroe and Alsen abound in Anise-seeds, which are much used to season their Meat, and mix with their Bread. Bornholm, Samsoe, with the other Islands, nourish Cattle, and afford Corn for the use of the Inhabitants. But Amack deserves to be particularly remembered; this little Island joins close to the City of Copenhagen, from which 'tis only separated by a small Arm of the Sea, which is passed over by a Draw-bridge, and exceeds in fruitfulness any spot of Ground in Denmark. This Land was given many Years ago to several Families of North Hollanders, who were planted there to make Butter and Cheese for the Court; the Descendants of whom retain to this day the Habit, Language, and Customs of their Predecessors, together with their Cleanliness and Industry; neither will they mix with the Danes, but intermarry with each other. They had formerly extraordinary Privileges granted to them, whereof some continue to this time, but others are retrenched; and by degrees it is to be feared they will be treated like the other Subjects.

This Island of Amack, through the Industry of these laborious People, is as it were the Kitchen-Garden of Copenhagen, and supplies its Markets plentifully with all sorts of Roots and Herbs; besides Butter, Milk, great quantities of Corn, and some Hay; whatever it produces being the best in its kind that is to be found in the whole Kingdom.

Jutland, part of the ancient *Cimbrica Chersonesus,* is the biggest part of the Kingdom of Denmark, and may amount to about two thirds of the whole. It is divided into four Stifts Ampts, or principal Governments. The present Governors are, the Count de Frize, the upper Mareschal Speckhan, Monsieur Edmund Schele, now Envoy Extraordinary to his Majesty from the King of Denmark, etc.

This is a plentiful Country, abounding more especially in Cattle; it wants good Sea-Ports towards the Ocean, notwithstanding which the Hollanders transport yearly great quantities of lean Cows and Oxen from hence to their more fertile Soil, where in a short time they grow so prodigiously fat, through better feeding, in the rich Grounds of Holland, that a vast Profit is made by this Traffick. The Horses and Swine of this Country are excellent, and in great numbers. It affords Corn in sufficient quantity for the use of its own People. The Land is more Fertile near the Sea-Coasts; the Inland being full of Heaths, Lakes, and Woods. In short, it is the best Country the King of Denmark is Master of, and appears to be least declining, because most remote from Copenhagen. *Procul a Jove, Procul a Fulmine.*[12] It being observed, that in limited Monarchies and Commonwealths, a Neighbourhood to the Seat of the Government, is advantageous to the Subjects, whilst the distant Provinces are less thriving, and more liable to Oppression: but in Arbitrary and Tyrannical Kingdoms the quite contrary happens.

[12.] "To retire from Jove is to retire from the thunder-bolt." This is a proverb indicating "far from court, far from fear." See definition in R. Ainsworth, *Thesaurus Linguae Latinae Compendiarum,* 1751, under "a princes court."

CHAPTER V

Of the Rest of the King of Denmark's Countries

The Dutchy of Sleswick is in general a very good Country; its convenient Situation between two Seas, the Ocean and the Baltick, rendering it considerable for Trade, although the natural Commodities, fit for Exportation, are in no great quantity. Some Corn, Cattle, Horses, and Wood for Firing it affords to its Neighbours, over and above a sufficient store of each for its own Inhabitants. It is divided between the King and the Duke of Holstein. The principal Town which gives Name to the Dutchy, belongs to the Duke of Holstein, who resides near it in his Palace of Gottorp, one of the most delicious Seats that is to be seen in all the Northern Parts of Europe; nothing can be more Pleasant and Romantick than the Situation of this Castle. It stands in an Island, surrounded by a large Lake made by the River Sley, whose rising Banks are clothed with fine Woods, the Waters clear and full of Fish, carry Vessels of small Burden to and from the Baltick Sea, into which it empties it self. The Gardens are large, with great Cost and Art cut out of the declivity of a Hill on the other side the Lake, and are as well disposed and laid out with Fountains, Parterres, Walks, and Water-works as many of the most famous Villa's in

Italy. A noble large Park, or rather Forest, full of Deer, Wild-boars, and all sorts of Game, joins close to this Garden, cut through with pleasant Walks and Ridings.

This Residence of the Duke of Holstein suffered much during the Misfortunes of its Master; many of the Improvements being not only suffer'd to run to ruine and decay, but industriously and as some say, by order, pull'd down and destroyed; which at present, since the Reestablishment of the Duke, are repairing and restoring to their former Splendour. Among several other things of value, none had better luck than an admirable Library, being a choice Collection of Books which many Dukes of Holstein had of a long time been gathering; this escaped, and in the Year 1692 I saw it with the rest of the Rarities of this place in a good Condition, and tending to a better.

Holstein is divided among several of the Branches of that Family, all whose Descendants call themselves Dukes of Holstein; and according to the German Custom, (as well younger Brothers as elder) assume the Title and Quality of Princes: only the chief and estated Men of these several Branches are distinguished by the Additional Title of the Place of their Residence; as the Duke of Holstein Ploen, Holstein Sunderburg, Holstein Norburg, etc. the Cadets of each, contenting themselves with the bare Title of Princes, till they come to be Proprietors of Land; whose Denomination they may add to that of Duke. But the King of Denmark, (who is likewise Duke of Holstein) and the Duke of Holstein Gottorp, are possessed of the greatest part of it, and both hold it as a Fief of the Empire.

Here, as well as in Sleswick, the Jurisdictions and Interests of these two Princes are very much intermixed; so that the People scarce know whose Subjects to reckon themselves, since they often swear Allegiance, and pay Tribute to both. In some Towns and Balliages both the King and Duke elect the Yearly Magistrates, and divide the Revenue; in others they do this by turns: So that upon any Quarrel or Difference between these two Princes, the poor People are strangely divided, and in a most miserable Condition; their Inclination leading them to the Duke's Interest, who being the weaker, finds it his Advantage to use them better; but their fear causing them to appear for the King as the stronger, though more Arbitrary.

This Country is very fruitful and pleasant; excellently well seated for Trade, lying between the two Seas, and having the advantage of the Neighbourhood of the River Elbe, and of Hamburg; which being a free City, and consequently a rich one, imparts a large share of its Blessings to the Territories of those Princes which lie any thing near it. This is apparent enough in the visible Prosperity of such Lands and People as are within a Day's Journey or more of that City, above such as lie remote from its Influence. The Inhabitants of Holstein use to brag that it resembles England in its variety of Hills, Meadows, Woods, Rivers, and Cornfields; as also that we are beholding to them and their Neighbourhood for our Original; the People of those Parts called Angles, having planted, and at the same time given the Name of Anglia to our Island.

The Danes, when they travel abroad, choose to call themselves Holsteiners, thinking it more honourable to be born within the Confines of the Empire, than otherwise.

Stormar and Ditmarsh lie the nearest to the River Elbe, and are for the most part low and rich Countries, the Soil being fat, and in most places resembling Holland, as well in its Fertility as manner of Improvement. These Countries enjoy also the benefit of having Hamburg and the River near them, with the additional Advantage of the Ocean; though it sometimes proves too troublesome a Neighbour, and overflows great part of their lower Grounds, notwithstanding the Banks and Dyckes that are raised to keep it out.

'Tis to be noted as a great natural defect, that the King of Denmark has not in all his Dominions one Navigable River for Vessels of any considerable Burden (for I do not count the River Eyder as such) unless we reckon the Elbe, which is rather to be esteemed one of the Confines and Boundaries of his Territories, than any way belonging to him; yet he has often, and does even to this day, endeavour to set up and establish a Toll at Glucstadt, being not without hopes, that taking the advantage of the Necessity of the Empire, during this expensive War, he may engage it to consent to this Toll against all other Considerations: But the Neighbouring Princes, the English and Dutch, and above all the City of Hamburg, will hardly be brought over to comply with an Innovation so prejudicial to their Trade and Interests.

Oldenburg for the most part is a flat Marish Country; much exposed to the Inundations of the Ocean; the Banks which should keep it in its due Bounds, not being maintained in good repair. It abounds in Cattle, and has a good Breed of Horses, which are much sought after for Coaches, by reason of their Colour, which is a yellowish Cream Colour. They are generally wall-ey'd, and tender-hoof'd, not able to last long, or endure hard labour. The Town of Oldenburg is but a very indifferent one, and its Castle much out of Repair. Upon the Death of the late Prince Anthony, this County came to be annexed to the Crown of Denmark.

Delmenhorst is a more rising Ground, and pretty well wooded. Both these lye together, and the Inhabitants are used the more gently, by reason of their distance from his other Territories.

Of Norway little can be said; but that it is divided into two great Provinces, the Southern and Northern; whereof one small County, called Yempterland, formerly belonging to the King of Denmark, is now in the Possession of the Swedes. His High Excellency Guldenlieu (which is the Title usually given him by the Danes) is Vice-Roy, or as they call him Stadtholder of the whole. It is sub-divided into four Stifts Ampts, or Principal Governments; Viz. Dronthem, Bergen, Christiania, and Larwick. The Governors are young Guldenlieu, natural Son to the present King, and Monsieur Stocfleet late Envoy extraordinary from Denmark to Sweden, etc. It is a very barren Country, affording neither Corn nor Cattle sufficient for the subsistence of its Inhabitants, although they be not numerous in proportion to its vast extent. There are Silver Mines in it, but whether the working of them turns to account is a question.[13] The Commodities which it yields fit for Exportation are Timber of all kinds, especially Fir, Stockfish, Masts for Ships, and Iron; of these it has a tolerable store; most of which the English and Dutch purchase yearly with ready Money: And herein Norway exceeds the other Dominions of the King of Denmark, that it affords Commodities for Exportation, which none of the rest do in any quantity. The Inhabitants are a hardy, laborious, and honest sort of People; they are esteemed by others, and esteem themselves much superior to the Danes, whom they call upbraidingly Jutes.

13. Note in margin: "The Exportation of Oak Timber is forbidden."

Iseland and Feroe are miserable Islands in the North Ocean; Corn will scarce grow in either of them, but they have good stocks of Cattle. No Trade is permitted them but with the Danes; the Inhabitants are great Players at Chess. It were worth some curious Mans enquiry how such a studious and difficult Game should get thus far Northward, and become so generally used.

The King of Denmark's Factories in the East and West-Indies, and in Guinea are esteemed of very little worth and consideration; yet I have seen several East-India Ships return home to Copenhagen well laden with the Merchandize of those Countries; and there is an East-India Company lately set up, whereof most of the Men of Quality are Members and Adventurers: But whether the Lading of those Ships I mentioned were the lawful Product of Trade, or acquired by other means, will in time be worth the inquiry of those Kingdoms and States whose Interest it is to preserve in the Indians and Persians a good Opinion of the honesty and fair dealing of the Europeans.

And thus I have said as much as I think requisite touching the Situation, Extent, and Qualities of the Lands and Dominions belonging to the King of Denmark, which amounts in general to this, that they are very large, disjoined, and intermixt, producing but a moderate Plenty of Necessaries for the Inhabitants, but few Commodities for the Merchant, and no Manufactures, if we except a little Iron. Whether these Defects in Countries well situated and indifferent fertile be altogether natural or partly accidental, will better appear when I treat of the Form of the Government, and the present Condition, Customs, and Manners of the Natives; but because these last do in a manner depend upon, and are influenced by the former, I shall choose to begin with it.

CHAPTER VI

Of Their Form of Government

The Ancient Form of Government here was the same which the Goths
and Vandals established in most, if not all, Parts of Europe, whither they
carried their Conquests, and which in England is retained to this day for
the most part.[14] 'Tis said of the Romans, That those Provinces which
they Conquer'd were amply recompensed, for the loss of their Liberty,
by being reduced from their Barbarity to Civility; by the Introduction of
Arts, Learning, Commerce, and Politeness. I know not whether this man-

[14.] Note in margin, from Guido Bentivoglio *Relatione delle provincie unite di
Flandra* (1611), bk. 3: "Furono veramente tutti i Re da principio Capi e non Re, di
Repubbliche e non di regni: ma poi il lungo uso ha fatto che i popoli si sìano disposti
all habito dell' intiera ubbidìenza, come apunte suole assuefarsì una pianta e un
corpo humano a vivere, in terreno e sotto clima diverso dal suo naturale." Translated as "'Tis true, at first all Kings were Heads of the people, and not Kings; of
Commonwealths and not of Kingdoms. But afterwards Custom hath so prevailed,
as people have been disposed and accustomed to the habit of intire obedience: just
as a plant, or humane body we see are accustomed to live in other earth, and under
other Climats, which differ from their own natural ones." In *Historicall relations of
the United Provinces & of Flanders written originally in Italian by Cardinall Bentivoglio; and now rendred into English by the Right Honourable Henry, Earle of Monmouth*
(1652), p. 47.

ner of Arguing hath not more of Pomp than Truth in it; but with much greater reason may it be said that all Europe was beholding to these People for introducing or restoring a Constitution of Government far excelling all others that we know of in the World. 'Tis to the ancient Inhabitants of these Countries, with other neighbouring Provinces, that we owe the Original of Parliaments, formerly so common, but lost within this last Age in all Kingdoms but those of Poland, Great Britain, and Ireland.

Denmark therefore was till within these Two and Thirty years governed by a King chosen by the People of all sorts, even the Boors had their Voices, which King Waldemar the Third acknowledged in that memorable answer of his to the Popes Nuncio, who pretended to a great power over him. *Naturam habemus à Deo, regnum à subditis, Divitias à parentibus, Religionem à Romana Ecclesia; quam si nobis invides, renuntiamus per praesentes.*[15] The Estates of the Realm being convened to that intent, were to Elect for their Prince such a Person as to them appeared Personable, Valiant, Just, Merciful, Affable, a Maintainer of the Laws, a Lover of the People, Prudent, and Adorned with all other Virtues fit for Government, and requisite for the great Trust reposed in him; yet with due regard had to the Family of the preceding Kings. If within that Line they found a Person thus qualified, or esteemed to be so, they thought it but a piece of just Gratitude to prefer him before any other to this high Dignity, and were pleased when they had reason to choose the Eldest Son of their former King, rather than any of the younger, as well because they had regard to Priority of Birth, when all other Virtues were equal, as because the greatness of his Paternal Estate might put him above the reach of Temptations to be covetous or dishonest, and in able him in some degree to support the Dignity of his Office. But if after such a Choice they found themselves mistaken, and that they had advanced a Cruel, Vitious, Tyrannical, Covetous, or Wasteful Person, they frequently Deposed him, oftentimes Banished, sometimes Destroyed him; and this either formally, by making him Answer before the Representative Body of the People; or if by ill

[15.] King Waldemar III (1314–64): "We have our nature from God, our realm from our subjects, our wealth from our parents, our religion from the Roman church; if you begrudge her to us we shall renounce her by these presents." The account is from Johannes Clüver's *Historiarum Totius Mundi Epitome* (Amsterdam, 1667), p. 523.

Practices, such as making of Parties, levying of Soldiers, contracting of Alliances to support himself in opposition to the People's Rights, he was grown too powerful to be legally contended with, they dispatched him without any more Ceremony the best way they could, and Elected presently a better Man in his room; sometimes the next of Kin to him, sometimes the Valiant Man that had exposed himself so far as to undertake the Expulsion or the killing of the Tyrant; at other times a private Person of a good Reputation, who possibly least dreamt of such an Advancement.

Frequent Meetings of the Estates was a part of the very Fundamental Constitution: In those Meetings all Matters relating to good Government were transacted; good Laws were enacted, all Affairs belonging to Peace or War, Alliances, disposal of great Offices, Contracts of Marriages for the Royal Family, etc. were debated. The imposing of Taxes, or demanding of Benevolences was purely accidental; no constant Tribute being ever paid, nor any Money levied on the People, unless either to maintain a necessary War with the advice and consent of the Nation, or now and then by way of Free-gift, to help to raise a Daughters Portion: the King's ordinary Revenue at that time consisting only in the Rents of his Lands and Demesnes, in his Herds of Cattle, Forests, Services of Tenants in manuring and cultivating his Grounds, etc. Customs upon Merchandize being an Imposition of late crept into this part of the World; so that he lived like one of our Modern Noblemen, upon the Revenues of his own Estate, and eat not through the Sweat of his Subjects Brows.

His business was to see a due and impartial Administration of Justice executed according to the Laws; nay, often to sit and do it himself; to be watchful and vigilant for the welfare of his People, to Command in Person their Armies in time of War, to encourage Industry, Religion, Arts and Learning; and it was his Interest, as well as Duty, to keep fair with his Nobility and Gentry, and to be careful of the Plenty and Prosperity of his Commons.

This was the Ancient Form of Government in this Kingdom, which continued with very little variation (excepting that the Power of the Nobles encreased too much) till about Two and Thirty years ago, when at one instant the whole Face of Affairs was changed: So that the Kings have ever since been, and at present are, Absolute and Arbitrary; not the least remnant of Liberty remaining to the Subject; all Meetings of the Estates in Parliament intirely abolished, nay, the very Name of Estates and Liberty quite forgotten, as if there never had been any such thing; the very first and principal Article in the present Danish Law being, *That the King has the Priviledge reserved to himself to explain the Law, nay, to alter and change it as he shall find good.*[16]

It is easie for any considering Person to guess the Consequences of this, which are, frequent and arbitrary Taxes, and commonly very excessive ones, even in Times of Peace; little regard being had to the Occasion of them: So that the value of Estates in most parts of the Kingdom is fallen three Fourths. And it is worse near the Capital City under the Eye and Hand of the Government, than in remoter Provinces: Poverty in the Gentry, which necessarily causes extremity of Misery in the Peasants, Partiality in the distribution of Justice when Favourites are concerned; with many other Mischiefs which shall be hereafter more particularly mentioned; being the constant Effects of Arbitrary Rule in this and all other Countries wherein it has prevailed.

And because it is astonishing to consider how a free and rich People (for so they were formerly) should be persuaded intirely to part with their Liberties, I thought it very proper to give an account by what steps so great a Change and Revolution was brought about: The Particulars of which I have received not only from Eye-witnesses, but also from some of the principal Promoters and Actors in it.

[16.] See the edition translated into English by a "Lover of the British Constitution" [Jenkin Thomas Phillips], *Lex regia or the Royal Law of Denmark* (1731), p. 10.

CHAPTER VII

The Manner How the Kingdom of Denmark Became Hereditary and Absolute

After the Conclusion of the Peace between the two Northern Crowns Anno 1660, some considerable care and time was necessary to redress the Disorders occasioned by so terrible a War. Denmark had been most violently shaken; and although the Fury of the Tempest was over, the Agitation caused by it still continued: The Army was not yet disbanded, nor could be for want of Money to discharge its Arrears; this caused frequent Insolencies in the Soldiers, with a further Oppression of the Burgers and poor Country People, who had been in a manner already ruined by the Miseries attending the War. The Nobility, though Lords and Masters, were full of Discontents, and the Clergy not in the condition they wished.

To redress all which Grievances, and reduce Affairs into some Order, by procuring Money for the Payment and Disbanding of the Army, the King thought fit to appoint a Meeting of the Three Estates at Copenhagen, viz. the Nobility, Commonalty, and Clergy; which accordingly followed about the beginning of October: After some few days Session (during which the Nobility, according to their usual practice debated how the Sums of Money requisite might with greatest ease and conveniency be levied upon the Commons, without the least intention of bearing any proportionable share themselves). Several Disputes arose, and many sharp Expressions passed between them and the Commons; on the one hand the Nobility were for maintaining their ancient Prerogative of paying nothing by way of Tax, but only by voluntary Contribution; and shewed themselves too stiff at a time when the Country was exhausted, and most of the remaining Riches lodged in their hands: They seemed to make use of this Occasion, not only to vindicate, but even to widen and enlarge their Privileges above the other two Estates, by laying Impositions on them at pleasure, which weight they themselves would not touch with one of their Fingers any further, than as they thought fitting. On the other hand, the Clergy for their late adherence to the interest of their Country, and the Burgers for the vigorous Defence of their City, thought they might justly pretend to new Merit, and be considered at least as good Subjects in a State, which they themselves had so valiantly defended. They remembered the great Promises made them when dangerous Enterprises were to be taken in hand, and how successfully they had executed them; thereby saving from a Foreign Yoak, not only the City of Copenhagen, but the whole Kingdom, the Royal Family, nay those very Nobles that now dealt so hardly with them: They judged it therefore reasonable, that the Sums of Money necessary should be levied proportionably, and that the Nobility who enjoyed all the Lands, should at least pay their share of the Taxes, since they had suffered less in the common Calamity, as well as done less to prevent the progress of it.

This manner of arguing was very displeasing to the Nobles, and begat much Heat and many bitter Replies on both sides: At length a principal Senator called Otto Craeg, stood up, and in great Anger told the President of the City, That the Commons neither understood nor considered the Privileges of the Nobility, who at all times had been exempted from Taxes, nor the true Condition of themselves, who were no other than Slaves; [the word in the Danish is *unfree*] so that their best way was to keep within their own Bounds, and acquiesce in such Measures as ancient Practice had warranted, and which they were resolved to maintain. This

word *Slaves* put all the Burgers and Clergy in disorder, causing a loud
Murmur in the Hall; which Nanson the President of the City of Copenhagen, and Speaker of the House of Commons, perceiving, and finding
a fit occasion of putting in practice a Design before concerted (though
but weakly) between him and the Bishop; in great Choler rose out of his
Seat, and swore an Oath, *That the Commons were no Slaves, nor would from
thenceforth be called so by the Nobility, which they should soon prove to their
cost:* And thereupon breaking up the Assembly in disorder, and departing
out of the Hall, was followed by all the Clergy and Burgers; the Nobles
being left alone to consult among themselves at their leisure, after a little
while adjourned to a private House near the Court. In the mean time the
Commons, being provoked to the highest degree, and resolving to put
their Threats in Execution, marched processionally by Couples, a Clergyman and a Commoner, from the great Hall or Parliament-House to the
Brewers-Hall, which was the convenientest place they could pitch upon
to sit apart from the Nobles, the Bishop of Copenhagen, and the President of the City leading them: It was there thought necessary to consider
speedily of the most effectual Means to suppress the intolerable Pride of
the Nobility, and how to mend their own Condition: After many Debates
they concluded, That they should immediately wait upon the King, and
offer him their Votes and Assistance to be absolute Monarch of the Realm,
as also that the Crown should descend by inheritance to his Family, which
hitherto had gone by Election. They promised themselves the King would
have so great Obligations to them for this piece of Service, that he would
grant and confirm such Privileges, as should put them above the degree of
Slaves. They knew he had hitherto been curbed by the Nobility to a great
Measure; and now saw their own force, being able (since they had Arms
in their Hands, and the concurrence of the Soldiers) to perform what they
undertook: At the worst, they supposed they should only change many
Masters for one, and could better bear hardships from a King than from
inferior Persons: Or if their Case were not better'd, at least they thought
it some comfort to have more Company in it; besides the satisfaction of
Revenge on those that had hitherto not only used them ill, but insulted
over them so lately. They knew the King, and had seen him bear with an
admirable Patience and Constancy all his Calamities; were persuaded that

he was a Valiant Prince, who had often exposed his Person for the sake of the Publick, and therefore thought they could never do enough to shew their Gratitude; which is the usual Temper of the People upon any benefit received from their Prince. Scarce was this proposed but it was agreed to; and nothing but the unseasonableness of the time, (it being now near night) deferred the immediate Execution of it; but all the necessary Measures were taken against next Morning. The Clergy had a further drift in this Change of Government; for having been hitherto kept under by the Nobility, they forecasted to have no other Superior but the King, whose new Authority they engaged to maintain by the influence they had on the Consciences of the People; expecting with reason the like Favour and Protection from the King, together with an encrease of their Power; since he was in a great measure obliged to them for his own; and the benefits were likely to be mutual for the future, the one having the force, the other the tie of Religion in their Possession. Which Contract subsists to this very day, to the great advantage of both sides.

The Court all this while was not ignorant of what passed; there wanted no Spies nor Messengers to give notice of the Discontents of the Commons, Hannibal Seestede, a cunning Man, was prime Minister; and the Bishop or Superintendent Swan, with Nanson the Speaker of the House of Commons, were his Creatures: These had formerly in secret laid with him the Design, which was now upon the point of disclosing, though their hopes were hardly raised so high, as to promise themselves such mighty Success. The whole Night passed in Brigues and Messages, the Commons anger was to be kept up to the requisite height, and the Resolution they had taken the Night before not to be suffer'd to cool, but persisted in betimes next Morning. The Queen, a Woman of Intrigue and high Spirit, wrought strongly in it by all manner of ways, whilst the King, either through doubt of the Event, or sense of the Dishonesty and Crime of the Action, in procuring after such a manner the absolute Dominion of a free Country, could hardly be brought to comply with it. He declared that indeed he should be pleased the Sovereignty were entailed on his Family, provided it were done by Universal Consent; but to become Absolute and Arbitrary, was neither his desire, nor did he think it for the benefit of the Kingdom; that he was satisfied he should not make ill use of such an unlimited Authority; but no body knew what Successors he might have; that it was therefore dangerous both for them to give, and for him to receive such a Power as might be abused in future times to the utter ruin of the Nation. But these Reflections, whether they were real, or only pretences, whether caused by the Piety or Weakness of the King, were soon overruled by the more Ambitious and Masculine Spirit of the Queen, who desired him to sit still, and see how she and her Emissaries would work for him; told him, That the Plot was well laid, and had begun to operate prosperously; that he must not obstruct his own and his Families good Fortune; and in fine, so far prevailed on him, that he seemed with fear to consent to, and permit that which most think he very much desired: Having however by this shew of unwillingness, left open to himself a door of Reconciliation with his People, in case the business did not succeed.

All this while the Nobles either had none, or but small intimation of the Designs of the Commons, they had been used so long to slight and tyrannize over them, that they were not now sensible of any impending danger from thence, contemning their Threats as well as their Persons, and imagining they would have repented next day, and complied with all that should be demanded of them; but the Plot was deeper laid than they supposed; for not only the prime Minister, but some other Members of their own Body, who had Employments depending on the Court, were engaged in it. This inadvertency, with the want of requisite Courage upon occasion, brought upon them the Mischief on a sudden; so that except two or three who were more than ordinary doubtful of what might happen, and slipt out of Town that Night, the rest were altogether fearless of danger, till the very instant that the Evil was remediless.

Schack the Governor of the Town had been gained by the Court to favour the Design, which he performed effectually, though not with so servile an intention as others; for when the King, upon the first news of the Resolution of the Commons, did often openly promise that he would in Gratitude and Recompense declare them all Free as soon as it lay in his power, by the Gift they were about to make him; and the People were willing to trust the King's goodness, and to depend on the performance of this Promise, encouraged thereunto by the Clergy, who alledged it a thing unbeseeming and dishonourable to require any other Security from the King than his bare Word; yet Schack urged vehemently that the Commons should insist to have this Promise under the King's Hand, and make themselves sure of the Reward for so considerable a Present as they were going to make, whilst they had so fair an opportunity in their hands. But all his Instances were in vain; they were in the giving humour, and resolved to do it generously, trusting the King for the performance of his Word: A thing which they have since often, though too late repented of.

Next Morning the Nobles met in the Council-House, and the other two Estates in the Brewers-Hall; the Resolution of the Commons could not be kept so secret, but by this time some warm rumours of it had reached the Nobility; but scarce had they leisure to consider what was fittest to be done on that occasion, when they were informed that the Commons were marching towards them: For the Bishop and the President had so well performed their Parts, and urged the necessity of speedily executing what had been resolved the day before, that all time was judged lost which was not employed in putting it in practice; they immediately agreed to go to the Council-House, and there propound to the Nobility their design, desiring their Concurrence in such a necessary Work for the welfare of the Kingdom. They marched through the Streets with great Gravity, and Silence, by Couples, as before, whilst the Mobb by repeated Shouts applauded what they were going to do. And thus they came to the House where the Nobles were assembled, who had scarce warning sufficient to receive them.

The President Nanson made a short Harangue, setting forth that they had considered the state of the Nation, and that they found the only Remedy for the many Disorders which afflicted it, was to make the Crown Hereditary, and to give more Power to the King than hitherto he had enjoyed; that this Resolution was already taken by the Commons and Clergy, in which if the Nobility should think fitting to concur, they were ready to accompany them to the King, and make him a tender of an Hereditary and Sovereign Dominion; if not, that they were going themselves, and the matter should be done without them: That a speedy Resolution was necessary, for they had already sent word to the Court of their coming, and his Majesty expected them in the Hall of his Palace; therefore desired to be informed in few words what they resolved to do.

The suddenness of such a Proposition, and briskness in the manner of its delivery, caused a general astonishment in the Nobles; one might have seen those who but the day before carried it so proudly, in an instant fall to an excess of Complacency, and betray their Fear by their Speeches and Countenances, as they formerly had done their Arrogance. The Mischief no sooner appeared to them, but they saw it was unavoidable; there was no leisure allowed them to consult; and to deny their compliance, or even to delay it, was dangerous. To give up at once their beloved Power, and submit their Necks to a heavy Yoak, was an intolerable Grievance: But they saw they were no longer the Masters; the Commons were armed, the Army and Clergy against them; and they found now too late, that that which the day before they had considered only as the Effort of an unconstant giddy Multitude, was guided by wiser Heads, and supported by Encouragements from Court; nay possibly by some of their own Body: They suspected each other, and no Man knew whether his next Neighbour was not in the Plot against the Publick Liberty. It is easie to imagine what distracted thoughts afflicted them on a sudden; they were altogether unprepared for such a dismal stroke: But some Answer must be given, and that speedily. Such a one as they had a mind to give, they durst not; for they were assembled in a Fortified Town, remote from their several Countries and Interests (where they had governed like so many Princes) in the power of those who could, and certainly would be revenged in case they proved refractory. The best way therefore was to seem to approve of what they could not hinder. They answer that the Proposition made to them by the Commons was not displeasing, but the manner of it wanted the requisite Formalities; that previous deliberation was necessary to an Affair of so great moment; that they could not but take it ill, a Resolution of such Consequence should be concluded on by the Commons without the least acquainting of the Nobility with it, who were the Chief Estate of the Realm: That they also aspired to the Honour of bearing their part in bestowing such a material Gift on the King and his Posterity, but desired that the Matter might be proceeded on with that gravity, and solemnity, which the nature of it required. That it was not fit such a weighty Trans-action should have the appearance of a Tumult, and seemed forced rather than a free Choice. The Conclusion of all was, That they hoped the Commons would a little defer the putting in Execution their Design; and in the mean time consult with them, till the Affair were done orderly, and with unanimous Approbation, as well as to mutual Advantage.

This was with great vehemency by the President denied. He replied, These were Shifts only to gain time, that the Nobles might be in a Condition to frustrate the Intention of the Commons; that the Point was already agreed, and the Resolution taken; that they came not thither to consider, but to act; if the Nobles would join with them, they were ready; if not, they would do what was to be done alone; and doubted not but his Majesty would make his use of it.

During these Disputes the Nobility had privily sent some of their Body to Court to acquaint the King, that the Commons were now at their House, and had made them sudden Proposals, out of form, but such as they should rather concur with, than be averse to; that they were ready to join with them in offering an Hereditary Crown to his Majesty, and the Heirs Males of his Family for ever; which they hoped his Majesty would accept in good part: But desired to proceed in the usual Methods, which such weighty Affairs merited, viz. by Conferences and Delibera-tions, that it might appear rather an effect of their just Sentiments of his Majesty's Valour and Conduct, than the sudden Motions of a Tumultuous Assembly.

The King, with a great deal of mildness, as if he had been wholly un-concerned and passive in the Case, replied; That he was obliged to them for their Designs in favour of Him, and the Royal Family; that he hoped what they were about would tend to the benefit of the Nation; but that a Crown intailed only on the Heirs Males could not be so acceptable to him, as if it were given without that Limitation; that the Government of Females had neither been a new thing at home, nor unprosperous in Neighbouring Countries: That they might consider of it, and since it was their Gift, he would not prescribe, but it could not be accepted by him unless it were more general.

In the mean time the Commons grew impatient, the Answer given them was not satisfactory, and the Nobles had not yet resolved on an entire Compliance, nor were ready to accompany them, because they had not yet an account of the Success of their Members sent to sound the Mind of the Court. The Clergy and Burgers therefore, led on by their Bishop and President, proceed without them to the Palace, and were met by the prime Minister, and conducted by him to the Hall of Audience, whither after some short time the King came to them. The Bishop makes a long Speech, setting forth the Praises of his Majesty, and the Cause of their waiting on him; concluding with an offer, in the name of themselves, the two most numerous, and if he pleased most powerful Estates, of an Hereditary and Absolute Dominion; together with the assistance of their Hands and Purses, in case any Body should go about to obstruct so necessary and laudable a Design for the good of the Country. The King told them in short, That he thanked them; and in case an Universal Consent established this good Desire of theirs, he would accept the Present they made him; but that the Concurrence of the Nobles was necessary; which he doubted not of in the least, when they had time to make the offer with the necessary Formalities: That he assured the Commons of his Royal Protection, and should not be unmindful of their Kindness, by easing them of their Grievances, and by encouraging Subjects who had behaved themselves so valiantly, and deserved so well from him. Concluding with his Advice to them to continue their Session till such time as Matters were brought to perfection, and he could receive their Gift with the Solemnity that was fitting: And thereupon dismissed them.

But the Nobles were all this while in a grievous distraction; they saw the Commons were gone to the King without them: Their Messengers brought News back that their Proposition of entailing the Crown on the Heirs Males, was not pleasing, because a greater Advantage was in prospect; that this offer was looked upon to proceed from Persons that would not have bestowed any thing, if they could have helped it. That it was thought they pretended to merit in giving only a part, when it was not in their power to hinder the taking the whole. In this irresolution they broke up; and since they were to meet again at Noon upon another Solemn Occasion, they resolved at that time to consider how to proceed in an Affair so delicate.

Monsieur Schele a Senator, and principal Man of the Country, was that Afternoon to be buried in great Pomp; his Body had lain some Months in State, and according to the Custom, was to be accompanied to its Interment by all the Nobility then in Town; this being a Parliament time was chosen for the Ceremony, because the Nobles were all together, and a magnificent Dinner was prepared, as is usual on the like occasions: In the height of their Entertainment an Officer comes into the Room, and whispers some of the principal Men that the City Gates were shut, and the Keys carried to Court: For the King having been informed by the Governor, that two or three had privily slipt out of Town the Night before, and being resolved that no more should Escape out of the Net, till he had done his business, had ordered the Governor that Morning to lock the Gates, and to let no Person in or out without special Order. The Governor sent one Bill, the Town Major, to put this in Execution; who as soon as he had done it, came to the House where they were met, and sat down at Table among the Senators. This dismal News of the Officer was presently whispered round the Company; who immediately applied themselves to him to know what the meaning was of such an unusual Proceeding at the time of a General Convention; They asked him what destiny was appointed them, whether they were there to be Massacred, or what else was to be done with them? The Town-Major calmly answered, That he believed there was no Danger towards them, that such violent Measures would not be taken by so gracious a King; though he had indeed given the Orders himself for the shutting the Gates; and that no Body was to stir out of Town without leave; but that this needed not disturb or hinder them from finishing the Work of the Day, and pursuing the Publick, as well as their Private Occasions. There wanted no more than this Confirmation from the Officer to overthrow all the Resolution, and Consultations of the Nobles; the dread of losing their Lives took away all thoughts of their Liberty. They immediately dispatched Messengers both to the Court, and the Commons, to give notice of their disposition to comply with what was formerly proposed; assuring them likewise, that they were ready to agree to all that should be asked of them.

But the King, who had began and played his Game so well hitherto, determined to pursue it to the utmost, and would not suffer the Gates to be opened, till the whole Ceremony of the Inauguration was concluded, and the Homage done in due form, and therefore ordered they should stay, till in the Face of the People, and the Army, they had sworn Fealty, and divested themselves of all Right, as well as Power, to cause any Disturbance, or Alteration for the future.

Three days time was requisite to prepare Matters for that fatal hour, wherein they were to make a formal Surrender of their Liberty; the Scaffolds were raised in the place before the Castle, and adorned with Tapestry; Orders were given for the Soldiery, and Burgers to appear in Arms under their respective Officers: And when all things were ready, on the 27th of October in the Morning, the King, Queen, and Royal Family mounted on a Theatre erected for that purpose, and being placed in Chairs of State under Canopies of Velvet, received publickly the Homage of all the Senators, Nobility, Clergy, and Commons; which was performed kneeling. The Oath, which they were obliged to take, was in these words:

I A. B. do Promise, and Declare, that I will be True, and Faithful to Your Majesty, as my most Gracious King and Lord, as also to Your Royal Family; that I will Endeavour, and Promote Your Majesties Interest in all things, and to the best of my Power defend you from all Danger, and Harm; and that I will faithfully serve Your Majesty as a Man of Honour, and an Hereditary Subject ought to do. So help me God, etc.[17]

This Oath they were all obliged to pronounce aloud, and some Men of Quality that were sick, or pretended to be so, were brought in Chairs. Among others one Gersdorf, a Principal Senator, who was the only Man that opened his Mouth in the behalf of their Expiring Liberties, saying, That he hoped, and trusted, that his Majesty designed nothing but the Good of his People, and not to govern them after the *Turkish* manner; but wished his Majesty's Successors might follow the Example, which his Majesty would undoubtedly set them, and make use of that unlimited Power for the good, and not the harm of his Subjects. Not one of the rest spoke a word, or seemed to murmur in the least at what was done; and it is observable, that among so many Great Men, who a few days before seemed to have Spirits suitable to their Birth and Qualities, none had

[17.] See *Lex regia*, p. 12.

the Courage during those three last days, either by Remonstrance, or any other way, to oppose in any manner what was doing. And I have heard very intelligent Persons, who were at that time near the King, affirm, That had the Nobles shewed ever so little Courage in asserting their Privileges, the King would not have pursued his Point so far as to desire an Arbitrary Dominion: For he was in continual doubt, and dread of the Event, and began to waver very much in his Resolutions; so that their Liberties seem purely lost for want of some to appear for them.

From the Theatre, those that had done Homage, went to the Council-House, where the Nobles were called over by Name; and ordered to Subscribe the above-mentioned Declaration, which they all did.

Thus this great Affair was finished, and the Kingdom of Denmark in Four Days time changed from an Estate little differing from Aristocracy, to as absolute a Monarchy as any is at present in the World. The Commons have since experienced, that the little Finger of an Absolute Prince can be heavier than the Loins of many Nobles. The only comfort they have left them being to see their former Oppressors in almost as miserable a Condition as themselves; whilst all the Citizens of Copenhagen have by it obtained the insignificant Privilege of wearing Swords: So that at this day not a Cobler, or Barber stirs abroad without a Tilter at his side, let his Purse be never so empty. The Clergy, who always make sure Bargains, were the only Gainers in this Point; and are still much encouraged by the Court, as the Instruments that first promoted, and now keep the People in a due Temper of Slavery; the Passive Obedience Principle riding Triumphant in this unhappy Kingdom.

It was but Justice, that the Court should pay well the principal Contrivers of this great Revolution; and therefore notwithstanding the general want of Money, Hannibal Seestede had a Present of 200,000 Crowns. Swan the Superintendent, or Bishop, was made Archbishop, and had 30,000 Crowns. The President or Speaker Nanson, 20,000 Crowns. And to the People remained the Glory of having forged their own Chains, and the Advantage of Obeying without reserve. A happiness which I suppose no English Man will ever envy them.

CHAPTER VIII

The Condition, Customs, and Temper of the People

All these do so necessarily depend upon, and are influenced by the Nature and Change of Government, that 'tis easily imagined, the present Condition of these People of all Ranks must be most deplorable; at least it appears so to an English Man, who sees it, possibly more than to them that suffer it: For Slavery, like a sickly Constitution, grows in time so habitual, that it seems no Burden nor Disease; it creates a kind of laziness, and idle despondency, which puts Men beyond hopes and fears: It mortifies Ambition, Emulation, and other troublesome, as well as active qualities, which Liberty and Freedom beget; and instead of them affords only a dull kind of Pleasure of being careless and insensible.

In former Times, and even till the late Alteration in the Government, the Nobility or Gentry (for they are here the same thing) lived in great Affluence and Prosperity; their Country Seats were large and magnificent, their Hospitality extraordinary, because their Plenty was so too; they lived for the most part at home, and spent their Revenues among their Neighbours and Tenants, by whom they were considered, and respected as so many petty Princes. In times of Convention of the Estates, which ordinarily happened once a year, they met their King with Retinues almost as large as his; they frequently eat, and drank at the same Table with him, and in the debate of Publick Affairs, their Suffrages were of greatest weight, and usually carried the Point: For the Commons were willing in a great measure to be directed by them, because they much depended on them. In process of time this Excess of Power, as you have heard, made most of them grow insolent, which was the chief occasion of their fall, together with the loss of the Liberties of the whole Country. So that now they are sunk to a very low Condition, and diminish daily both in Number and Credit; their Estates scarce paying the Taxes imposed on them: Which makes them grind the Faces of their poor Tenants to get an Overplus for their own Subsistence. Nay, I have been assured by some Gentlemen of good Repute, who formerly were Masters of great Estates, that they have offered to make an absolute Surrender to the King of large Possessions in the Island of Zealand, rather than pay the Taxes; which offer, though pressed with earnestness, would by no means be accepted. And upon my further enquiry into the Reason of it, I have been informed, that Estates belonging to those Gentlemen, who made this offer, lying in other places, which had the good Fortune to be taxed less than the full value of the Income, were liable to pay the Taxes of any other Estate appertaining to the same Person, in case that other Estate were not able; so that some have been seen with a great deal of joy declaring that the King had been so gracious as to take their Estates from them.

Through these, and several other means, many of the ancient Families are fallen to decay; their Country Habitations, which were like Palaces, being ruinous, they are forced to live meanly, and obscurely in some corner of them: Unless it be their good Fortune to procure an Employment, Civil or Military, at Court, which is the thing they are most Ambitious of; it being indeed necessary to secure to their Families any tolerable Subsistence, or to afford them some shelter from the Exactions, and Injustices of the Collectors. The Civil Employments are in no great number, nor of great value; as they seldom are in a poor Country governed by an Army; so that few are provided for this way: The greatest part patiently enduring their Poverty at home; where, in a short time, their Spirits, as well as their

Estates, grow so mean, that you would scarce believe them to be Gentle-men, either by Discourse or Garb.

Ancient Riches and Valour were the only Title to Nobility formerly in this Country; the Nobles and Gentry being, as I said before, the same thing. None took either their Degree, or Patents of Honour from the King: But of late years to supply the want of Riches, some few Titles of Baron or Count, and nothing higher, have been given to Favourites; who enjoy not the same Privileges by those Titles, as our Lords in England do, but content themselves with a few Airy insignificant ones, which distin-guish them from the Common People; there are not many, even of this kind of Nobility, I believe fifteen or twenty are the most; these are such, who are most easie in their Fortunes, and are obliged (that they may pre-serve them) to keep in with the Court by all manner of ways; as indeed all are, who have a mind to live and eat Bread.

'Tis only this kind of Nobility with Titles, that have liberty to make a Will or Testament, and thereby to dispose of any Estate otherwise than as the Law has already determined, that it shall fall of course: Unless such Will be during the Life of the Testator, approved of and signed by the King; and then it shall be of force, and valid.

'Tis almost needless to mention that there is no buying, or selling of Land here; for where an Estate is a Charge, there will be few Buyers. Neither do I remember any one Alienation of Lands for Money, dur-ing all the time I stayed in that Country, except some Estates, which the Queen purchased; where she paid after the rate of 16000 Crowns for that which Thirty Years ago was valued at 60000 Crowns. There were indeed some Persons, who took Lands from the King in lieu of Money, which they had lent the Crown; and among these I remember to have heard of two, Monsieur Texera a rich Jew of Hamburg, and Monsieur Marseilles, a Dutch Merchant, who was formerly established at Copenhagen. These were forced to take Lands, or Nothing, for their Debts, which amounted to some Hundred Thousands of Crowns; yet did these Lands yield them so little Income, by reason of the Taxes imposed on them, though they were vast Tracts of fertile Ground, that they would willingly have parted with them (as I was informed) for one fifth part of their Principal.

However, in case it should happen that one who has a mind to transplant himself to another place, could find a Purchaser for his Estate, the Law is, That one third part of such Purchase-Money shall accrue to the King; and indeed if there were not such a severe Law against Alienations, it is possible most of the present Possessors would quit the Country the first Opportunity.

The King assumes to himself the Power of disposing of all Heirs and Heiresses of any Consideration, as it is practised in France: Not that there is any Law for it, but upon pain of his Displeasure; which here is too weighty to be born.

Military Employments are mightily coveted by the Native Gentry, almost as much as the Civil; and purely for the same reason that the Priest's Office was among the Jews, viz. That they may eat a piece of Bread. For it is a sure way to find Soldiers (as long as there are Men in a Kingdom) to imitate the French King's practice in this particular, make the Gentry poor, and render Traffick unprofitable or dishonourable, Men of Birth must live, and one half of the Nation, by giving up themselves to Slavery, will contribute their Assistance afterwards to put Chains upon the other.

Yet in Denmark the Natives are considered much less than Strangers, and are more out of the Road of Preferment, whether it be that the Court can better trust Strangers, whose Fortunes they make, than the Posterity of such whose Fortunes they have ruined: Or whether they think their very Parts and Courage to be diminished in proportion to their Estates and Liberty, (which appears to be plainly the case of their common People) or for what other reason; certain it is, that all sorts of Places, Civil and Military, are filled more by Foreigners than Gentlemen of the Country: And in their disposal of Offices it is remarkable, that such as are of ordinary Birth and Fortunes, are much sooner preferred than those of contrary qualities: So that here may be found several in the most profitable and honourable Employments who have formerly been Serving-men, and such like; and these prove the best Executors of the Will and Pleasure of Arbitrary Power, and therefore are caressed accordingly. There is one further advantage in the promotion of these kind of Men; that after they are grown rich by Extortion, and have sucked the Blood of the Poor, when Clamours grow loud against them, the Court can with ease squeeze these

Leaches, laying all the blame of its own Oppression at their Doors; and this without the danger of causing the discontent of any of the Nobles, upon the score of Kindred or Alliance.

The difficulty of procuring a comfortable Subsistence, and the little security of enjoying what shall be acquired through Industry, is a great cause of Prodigality, not only in the Gentry, whose Condition is more easie, but also in the very Burgers and Peasants: they are sensible that they live but from Hand to Mouth, and therefore as soon as they get a little Money they spend it. They live to day as the Poet advises, not knowing but what they now have may be taken from them tomorrow. And therefore expensiveness in Coaches, Retinue, Clothes, etc. is no where more common, nor more extravagant in proportion to their Income, than in this Country. Parsimony is often, not only a cause, but a sign of Riches; the more a wealthy Man has, the more he endeavours to acquire, and to encrease his stock: But here the Courtier buys no Land, but remits his Money to the Bank of Amsterdam, or of Hamburgh; the Gentleman spends presently on himself and his Pleasures all that he can get, for fear he should have the Reputation of being Rich, and his Money be taken from him by Taxes, before he has eaten or drank for it; the Merchant and Burger do the like, and subsist purely upon Credit; there being very few of this sort in the King's Dominions that can be called rich, or worth 100,000 Rix Dollars. The Peasant or Boor, as soon as he gets a Rix Dollar, lays it out in Brandy with all haste, lest his Landlord, whose Slave he is, should hear of it, and take it from him. Thus *Torva leaena lupum sequitur, lupus ipse capellam.*[18] The Trading Towns and Villages, (if we except Copenhagen, whose Situation and Haven make it thrive a little in spite of ill usage) are all fallen to decay. Those Burroughs which formerly lent good Sums of Money to the Prince upon extraordinary Publick Occasions, and furnished the Hollanders yearly with ten or twelve great Fly-boats Lading of Corn, being now not in a condition to raise 100 Rix Dollars, or to Lade one small Ship of Rye; as may be instanced in Kiog, once a flourishing little Seaport-Town, twenty Miles from Copenhagen, which in King

[18.] Virgil, *Eclogue* 2, line 64: "The fierce lioness pursues the wolf, and the wolf in turn the goat."

Christian the Fourth's time raised for that King's Service, in four and twenty hours time, 200,000 Rix Dollars; yet upon occasion of the last Poll Tax, I heard that the Collectors were forced to take from this and other Towns (in lieu of Money) old Feather beds, Bedsteads, Brass, Pewter, Wooden Chairs, etc. which they violently took from the Poor People, who were unable to pay, leaving them destitute of all manner of Necessaries for the use of Living.

Some Manufactures have been endeavoured to be introduced, not so much with a design of benefiting the Publick, as private Courtiers, and great Men who were the Undertakers, and expected to profit thereby: particularly that of Silks and Drinking glasses; but in a little time all came to nothing; it being a very sure Rule, that Trade will not be forced in a place where real Encouragements and Advantages are not to be found, and where Property is not secured; the very Credit of the Subject being as slender as his Riches are uncertain.

If this be the Case of the Gentleman and Burger, what can be expected to be that of the poor Peasant or Boor? In Zealand they are all as absolute Slaves as the Negroes are in Barbadoes, but with this difference, that their Fare is not so good. Neither they, nor their Posterity, to all Generations, can leave the Land to which they belong; the Gentlemen counting their Riches by their Stocks of Boors, as here with us by our Stocks of Cattle; and the more they have of these, the richer they are. In case of Purchase, they are sold as belonging to the Freehold, just as Timber-Trees are with us. There is no computing there by numbers of Acres, but by numbers of Boors, who, with all that belongs to them, appertain to the Proprietor of the Land. Yeomanry, which is the strength of England, is a state not known or heard of in Denmark; but these poor Drudges, after they have laboured with all their might to raise the King's Taxes, must pay the Overplus of the Profit of the Lands, and their own Toil, to their Landlords, who are almost as poor as themselves. If any of these Wretches prove to be of a diligent and improving Temper, who endeavours to live a little better than his Fellows, and to that end has repaired his Farm-house, making it convenient, neat, or pleasant, it is forty to one but he is presently transplanted from thence to a naked and uncomfortable Habitation, to the end that his griping Landlord may get more Rent, by placing another on the Land that is thus improved: so that in some years 'tis likely there will be few or no Farm-Houses, when those already built are fallen through Age or Neglect.

Another Grievance is, the Quartering and paying of the Soldiers.[19] Those that know what a vexatious thing it is (over and above the Charge) to be constantly plagued with insolent Inmates, who Lord it whereever they dwell, will soon allow this to be a Mischief scarce supportable.

And although this Country have a tendency to be extremely populous, the Women being exceeding fruitful, which is sufficiently proved by the vast Swarms that in former Ages, from these Northern parts, over-ran all Europe; yet at present it is but competently Peopled; vexation of Spirit, ill Diet, and Poverty, being great Obstructions to Procreation. Within Man's Memory the Peasants lived very happily; there was scarce any Family of them that was not Owner of a large piece of Plate or two, besides Silver Spoons, Gold Rings, and other odd Knacks, which they are fond of to this day, (and whenever they have any Money, will lay it out in such-like things, because they dare not trust themselves with the keeping of Money, the inclination to spend it presently is so general) but now it is a great rarity to find in a Boor's House any thing made of Silver; or indeed any other Utensil of Value, unless it be Feather-Beds, whereof there are better, and in greater plenty than in any place I ever saw; and which are made use of, not only to lye upon, but also to cover with instead of Blankets.

Among all the Hardships which are imposed on these poor Peasants, that which seemed to me one of the greatest, was the Obligation they lye under to furnish the King, Royal Family, and all their Attendants, their Baggage and Furniture, with Horses, and Travelling Wagons, whensoever he makes any Progress (which he often does either to Jutland or Holstein) or takes any lesser Journey in Zealand; nay, although it be only to his Country-Houses of Fredericksburg and Yagersburg. In these Cases all the Peasants that lye near the Road, or in that District, are summoned to attend with their Horses and Wagons at certain Stages, where they are to relieve each other; and this they often do, always at their own Charges for

19. Note in margin: "This was once known in England, when the Lord Dane or Danish Soldier, quartered in the English Yeoman's house and domineer'd to purpose: whence came the nick-name of Lazy Lordane."

Man's, and Horse-meat, for two or three days together, no regard being had to the Season of Harvest, (which is the usual travelling time) or to any other Conveniency of these poor Wretches. I have frequently seen them with hundreds of Wagons in a Company, attending the Arrival of the Court, bewailing their sad Condition; and as soon as the King came up, and his Coaches, with those of the other Persons of Quality, were fitted with six or eight Boors Horses each, (for they are little bigger than Calves) then every Lacquey seizes on his Boor and Wagon, for his own proper use; at which time, unless his Pleasure be in all things complied with, the poor trembling Peasant (who drives on, and takes all patiently, without replying one word) is so beaten and abused, that it has often moved my Pity and Indignation to see it. Neither is it only when the King himself travels, that the Boors are put to this trouble, but whenever he pleases to give his Warrant to any Person of Quality, or Officer, that has a Journey to make, they are obliged to this Service and Attendance.

Apoplexies and the Falling-Sickness are the Epidemical Distempers here; one shall hardly pass through the Streets of Copenhagen, without seeing one or two poor Creatures grovelling on the Ground in a Fit, and foaming at the Mouth, with a Circle of Gazers and Assistants about them: I know not what to impute this to, unless to the ill Diet of the Common sort, which is generally Salt-meats, Stock-fish, and such-like. Apoplexies among the better sort, often proceed either from excessive Drinking, or from Discontent; it being very usual here to have them die of a *Slacht*, as they call it, which is an Apoplexy, proceeding from Discontent and Trouble of Mind. But by way of amends for these ugly Distempers, there are few or none that are troubled with Coughs, Catarrhs, Consumptions, or such like Diseases of the Lungs; so that in the midst of Winter in the Churches, which are very much frequented, there is no noise to interrupt the Attention due to the Preacher. I am persuaded their warm Stoves, with the Plenty and Pureness of their Firing, (which is Beech-wood) contributes as much to their freedom from these kinds of Maladies, as the grossness and unwholsomness of our Coals in London does to our being so universally troubled with them; notwithstanding the ingenious Sir William Petty be of another Opinion: for in all other respects of Air and Situation, we have much the advantage of them.

The Tables of the better sort are usually well furnished with Dishes, yet I cannot commend the Cheer; because the Flesh is generally lean, and (except the Beef and Veal) ill tasted, especially the tame Fowl, the fattening of which is an Art not known by above two or three, who have been taught it by an English Poulterer, lately set up at Copenhagen. Wether Mutton is very scarce, and seldom good. Wild Ducks hardly to be eaten; and Plovers never. Here are no wild Pheasants, Woodcocks, Rabbits, or Fallow Deer. Red Deer there are, but they are the King's Game, and not to be bought for Money. The Hares are good, and the Bacon is excellent. Now and then you meet with a *Cheureuil*, or small Roe Buck in the Market, but it is generally lean. Sea-fish is scarce, and not good, but the River-fish makes amends, here being the best Carp, Perch, and Craw-fish that are to be found any where. One cannot expect extraordinary Fruits thus far North; yet the Gentry do not want such as are very tolerable, being extremely addicted to Gardening; and several of the Nobility being so curious, as to have Melons, Grapes, Peaches, and all sorts of Salads very early, and in great perfection. The Butter is very good, but the Cheese stark naught. In general, their way of Cookery would hardly be pleasing to an English Man.

They are much addicted to drinking; the Liquors that are most in vogue with Persons of Condition, are Rhenish Wine, Cherry Brandy, and all sorts of French Wine. The Men are fond of them, and the fair Sex does not refuse them. The poor People, who are able to indulge themselves, do it in bad Beer, and Danish Brandy, which is made of Barley.

The Gentlemen and Officers go very fine in their Dress after the French mode; but the Ladies Winter-dress is Danish, very becoming, and convenient. The Burgers, Servants, and even Peasants, are neat and cleanly; they love [a] change of ordinary white Linen, which is here made cheap; the Women-kind employing their leisure time in Spinning. All these People have a degree of Vanity; Pride and Poverty being often Companions to each other.

Their Marriages are usually preceded by Contracts, which will last sometimes three, four, or more years, before they proceed to a publick Wedding by the Minister; though often the young Couple grow better acquainted before these Formalities are dispatched. The Gentry give Portions with their Daughters; but the Burgers and Peasants, if they be able, give Cloaths, some Household stuff, and a great Wedding Dinner, but nothing else till they die.

Sumptuous Burials and Monuments are much in request with the Nobility; and it is usual to keep the Corps of a Person of Quality in a Vault, or the Chancel of some Church, for several Years together, till a fit opportunity to celebrate the Funeral. The poorer sort are buried in great thick Chests; and in the Towns, there are about a dozen of common Mourners belonging to each Parish, who are obliged to carry, and attend them to their Graves.

The Common People are mean spirited, not Warlike in their Tempers, as formerly; inclined to gross Cheating, and to suspect that others have a design to cheat them; therefore unwilling to go out of a road they have been accustomed to: insomuch that if you offer them great profit for a thing which they have not been used formerly to sell, they will refuse to part with it, as suspecting that you see an advantage in such a Purchase, which as yet is unknown to them, but which they hope to find out. I remember one instance: Seeing great Flocks of Green Geese in the Fields near the Town, I sent to buy some, but they being never used to sell, or eat Geese, in that Country, till they are big and old, it was not possible to persuade any body to part with one of them, though double the price of a big one were offered for each. They asked what we desired to buy them for? What we would do with them? etc., for they could not be persuaded, any one would be so foolish as to eat them whilst young, or little; after a Week, an old Woman, to whom Money had been offered for a dozen, came and brought four to sell, saying, *That neither she, nor her Geese, had thriven since she had refused to sell them at a good price; for the Kite had the night before kill'd eight of her stock, and that now the remaining four were at my service.* Thus the Superstition of this old Woman procured us the first Green Geese that I believe were ever eaten in Denmark; but after that they had taken notice that we fatted and killed them for eating, they furnisht us with them as often as desired. I would not omit this silly Story, because it gives a more lively Idea of the Temper of the Common People, than any Description I could make. In their Markets they will ask the same price for stinking Meat, as for fresh; for lean, as for fat, if it be of a kind. And the sure way not to obtain, is to seem to value, and to ask importunately, a thing which otherwise they themselves would desire should be done. This last Remark is not peculiar to the Common People only.

I do not see that they are good at imitating the Inventions of other Countries; and for inventing themselves, I believe none here, since the famous Tycho Brahe, ever pretended to it. Few or no Books are written, but what some of the Clergy compose of Religion. Not so much as a Song, or a Tune, was made, during three Years that I stayed there. Their Seasons of Jollity are very rare, and since the fatal Opera about four years ago, wherein many hundred Persons were burnt together in the old Queen's House,[20] they content themselves with running at the Goose on Shrove-Tuesdays, and taking their pleasure upon Sledds in the Winter, well wrapped up in Wool or Fur. A Divertisement much in request in this Court, and among all kinds of People. Perhaps it will be thought too nice here to remark, That no body presumes to go in a Sledd, till the King and Court has begun; That the King passes over a new Bridge the first. And that the Clocks of Copenhagen strike the hours after the Court Clock.

'Tis a difficult matter for Strangers to find conveniences of Lodging or Eating in Denmark; even in Copenhagen are few or no Lodgings to be Let in private Houses; and in the Taverns one must be content to Eat and Drink in a publick Room, into which any other Company may enter, and do the like at another Table; unless one pretends to higher matters than ordinary. The Language is very ungrateful, and not unlike the Irish in its whining complaining Tone. The King, great Men, Gentry, and many Burgers, make use of the High-Dutch in their ordinary Discourse, and of French to Strangers. I have heard several in high Employment, boast that they could not speak Danish. Yet very many of the Monosyllables in this Tongue are the same with the English; and without doubt we owe the Original of them to the Danes, and have retained them ever since they were Masters of our Country.

[20.] The 1738 edition notes in a lengthy comment that on April 19, 1689, 200 to 280 people perished in the fire that destroyed the entire castle and its contents.

CHAPTER IX

Of the Revenue

The Revenue of the King of Denmark arises from three Heads: First, The Taxes and Impositions of his own Subjects: Secondly, Customs paid by Foreigners: Thirdly, Rents of his own Estate, Crown Lands, and Confiscations. Each of these shall be treated of apart.

The Taxes paid by his own Subjects, are in some Cases fixed, and constant, in others arbitrary. When I distinguish between these two, it is not meant that the King's Power is limited in any wise; but only that he chooses, in some Taxes, to follow Rules and Measures established by himself, in all others he varies often. Of the first sort are, First, The Customs, or Toll, for Import and Export: Secondly, The Excise, commonly called the Consumption; which is upon Tobacco, Wine, Salt, Grain, etc., and all Eatables and Drinkables brought into any Town of the King of Denmark's Dominions to be spent. These are the great Taxes, and the last is severe enough. There are besides, of this kind, smaller Taxes; as that 3*dly* upon Marriages, where every couple Marrying, pay so much for the Licence, according to their quality; this is pretty high, and comes in some Cases to a good number of Rix Dollars for a Licence. 4*thly*, A Tax for marked Paper, whereon all Bonds, and Contracts, Copies of Judicial Proceedings, Grants, Passports, etc. must be written, otherwise they are invalid. And this is an uneasie Tax; there being of this kind of Paper, which amounts to several Rix Dollars a Sheet. Fifthly, Taxes for Brewing, Grinding, and other things, which shall be hereafter spoken of. But these, and such like, are certain; that is to say, every one knows how much he is to pay, according to an Ordnance at present in force; which however may be altered as the King pleases.

Of the second sort are Impositions upon Land; which is reckoned, not by Acres, but Farms; viz. so much for every proportion of Land that will bear the sowing of a Tun of hard Corn. Wheat and Rye are called hard Corn, and according to the Fertility of the Land, Seasonableness of the Year, Ability of the Landlord, each Farm is taxed higher or lower; but seldom too low.

Secondly, Poll-money, which is sometimes raised twice in a year, and is imposed according to the Substance of the Person taxed; which is guessed at, not fixed, as in other places, where all of a Rank pay equally.

Thirdly, Fortification-Tax, or Money raised for, or upon pretence of making Fortifications for the Defence of the Kingdom, etc.

Fourthly, Marriage-Tax, when a Daughter of Denmark is to be disposed of; whose Portion commonly is but 100,000 Crowns: but under this Name, occasion is taken to raise more.

Fifthly, Trade-money, wherein every Trades man is taxed for the liberty of exercising his Trade, according to the Gain which it is computed he makes by it: and he is moreover obliged to quarter Soldiers.

Sixthly, Ground-Rent for all Houses in Copenhagen, or any other Towns in Denmark; which are taxed by the King, when he pleases, according to the goodness of the House, the ability of the Possessor, or the greatness of the Sum he intends to levy at that time.

In Holstein and Sleswick the Lands are taxed by Ploughs; each Plough paying so much a Month.

To begin with those of the first sort, whereof the Rates are known and fixed; it would be convenient, in speaking of the Customs and Excise, to transcribe the whole Book of Rates, but I fear to be too tedious; however not to be wanting in any thing material, and to give a taste, whereby to guess at the rest; and measure Hercules by his Foot, some Particulars shall be set down, whereof to make a right Judgment, a due regard must be had always, not only to the Plenty and Scarcity of Money in a Country, but also to the goodness of a Commodity. For instance, when I speak of a fat Ox, it must not be imagined that we mean such as are usual in our English Markets; but rather such as we see come from Wales or Scotland. And so of other things in the Consumption Tax. And a Rix Dollar, considering the scarcity of Money, ought to be computed to go further than three crowns with us.

Import Customs

1 Ship pound of:	RD.	Stiv.
Iron Bars imported, pays	02	00
of wrought Iron	05	16
of Copper	00	32
of Wire one sort	15	00
of Wire another sort	20	00
of Pewter Vessels	15	00
of Pewter unwrought	00	18
of Lead	00	12
100 weight of Steel	00	24
one pound of Quicksilver	00	02
one Ell of Cloth of any value	00	08
one Ell of plain Silks	00	12
one Hat	00	32
one piece of Kersey of 20 Ells	01	08
12 pair of Worsted Stockings	01	12
50 Ells of plain Ribband	00	24
24 Ells of Ribband with Gold or silver in them	00	13
12 pair of Gloves	00	24
one Waistcoat knit	00	12
one other Waistcoat	01	05

	RD.	Stiv.
one Horse	01	32
one dozen of Knives	00	33
one Last of Coals	00	15
100 of Lemons	00	08

100 pound:

	RD.	Stiv.
of Capers	00	40
of Currants	01	02
of Raisins	00	32
of Cinnamon	06	00
of Confections	04	08
of Cork	03	00
of Nutmegs	04	08
of Sealing-wax	04	08

	Customs or Toll.		Consumption or Excise.	
	RD.	Stiv.	RD.	Stiv.
one Barrel of Tallow	03	00	01	16
one pound of Tobacco Leaves	00	00½	00	03
one pound of Tobacco Rolls or Snuff	00	04	00	03
one Barrel of Barley	00	20		
one Barrel of Flour of all sorts	00	26		
one Barrel of salt Beef	01	05		
one Ream of Paper	00	05		
one Barrel of Butter	03	00	00	32
one Ship-pound of Cheese	03	00	00	14
one Last of Spanish Salt	15	00	00	36
one Last of French Salt	08	00	00	36
one Last of Lunenburg Salt	24	00	00	36
one Hogshead of French Wine	06	32	05	00

	Customs or Toll.		Consumption or Excise.	
	RD.	Stiv.	RD.	Stiv.
one Hogshead of Vinegar	04	32	03	00
one Ahm of Rhenish, Canary, or other Strong Wines	08	00	06	00
one Ahm of French or Rhenish Brandy	10	32	03	16
one Hogshead of Cider	04	32	02	16
one Barrel of				
salt Herrings	01	32	00	04
of salt Salmon	01	32	00	12
of Beer	02	00	00	32
Feathers, one Lispound	02	12	00	02

	RD.	Stiv.
An Ox brought into any Town pays at the Gate	01	16
But into Copenhagen	02	00
One Calf into Copenhagen	00	16
elsewhere	00	08
A Sheep, Swine, or Goat	00	06
A Chevreuil	00	32
A Pigg	00	01
A Hare	00	04
A Turky	00	03
A Goose	00	01½
A pair of Pigeons	00	01½
of Ducks	00	02
of Partridges	00	04
of Blackbirds or Thrushes	00	01
Twenty Eggs	00	00½
Twenty dried Eeles, Breams, or the like	00	02

	RD.	*Stiv.*
Twenty Pickerels dried	oo	o1
one Salmon	oo	o6
one Pail of Milk	oo	o2
one Barrel of salted Flesh or	o1	oo
Tripes which comes in by Land to Copenhagen	o1	oo
to other Towns	oo	32
the like by Sea to Copenhagen	oo	32
to other Towns	oo	24
one side of smoak'd or salted Pork	oo	o2
one Barrel of Tongues	o1	oo
one Firkin of Honey	oo	24
one Barrel of Beans or Pease	oo	o8
of Parsnips or Turnips	oo	o1½
one Bushel of Nuts	oo	o2
four Bunches of Onions	oo	oo½
one Barrel of Hopps	oo	o6
one Firkin of Soap	oo	12
of Mustard-seed	oo	o4
of Hempseed or Linseed	oo	o1½
a Horse-load of Hay entring the Gates	oo	o2
a Horse-load of Charcoal	oo	o4
of Straw	oo	o2
of green Keal or Colworts	oo	o1
of Turf or Wood by Land	oo	o1
of Beech wood by Sea	oo	o4
of short Wood	oo	o2
of Birch-wood	oo	o1
of Bark	oo	o2

Planks, Oak-boards, and Firdeals exported, pay One per Cent. per Last, according to the Ships burden.

	Custom.	
	RD.	Stiv.
a Mast for a Ship of 28 Palms long	30	00
of 21 Palms	11	00
of 13 Palms	01	24
Between 12 and 8 Palms per dozen	02	24
Under 5 Palms per dozen	00	12
The rest proportionably		

	Consumption or Excise.	
	RD.	Stiv.
one Doe-skin undressed	00	02
dressed	00	04
ten Calves-skins	00	02
ten Sheep-skins	00	01
one Ox-hide	00	02
Tanned	00	04
ten Hides of English Leather	00	24
one Barrel of Rye ground for Bread, pays to the King for the grinding	00	16
ground for Brandy	00	32
one Barrel of Wheat ground for flour	00	40
of Malt for a Brewer	00	32
for a private House	01	00
of Oats for Grout	00	08

A Rix Dollar is something short of an English Crown in value; a Stiver is more than an English Penny. 48 Stivers make a Rix Dollar. One Lispound is the same with that we call a Stone. One Ship-pound is 20 Lispound. A Danish Ell is a third less than an English, or thereabouts.

There are publick Mills appointed and farmed to certain persons by the King, where all the Inhabitants of Copenhagen are bound to grind upon a Penalty, and to pay the Sums above-mentioned for grinding: it being not permitted to any private Person or Brewer to grind his own Mault, nor Baker his own Bread-corn.

I need say no more of the Tax for Marriage Licences, or that for the use of mark'd Paper in Bonds and Contracts, than has been already mention'd.

Those of the second sort, viz. Land-Tax, House-Tax, Poll-Money, and Fortification-Money, which are sometimes laid high, and sometimes low, can have no settled estimate made of them; however, I shall endeavour to compute them in the summing up the total of the Revenue, according to what they have yielded of late years, which was pretty high; and according to the utmost they can bear at present, or may probably for the future.

Some years ago, since the last War with Sweden, the King caused a Valuation and a Register to be made of all the Houses in the Cities and Burroughs within his Dominions, as likewise an admeasurement of all Lands in the Country, that he might the better proportion the Taxes he should have occasion to levy. These are now applotted and raised according to the very utmost of the Peoples Abilities; neither do I believe that in case of a War or other exigency, they could possibly bear a greater burden; for in the Country the Gentleman and Peasant are in a manner ruined; in the Cities and Burroughs, Houses pay yearly for Ground-Tax four per Cent. of the whole value that the Ground is rated at, if it were to be purchased; and this is estimated by Commissioners appointed for that purpose, according to the quantity of the Ground, or the conveniency of the Station: moreover, for every hundred Rix Dollars which the Ground of any House is rated at, the Inhabitants are obliged to quarter one Soldier. Thus a Rhenish-Wine Vintner at Copenhagen, and he none of the richest, has the Ground of his House valued at 900 Rix Dollars, he consequently pays 36 Rix Dollars yearly for Ground-tax, and quarters nine Soldiers upon the account of his House, and three more upon the account of his Trade. The like proportion is observ'd towards all others, with respect to their Houses and Trades.

Here is commonly one Poll-Tax at least every year; or if it chance to miss one year, it is usually doubled the next. The lowest Assessment is according to the following proportion, viz. a Burger esteemed worth eight or ten thousand Rix Dollars, pays for himself four Rix Dollars, for his Wife four Rix Dollars, for every Child two Rix Dollars, for every Servant one

Rix Dollar, for every Horse one Rix Dollar. An ordinary Alehouse-keeper pays for himself one Rix Dollar, for his Wife one Rix Dollar, for every Child 24 Stivers, for every Servant 16 Stivers.

About two years ago there was a Poll-Tax higher than ordinary; and at that time this proportion was observed: One of the Farmers of the Customs paid for himself 24 Rix Dollars, for his Wife 16 Rix Dollars, for her Maid two Rix Dollars, for every other Servant one Rix Dollar. A Burger esteemed worth six or eight thousand Rix Dollars paid for himself six Rix Dollars, for his Wife four Rix Dollars, for every Child two Rix Dollars, for every Servant one Rix Dollar; and thus did others according to their several Abilities.

The Fortification *Schatt* is a Tax with a witness: in that which was levied in the Year 1691, these were the Rules for payment. All the King's Servants paid 20 per Cent. of their yearly Salaries. All the Officers of the Army, beginning with Captains, and so upwards, 30 per Cent. of their Pay. (These used to be freed from former Taxes of this kind.) The Nobility and Gentry paid in proportion to their Rank and Estate. The highest, as Count Guldenlieu, etc., from seven hundred to one thousand Rix Dollars each. Burgers were taxed according to their supposed Abilities; the richer sort from one hundred to four hundred Rix Dollars, each; the middle sort of Merchants worth six or eight thousand Rix Dollars paid forty Rix Dollars; an Apothecary sixty eight Rix Dollars; a Vintner fifty five Rix Dollars; ordinary Burgers eight or ten Rix Dollars each: the poorer sort one or two Rix Dollars, and so forth. This sort of Tax has been accounted equal with another called the *Kriegs Sture,* imposed at the beginning of the War; and that amounted to near seven hundred thousand Rix Dollars in all. But 'tis most certain, the People are not now able to pay it as they were then, and consequently it will not be so much by a great deal.

When the King's only Daughter was about to be married to the present Elector of Saxony, a Marriage-Tax was intended, and had certainly been levied in case the Marriage had gone forward: but the one, as well as the other, is now no more spoken of, though no Kingdom in Europe can boast of a more deserving Princess.

I suppose by this time an English Reader has taken a Surfeit of this Account of Taxes which the Subjects of Denmark do pay; but it ought to be a great Satisfaction to him to reflect, that through the Happiness of our Constitution, and the Prudence and Valour of our King, the People of this Nation, though enjoying ten times more natural and acquired Advantages than the Danes, which causes more than ten times their affluence; do not for all that pay towards the carrying on the most necessary and just War, the third part in proportion to what the King of Denmark's Subjects do in time of a profound Peace: *Pax servientibus gravior est quam liberis bellum.*[21]

The second Head from whence proceeds a considerable Branch of this King's Revenue, is the Customs or Toll paid by Foreigners. These pay something more for imported Goods than the Natives and Burgers, and more Anchorage-money in the Ports. The Danes, from their own Ports to their own Ports, paying four Stivers per Last; from Foreign Ports ten Stivers per Last, whereas Foreign Ships pay twelve Stivers. But that which is most considerable to the King, is the Toll paid by all Strangers (except the Swedes) that pass the Sound; and the Customs of Norway.

I have in another place given an ample Account of the Original and Progress of this Toll, together with the Copy of a Letter which makes a Computation of the present Revenue arising from thence; so that I shall not need to repeat what I formerly said; only in general, that it is much fallen from what it was in the time of the last War, when all that passed paid; it came then to about 143,000 Rix Dollars yearly. In the Years 1690, and 1691, it amounted not to much more than 65000 Rix Dollars, at which rate we may judge it likely to continue. This belongs to the King's Privy Purse, and comes not under the Management of the Treasurer.

The Revenues of Norway arise chiefly from the Tenths of Timber and Tar, of Fish and Oil, and the Customs of the same; which being bought

[21.] The 1694 edition claims this as a citation of Tacitus, *Annals*, bk. 10, chap. 16. The 1738 edition corrects the author to Livy but not the title (which is *Ab urbe condita*, bk. 10.16). "They sued for peace because they could no longer endure war, they had taken to war again because enduring peace as slaves was worse than fighting war as free men."

and exported by Foreign Merchants, the Sums that come from thence into the King's Coffers are principally owing to them. It is true, there are Silver Mines, and Iron, and one of Copper, but these are of small value. The Excise, and the other Taxes of the Natives, are the same with those of Denmark; which these of Norway are better enabled to pay, because of their Foreign Trade; although this also is considerably diminished since their late Quarrel with the Dutch; who thereupon gave over their Traffick with them, and transferred it for some time to Sweden. These Differences have indeed been since adjusted, but it is a hard matter to reduce Trade thoroughly into the former Channel, when once it has taken another course. The Danes are of opinion, that neither the English nor Dutch can possibly want the Norway Trade for their Naval Stores: but if a right use were made of our Plantations in the West-Indies, they may chance to find themselves mistaken.

It may not be amiss to mention in this place, though it be something foreign to the Matter in hand; that just before the present War with France, the Trading Ships belonging to all the King of Denmark's Dominions, were computed to amount to about four hundred, besides little Barks that bring Wood, etc. because the number of them had been lessened almost two thirds within thirty years. But at present, since the Trade of Europe has been in a manner carried on by the Neutral Princes, it cannot otherwise be, but that the number must be considerably increased within these four years; though as yet it comes not up to what it formerly did. To conclude with Norway, which is divided into the Southern and Northern Provinces. The whole Revenue from the first of these amounts yearly to between five and six hundred thousand Rix Dollars; and from the last to between two and three hundred thousand Rix Dollars; and so the Total may be *communibus annis*[22] 800,000 Rix Dollars.

The exactest Computation that I have known made of the English, Dutch and French Trades to these Parts in Times of Peace, ran thus: Of English there passed the Sound yearly, from two hundred Vessels to three hundred; of Dutch from one thousand to eleven hundred; of French from ten to twelve; and the like proportion to Norway. By which it is easily

[22.] "Total for the year."

judged, that the Friendship and Trade of France ought to come in no competition with that of England and Holland; since the King of Denmark owes so large a share of his best Revenue to these last, and so little to the other.

The third and least considerable Branch of the Revenue arises from the Rents of the Crown Lands, and confiscated Estates. The latter are in the King's hands, either upon account of forfeiture for Treason, and other Crimes, or by reason of Debt and Non-payment of Taxes; and it is to be supposed these will encrease every day in proportion to the Poverty of the Country; since, as I formerly said, many would be glad, rather to surrender their Estates to the King, than pay the Taxes imposed on them.

But notwithstanding this Addition of Lands, the King is so far from being the richer, that he is the poorer for it: for upon the King's becoming possessor of any Man's Estate, immediately the great pains and care ceases which was formerly taken to improve it, and make it yield as much as it could; and it becomes almost desolate, either through the negligence or little encouragement of the Tenants: generally it turns to Forrest, and contributes to his Diversion, though little to his Purse; and the Houses run to decay. So do the Royal Palaces, whereof there are a great many on the Crown Lands, few of them, except Fredericksburg, being in a Condition to be dwelt in. For which reason it is a hard matter to make a just Calculation what yearly Revenue these afford: and that which they do yield goes for the most part among the Courtiers, who have the Government of the King's Houses, the Supervisorships of his Parks, Forests, and Farms, with the Services of his Boors, and Tenants. So that I believe we should rather over, than under reckon them, if we compute the clear yearly profit of these to amount to 200,000 Rix Dollars.

I endeavoured to know from an exact and understanding Person there, how much the running Cash of those Kingdoms might probably be: Whose Answer was in these Words: *It is very difficult to make any rational Computation of the running Cash of these Kingdoms; but certainly it is but very little, and not near the hundredth part of that of* England: *for excepting a very few, none have any Cash by them; the Trading People, through whose hands it runs, being generally Men of no Substance, but indebted over Head and Ears to their Creditors at* Amsterdam *and* Hamburg, *it comes no sooner in, but it is paid out. Moreover, the Cash of the Nation runs yearly out, by what the Officers of the Army, who are Foreigners, can clear; for all that they transport to other Countries: likewise by what divers of the Ministers of State can scrape together; since it is observed, that few or none of them purchase any Lands, but place their Money in the Banks of* Amsterdam *and* Hamburg. *Furthermore, by what the over-balance of Trade carries away; for this Country consumes more of Foreign Commodities, than its own Product can countervail. And all this makes me believe, that there is but an inconsiderable running Cash here; and very much of that which runs among the People is Brass-money, which is not worth any ones while to Export: Besides, the very Silver Coin has a great mixture of Brass in it.*

From the whole I conclude, that there is a moral Impossibility all these Taxes and Impositions should continue. The weight of them is already so great, that the Natives have reason rather to wish for, than defend their Country from an Invader; because they have little or no Property to lose, and may probably thereby mend their Condition, when there is scarce a possibility of making it worse. There seems to be a great sense of this in the Court, and therefore an Army composed of Foreigners is depended on. Here follow the Particulars of the Revenue.

	Rix Dollars.
Toll of the Sound	65,000
All the rest of the Toll of Denmark farmed at	165,000
The Consumption or Excise of Copenhagen, farmed at	140,000
The Consumption of the rest of Denmark	140,000
Smaller Taxes in Denmark	100,000
Poll-Tax, Fortification-Tax, Ground-Rents, Hardcorn-Tax	1,000,000
All the Revenue of Norway	700,000
King's Estate, Crown-Lands, etc.	200,000
Iseland farmed for	27,000
Oldenburg and Delmenhorst	80,000
Toll upon the Weser	5,000
Feroe, Greenland, etc.	0
Rix Dollars	2,622,000

It must be observed, that the Poll-Tax, and the Fortification-Tax, are never both raised the same year; so that there must be deducted out of that Sum about 400,000 Rix Dollars in lieu of one of those Taxes; and then the Sum total of the whole Revenue of the King of Denmark will amount every year to about two Millions two hundred twenty two thousand Rix Dollars.

CHAPTER X

Of the Army, Fleet, and Fortresses

Having done with the Revenue, I come in the next place to shew how those Sums are expended: And it is certain, that the levying of them is not more grievous to the Subject than the Reason for which they are levied, viz. the Maintenance of a great standing Army: so that the People are Contributors to their own Misery; and their Purses are drain'd in order to their Slavery. Thus the King of France makes the rich Towns he takes be at the Charge of building Citadels to keep themselves in awe: and it is that Master of the Art of Reigning, as his Flatterers call him, that has instructed the Court of Denmark, as well as the other Princes and States of Europe, the pernicious Secret of making one part of the People, both the Bridle and Scourge of the other; which in time must needs end in a general Desolation.

The King of Denmark has been but too apt a Pupil to such a Master, and has endeavoured even to exceed his Original; which he finds to his cost at this day, in raising more Men than his Country can maintain. Soldiers are, through I know not what mistaken Policy, esteemed the Riches of the Northern Kings, and other German Princes; for when they make an estimate of each others Wealth, it is not by the usual and ancient manner of Computation, the Fertility or Extent of the Territory, the Traffick, Industry, Number, or Riches of the People; but by so many Horse and Foot. For the subsistence of which they are forced, after they have eaten up their own Subjects, to make use of a hundred cruel and unjust Shifts, to the Ruin of their Neighbours. And when they cannot accomplish such a destructive Project in the manner they wish, then they are constrained to foment Quarrels between more potent Princes, that they may have the opportunity of selling to one or other those Forces which themselves cannot possibly maintain: so that at present Soldiers are grown to be as saleable Ware, as Sheep or Oxen, and are as little concern'd when they are sold; for provided the Officers be rendered content by the Purchaser, in having liberty to plunder the laborious and honest Country People in their Marches, and a fat Winter-quarter, with Permission to defraud their own Men of their Pay: the common Soldier goes with no more sense than a Beast to the Slaughter; having no such Sentiment, as Love of Honour, Country, Religion, Liberty, or any thing more than mere fear of being hanged for a Deserter.

But this mischievous Custom of Princes esteeming Soldiers the only true Riches, was first begun and established by the French King, and is grown general by his Care to cultivate this Opinion in the Minds of the German Princes, whose poor Countries he foresees will be soon ruined by such a practice. This he principally aims at, and it has brought Matters to such a pass, that War and Destruction are grown absolutely necessary. For as all Men that lay up Wealth never think they have enough; so these that consider Soldiers as the only Riches, never cease enlarging their Number, till they are necessitated for their Subsistence, either to come to Blows with their Neighbours, or to create Animosities between other; wherein they have found the knack of being employed, and receiving Pay without interesting themselves in the Quarrel. Where this will end, God Almighty knows, and can only prevent the apparent Mischiefs threatened by it, viz. the universal Misery and Depopulation of Europe. For since this Practice is grown so general, none of these Kings or Princes, though endowed with a more peaceable Spirit and better Judgment than the rest, dares lead the

Dance, and disarm, for fear of his Armed Neighbours, whose Necessities make them wait only for an opportunity to fall upon him that is worst provided to make Resistance: And this is none of the least Calamities which the French Tyranny has forced upon the World, having reduced all the Princes and Commonwealths of it to this hard choice; either to submit themselves to an intolerable Foreign Yoak, or maintain Vipers at home to gnaw their own Bowels.

But the Consequences of these unjust Practices have been more pernicious to Denmark, than to the French King that set the Example; the Toad may emulate the Ox, and swell, but he shall sooner burst, than equal him. The one goes on in a course of prosperous Tyranny; but the other through an ill Calculation of his own Strength, which is no way proportionable to his Ambition, never hitherto throve in any of his Attempts upon his Neighbours. Hamburg is yet a Free City, and the Duke of Holstein restored to his Possessions; whilst Schonen, Halland, Bleking, and Yempterland remain in the Possession of the Swedes; who in taking up Arms for their own Defence, have had the Fortune to revenge the Injury. And the Danes are constrained to acquiesce in the Loss of those their best Provinces, without any rational hopes of ever recovering them.

A List of the Horse and Foot in the Service of the King of Denmark, *which belonged particularly to* Denmark, Holstein, *and* Oldenburg.

Horse.	*Men.*
Regiment of Danish Guards, consisting of six Troops, 75 Men in each Troop, Lieutenant General Pless Colonel, with Officers of all sorts	500
Regiment of Holstein Guards, consisting of nine Troops, each fifty with the Officers, Colonel Bass	450
Col. Berensdorf's Regiment, nine Troops	450
Col. John Rantzaw nine Troops	450
Col. Rave nine Troops	450
Col. Swanwedle nine Troops	450
Col. Bassum nine Troops	450
Col. Nemerson nine Troops	450
Col. Hulst nine Troops	450

Horse.	*Men.*
Col. Sturk nine Troops	450
Col. Otto Rantzaw nine Troops	450
Col. Gam nine Troops	450
Total	5450

Dragoons.	*Men.*
Baron Lyondale Colonel	500[23]
Col. Bee	500
Col. Habercas	500
Total	1500

Foot.	
Regiment of Guards, Duke of Wirtemberg Colonel	1400[24]
Queen's Regiment, Col. Passaw	1200
Prince Royal's Regiment, Col. Crage	1200
Prince George's Regiment, Count Alefeldt	1100
Prince Christian's Regiment, Brig. Elemberg	1000
Zealand Regiment, Col. Tramp	1200
Funen Regiment, Col. Browne	1100
Lieutenant General Schack's Regiment	1800
Lamsdorf's Regiment	1200
Regiment of Curlanders, Col. Pottcamer	1000
Marine Regiment, Col. Gersdorf	1000
Oldenburg Regiment, Col. Bieulo	2000
Total	15200

Note, That by virtue of a Treaty concluded with the Emperor, there were sent lately into Hungary part of the fore-named Troops under the Command of Col. Rantzaw; Viz.

23. Note in margin 1738: "Raised most in Norway."

24. Note in margin: "Note, that these 7 Regiments were greater before that Battalions were taken out of each of them, which were sold to his Majesty, and now serve under the Duke of *Wirtemberg's* command in *Flanders.*"

One Battalion of Lieutenant-General Schack's Regiment.
One Battalion of Col. Pottcamer's Regiment.
One Regiment of Horse taken from the former Colonel, and given to one Colonel Wyer.
Colonel Bee's Regiment of Dragoons, which may be deducted from the Sum Total at the end.

	Men.
Fuzeliers, Canoniers, and Bombardiers in Denmark, Norway, Holstein, etc.	1800
Sum Total of the Foot besides Officers	17000

A List of the Forces in Norway.

One Regiment of Horse consisting of 9 Troops, Commanded by Col. Rechle	456
One Regiment of Dragoons, Commanded by Col. Marshal	800
	1256

Foot.

Bergen Regiment, Col. Ed. Ken	1200
Aggerhuy's Regiment, Col. Housman	1000
Smaland Regiment, Brigadier Tritstaw	1000
Upland Regiment, Col. Brockenhuysen	1000
Westland Regiment, Col. Arnauld	1100
Drontheim Regiment, Col. Schults	1200
A *Marine* Regiment	600
Two new raised Regiments, one Commanded by Col. *Bunenberg,* the other by	2000
Two free Companies as *Drontheim*	200
	9300
Reserves	5000

These Reserves are such as receive no Pay in time of Peace, but are like our Militia, only they have Clothes given them once in two years; and are obliged to meet and Exercise every Sunday, if the Weather be fair.

So that the King of Denmark's Land-Forces, consisting

of Horse and Dragoons in Denmark, Holstein, etc.	6950
Foot in the same	17000
Horse and Dragoons in Norway	1256
Foot in Norway, including the Reserves	14300
In all are	39506
But if you exclude the Reserves, with about 2500 men that were sent to Hungary, the Sum total will amount to (besides Officers of the Foot)	32006

A great Regiment of Foot before the Battalions were drawn out of them for the King of England's Service, consisted of Nineteen Companies, and so it will be again when these Forces return to Denmark. In the Guards were a great many more.

The charge of one of these great Regiments of Foot amounts to 90,000 Rix Dollars a Year, thus;

	R.D.	Stiv.
1 Captain's pay per Month	20	00
2 Lieutenants, 11 Rix Dollars each	22	00
3 Serjeants 1 Fourier pay 4 R.D. bread 32st. to each in all	18	32
3 Corporals pay and bread, 3 R.D. 32 Stivers each	11	00
2 Carpenters 10 Gefreiders 2 Drummers 3 R.D. 8 St. each	44	16
88 Common Soldiers 2 R.D. 32 Stivers each	234	32
	350	32
For nineteen Companies	6662	32
The Grenadiers have half a Rix Dollar per Man more	54	24
This is per Month	6717	08
And per Year	80606	00
Each Captain hath per Month for recruiting, 8 R.D. which for 19 Companies in 12 Months amounts to	1824	00

The Colonel hath more than his
Captain's pay per Month 30 R.D.

	R.D.	Stiv.
2 Lieut. Colonels per Month more 40 RD		
2 Majors per Month more 20 RD		
And to a Regiment are 5 Ensigns 50 RD per Month 140 RD		
And in a year	1680	00
Total	84110	00

The Remainder of the 90 thousand Rix Dollars runs up for the other Officers, Auditor, Quartermaster, Surgeon, Powder, Shot, and other necessary Expenses.

The Common Soldier receives but 17 Stivers a week; the rest goes for Bread, Quarters, and Cloaths, which they have once in three years from head to foot; and in the midst of those three years, Shoes, Stockins, Breeches, Shirt, and Cravat. 'Tis permitted to the Common Soldiers to work where they are quartered; but then during this permission, their Officers receive all the benefit of their pay. The Foot, both Officers and Soldiers, are for the most part Strangers of all Countries, whom Choice or Fortune brings thither; Germans, Poles, Courlanders, Dutch, Swedes, Scotch, Irish, and now and then an English Seaman, whom they make drunk after a long Voyage, and inveigle him by fair Promises, in that humour, to take some of the King's Money. The Natives are, through their dispirited temper, thought very improper to make Soldiers; and besides, the Landlords, whose Slaves they are, can hinder them from entering into the King's Service, and can remand them, if any should offer so to do; as has been frequently practised by them, to avoid Misery at home, and to exchange one Slavery for another.

The Officers of the Horse receive no more Pay in time of Peace, than those of the Foot. The Troopers, who are generally Natives, and none of the best Soldiers, are maintained every one by his Peasant, who is bound to give him and his Horse, Meat, Drink, House-room, etc. besides to the value of six shillings sterling a Month; half of which Money goes to his

Colonel towards his mounting. The Dragoons are in somewhat a better condition, because they are not obliged to keep Horses, but in time of War; besides, in Holstein they have larger Pay than in Denmark.

In Norway the Forces cost but little, in comparison of what they do elsewhere; for besides the Pay of the Officers, and the Clothing of the Soldiers, not much Money is expended; each single Soldier having Free Quarter amongst the Boors. It is to be noted, that the Officers of this Army are, for the most part, fourteen or eighteen Months in Arrear of Pay; so that the best part of their Maintenance is out of the Common Soldier's Subsistence Money.

The Names of the General Officers

Lieutenant-Generals.
Count Wedel Mareschal.
Count Guldenlieu Viceroy of Norway.
Duke of Wirtemberg.
Commandant Schack.
Monsieur Plessen of the Horse.
Monsieur Dumeny.
Major-Generals.
Monsieur De Cormaillon.
Monsieur Maspack of the Horse.
Master of the Ordnance is Coll. Monk.

Thus much shall suffice for the Land. I come now to speak of the Sea-Forces.

The Names of the Admirals, are

Admiral General Monsieur Juel.
Vice-Admiral Bielk.
Vice-Admiral Spaan.
Vice-Admiral Gedde.
Rear-Admiral Hoppe.
Rear-Admiral Van Stucken.

There are in Copenhagen 3000 Seamen kept in constant Pay, who go not to Sea unless in time of War, but have a certain small allowance of Money, with a constant weekly provision of Salt Flesh, Stock-fish, Meal, Grout, etc. given them out of the Publick Store-Houses, for the maintenance of themselves, and Families. They have moreover several Streets of small Houses, like Baraques, built regularly for them, by King Christian the Fourth, in one of the Out-skirts of Copenhagen within the Works; where they live Rent-free, and where they leave their Wives and Children when they go to Sea. Their business in time of Peace is to work on the *Holm;* which is a large Yard with Docks in it, to build Shipping, over-against the King's Palace in Copenhagen. Here they are employed by turns in all laborious Works belonging to Ships, Guns, Anchors, Cables, drawing of Timber, etc. and so painful is this Toil esteemed, that Criminals of the highest kind are usually condemned to work on this *Holm* for a certain number of years, or during life, according to the nature of the Offence. Once a year generally, to find exercise for these, some of the Men of War are rigged and equipped with their Guns, etc. and drawn out of Port to sail up and down, between that and Elsignor, for three or four Weeks, or longer, according as the good Weather lasts. The pay of these Mariners in Money is but 8 Rix Dollars yearly for each; and as small as it is, it is so ill discharged, that they mutinied several times, of late years, for want of it, and even besieged the King in his Palace, till some signal Severity towards the principal Mutiniers quelled them. There is usually a year and a halfs Arrears owing to them, and often more; which is the better born, because of their weekly Allowance in Provision; although that be very scanty, especially to such as have many Children to feed.

The best Seamen belonging to the King of Denmark are the Norwegians; but most of these are in the Service of the Dutch, and have their Families established in Holland; from whence it is scarce likely they will ever return home, unless the Dutch use them worse, or the Danes better than hitherto they have done; for the Danish Sea-provision is generally very bad.

All the Officers of the Fleet are in constant Pay, as well in time of Peace as War, which makes them less given to plunder, than those who make use of the short time they are in Commission to enrich themselves as fast as they can.

A List of the King of Denmark's Fleet.

Ships.	Guns.	Men.
Christianus Quintus	100	650
Prince Frederick	84	600
Elephant	84	600
Three Crowns	84	600
Norway Lion	84	600
Prince George	82	600
Cour Prince	82	590
Mercurius	76	510
Mars	76	500
Three Lions	70	490
Drake	70	490
Charlotta Amelia	68	480
Anna Sophia	66	470
Swan	66	470
Christianus Quartus	64	430
Fredericus Tertius	56	400
Guldenlieu	56	390
Christiania	58	390
Oldenburg	56	360
Lintworm	49	330
Sleswick	42	300
Feroe	54	380
Angel	52	300
Delmenhorst	50	300
Swedish Falcon	48	250
Neptune	46	220

Sword-fish	44	210
Tumbler	42	200
Hummer	34	160
Ships.	*Guns.*	*Men.*
Danish Mermaid	30	140
Dragon	28	140
White Falcon	26	120

Small Ships and Snaws.
The Tyger.
New Elephant, a Yacht.
Phoenix Galley, a Bomb-boat.
Minden.
Pacan.
Little Elephant, a Yacht.
Swermer.
The Ape.

No Fire-Ships.
In all 32 Ships. 1927 Guns. 12670 Men.

This Fleet was never set to Sea thus equipped; but this is the Computation the Danes make of their Sea-Forces; and thus much they say in case of necessity they are able to perform.

Some of the biggest of these Ships draw more Water by five or six Foot at the Stern than at the Head, which denotes they are broken-backt; they are all generally lower Masted than ours, and seem more unwieldy. I believe them more proper for the Baltick than the Ocean; if we except some few of the Cruisers, and other Ships which Convoy their Merchant-men to France, Spain and Portugal.

Fortresses Belonging to the King of Denmark

On Bornholm, a Fertile Island in the Baltick Sea, nearest to Sweden of any of this King's Dominions, are two Fastnesses; one an ancient Castle, the other a Citadel, according to the Modern manner of Fortification, which commands the best Road in the Island called Roena. It was finished in the Year 1689 and has good Bastions and Out-works.

Christian's Oye, about seven English Miles North-west from Bornholm, being a number of little Islands which enclose a safe Harbour for thirty Sail; the largest Isle, in form of a Crescent, is well fortified. In the Island Mûne at Stege, a small Town, is an ancient Castle of little Defence, where there is a Garrison.

In Laland, all that looks like strength, is the Town of Naxkew, and an old Castle called Allholm; but they are of no great Defence.

In Zealand, first, the Town of Copenhagen is well fortified, but the Works are only Earth. Secondly, The Castle of Cronenberg near Elsignor, which is now near finishing, and is faced with Brick. It is an irregular, but good Fortification. Thirdly, Corsoer, a small Earthen Fortress over against Funen.

In Funen, the Town of Nyburg is pretty well fortified towards the Sea; but towards the Land the Works are out of repair.

In Holstein there is, first, Glucstadt, a well fortified Town upon the River Elb, which because of its Neighbourhood to Hamburg is kept in a good condition. Secondly, Cremp, a Town within three English Miles of the former, near the River Stoer, in no extraordinary repair. Thirdly, Hitlar Scance on an Island, twelve English Miles from Hamburg. Fourthly, Rendsburg, on the Borders between Holstein and Sleswick, and on the River Eyder; this Place is now enlarging, the Bulwarks and Outwarks are facing with Brick; it will be a Royal Fortification, and is the most considerable Place the King of Denmark has, both for Strength and Situation. Fifthly, Christian's Prize, or Frederick's Ort, (for it has two Names) situated at the entrance of the Haven of the City of Kiel on the Baltick. It is commanded by a Hill one hundred and twelve Roods North from it.

In Jutland, first Fredericia, a very well fortified Town, being a Pass over the Little Belt. Secondly, Hall, a small Fortress on the North-side the Entrance of the River that leads to Alburg. Thirdly, at Flatstrand, twenty English Miles South of the Scagen Point, is a Schance and a small Fort for the Defence of the Haven.

To the Southward of the North Cape of Lapland is a Fort of six Bastions, called Wardhuys. And in Norway there is, first, Drontheim, guarded to the Sea by a strong Castle, called Monkholm, (where Monsieur Griffenfelt is at present kept close Prisoner) and to the Land by a strong Citadel. Secondly, Bergen, a very strong Place towards the Sea, and environed with high Mountains, which make it inaccessible by Land; 'twas here the Dutch East-India Ships sheltered themselves, when the English Fleet, under the Command of the Earl of Sandwich, attacked them unsuccessfully. The Danes had passed their word, that they would deliver them up; but some seasonable Presents which the Hollanders made at Court, prevailed so far, as to make them break it; which occasioned the Hollanders Safety, and our Disgrace. Fourthly, Christiania, the Capital of Norway; it has a strong Citadel. Fifthly, Larwick, a slight Fortification. Sixthly, Frederickstadt, a place which has good Works, but built on a bad Foundation. Seventhly, Wingar Castle, a Pass on the Borders of Norway. Eighthly, Frederick's-hall, a place well fortified, but much commanded by a Hill one hundred Rood from it. Ninthly, a Fort at Fleckero, near the Town of Christiansandt.

In the East-Indies the King has a small Fortress called Tranquebar, on the Coast of Coromandel: In Guiney another called Christiansburg; and a third in the Island of St. Thomas in the West-Indies, which commands the only good Port in all those Parts, wherein Ships take shelter during the Season of the Hurricanes.

One may easily judge that such an Army and Fleet, with so many Fortresses, cannot be maintained as they ought, without a very great Purse. The former Chapter gives a just account of the Revenue; and the Military Expenses may be guessed at by this: There is over and above all these, the Charge of the Civil List, the maintenance of the Court, King's Children, Publick Ministers, etc. Whether the Income bears proportion to all these Expenses, and would be sufficient without the assistance of Foreign Money, is left to the determination of such as are skill'd in Calculating.

CHAPTER XI

Of the Court

Under this Head I comprehend the King, Queen, Royal Family, Ministers of State, Knights of the Order of the Elephant, and of Dannebrug, with other principal Officers belonging to the Court.

The present King of Denmark, Christian the Fifth, is but of a moderate stature, rather lean than corpulent, yet well proportioned, and strongly built; his Complexion is Sanguin, he wears a black Perriwig; the Lines of the lower part of his Face are not unlike those of King Charles the Second; his Constitution has been very robust, capable to endure, and loving to undergo all manner of fatigue; until that within these few years, having had some fits of the Gout, he thought it better to dispense with Exercises which might disturb his Ease; especially there being less need in time of Peace of his taking such pains as he easily could, and yet would do, were there occasion. He began the six and fortieth year of his Age the fifteenth of April 1692. His Habit is usually modest, but gentile; he seldom appears at Court times with either Hat or Gloves, though always (after the German fashion) with a good Sword girt close to his side.

As to his qualities, he is a Prince of singular affability and good nature; temperate if you consider the humour of that Country; being neither luxurious in his Meat or Drink, and of late years very seldom making any Debauch. His Amours have not been many, and in those he has continued very constant. He is Religious as a Prince ought to be, without doting on his Clergy, though they seem to adore him; in his own temper a lover of Justice and Moderation; but often over-ruled by those about him, to whom he leaves the whole management of Affairs; because he neither loves, nor has a Genius for business. He speaks little, unless to his Ministers, and immediate Servants; yet he gives all opportunity and encouragement to others to entertain him; as it were emboldening them by a gracious Smile, and advancing towards them. He is Master of three Languages besides his own, the High and Low Dutch, and the French, using them with great ease upon occasion. He was not bred up to any sort of Learning, yet takes a particular delight in Geography; and is never better pleased than when an exact Chart of any Country, or Delineation of any Fortress is brought to him: his Genius for the War inclining him to love Fortification. He is of a clear undoubted Personal Courage, as has been often demonstrated in the late Wars with Sweden: but eases himself of the greatest part of the Conduct, which he leaves to his Generals, not relying on his own Judgment either in occasions of Action or Negotiations; though 'tis probable the greatness of his Courage in the one, and the sincerity of his Intentions in the other, would produce better effects, did he trust himself more, and others less. In fine, he is a very mild, and gracious Prince, beloved rather than reverenced by his People; who are sensible that the present Form of Government, concurring with a King of a severe temper, would be altogether intolerable. His Motto under his Arms and Cypher is, *Pietate* & *Justitia;*[25] and his Subjects do really believe the preservation of these to be his true Inclinations; and that all hardships that fall upon them, have their rise from the Ministry. Therefore they complain of his permitting, rather than his acting, and attribute all the Evils they endure, to the easiness of his Temper, and unhappiness of their present Constitution; which is not redressed by any Advantages derived from his Education.

The Queen, Charlotta Amelia, is a Princess that deserves to be mentioned with all honour, even though she were not of that high Quality.

[25.] "With piety and justice."

She is fair, and well shap'd; her Complexion being a mixture of Fleg-matick and Sanguin; and although she be in the forty first year of her Age, continues still handsome; her Carriage is very engaging, affable, and free; her great Accomplishments secure to her the Hearts of her Subjects, not-withstanding her differing from them in Religion, and stop the mouths of the bigoted Lutherans, which would be apt enough to exclaim against her, did not a most unreproachable Life set her above Malice. They have made several Attempts to wound the Calvinist Religion through her sides; but she has hitherto frustrated them all, and preserved not only her self, but the little French Protestant Church (lately founded in Copenhagen by her Bounty, and subsisting through her Protection) from all the Assaults made against it by Persons in Power. And this she does the more effectu-ally, through a prudent compliance with the King in matters indifferent, going frequently with him to the Lutheran Service and Sermons: thereby not only shewing the charitable and good Opinion she has of the Publick established Worship, but getting a greater freedom of going every After-noon to hear the French Ministers in her own Church. She is the common Refuge of distressed People, who never fail of their account in approach-ing her. Neither is Access to her difficult; she often prevents those that have need, and does good before she be sought unto. In short, she is Sister to the present Landgrave of Hesse Cassel; worthy of such a Brother, and the illustrious Stock from whence she proceeds.

The King of Denmark has five Children; four Princes and one Prin-cess. Prince Frederick the eldest, who is also called the Prince Royal, is about twenty years old; it were to be wished his Education had been more conformable to his quality; for his former Governor being somewhat pe-dantick, had infused a little stiffness and formality into the Pupil, which People that judge by outward Appearances, are apt to misconstrue Pride; but doubtless his Travels have reformed that ill habit. Prince Christian, the second Son, is about eighteen years of Age, of a more lively and affable temper than his elder Brother, as well as taller, and of a more robust Con-stitution; much addicted to Hunting, and riding the great Horse; he longs for nothing more than to see and shew himself to the World. Prince Charles, the third Son, is about nine years old, and Prince William, the Fourth, about six. The former is a very forward hopeful Youth; the latter does not yet stir out of the Nursery, so that no Judgment can be made of him.

The Princess [Sophia Hedwig] is about sixteen, a very beautiful sweet tempered and well-educated Lady; she was contracted to the present Elector of Saxony her own Cousin Germain; but the Match was afterwards broken off.

The King has besides these, two Natural Sons by Mrs. Mote, a Citizen's Daughter of Copenhagen, whom he had made Countess of Samsoe (an Island which he has given to her) he sends her moreover, as it is confidently reported 1000 Rix Dollars every Saturday Night. The young Gentlemen, her Sons, are very handsome and hopeful. The eldest is in the Service of France, where he has a Regiment of Horse, and is called young Guldenlieu, to distinguish him from the Elder, who is Viceroy of Norway; the King gives him the Revenue of the Post-Office. This Appellation of Guldenlieu is appropriated to the Bastard Sons of the Kings; I know not whether it began with the present Viceroy of Norway, or not; but it is likely to continue hereafter, and a young Guldenlieu will become as necessary an Ornament to the Court, as an Heir of the Crown.

The second of the King's Sons, by the Countess of Samsoe, is designed for the Sea; and to that end has been sent several Voyages in a Man of War under the Direction of a trusty Person, in order to fit him to be one day Admiral-General.

His high Excellency, Count Guldenlieu, Viceroy of Norway, and Natural Brother to the King, will be more properly mentioned here, as one of the Royal Family, than when we come to speak of the Ministers; for though he be one of them, yet he cares not to embark himself deep in the Publick Affairs, having formerly, in some Occurrences, burnt his Fingers; he thinks it wisdom rather to enjoy his Divertisements, and the favour of the King, which he now firmly possesses. His Father, King Frederick, loved him so well, that he once thought of making him King of Norway; which has been remembered to his prejudice, and obliges him to carry himself with great care, under a Government so Arbitrary as this is. He is about fifty six years of Age, has been one of the handsomest, and continues one of the finest Gentlemen that Denmark has produced: having to his Natural Accomplishments, added all the advantages of Travel, and

Knowledge of the World. He is a Man of Pleasure, and understands it in all its Refinements; his Palace, his Gardens, his Entertainment, manner of accosting, etc., excelling by many degrees any thing that can be found elsewhere in that Kingdom. He was formerly Ambassador Extraordinary from King Frederick his Father to King Charles the Second, who shewed such a particular esteem for him, that he made him the Partner of his Pleasures. And this is returned by so deep a sense of that King's Kindness, that he scarce ever mentions his Name without great concern. He speaks a little English, and is very obliging to any Person that belongs to this Country, in gratitude for the great Civilities he received here.

The King of Denmark's Court, as to Pomp and Magnificence, can hardly be called a Royal one; the Luxury and Extravagance of the more Southern Courts of Europe having not reached thus far North, no more than their Riches. It is true indeed, since their good correspondence with France, their Manners are somewhat refined above what they formerly were; they affect French Modes, French Servants, and French Officers in the Army; whereof they have one Lieutenant General, and one Major General, who have quitted France for fighting Duels there. And this is either really true, or at least the pretence of such as seek Service in Foreign Countries on purpose to do the business of France, whose interest they always cultivate industriously, though they seem never so much in disgrace with their Prince.

In this Court no Ensigns of Majesty appear; let the occasion be never so solemn, except such as are Military, all those which a standing Army can afford, such as Horse and Foot Guards, Trabands, which answer our Beef-eaters, Kettle-Drums, and Trumpets, etc. are there in perfection, and used every day as much as in a Camp: but Badges of Peace, viz. Sword of State, Heralds, Maces, Chancellor's Purse, etc. are not known.

The King sits down to Dinner with his Queen, Children, Relations, prime ministers, and General Officers of the Army, till the round Table be filled. The Court Mareschal invites whom he thinks fit to eat with the King, speaking sometimes to one, sometimes to another, till all have had their turns in that honour. A Page in Livery says Grace before and after Meat, for no Chaplain appears either here, or in any other of the Protestant Courts abroad, but in the Pulpit. There is a plentiful Table; but the

Meat dressed after their own manner. The King's particular Diet every day, is a Loin of roasted Veal, and his Drink Rhenish-Wine; whereof a silver Beakerfull stands at every one's Plate, which generally serves for the whole Meal. The Attendants are one or two Gentlemen, and the rest Livery Servants. No Ceremony of the Knee is used to the King. The Kettle Drums and Trumpets, which are ranged in a large place before the Palace, proclaim aloud the very Minute when he sits down to Table. Sunday is his Fasting day, and by his Example, is so to many of the Courtiers.

Court times, wherein those that have business, may most easily have Audience, are an hour before Dinner constantly, and sometimes before Supper. At such times the King's Children, Domestick and Foreign Ministers, Officers of the Army, and Household, appear in the Anti-chamber and Bedchamber: these compose the Court, and seldom amount to above the number of twenty or thirty. Few or no Gentlemen, that have not Employments, are seen at Court, or in Copenhagen, for Reasons formerly given.

The Officers of the Household are, The Marshal, who regulates the Affairs of the Family, and gives the King notice when Dinner or Supper is ready. The Comptroller of the Kitchen, who places the Dishes of Meat upon the Table, and is likewise Master of the Ordnance. The Master of the Horse, who looks after the King's Stables, and Studs of Mares, whereof the King has very many, and very good, especially those of one Breed particular to him, which are light Iron-Grey, with black Heads, Tails, and Mains. But one forms a nearer Idea of the Grandeur and Revenue belonging to these several Offices, by imagining them like the same in the Families of some of our English Noblemen, rather than of those belonging to Whitehall. The Master of the Ceremonies is obliged by his Employment to be a constant Attender at Court.

But the principal Favourite of the King is Monsieur Knute, a Mecklenburger, and only Gentleman of the Bedchamber. He has been bred up all along with the King, as his Confident and Companion in his Pleasures; is a civil well-natur'd Gentleman, speaks no Language but his own, and loves least of all the French; meddles rarely with publick business, yet when he undertakes any thing with the King, seldom fails of Success. There are several Grooms of the Bedchamber subordinate to him. And the

Queen has many Gentlemen, Sons of Persons of the best Quality, which are Attendants upon her, and eight Maids of Honour.

The King's Ministers are, first, Monsieur de Guldenlieu, who has the precedence at the Council-Board, and in all other Commissions where he is employed with the rest; but business, as I intimated before, being not his Talent, or at least not his Choice, it is rather out of respect to his quality, than otherwise, that he is reckoned among them.

Secondly, Count Raventlau, Great Master of the Game, which is the Employment of greatest Profit in the King's Gift, after the Viceroyship of Norway: he is a Native of Holstein, and is lookt upon as Prime Minister; therefore all Foreign Ministers address themselves to him. He takes it not ill to be stiled so; though he seems upon some occasions modestly to decline it. He is very affable civil, and of easy access; a Man of Pleasure, and an admirer of the fair Sex, as well as Monsieur de Guldenlieu: his Parts and Learning are of a moderate size; though of late, through a more diligent application to business he be much improved; so that he seems to fill worthily enough the Post wherein his Master has placed him. He is about Three and forty years of Age, his Complexion fair, and his Constitution robust; his Inclinations were but indifferent towards the French (as being convinced that the low Ebb of his Country's Prosperity, and his Master's Honour, were in a great measure owing to their Counsels and Practices) till within this year or two, that private Interest has reconciled him to that Court: the benefit of the French Traffick, during this War (wherein he is deeply concerned, as well by several Ships of his own, as by giving Protection to others that manage that Trade) has made him think that it is his Master's Advantage, as well as his, to keep firm Friendship with France. On the other hand, the English obstructing that Traffick, by taking and confiscating several Ships wherein he was concern'd, seem to have quite lost his favour. Yet after all, 'tis believed, if he could procure the same, or equivalent Advantages for himself and his Master, his Inclinations would more willingly lead him to accept of them from England than France; but the unhappy Circumstances of this present Conjuncture do render that matter scarce possible.

Thirdly, Baron Juel, younger Brother to the Admiral General, and a Dane by Birth, about sixty years old; he is very corpulent, and of a fleg-matick Complexion; more easy in his Fortunes than any about Court, which is in part owing to his remarkable parsimonious temper. The Danes look on him as one of the cunningest men among them, who under the disguise of a seeming Simplicity covers a great deal of Craft. His words are very few and smooth, and his behaviour Civil. It is thought that he sees with regret the Misery his Country is reduced to, as being one of the Stock of old Nobility, who have suffered by the change of the Constitution: yet his Advice cannot be wanted, where there is such a scarcity of good Heads; and therefore he is employed in all difficult Affairs, which he manages with great dexterity and success.

Fourthly, Monsieur Ehrenschild, a German by birth, and formerly Secretary to Monsieur Terlon the French Ambassador at this Court, which makes him French in his Inclinations to this day. The King enobled him, and gave him the Name of Ehrenschild, instead of that of Beerman, by which he was formerly known. He is about 65 years old, of a weakly constitution, and therefore most commonly resides at Hamburg, under pretence that the Air is necessary for his Health; but in reality to manage the King's Affairs with that Town; wherein is constantly maintained a Faction, which must have Life kept in it by the Residence of a Minister of Quality. Moreover, that City being conveniently seated for the Correspondence with all Germany, from whence a nearer inspection may be made into the proceedings of the neighbouring Princes, as well as the management of the French Traffick during this War; it is thought necessary to keep an able Man there: this Monsieur Ehrenschild has been bred a Scholar after the German way, and is well skill'd in negotiating; wherein he has been constantly employed since he first entered into business. He is esteemed a Cunning man, but has no great reputation of Integrity; he affects to find out difficulties, and is excellently skill'd in prolonging a business. The Foreign Ministers call him by the Name of *Pater difficultatum*,[26] and say that he has a peculiar knack in finding *nodum in scirpo*.[27] Therefore they care not for Treating with him, because he values Argumentation, and seeks Sophisms rather than Truth, or the Decision of the Matter.

[26.] "Father of difficulties."
[27.] A proverb meaning "to seek a difficulty where there is none."

You can never bring him to say such a thing is, though it be as clear as the Sun; but *cela peut êstre:*[28] thereby leaving always a Hole open to creep out at. He hoards up all his Money, or puts it in the Banks of Hamburg and Amsterdam, having small prospect of a future happy establishment for his Family in Denmark. And this is the common Maxim of all the most intelligent Heads in that Kingdom, as appears by their making few or no Purchases.

Fifthly, Monsieur Plessen, a Gentleman of Mecklenburg, and formerly the Manager of Prince George's Revenue in Denmark. He is now the Ober-Rent Master, or Comptroller of the Finances, in the room of Monsieur Branat, lately removed from that Employment. The State of the Finances and Expenses were very much embroiled, and the King some Millions of Crowns in Debt when he undertook the difficult Task of setting things right; which it is generally thought he will accomplish as far as they are capable: and 'twas high time to set seriously about redressing Affairs, for the King's Credit both at Hamburg, and every where else, was in a manner absolutely lost, through the ill Payment of all Assignments. He is about Six and forty years old, of a Melancholy Complexion, and weakly Constitution; is esteemed to have a good Judgment, and to understand the World; though his Distempers make him sometimes particular in his Humour. He speaks four or five Languages, and English among the rest. His Inclinations seem to be rather English than French; as well on the account of his Dependence on Prince George, as because he is convinced 'tis more the Interest of his Master to be well with England and Holland, than with France. He appears to be disinterested, and is very easy in his Fortunes, which consist most in ready Money. In short, he is a Man of Business, and seems to be more downright in his manner of dealing than many of the rest.

These Five compose the King's whole Privy Council. Four of them are constantly at Court, and the fifth at Hamburg; by the weekly Advices of whom the others do for the most part regulate all their Deliberations.

The King in this Council determines all Affairs; deliberates of Peace or War, of Alliances, and other Treaties; of Taxes, Fortifications, Trade, etc.

[28.] "This being the way things are."

without the intervention of any other Person, unless it be the Secretaries of State; who are yet esteemed here rather as Ministerial Officers and Assistants, than principal Counsellors. There are four of these Secretaries that are not Secretaries of State, in the sense that ours in England are, that is to say, Prime Ministers; but carry the Pen, and have the management of the business relating to their several Provinces; the first is the Secretary for the Affairs of Denmark, and is at present Monsieur [. . .].[29] The second for the Affairs of Norway, is Monsieur Mote, Brother to the King's Mistress the Countess of Samsoe. The third for Foreign Affairs, is Monsieur Jessen; and the fourth, who is Secretary at War, is Monsieur Harboe. When any thing which concerns the Province of any of these is debated at Council, the Secretary it belongs to is to be present; but Monsieur Jessen never misses, because there is always business relating to Foreign Affairs; and the usual times of the sitting of the Council being after the Posts come in, his Employment is to read all the Letters, and to make Remarks on them. This renders his Office more considerable than that of the other Secretaries, and makes him enter into the Secrets of the Cabinet, which pass for the most part through his sole management. He has also liberty to speak his Sentiments; and because he has been bred a Latin Scholar, that, as well as his Employment, entitles him to the penning of all Treaties with Foreign Ministers. Therefore he is constantly one of the Commissioners appointed to treat with them; and to whom they are to have recourse almost as necessarily as to the Prime Minister, who suffers himself to be in a great measure guided by this Secretary. He is about forty, of a civil behaviour and humility, even to affectation; speaks four or five Languages very well, and very much; whereby he sometimes gives advantages to those that have business with him. He has but a moderate reputation for Sincerity, or Parts; yet so much used to the Road of Publick Affairs, that he cannot be wanted, because they have no fitter Man to put in his place. He is Son-in-Law to Monsieur Ehrenschild, by whom he is much governed, and of the same Inclinations as to France. This Affinity is a great support to his Fortune, as long as that old Gentleman lives; and his diligence in his Employment, (if there were nothing else) will secure to him his Post

[29.] No editions identify this person.

and his Princes Favour; provided always that he keep fair with the Prime Minister, (as at present he does) and act in concert with him.

The ordinary Diversions of the Court are Progresses, which are made once a year at least, to Sleswick, or Holstein, either to make a review of some Troops, or to see the Fortifications at Rendsburg; besides smaller Journeys to Laland, and elsewhere, up and down the Country. These are of no Expense to the Treasury, because the travelling Wagons and Horses are found by the Boors, who are also to pay their Personal Attendance, and be ready for all necessary Services. During five or six Weeks every Summer, the Court removes to Jagersburg, a small Hunting-House, situated upon a little Lake within four English Miles of Copenhagen, and not far from the Sea: and for five or six Weeks more it resides at Fredericksburg, the chief Country Palace of the Kings of Denmark, about twenty English Miles from Copenhagen, began by Christian the Fourth, and finished by this King's Father, Frederick the Third: this is that House which the Danes boast so much of, and tell wonders of the quantity of Money it cost in building. It is seated in the midst of a Lake, the Foundations of it being laid in the Water, which probably occasioned the greatest part of the Expense; you pass into it over several Draw Bridges. This watery Situation in so moist and cold a Country, cannot be approved by the Critical in Seats, especially when the rising Grounds about this Lake (which are clothed with fine Woods) afforded much better places both for health and prospect: but it is the humour of all this Kingdom, to build in the midst of Lakes; which I suppose was at first practised upon the score of Security. This Palace, notwithstanding the great cost they talk of, is far from being magnificent, or well contrived; for the Rooms are low, the Apartments ill disposed, the fine Chapel much too long in proportion to its breadth, and has a Gallery over it, which has one of the worst contrived Entrances that can be imagined. In fine, it falls far short of many of our Noblemen's Country-Houses in England; yet is esteemed by the Danes as a Nonesuch. There is indeed a fine Park about it, well filled with Red Deer; having large Ponds, high Trees in great quantity, a good Bathing-House, and other Country Embellishments; so that it is by far to be preferred to all the rest of the King's Houses, which except these two last mentioned, are for the most part out of repair: that of the Fortress of Cronenburg near

Elsignor, and of Coldingen in Jutland, with others, being scarce habitable even during one Fortnight in the Summer Quarter.

At Fredericksburg the Court spends most of its time in Stag-hunting, for there are few Fallow-Deer in Denmark; during which Sport the King allows great freedom to his Domesticks and Ministers, who commonly do all accompany him where ever he goes; insomuch that he seems to lay aside all Majesty, and the Formalities of it for that Season; they eat and drink together, the latter sometimes to Excess, after a hard days hunting; when as soon as Dinner is done, they adjourn to the Wine-Cellar. About five or six in the Afternoon the Hunting-Assizes are solemnly held in the great Court before the Palace, the Stag is drawn into the midst of it by the Huntsmen, who are all cloathed in Red, having their great Brass Hunting-horns about their Necks; and 'tis there broken up with great Ceremony, whilst the Hounds attend with much Noise and Impatience. One that is likeliest to give a good Gratuity to the Huntsmen, is invited to take Essay, and presented with the Deer's foot. Then Proclamation is made, if any can inform the King (who is both Supreme Judge and Executioner) of any Transgression against the known Laws of Hunting that day committed, let him stand forth and accuse; the accused is generally found guilty; and then two of the Gentlemen lead him to the Stag, and make him kneel down between the Horns, turning down his Head with his Buttocks up, and remove the Skirts of his Coat, which might intercept the blows; then comes his Majesty, and with a small long Wand gives the Offender some Lashes on his Posteriors, whilst in the mean time the Huntsmen with their Brass Horns, and the Dogs with their loud Openings, proclaim the King's Justice, and the Criminal's Punishment. The whole Scene affording Diversion to the Queen, Ladies, and other Spectators, who are always assisting, and stand in a Circle about the Place of Execution. This is as often repeated as there happen to be Delinquents; who as soon as the Chastisement is over, rise up and make their Obeisance, "proudly boasting Of their magnificent Rib-roasting."[30] After all is done, the Hounds are permitted to fall to, and eat the Deer.

At another season Swan-hunting is the Royal Pastime; the wild Swans

30. Note in margin: "Hudibras."

haunt a certain small Island not far from Copenhagen, and breed there; about the time that the Young ones are near as big as the Old, before their Feathers are grown long enough to fly, the King with the Queen, Ladies, and others of the Court, go to the killing of them; the Foreign Ministers are usually invited to take part in this sport: every Person of Condition has a Pinnace allotted to him, and when they come near the haunt, they surround the place, and inclose a great multitude of young Swans, which they destroy with Guns till they have killed some thousands. What is killed by the whole Company is brought to the Court, which challenges the Feathers and Down of these Birds, the Flesh of them being good for nothing.

On Shrove-Tuesdays the King, Queen, Royal Family, Home and Foreign Ministers, and all the other Persons abovementioned, that usually compose the Court, cloath themselves in the habit of the North-Holland Boors, with great Trunk-hose, short Doublets, and large blue Thrum-Caps; the Ladies in blue Petticoats, and odd Head-dresses, etc. Thus accoutred they get up in their Wagons, a Man before and a Woman behind, which they drive themselves, and go to a Country Village called Amak, about three English miles from Town; there they dance to Bagpipes, and squeaking Fiddles, and have a Country Dinner, which they eat out of Earthen and Wooden Platters, with wooden Spoons, etc. and having passed the day in these Divertisements, where all are equal, and little regard had to Majesty, or other Quality: at Night they drive in like manner home again; and are entertained at a Comedy and Magnificent Supper by the Viceroy Guldenlieu, spending the Remainder of the Night in Dancing in the same Habits, which they put not off all that day.

Every Winter, as soon as the Snow is firm enough to bear, the Danes take great delight in going in Sleds. The King and Court first giving the Example, and making several Tours about the Town in great Pomp, with Kettle-Drums and Trumpets; the Horses which draw the Sleds being richly adorned with Trappings, and Harness full of small Bells, to give warning to such as stand in the way. After the Court has been abroad, the Burgers and others trot about the Streets all night, wrapt up in their Fur Gowns, with each his Female in the Sled with him; and this they esteem a great and pleasant Pastime.

In travelling to Fredericksburg, Jagersburg, and many other places from

Copenhagen, there are two Highways; one the common Road, which is usually bad; the other the King's Highway, very fair and even, peculiar to the Court, and such as it has a mind to favour in bestowing on them a Key to open the several Gates that are upon it.

In this Chapter of the Court, it will not be improper to take notice that there are in Denmark two Orders of Knighthood, viz. that of the Elephant, and that of Dannebrug; the former is very honourable, and the Companions of it are of the highest Quality, or extraordinary Merit. Their Badge is an Elephant with a Castle on its back, set with Diamonds, and hung on a watered Sky-coloured Ribband, worn as the George is in England. The later is the honorary Reward of inferior Gentlemen or Noblemen: their Badge is a white Ribband with red Edges, worn over the contrary shoulder with a small Cross of Diamonds hung to it, and an Embroidery on the Breast of their Coats like a Star, in which is the Motto, *Pietate & Justitia*. They say that the Order of the Elephant was instituted about Two hundred and ten years ago by King Christian the First, at the Wedding of his Son.

A List of the Present Companions of It Follows

The King Sovereign of the Order.
Prince Royal.
Prince Christian.
Prince Charles.
Prince George.
The King of Sweden.
Elector of Brandenburg.
Elector of Saxony.
Viceroy Guldenlieu.
Duke of Holstein.
Duke of Holstein his Brother.
Landgrave of Hesse.
Count Rantzaw of Bredenberg.
Duke of Holstein Plôen.
Duke of Holstein Norburg.
Duke of Holstein Brieg.
Landgrave of Hesse Hombourg.

Markgrave of Anspach.
Markgrave of Baden Durlach.
Duke of Ostfrize.
Duke of Saxe Cobourg.
Prince Frederick of Saxe.
Duke of Wirtemberg.
The Mareschal Count Wedell.
Count Reventlau.
Count Alefeldt.
General Admiral Juel.
Baron Juel.
Justin Hoeg under Viceroy of Norway.
Godtske van Buckvalt, a Gentleman of Holstein.
Monsieur de Ginkle, Earl of Athlone.

They pretend that the Order of Dannebrug is more Ancient, and recount many Fables of its Original, viz. That one King Dan saw a white Cross with red Edges, descend from Heaven, and thereupon instituted the Order, and gave it this compound Name, from Dan and Brug, which signifies Painting. The Knights of this Order are almost as common here, as Baronets with us, and therefore I omit their Names.

The following Ordinance for Rank and Precedency was published in Danish and French, Anno 1680. But most of the Offices therein marked * are now vacant.

An Ordinance for Rank and Precedency in the Kingdom of Denmark.[31]

I.

The Kings natural Children.

II.

1. *The High Chancellor.
2. *The High Treasurer, call'd Schatz-meister.

[31.] This passage appeared in French in the 1694 edition, but it was translated subsequently in the 1738 edition. We have substituted the English version as the main text. For the original French passage, see Appendix 2: "Ordonnance pour les Rangs du Royaume de Danemarck," p. 361.

3. *The High Constable of *Norway*.
4. *The Marshal de Camp General.
5. The Admiral General.
6. The Counts who are Privy-Counsellors.
7. The Knights of the *Elephant* who are Privy-Counsellors, or hold the same Rank with them.
8. *The other Constables.
9. The Vice-Chancellor.
10. *The Vice-Treasurer.
11. The Vice-Constables.
12. The other Privy-Counsellors.

III.

1. *The Great Master of the Ordnance.
2. *The Great Lieutenant Marshal.
3. The Lieutenant General Admiral.
4. The Generals of Cavalry and Infantry.
5. The Lieutenants General of Cavalry and Infantry.

IV.

1. The Counts who are created Counts, or naturalized by the King.
2. The Barons who are created Barons, or naturalized by the King. And after them, the Knights of *Dannebrug*, or of the *White Ribband*.

V.

1. *The Great Marshal of the Court.
2. *The first Privy Secretary, and Secretary of State.
3. The first Gentleman of the Bed-Chamber.
4. The Great Master of the Horse.
5. The Great Huntsman.
6. *The Great Cup-Bearer.

VI.

1. The Counsellors of State.
2. The Counsellors of Justice.
3. The Commanders of Dioceses, and the Treasurer.

VII.

1. The Majors General, the Admirals, the Commissary General of the Army, the Colonels of the Life-Guards or Trabants.
2. The Brigadiers.
3. The Marshal of the Court.

VIII.

1. The Counsellors of the Chancery, the King's Envoys Extraordinary, and the Master of the Ceremonies.
2. The Counsellors of the Chamber of Accompts, the Attorney General.
3. The Counsellors of War.
4. The Counsellors of the Admiralty.
5. The Counsellors of Trade.

IX.

1. The Superintendant of *Zealand.*
2. The King's Confessor.
3. The Rector of the Academy for the time being; the President of the City of *Copenhagen.*

X.

1. The Colonels of the Regiments of Horse and Foot Guards, the Vice-Admirals, the Colonels of the Artillery.
2. The other Colonels of Horse and Foot.
3. The Lieutenant-Colonels of the Life-Guards or Trabants, and after them the Bailiffs.

XI.

1. The Gentlemen of the King and Queen's Bed-Chamber.
2. The Master of the Horse.
3. The King's Huntsman.
4. The Secretary of the King's Chamber.
5. The Secretary of the Militia.
6. The chief Pay-Master.

XII.

1. The Assistants of the High Court of Judicature, the Assistant Counsellors in *Norway,* and the Super-Intendants of the other Provinces.
2. The Provincial Judges.

XIII.

1. The Auditors General, the Quarter-Masters General.
2. The Lieutenant-Colonels, Rear-Admirals, and Majors of the Life-
Guards or Trabants.

XIV.

1. The Assistants of the Chancery, and of the Court of Justice in *Norway.*
2. The Assistants of the Consistory, the Burgomasters of *Copenhagen,*
and the King's Physician.
3. The Assistants of the Chamber of Accompts, and after them the
Commissaries of the Provinces.
4. The Assistants of the Court-Marshal.
5. The Assistants of the Court of Admiralty.
6. The Assistants of the Commissioners of Trade.

XV.

The Masters of the Kitchen, the Gentlemen of the Court, the Adju-
tants General, the Majors, the Captains of the Horse-Guards, the
Captains of Men of War.

XVI.

1. The Secretaries of the Chancery, and of the Court of Justice.
2. The Secretary of the Chamber of Accompts.
3. The Secretary of the Court-Marshal.
4. The Secretary of the Admiralty.
5. The Secretary of Trade.

It must be observed that when several Persons in Office are named
together, and are not distinguished by a separate Figure, they take place
among themselves according to the Date of their Commissions.

The King's Ministers who hold Offices that are not mentioned in this

Ordinance, shall keep the same Rank they have hitherto enjoyed; and those to whom the King has given, or shall give, the Title of Privy Counsellors, shall have the same Rank as if they were really and effectually such.

They who actually exercise an Office, shall have the Precedency before such as have only the Title of it, and do not officiate.

They whom the King dispenses with from exercising their Offices, shall yet keep the same Rank they had when they actually exercised them; and if any one takes another Office of an inferior Rank to that he had, he shall nevertheless hold the Rank of the former.

The Precedency with respect to Women shall be thus: After the Countesses follow the Governesses, and Ladies of the Bedchamber, and of the Court, while they are in Waiting: Next come the Wives of Privy-Counsellors, and of such as have the same Rank with them: Afterwards the Baronesses, and other Wives, according to the Rank of their Husbands when living, and also after their Deaths while they continue Widows.

The Noblesse [Nobility and Gentry] who have no Offices, and the Captains of the Horse and Foot, and other Persons ecclesiastical and secular, shall hold among themselves the same Rank they did formerly.

To these Regulations all Persons are to conform, on pain of forfeiting the Royal Favour. And if, contrary to all Expectation, any one should, of his own Authority, act or do any thing contrary to this Ordinance, he shall immediately, after being convicted of such Crime, pay a Fine of One thousand Rix-Dollars; and moreover be prosecuted by the King's Attorney-General, as a Transgressor of His Majesty's Royal Orders.

Given at Copenhagen, December 31, 1680.

CHAPTER XII

The Disposition and Inclinations of the King of Denmark towards his Neighbours

The Kingdoms and States which border upon the King of Denmark, are towards the North and Northeast, the Territories belonging to Sweden; towards the South, the Duke of Holstein's part of Sleswick and Holstein, the City of Hamburg, and the Dutchy of Bremen. Towards the West and Southwest, England, and Scotland; which are separated from them by the main Ocean. Towards the South-east the Dukedoms of Saxe Lawenburg, of Mecklenburg and of Lunenburg. The Dominions of Brandenburgh, etc. lye also this way not far distant from them.

Between the King of Denmark, and most of these Neighbours, it may be said in general, that there always is a reciprocal Jealousy and Distrust, which often breaks out into open Hostilities; with those nearer more frequently, with the remoter more seldom, according as the occasions of quarrel or revenge do happen.[32]

The interposition of a vast Ocean has hitherto kept the Danes in pretty

32. Note in margin: "England."

good terms with England and Scotland, and the Trade they have with those Kingdoms is very considerable to them; their Maritime Forces are in no measure sufficient to cope with us and others concern'd, otherwise they have had a good mind to challenge the sole right of the Groenland Whale-fishing; as pretending that Country to be a discovery of theirs, and therefore to belong to them.

Since the present Wars with France, and our strict Union with the Hollanders, they have shown themselves extreme jealous of our Greatness at Sea, fearing lest we should ingross and command the whole Trade of the World; and therefore have favoured France on all occasions, as much as they durst, furnishing it with Naval Stores, and other Commodities which it wants. And for this reason (notwithstanding their scarcity of Money) they will hardly be persuaded either to lend or sell any more Forces to the Confederates. Neither is it to be doubted, but that as well to keep the balance of the Sea Power even, as to secure the liberty of their Commerce, which brings them in great Gains, they will leave no Stone unturned to do us a Mischief, in order to humble us to such a degree as may put them out of fears, that we shall give law to the Ocean. To this end they have entered into stricter Alliances with Sweden of late, for a mutual Vindication of open Commerce, than the natural Animosities between those Northern Crowns did seem to admit of; but the present apparent necessity of restraining within Bounds our growing united Power at Sea, works more prevalently with them both, than the ancient hatred which they retain for each other; and which may break out again, as soon as they are out of fear of us.[33]

For Sweden is the most powerful, most dreaded, and nearest Neighbour of Denmark; the Territories of that King lye as it were at the Gates of Copenhagen, the Capital City, and may be seen from the very Bedchamber of this King, ever since the Danes lost three of their best Provinces on the other side the Baltick; so that as well the Resentment of past Injuries, as the dread of future Mischiefs from the greatness of Sweden on the one side; the consciousness of being violent possessors of another's Right, the certainty of their being hated and envied for those Acquisitions, the fear

33. Note in margin: "Sweden."

of losing them in case Denmark grow powerful on the other, are unsur-
mountable Obstacles to any firm Friendship between these two Crowns.
The ancient Quarrel, like a Wound ill healed, is but skinned over, and fes-
ters at the bottom, although our equally disobliging them in the interruption of their Traffick, has made a greater step towards their mutual Reconciliation, than was thought to be practicable. But whenever we please to
caress the one at the expense of the other, this seeming Knot will discover
the weakness of its contexture, and probably dissolve of it self.

Neither is the Alliance by the King of Sweden's having married the
other's Sister,[34] of any moment towards a good Correspondence, but rather
the contrary. The King of Sweden, though a very virtuous Prince, shews
coldness and indifference enough (upon this account, as it is thought)
towards his Queen, who is a very accomplished Princess; and either has,
or thinks he has reason to avoid a further Matrimonial Tye with the Dane:
therefore he chose rather to Contract his only Daughter with the young
Prince of Holstein Gottorp, whose Estates are in a manner wasted and
ruined, than with the Prince Royal of Denmark; for having but one Son,
in case of whose death this Daughter would be Heiress of his Crown, he
thinks it not prudence to leave it to so near a hazard and probability, that
the Dane may be one day Master of both Kingdoms.

Upon the Foundation of this mutual Jealousy, are built the Friendships
and Enmities which each of them (but especially Denmark) have with
most of their other Neighbours, and the rest of the German Princes. And
upon this account it is principally that the Animosity is so great between
this Crown and the Princes of Lunenburg;[35] with whom, on the contrary,
the Swede has always kept a good Correspondence, that upon occasion
of any Attack made on his Territories in the Circle of Lower Saxony, or
in Pomerania, (which are looked upon by the rest of the German Princes
with an evil Eye) he may secure to himself the Assistance of that powerful
Family against the Dane or Brandenburger; therefore the neighbourhood

[34.] Note in margin: "Quae apud concordes vincula caritatis, incitamenta irarum
apud infensos erant. Tacit." Translation: "What are bonds of love between united
hearts, became with bitter foes incentives to fury." Tacitus, *Annals,* bk. 1, chap. 55.
35. Note in margin: "Duke of Lunenburg."

of the Lunenburg Princes will always be grievous to, and suspected by Denmark, which will obstruct by all means it can, the Accessions either of Territories or Honours to that Family. So that it is not to be supposed that the Dane will quietly sit down with the Duke of Zell's thrusting himself into the possession of the Dutchy of Saxe Lawenburg, which borders immediately upon Holstein; nor with the determination of the Imperial Diet in favour of the Ninth Electorate conferred on the Duke of Hannover. On the other hand it is thought that the Swede, in order to the further curbing of Denmark, will uphold the Lunenburg Family in its Acquisitions; in the matter of the Electorate openly and aboveboard; in the other of Saxe Lawenburg secretly, because of the invalidity of the Title of that Family to that Dutchy; which seems to be no longer good than it can be maintained by force or connivance.

The Princes of Lunenburg have also hitherto seconded the Swedes Intentions, in being the Guardians of Hamburg,[36] upon which City the King of Denmark casts a longing Look, and has made frequent Attempts. His pretensions to it as part of his Dutchy of Holstein, are none of the weakest, but his Arms and Councils in order to the Reduction of it under his Power, have been unsuccessful. He encourages his new Town of Altena (which is built close under its Walls) as a Rival, and which one day may be a curb to it. And in truth, this rich City has great reason to be jealous of such a Neighbour, whose chiefest Ambition is to destroy its Liberty, and render himself its Master. But the Duke of Zell (whose Territories lye next) has always some Forces posted near enough to prevent the King of Denmark's Designs upon it; therefore this City pays a great deal of respect to those Princes, whom it looks on as its best Protectors. With the other German Princes it keeps also as good a Correspondence as possible; and they on their part shew an affection to the Liberty of that City, the Reduction of which, under the Power of the Danes, would be extremely inconvenient to them, as well upon the score of the Trade of great part of Germany, whereof it is the Seat and Principal Mart by its convenient Situation on the River Elb; as upon the score of the great Addition

36. Note in margin: "Hamburg."

such a Conquest would make to the Power of the Danes; who are usually ill Neighbours when they are weak, but would be insupportable were their Force proportionable to their Inclinations.

Nor would the Brandenburgers[37] wish that this City, or the Town of Lubeck, should have any Master, but would endeavour to their utmost to frustrate Attempts upon them, and yet the Elector of Brandenburg is esteemed the firmest Ally the King of Denmark has; for their common interest to prevent the Greatness of the Swedes, (whereof they are equally jealous and fearful) unites these two Princes stronger than any tie of Blood could do. The Ducal Prussia, and that part of Pomerania which belongs to Brandenburg, lies open to the Swedes; and the least transport of Forces from Sweden to Germany side of the Baltick gives a terrible Alarm to all the Neighbours. They cannot forget the strange Successes of Gustavus Adolphus, nor the Encroachments of Sweden in the late Wars; neither can they be otherwise persuaded, but that there is always impending danger of the like Attempts from the same Nation, abounding in Soldiers, and ruled by a frugal, diligent, and active young King. So that, as I said before, their common danger makes them strangely concur in this design of keeping the Swede within his due Bounds, although in other matters some disagreement may happen between them; as may be more particularly instanced in the Affair of St. Thomas's Island, and in the Branden-Burgers endeavours to force the Dane to a Restitution of the Duke of Holstein Gottorp to his Country; which was so happily accomplished by his Majesty of Great Britain, the very first year of his Exaltation to the Throne.

The Duke of Holstein Gottorp (whom I have purposely mentioned last of those Princes that confine with Denmark, that I may have an opportunity to speak more amply concerning his Case) is nearly related to the King of Denmark, both by Consanguinity and Affinity. They are of the same Family of Oldenburg; the Ancestor of the present Duke refused the Kingdom of Denmark, in favour of the Ancestor of the King; whom he recommended to the Peoples Election. This Duke is married to the King's Sister, by whom he has Issue a very hopeful Prince; his Territories

37. Note in margin: "Brandenburg."

are intermixt both in Sleswick and Holstein with the King's, but much to his disquiet and inconvenience; for Ambition knows no bounds, especially when joined with Power sufficient to oppress a weak Opponent. The King thought it for his Interest (and that is esteemed reason enough with most Princes) to be Master of the whole Country; which the Duke being sensible of, and convinced that the first convenient opportunity would be taken to dispossess him, to secure himself, cultivated as strong a Friendship as he could with the King of Sweden his Brother in-Law, and one who upon many accounts was bound to hinder the Greatness of the Danes. Yet this Confederacy reached no farther, nor was ever intended to be made use of by the Duke otherwise than as a Defensive Guard, the Reputation whereof might possibly shelter him from Oppression. For the Duke was of himself much too weak to oppose the King, and the Succours of the Swede too far distant to frustrate a sudden Attempt, to which he lay constantly exposed. But in regard that at long run this Alliance would stand him in greatest stead (as he has found by Experience) it was always most carefully cherished and maintained on the Duke's part, and no less on the King's, who did, and ever will think it of great advantage to him to uphold the Duke of Holstein in his lawful Rights; and no less detrimental to his Enemy; this Duke being the severest Thorn in the Foot of the King of Denmark, and the greatest Mortification to him that can possibly be imagined; who now of a near Kinsman and Brother, by his ill usage has made an utter Enemy, that (notwithstanding the present Composure of Differences) can neither trust him, nor be trusted by him. For the better understanding of which it will not be amiss in another Chapter to give a short account of the Proceedings in that whole Matter.

CHAPTER XIII

The manner of dispossessing, and restoring the Duke of Holstein Gottorp

The Affairs between the King and Duke being on the terms above-mentioned, that is to say, Ambition and Reason of State guiding the Designs of one Party, Fear and Weakness of the other, Hatred and Distrust of both; there seemed to be wanting nothing but a fair Opportunity to put in practice what had been long projected by the Danes, which at length happened in the year 1675.

Among other Differences which remained to be adjusted between the King and Duke, the Succession to the Counties of Oldenburg and Delmenhorst was the greatest; this was at length left to the determination of the Imperial Court; but whilst it was under debate there, several meetings between the Ministers of Denmark and those of Gottorp were appointed, in order to an amicable composure of this and all other Quarrels; which Meetings were principally sought after by the King, with all the seeming desires of Amity, and Appearances of Friendship imaginable, the better to lull the Duke into Security, and a Persuasion of the Sincerity of his Intentions. Sometimes an Equivalent for the sole possession of those Counties was proposed and hearkened to, and the whole Matter seemed to want nothing but fair drawing up, and the Ratification. At other times fresh Disputes arose touching the Taxes of the Dukedoms of Sleswick and Holstein, whereof the King challenged the greater part to himself, in proportion to the share of Forces which he maintained for Defence of the Country. On the other side, the Duke insisted on it, that the Taxes ought equally to be divided; and if the King kept up more Troops than were necessary, that did not any way prejudice his right to an equal share of the Revenues, especially since the King's undertakings were managed neither with any previous Communication with, or consent of the Duke; nor were agreed unto by the States of the Dukedom, both which by ancient Treaties ought to have been done. But this Ball was either kept up, or let fall, according to the Circumstances of Affairs abroad, which the Danes had a watchful Eye upon, at the same time that they treated with the Duke.

For the Swedes having taken the part of France against the Empire, were at this time engaged in a War with the Elector of Brandenburg. And the Danes who had long since resolved to break with Sweden, thought no time so proper as this to revenge their ancient Quarrel, and to regain their lost Provinces. But looking upon the Duke of Holstein as a Friend to Sweden, and a main Obstacle to their Intentions, they durst not march their Army out of the Country, till they had so ordered Matters as to apprehend no danger from him.

A deep Dissimulation was necessary to the carrying on this Design upon the Swedes and House of Gottorp; and was made use of with so much Address, that the Swedish Ambassador, who was then residing at Copenhagen, and negotiating a Marriage for the King his Master with the Daughter of Denmark, was caressed in an extraordinary manner, and treated with the greatest Demonstrations of Friendship possible: And at the same time the Prime Minister of Denmark wrote most obligingly to the Duke's Resident then at Hamburg, That he was ready to meet him half way, and would join endeavours with him to adjust all Differences, and establish a firm Correspondence between their Masters, which he said he desired above all things. He added moreover, that when willing Minds met together about the Composure of Differences, a few hours would put an end to that which had been transacting many years; and therefore conjured him to meet him. The King also did often declare himself to this purpose to the Duke's Ministers, That he would acknowledge, as a great Obligation conferred on him, the furthering an Accommodation between him and the Duke.

'Tis the Custom of the King of Denmark to make once a Year a Voyage into Holstein, where he assembles and takes a review of his Troops. This is done not only upon the score of Diversion, and to see that the Forces be in good Condition; but also to use the neighbouring Princes and Hamburgh to such a practice; that when they see it performed several years without any ill Consequence, or Attempts upon them, they may take the less Umbrage, and be less upon their Guard, whenever he should have any real Design. About this time the King was beginning such a Journey, in order to put his Projects in Execution; and to lull the Duke into a deeper Security, writes to him very kind Letters, desiring him not to be concerned at it, since he had no other end in it than formerly in the like Voyages, unless it were to put a final determination to all Differences between them to their mutual satisfaction. The Duke was so pleased by these Assurances under the King's Hand, that he went in Person to meet his Majesty, accompanied by his Brother the Bishop of Lubeck, and many others of the Nobility; and afterwards treated him very splendidly at a House of his upon the Road near his Residence of Gottorp; the King then caressing him, and desiring him earnestly to come and see him at Rendsburg (a fortified Town about fourteen English miles from thence) near which the Rendezvous of the Troops was appointed. Towards the conclusion of this Feast several large Healths were drank to the future good Agreement, with so much appearing Sincerity, that the good Duke thought he had no reason to doubt the reality of it; but ordered his Chief Minister to wait upon the King and his Ministers at Rendsburg; where they so far accommodated all Matters, that the whole Affair was supposed near its Conclusion.

Upon this the Duke sends three of his chief Counsellors, impowered by a special Commission, to treat and conclude at Rendsburg; with whom three of the King's Council met, and conferred. The business of the Conference was principally about the Exchange of other Lands for the Counties of Oldenburg and Delmenhorst; but in it the King's Commissioners took occasion to renew the Debate about the division of the Taxes, whereof, as I have said before, the King challenged the greater part: This did a little surprize and displease the Duke's Commissioners, who thought it foreign to the matter in hand, and would not hearken to Proposals of that nature.

At the very same time, and during this Conference, the King's Prime Minister wrote to the Duke's, That he thought it necessary for both Princes, that the Duke of Gottorp would please to come to Rendsburg to the King, who was ready to conclude a Treaty; because the Presence of so near a Relation would contribute more than any thing else to a Friendly Composure of all these matters. And the Duke, as well upon the account of the former Invitation, as upon this fresh one, withal to shew his forwardness towards a Peace, resolves upon the Visit; first sending a Gentleman to acquaint the King with his intention, and desiring his permission to come and wait upon him. The King's Answer was, That he should be heartily welcome, and his Chief Minister also, whom he desired to bring along with him. Thus the Duke being fully persuaded that all was meant honourably, on the 25th of June began his Journey, accompanied by his Minister and other Nobility, and arrived at Rendsburg; where he was welcomed by a discharge of all the Cannon of that Fortress, and other demonstrations of Joy.

The next day, being the 26th of June 1675, a fatal one to that unfortunate Prince and his Family, an Express arrives with Letters of the great Defeat given the Swedes by the Brandenburgers at Fehr Berlin: this was what the Danes wished and waited for; but could scarce promise themselves it should succeed so fully according to their expectations, or nick the time so justly as it did. They thought Heaven it self concurred with their Intentions; and not to be wanting on their parts, immediately give orders to shut the Town Gates, to call a Council of War, to send their Soldiers up and down, and seize all the Duke's Towns and Fortresses. These Orders were as suddenly executed: the Duke's Troop of Guards were disarmed, himself confined a Prisoner to his Apartment; his Dinner, which he thought to have eaten with the King, was brought in to him by Officers and Soldiers, who watched him so narrowly that he could not stir; the poor Duke exclaiming in the mean while, and complaining that he was ill used; that he was a Sovereign Prince of the Empire, independent of any other Power; that he was a near Kinsman, a Brother-in-Law, nay, an invited Guest of the Kings; that all the Laws of Justice, of Blood, of Friendship and Hospitality were violated by this Action, wherein the King had broken his Parole, and the Sanctuary of his own House. But all this was in vain; the Duke had no Remedy prescribed to him, but Patience; the Blow which was begun, must be followed, and more Evils must succeed that which had already happened.

For the Duke being thus seized, his Ministers were presently sent for, and told, That now there was an end of all Treating, that the King was Master, and would act as such: To which purpose he would take possession of the Duke's whole Country, and put Garrisons into all the strong Places which he thought proper to secure to himself, because he had an intention to lead his Army elsewhere against the Swedes; that the Inclinations of the House of Gottorp were always malevolent towards the King, and by him considered as such; however if the Duke would fairly and freely renounce his Right to the Lands in question, the King might, at the Duke's request, be prevailed upon to give him an hundred and fifty thousand Rix Dollars at Copenhagen for it.

Notwithstanding the Extremity the Duke was reduced to, he could not be brought to consent to such a severe Condition; but offered, since Matters could be no better, that the King without prejudice to his Right, should have the Taxes so much contested, in the manner he desired; that his Majesty should put one half of the Garrison into the strong Town of Tonningen, provided that all therein did take the Oaths of Allegiance to both Princes, till such time as the Exigencies of Affairs would permit the entire Restoration of it to its former Master: That if the King would dispose of his Country solely, the Duke must yield to force, but hoped his Right should be reserved entire, and desired that his Residence and Habitation of Gottorp, which was neither by Nature nor Art strong enough to be formidable, might be left free to him: Lastly, That the King would grant him and his liberty to dispose of themselves as they thought fit.

The Danes Answer was, That these Offers and Demands were no other than Trifles; That the King would proceed to the Execution of his own Will and Pleasure by Force and Arms; that neither the Duke, nor any of his, should ever be restored to their Liberty till he had signed an Instrument there ready drawn up, to order the Commander of Tonningen to Surrender it to the King; which the Duke at last, through despair of his Life, was forced to consent to; and accordingly that Fortress, with all its Cannon and Stores, was delivered up to the Officer sent by the King for that purpose.

Things being brought to this pass, the Duke was removed to his own House at Gottorp. His Dutchess, who had been all this while at Copenhagen, and as it was thought consented to all the Injustices acted against her Husband and Family, was restored to him; but he was in effect a Prisoner still; for Guards were placed at all the Avenues, every day some new severe Conditions were proposed to him, and Articles offered him which he was forced to sign: one of which was a Renunciation of his Supream and Independent Right over the Dukedom of Sleswick. Being at last quite tired with so many Violences, not knowing where they might end, he began to think of his Escape: so that one day taking the Advantage of his Dutchesses being sent for again by her Mother, the Queen Dowager of Denmark, he pretended to accompany her part of the way; and by the means of some trusty Servants, had re-lays of Horses placed in convenient stations. After a few hours travelling with her, he took his leave of her, and pretending to hunt, set Spurs to his Horse, and rid away as fast as he could towards Hamburg.

The Allarm was presently given of the Duke's flight, and many Horsemen were dispatched after him, which he being aware of, took not the direct Road, but went about by Kiel; so that, after a narrow escape, he arrived safely where he designed. This mightily vexed the King, who used all means to get him out of that City, because Hamburg being so populous a Town, the fame of the Barbarity exercised against him flew from thence all over Europe. But the Duke had been taught by former Misfortunes not to trust his Enemy; and as soon as he got to Hamburg, solemnly protested against the validity of all that he had been constrained to agree to, whilst he was in Durance; yet withal declared, That he was as ready as ever to come to an amicable Composure of Differences with the King, to prevent the ruin of his Subjects, and other Mischiefs; provided the King would redress some of the greatest Grievances. This Proposition was so little regarded, that instead of hearkening to it, the King ordered the Fortress of Toningen to be demolished, the Dukedom of Sleswick to be sequestred, the Magistrates and People to be absolved from their Allegiance to the Duke, and obliged to an Oath of Fidelity to the King; all the Revenues of the Duke to be brought into his Treasury; Garrisons to be continued in the Duke's Forts and Mansion-house, and unless the Duke came to accept of the King's terms in relation to that Fief, that it should for ever be annexed to the Crown of Denmark.

For the more speedy publication of these new Orders, Proclamations were made and affixed to that effect in all the Towns of the Dukedom. The Duke on his part publishing others in opposition to this Usurpation, together with a Solemn Protestation against all that had been done; concluding with a Command to the States of the Dukedom, and the rest of his Subjects, to continue firm in their Loyalty and Obedience to their Natural Prince.

But the King, who was resolved no longer to keep any Measures with him, nor to preserve that Country in any tolerable condition which he knew not how long he might enjoy, exacted vast Contributions from the poor Subjects, to the value of many Millions of Gold, and to the ruin of as flourishing a Province as any in the Circle of Lower Saxony; thereby disabling the Duke's Subjects from contributing any thing towards the Subsistence of their Master; who continued all this while at Hamburg in a state little befitting his high Quality; whilst he sent his Son abroad to raise the Compassion, and implore the Assistance of all the Neighbouring German Princes; on which Errand I had the Fortune to meet him at the Courts of Hannover and Wolfenbuttel. He made also strong Application to the Crown of England, as Guarantee of the Northern Peace, and caused a full Representation of his disconsolate Condition to be printed in English, which contains at large most of the Particulars above-mentioned; but all in vain: the Duke continued a Sufferer notwithstanding his many Appeals to those who ought to have interested themselves in his behalf: until such time as the King of Sweden began in earnest to take his Cause in hand. This King having at last brought the Affairs of his own Kingdom into such a Posture as permitted him to resent the Injuries done to his near Relation, threatened the Dane with a War in case he delayed Restitution;

and to this effect, in the Year 1689 set a Fleet to Sea, with intention to second his Threats by Blows; which he might the better then do, because the chief Support of the Danes in their Injustice, (the French King) was at that time attacked by the Forces of the Confederates; and England, by the Accession of his present Majesty to that Crown, was become a principal Party in so just a War. So that France was likely to have its Hands full at home. Besides, his Majesty of Great Britain being become Guarantee of the Northern Peace, thought himself obliged in honour to maintain it; and in order to that end, gave such Instructions to his Envoy Extraordinary, then going to the Danish Court, as might induce it to comply with Justice, and prevent that Effusion of Blood which was threatened. These Remonstrances had their due weight with the King of Denmark; who at last yielded to the necessity of his Circumstances, and to the Solicitations of the Elector of Brandenburg, who pressed among the rest the Restoration of the Duke, and had sent his Ministers to the Congress for the Accommodation, to propose a Project to that end; not so much out of kindness to the Family of Gottorp, as for fear the Swedish Arms should by any just occasion be brought over the Baltick; the event of which might be fatal to all the Neighbourhood, and to the Brandenburgers in particular. Thus the Danes, with reluctancy, consented at last to give up what they had unjustly detained above thirteen years from its right Owner, after having raised vast Sums of Money from the Country: for the Duke's part of the Dutchy of Sleswick only, had about 28,000 Ploughs in it, each of which were taxed to pay four Crowns a Month: besides innumerable other Extortions, which filled the Purses of the Ministers of Denmark, who shared the Revenues among them. The Swedish and Danish Fleets had been about a Fortnight at Sea, but no Action had happened between them. After the Accommodation was published, and the Duke restored, (yet without any reparation of Damages past) the two Fleets returned to their several Ports, and the Duke to his Habitation of Gottorp, which he found in a desolate Condition, compared to what he left it in. The Dutch had a principal Hand in the Conclusion of this Agreement, by the means of Myn Heer Heemskirk their Minister; and his Majesty of Great Britain a large share of the Glory of redressing a Wrong, which through so many years possession pleaded a kind of Prescription to warrant it; the very first half year of his Reign vindicating the Honour of the Crown of England, which was engaged as Guarantee; and securing the Peace of the North, in order to the procuring the Assistance of one, or both of those Princes, towards the humbling the common Enemy. This he effectually did; for the Danes immediately afterwards, sent by Treaty seven thousand Soldiers, which are yet in his Majesty's Pay; and the Swedes remain at liberty to continue such of their Troops in the Dutch Service as formerly were stipulated for, and which (had a War broken out) they might have been forced to recall.

CHAPTER XIV

The Interests of Denmark in relation to other Princes

In treating of the Interests of the King of Denmark in relation to other Princes or States which do not confine upon his Dominions, and of his Affections towards them, it will not be necessary to observe strictly the order and rank which those Princes hold in the World, I shall therefore take them as they come indifferently.

With the Emperor the King of Denmark is obliged to keep always a good outward Correspondence, he being himself a Prince of the Empire, as Duke of Holstein; and the Emperor having it often in his Power to do him several Kindnesses or dis-kindnesses. The King has a great desire to establish a Toll at Glucstadt upon the River Elb; and although the Emperor's consent would not absolutely secure the business for him, there being many other Princes, together with all those who are concerned in the Trade of Hamburg that would obstruct it: yet it would strike a great stroke, and must always be a necessary Preliminary. He keeps therefore very fair with his Imperial Majesty, and when pressed by the Ministers, sends (for valuable considerations) some Troops to serve in Hungary against the Turks; notwithstanding which he is inwardly troubled at the

Power of the House of Austria, and the Increase of its Dominions; being jealous, as most of the other German Princes are, that the Greatness of that Family may one day turn to the detriment of the Liberty of Germany: and therefore is not displeased at the Successes of the French, or of the Turks. He has been heard to complain of the neglect which the Imperial Court shows of him, and its partiality for the Swedes; this occasioned the Emperour's sending a Minister lately to Reside at Copenhagen, as well as at Stockholm; since which he seems to be better satisfied. But at the bottom it is to be supposed, that the Dane is no true Friend of the Emperor's; because he thinks his Imperial Majesty favours some Interests opposite to his, in conniving at the Lunenburgers forcible possession of the Dukedom of Saxe-Lawenburg, and bestowing the Electoral Dignity on that Family; the confirmation of which the King of Denmark opposes with all his Power.

With Poland the King of Denmark has at present little occasion either of Friendship or Enmity; there being but small Correspondence between them; yet he will rather chuse to keep that Crown his Friend, than otherwise; because it may one day stand him in stead against the Swedes: And for this reason it is that the Elector of Brandenburg, whose Interest in that particular is much the same with Denmark's, maintains a good Correspondence, and Entertains a constant Minister at Warsaw. Besides, the Port of Dantzick is convenient for all that Trade in the Baltick, and the Danes bring Corn, as well as other Merchandize from thence. They keep likewise good Amity with the other Hans Towns.

The King is upon fair terms with the Duke of Courland, who has permitted him to raise Men in his Country, the Commander of which, one Poteamer, is Brother to that Duke's prime Minister; and the Soldiers are the best able to live hardily, and to endure Fatigue of any in the World.

It is the Interest of Denmark to be well with the Dutch above all other Princes in Europe, because of the great Revenue it receives from their Traffick, and the Toll which they pay in the Sound: Because also in case of a quarrel with Sweden, or any other extremity, the King of Denmark is certain of the Assistance of the Hollanders; which is always sufficient and ready to protect him, as has been experienced in the former Wars between the Northern Crowns: for the Dutch will never suffer the Balance of the North to lean too much to one side, their Interest in the Trade of the Baltick being so considerable; but will take care to assist the weaker with proportionable Succours; which the conveniency of their Situation, and their Naval Force permits them to do with greater ease than any other. Notwithstanding all which Considerations, there are frequent Occasions of Quarrel between the Dutch and Danes; and the Friendship which the latter have for the former (especially since this War with France, and the Convention made with England for the Interruption of all Commerce with that Kingdom) is very weak and unstable; for besides that an Absolute Monarchy, for other Reasons, can never thoroughly love a Republick, the Danes are envious at the great Trade of the Dutch; and count it a Disparagement that Merchants, as they call them, should have it in their Power to give Law to a Crowned Head. However, at the bottom, Denmark would not be pleased that Holland should sink under the Force of its Enemies, but would use its best Endeavours to prevent it, though possibly not before Matters were reduced to so great an Extremity, as it might be beyond the Ability of the Danes to afford a timely Remedy.

The King of Denmark loves the Alliance of France, and keeps a stricter Correspondence with that Crown than with any other; though it be most certain that the Maxims which he has learnt from thence, and the Practices which followed those Maxims, have been the principal Occasion of that Kingdom's present ill condition. But the King of France by fair Words, large Promises, and a little Money seasonably bestowed, has had the knack to amuse this Court, and to make it act as he pleases; notwithstanding the many Affronts, the ill Successes, and the universal Misery which through his means have attended it. The Emissaries of France are thick sown here; nothing pleases that is not according to the French Pattern, either in Dress, Military Discipline, or Politicks: and it is certain that a fitter could not be followed by any Arbitrary Prince, provided a due regard were had to the force and strength to perform in proportion to the Design undertaken. But the want of this Consideration has been fatal to Denmark; France had told this King, that Soldiers are the only true Riches of Princes, and this has made him raise more than he knows what to do with, unless he disturb his Neighbours; which generally he does for the Interests of France, though at last it turns to his loss. So that Denmark resembles in this point a Monster that is all Head and no Body, all Soldiers and no Subjects; and whenever a General Peace comes to be established in Europe, which shall set open Foreign Trade, and consequently spoil all the Advantages that his Country enjoys at present, I cannot see what will become of the Publick Affairs here; for the Soldiers when disbanded, being most of them Strangers, will return to their respective Homes; and the Revenues of these Kingdoms must sink extreamly through the want of People, and their Poverty. It seems therefore no less than madness for the least and poorest Kingdom of Europe to think of emulating with Success the richest, greatest, and the most populous, and to take its Measures from thence; as if there were no difference between King and King: So have I heard that the little Republick of St. Marino in Italy, which consists but of one small Town with the Mountain it stands upon, and is scarce taken notice of by Travellers, takes occasion to write to the Republick of Venice sometimes, and to stile it Our Sister, with as much Gravity and Pride, as if it equalled the other in Power. But the vanity of these poor Italians proceeds no farther than words, which does them no harm.

But the true Reasons which renders it the Interest of Denmark to keep well with France (and they are no weak ones) are first, because they look upon that Crown as the sole Balance against the Grandeur of the Emperour, and the House of Austria, whose Power, as I said before, is looked on by all the Princes of Germany with a very jealous Eye; the late Addition of the Crown of Hungary to it, with its other Conquests on that side from the Turks, the probability of the Spanish Dominions falling to some active Branch of it, and the remembrance what havock the Emperour Charles the Fifth, and his Successor, made among the German Princes, when possess'd of the like Advantages, makes the Danes as well as the others, reflect seriously upon what may happen hereafter, should France be reduced to too low an ebb: A second reason is, because they know no other Naval Force able to contest the intire Dominion of the Seas with the English and Dutch; and they are willing to keep the dispute about that Dominion undetermin'd between the French and us, that no Laws may be laid upon Traffick, but that they may reap their share of the Trade of the World; which they think would be but small, should that Point be once finally decided to our Advantage. A third Reason and the most forcible is, the Subsidies which the King of Denmark draws from time to time from France: a little ready money among a necessitous People, carrying irresistable Charms with it; And this has been the drift of the French Policy in advising that King to a greater Charge than he was able to bear, under pretence that they consulted his Honour and Grandeur, whereas they only consulted their own ends; being sure, after they had rendered him and his Country Poor, that they could buy him when they pleased. Yet whenever the French Treasure shall come so far to be exhausted, that a fairer bidder appears; this piece of Policy will not only fail the French, but turn to their disadvantage.

With the Kings of Spain and Portugal the Dane is in a state of indifferency. Their Dominions are so far asunder, and the business so little which they have with each other, that there happen few or no occasions, either of a Quarrel or Friendship between them. Yet the Danes have some small Trade for Salt and Wine with each of these Princes Subjects; and during this War make some benefit of their Neutrality, by transporting in their Ships the Effects of French, English, and Dutch from one Port to another. They have indeed some Pretensions on the Spaniard for Arrears of Subsidies owing to them ever since the Danes took the part of the Confederates against France in the former War; but they despair of obtaining them, unless some unforeseen Accident put them in a way of getting that Debt, the Accompts of which have hardly ever been adjusted between them.

With the late Elector of Saxony the King of Denmark kept a very good correspondence; the Elector having married one of the King's Sisters, that Affinity produced as amicable effects as could be desired; insomuch that it begat a Resolution of a nearer Union of the two Families in a Match between the present Elector (then Prince) and the King's only Daughter; this proceeded as far as a formal Contract, and the usual Marriage presents were Solemnly exchanged in order to Consummation; when on a sudden the old Elector died last year, as he was leading an Army towards the Rhine against the French, for the common cause of Europe; the Death of this Prince, among other Alterations, produced this, that his Successor the present Elector being thereby become at his own disposal, and having been formerly very much in love with another Lady, who is the present Electress; refused to compleat his Marriage with the Daughter of Denmark, and sent back the Presents which were given at the time of the Contract. This Action of his highly disgusted the King, Queen, and the whole Danish Court; however, there was no Remedy but patience; the Elector was too remote to fear any Effects of the Danes displeasure, and resolved to pursue his own Inclinations in the choice of a Wife, let the World say and do what it would. Accordingly he presently courted and married where he fancied; leaving the Danes to digest this Affront as well as they could; which they will scarce forget this great while. So that it is to be supposed the ancient Knot between the King and the Electoral Family of Saxe is hereby very much loosened; yet not so far as to proceed to any open Breach, the Elector's Excuses for this Action having been received and accepted of as some sort of satisfaction.

With the Bishop of Munster, the King of Denmark lives in good Amity, by reason of his Neighbourhood to the Counties of Oldenburg and Delmenhorst; and for the most part has a Minister residing in that Court. The like Friendship is between him and the other Princes of Germany; particularly with the Landgrave of Hesse Cassel, who is Brother to his Queen, and extreamly beloved by her.

The King of Denmark has one Brother, viz. Prince George, born 1653 and married to her Royal Highness the Princess Ann, Sister to her Majesty of England: And four Sisters, viz. Anna Sophia, the Widow of the late Elector of Saxony. Frederica Emilia, the Wife of the Duke of Holstein. Guillimetta Ernestina, Widow of the Palatine of the Rhine. Ulrica Eleonora Sabina, the Queen of Sweden.

CHAPTER XV

Of the Laws, Courts of Justice, etc.

Some Naturalists observe, that there is no Plant or Insect, how venomous or mean soever, but is good for something towards the use of man if rightly applied: in like manner it may be said, That several useful Lessons may be learnt, conducing to the benefit of Mankind, from this Account of Denmark, provided things be taken by the right handle.

Hitherto we have indeed met with many things in it to be avoided, and little deserving imitation: but being now to speak of the Danish Laws, I must needs begin with this good Character of them in general, That for justice, Brevity, and perspicuity, they exceed all that I know in the World. They are grounded upon Equity, and are all contained in one Quarto Volume, written in the Language of the Country, with so much plainness, that no Man, who can write and read, is so ignorant, but he may presently understand his own Case, and plead it too if he pleases, without the Assistance of Counsel or Attorney.

Here is none of that Chicane to be found which destroys and raises so many great Estates in England; a very few Advocates do the business of all the Litigious Persons in these Kingdoms. Neither are their Fees arbitrary or exorbitant; no Suit of what importance soever hangs in suspence longer than one Year and a Month: since a Man may go through all the Courts, and have Execution done within that time, unless he be wanting to himself.

It may be replied to this, That the scarcity of Money may be the principal occasion of few Law-Suits and Lawyers. It is not denied, and perhaps a right sense of this was the first cause of so good a Regulation of Justice: for since the King was resolved to empty the Pockets of his Subjects, it was not for his advantage to permit others to do it, and share the Gains with him. However, thus much may with certainty be averred, That the like Regulation would not only agree with, but consummate the happiness of a rich Country; and this Instance of Denmark makes it evident that such a Regulation is practicable.

But to return to our purpose. In Denmark, in the ordinary Proceedings between Man and Man, there are three Courts, every one of which has power to give a definitive Sentence, and must either Acquit or Condemn. Yet there lies an Appeal from the lower to the higher; and if the inferior Judge has wilfully varied from the positive Law, the Party wronged has Damages given him, both from the Judge and his Adversary. Here is no removal of Actions from one Court to another, where the Parties may begin all again; but by way of ordinary procedure from the lower to the higher. The three Courts are these, first, In Cities and Towns the Byfoghts Court, to which in the Country does answer the Herredsfougds Court. Secondly, From thence lies an Appeal to the Landstag or general head Court for the Province. Thirdly, From thence to the Court called the Highright in Copenhagen, where the King himself sometimes sits in Person, and it is always composed of the prime Nobility of the Kingdom. The Judges in the two former Courts are constituted indeed by the King's Letters Patents *durante beneplacito;*[38] but are punishable for any misdemeanors committed, and condemned to make Reparation to the Party injured for any Injustice by them done. The City of Copenhagen has this particular Privilege, that the Sentences past in the Byfoghts Court, instead of passing through the Provincial Court, are tried by the Burgomaster and Common Council, and so proceed to the highest Court; which resembles

[38.] "During the pleasure (of the king)."

so far our High Court of Chancery, that if any matter happen to fall in debate, for the decision of which there is not a positive Article to be found in the Law (which rarely happens) it is there determined by the King, or by the others present, who are as it were the Keepers of the King's Conscience: and all this were very well, were it not that the first Article of the Law reserves to the King the Privilege of explaining or altering it at his pleasure.

In Matters relating to the Revenue, the Rent-Chamber in Denmark resembles our Court of Exchequer: which has also a Paymaster General belonging to it; and sometimes there is a Court composed of some Members of this Rent-Chamber, the Admiralty, and the Colledge of Commerce; before which lyes the Appeals of Merchants whose Goods happen to be seiz'd for not having paid the King's Duties.

The Sentences passed in the inferior Courts are sometimes biassed and partial; but not often, for fear of the highest Court, where great regard is had to Justice; insomuch that I knew a Judge, who very hardly escaped being fined for a Sentence passed against an English Merchant; which Sentence was presently reversed.

Indeed, whilst Monsieur Griffinfeldt and Monsieur Wibbe were Chancellors, there were mutterings, that the High Court Sentences were not altogether up to the rigour of the Law; but this is very rare now, unless when a Courtier or Favourite is interested in such a Sentence; in which case, or in matters wherein the King is concerned, you are to expect little Justice, especially if it relate to Money.

The Salaries of the Judges are but small; they are paid out of the Exchequer, and do not consist in Fees. The Byfogd may have about one hundred Rix Dollars yearly; and he pays himself out of the Fines of Delinquents. In the Country the Herredsfogds have each of them the Rent that is due to the King for a Farm that stands rated at ten Tuns of Hard-corn; he has besides from the Plaintiff and Defendant for the Sentence he passes, ten Stivers from each. And the Byfogd or Judge in Cities and Towns, double as much. Moreover, the contesting Parties are bound to pay the Clerk so much a sheet for the Paper, in which is set down at large the whole proceeding, and the Allegations of each Party, whether they be Verbal or by Libel, and at the close of all the Sentence it self. At the Byfogds Court, and the Landstag, the Judge inserts the Law, and adds the Reasons upon which his Judgment is founded; but in the High Right no Reason is given at all, or but very seldom. And that no Clerk may have it in his power to pick any Man's Pocket by filling up many Sheets of Paper, there are Limits set, beyond which no man is obliged to pay. Every one may plead his own Cause that pleases; however, it is the King's Order that the Magistrates take care to have one or more Advocates (such as they approve of) who are to plead for the Poor, and for such as cannot plead for themselves: upon the whole matter, the Charges of the Law are very easie; since a complaint may go through the three Courts for fifty Rix Dollars, which is less than twelve pound Sterling; unless the Sum in question be very great, and more than ordinary Evidences to be written on Sealed Paper. These Laws are so equitable and expeditious, that they are extreamly commended by Merchants and Strangers, who have occasion to have recourse to them. Neither is the smallness of the Expense any Encouragement to those that love going to Law; for the Laws themselves provide effectually against this Mischief, and take away the very Root of Litigiousness: being so plain and clear, that a troublesome Person never finds his Account in promoting vexatious Suits, but meets with all the Disappointments one would wish him.

In Criminal Matters a great Severity of Justice is practised. You never hear of any Person guilty of the Crime of Treason against the King; the Government has rivetted it self so fast upon the Bottom it now stands, that no Body offers to wag so much as the Tongue against it. There are no Clippers or Coiners, no Robbers upon the High-way, nor House-breakers; which conveniency of Arbitrary Government, among the multitude of Mischiefs attending it, I have likewise observed in France; perhaps because those Princes, who are entire Masters of their Subjects Purses at pleasure, take more effectual care of them as of their own, and therefore use such means that none shall plunder or cheat their People, for the same reason that Folks kill Vermin in Dove-Houses, viz. that they may make the greater profit themselves. The most usual Capital Crimes are Manslaughter and Stealing: Execution is done upon Offenders by beheading them with a Sword at one stroke very dexterously; the Headsman, though infamous by his place, so that no Body will come into his Company, yet is commonly rich, having other advantagious Employments that no Body else dares undertake, viz. the emptying all the Necessary Houses, the removing all dead Dogs and Horses out of Houses and Stables, or from before Doors; for no Danish Servant will upon any terms set a hand to either of these Works, and the Executioner has his own Rates for these base Offices, which he performs by his under Servant, called the Racker.

The Advocates are not bred as with us in England in Publick Societies, such as Inns of Court or Chancery; neither take they any degrees of Barrister, Serjeant, or the like; but may take up the Calling as they please, according to their Inclinations or Abilities.

There are besides the three ordinary Courts before mentioned, Commissioners of the Admiralty, which they call the Admiralty-Court; wherein Affairs relating to the Sea are determined, such as Prizes, Wrecks, Disputes with Privateers, and the like.

There is likewise a Chancellary, which consists of a number of Clerks, who write and issue all the King's Orders, give out Citations, transcribe Papers, make the Latin Projects of Treaties with Foreign Courts, according to the Directions they receive. In short, they are as it were under-Secretaries, and were formerly subject to the Government of one whom they called a Chancellor; but since Monsieur Wibbe's death, that Employment has not been filled: neither does it resemble our Place of Chancellor in England. The Clerks of this Office have some small Salary from the King, and have moreover so much for every Citation to the High Court, and so much for every Order they issue, which they divide among them.

In Copenhagen there is a Publick Officer appointed, called the Polity Master, whose business is to keep good Orders in Affairs relating to the City; he is to see that the Merchants sell warrantable Merchandize, that they do not interfere in one another's Trades; and to compose Differences on that account among them; that the Publick Buildings, Draw-bridges, and Canals be kept in repair; that the Streets be paved, cleansed, and free of the Incumbrances of Bulks and other Inconveniencies. That no prohibited Goods be brought in; that there be always plenty of Bread-Corn, and sold at a moderate Price; that the requisite Assistance in case of Fire be at hand. And indeed the Orders taken in this matter are very good; for there are select Companies appointed to watch and extinguish the Fire, no others daring to approach within a certain distance, lest under pretence of bringing help, they take the occasion to plunder. The Chimney-sweepers are bound to keep a Register of all Chimneys they sweep, that in case of any ill Accident, those by whose neglect or covetousness it happens, may be answerable for it. No Torches or Flambeaux are allowed to be carried in the Streets, by reason of the great quantities of Fir, Timber, and the constant high Winds which are here; instead of which all Persons, even the Court it self, make use of large round Lanthorns, carried at the end of long sticks. The Polity Master regulates also the price of Travelling in their open Wagons, and punishes such as exact more than the established rate, if they be complained of; also such as travel in the King's particular High-way without permission; and such as make use of Guns and Fowling-Pieces, and bring in Venison, Fowl, and Hares by stealth, or in times when they are prohibited to be killed. He takes care also to prevent and suppress Riots and Disturbances of the Soldiers, who are not permitted to walk the Streets after the Tattoo has gone about; and in general of all other matters relating to order, quiet, and decency.

Among other good Regulations in Denmark, I look upon that of the Apothecaries to be none of the least commendable; for no man is per-mitted to exercise that Trade, unless he be appointed by the Colledge of Physicians, and confirmed by the King himself. There are but two allowed to the City of Copenhagen, and one to every other considerable Town. Their Shops and Drugs are carefully visited twice or thrice a year by the Magistrates, accompanied by the Doctors of Physick; and such Drugs as are either naught or old, are taken from them and flung away. The prices of all these Drugs are fixed, so that any Child may be sent to an Apothe-caries Shop without hazard of being imposed upon; and nothing is sold that is not exceeding good, and at very moderate Rates. They sell all for ready Money, yet keep exact Books of what they sell, to whom, and by whose Prescription: so that the great Mischief of accidental or wilful Poy-soning, so frequent in other Countries, is either quite avoided; or if prac-ticed, easily discovered and punished.

The Government in the Country is managed, by dividing it into sev-eral Districts or Governments, called Stifts Ampts, whereof there are in all seven, of these, four are in Jutland, the other three in the Islands. Each of these is again subdivided into three lesser Jurisdictions, called Ampts. The Stifts-Ampts-man, or Governor of a County is commonly one of the best Quality and Fortune in that part of the Country; and this Charge answers to that of Lord Lieutenant of our Counties in England, or rather of Intendant in France. The Ampts-man, or under-Governor of a Hundred, or Balliage, is generally a Gentleman of lesser Fortune, who resides in the principal Town of his District, and takes care of all Matters relating to the Publick: as convenient quartering of Soldiers, providing for their March, collecting the King's Revenues, giving orders to the Peasants when employed about Publick Works, or when the King travels. All this they do themselves, or by inferior Officers, like our Bailiffs and Constables. These Employments are for the most part given by the King during life, and are the principal Rewards of such as have well deserved: he that has served long and faithfully as a Foreign Minister, or in any other considerable Civil Post, is usually promoted upon a vacancy to be Stifts-Ampts-man of his Province; provided his Estate and Interest there be some way correspondent. The Grooms of the King's Bed chamber, and other Officers of the Court, upon their Marriage, or retiring from Court, are gratified with an Ampt, and sent to live at home; provided they have served long, and be in any favour. The King pays to each of these a yearly Salary out of his Treasury; to a Stifts-Ampts man a thousand Crowns a year, to an Ampts-man four hundred Crowns. The principal Advantages they reap from these Employments, are these: First, That being more considered and favoured at Court than others, they escape better at the time of a Publick Tax, and can often find means to ease the Burthen off their own Lands by inhancing it upon others; neither will the Court willingly give ear to Complaints against them. Secondly, They are very much honoured and feared at home, and have the Privilege to domineer over the Peasants, and other their inferiors without control, unless they do it too grosly, and beyond measure.

Before I conclude this Chapter, I think it very pertinent to take notice, That in Denmark there are no Seditions, Mutinies, or Libels against the Government; but all the People either are or appear to be Lovers of their King, notwithstanding their ill Treatment, and the hardships they groan under. And I suppose one principal Reason of this to be the Equality of the Taxes, and the manner of Taxing. It is not to be imagined by those that see it not, what a comfort it is to the Sufferers to be ill used alike; for Poverty and Riches being only such in proportion; provided men be treated like their Neighbours, they grumble not; that which vexes the Oppressed in most Countries, (especially the Common People, who are more than ordinary envious) is to see their County, their Parish, or their House taxed more in proportion than their Neighbours: and they have reason to be discontented at this, for it brings real Poverty upon those that are over-taxed; it does not diminish the general Stock of the Subjects Money, which would keep all Commodities and Necessaries at equal and moderate Rates; but picks particular men's Pockets, whilst it leaves others rich and able to profit by the Necessities of the Poor.

'Tis a certain sign of an ill Government where there are abundance of Laws; but 'tis no certain sign of a good one, where there are but a few, as is plain in the case of Denmark. However, this Blessing of few and good Laws, is like a Grain of Consolation to sweeten a World of Bitterness, and enables them to bear their other Hardships with more Ease and Patience.[39]

[39.] Note in margin: "Corruptissima re publica plurimae leges." Translation: "The more corrupt the state, the more laws." Tacitus, *Annals*, bk. 3, chap. 27.

CHAPTER XVI

The State of Religion, of the Clergy, and Learning, etc.

When the Corruptions of the Roman Church grew so intolerable to many Nations in Europe, that an Universal Reformation became necessary, Denmark, among the rest of the Northern Countries (which had been less managed and more abused by the Priests than the Southern) shook off that yoke, and instead of the Roman-Catholick, embraced the Doctrine and Opinions of Martin Luther. King Frederick the First, about one hundred and fifty years since, brought these in, and established them so generally in his Dominions, that at this day there is no other Religion here professed than the Lutheran, if we will except the little Reformed French Church of Copenhagen, set up by the Queen, and one Popish Chapel at Glucstadt, permitted about ten years ago to a few Popish Families in those parts; which is the first that has been since the Reformation. This great Unity in belief in the North (for Sweden has it as well as Denmark) is owing to the Sincerity of those Princes that began the Reformation there: for it is likely they did it upon a pure religious account, and therefore went effectually to work in the Conversion of all their Subjects, using proper means for such a purpose; whereas in England, and elsewhere, Reasons of State and other Byends, had at least as great a share in it as Conviction of Conscience; so that the business was done by halves, through the unsettledness of our Princes in their Opinions, who encouraged or connived at a dissenting Party, according as their worldly Interests led them. The vast convenience to any Prince of having all his Subjects of one Opinion, is visible in Denmark; where there are no Factions nor Disputes about Religion, which usually have a great influence on any Government; but all are of one Mind, as to the way of Salvation, and as to the Duty they owe their Sovereign. This cuts off occasion of Rebellion and Mutiny from many, who otherwise would desire it, and seem to have reason enough, because of the heavy pressures they lye under. As long as the Priests are entirely dependant upon the Crown, and the People absolutely governed by the Priests in Matters of Conscience, as they are here, the Prince may be as Arbitrary as he pleases, without running any risque from his Subjects: in due consideration of which benefit, the Clergy are very much favoured, and have full scope given them to be as bigotted as they please; which indeed they are to a very great degree, having no common Charity for any that differ from them in Opinion, except the Church of England; and to that they are very kind, often saying, That there is no Essential Difference between it and theirs, and wishing that there were an union of them projected and perfected: wherein their Design is not so much to reduce our Ecclesiasticks to the low estate theirs are in, as to raise their own to the Splendour and Revenues of ours; which are the principal Virtues they admire in us. They have cast off the Opinions of Rome in the Supremacy of the Pope, and other Points; but they would retain the Grandeur belonging to that Church, and applaud us for doing both so dexterously: so that I am confident the business of Consubstantiation would make no difference, did Princes think it worth their while to promote this Union. On the other side, the Calvinist is hated by them as much as the Papist; and the reason they give is, because he is against absolute Monarchy, and has a resisting Principle.

Notwithstanding this Flattery of the Court, they are not admitted into civil Affairs, nor have any thing to do in the Government: neither are they encouraged to appear about Court, or on Publick Occasions; the Pulpit is their Province, and it is left free to them. Here they take a vast

Liberty of Reprehending not only Vices, but particular persons of the highest quality, which no body takes notice of, as long as they keep to their own Trade. The common People admire them for this boldness, and the best Subsistence of the Priests in Cities and Towns being voluntary Benevolence, they take care to cultivate the good Opinion of the Mobb, whom they keep likewise in awe by the practice of Confession before they Administer the Sacrament, which every one that receives is obliged to undergo; and this they retain of the Romish Church, as well as Crucifixes, and other Ceremonies.

There are six Superintendants in Denmark, who take it very kindly to be called Bishops, and My Lord; viz. one in Zealand, one in Funen, and four in Jutland: There are also four in Norway. These have no Temporalities, keep no Ecclesiastical Courts, have no Cathedrals, with Prebends, Canons, Deans, Subdeans, etc. But are only *primi inter pares;*[40] having the Rank above the inferior Clergy of their Province, and the inspection into their Doctrine and Manners. The Revenue of the Bishop of Copenhagen is about Two thousand Rix Dollars yearly; the other Bishops of Denmark have about Fifteen hundred Rix Dollars, and of Norway One thousand Rix Dollars; they are allowed to have two or three Parishes each; their Habit is common with that of the other Ministers, viz. A plaited black Gown, with short Sleeves, a large stiff Ruff about the Neck, and a Cap with Edges, like our Masters of Art, except that theirs is round, and the others square.

Most of them understand English, and draw the very best of their Divinity, as they confess themselves, out of English Books. Many of them have studied in Oxford, who are more valued than the others; they are very constant Preachers, and never read their Sermons, but pronounce them with a great deal of Action. Holy-days and Fast-days are observed as solemnly as Sundays; and in Copenhagen the City Gates are close shut during Sermon time, so that no body can go in or out. The Commonalty are great frequenters of the Churches, which are kept much more decently, cleanly, and better adorned than with us: so that they look almost as gaudy as the Popish Churches.

[40.] "First among equals."

They are all great Lovers of Organs, and have many very good ones, with skilful Organists, who entertain the Congregation with Musick, during half an hour, either before or after Service.

Denmark has formerly produced very Learned Men, Such as the famous Mathematician Tycho Brahe, the Bartholines for Physick and Anatomy, Borichius, who died lately, and bequeathed a considerable Legacy to the University of Copenhagen. But at present Learning is there at a very low Ebb; yet Latin is more commonly spoken by the Clergy than with us. The Books that come out in Print are very few, and those only some dull Treatises of Controversy against the Papists and Calvinists. The *Belles Lettres,* or Gentile Learning are very much strangers here, and will hardly be introduced till a greater affluence among the Gentry makes way for them. It is said that Necessity is the Mother of Invention; which may be true in some degree, but I am sure too much Necessity depresses the Spirits, and destroys it quite; neither is there any Invention here, or tolerable Imitation of what is brought in to them by Strangers.

There is but one University, which is at Copenhagen, and that mean enough in all respects; neither the Building nor Revenues being comparable to those of the worst of our single Colledges. The Students wear black Cloaks, and live scattered about the Town, after the manner of those in Leyden. Some of the Professors live in the House. Every year on the King's Birth day they have a kind of Act; the King honours them with his presence, and the Rector *Magnificus* harangues him with a Latin Speech, full of as fulsome Flattery, as if Louis le Grand were the Monarch to be entertained, and a fawning Jesuit the Orator. At certain Periods there are a few Danish Verses sung by the ordinary singing Boys to very indifferent Musick; and so the Farce ends.

There was in this King's Father's time an University at Sora, a Town very pleasantly situated about Forty miles from the City, where the Lodgings and Conveniencies for studying much exceeded those of Copenhagen: But the King had occasion for the Revenues; so that now it is desolate, and in its stead only a small Grammar-school erected.

The Provisions for the Poor are very inconsiderable; formerly there was a pretty store of Hospitals scatter'd up and down the Country, but at present the Revenues of most of these are diverted to other uses, and those not Publick ones.

To conclude; I never knew any Country where the Minds of the People were more of one calibre and pitch than here; you shall meet with none of extraordinary Parts or Qualifications, or excellent in particular Studies and Trades; you see no Enthusiasts, Mad-men, Natural Fools, or fanciful Folks; but a certain equality of Understanding reigns among them: every one keeps the ordinary beaten road of sense, which in this Country is neither the fairest nor the foulest, without deviating to the right or left; yet I will add this one Remark to their praise, that the Common People do generally write and read.

The Conclusion

It has been a great Mistake among us, That the Popish Religion is the only one, of all the Christian Sects, proper to introduce and establish Slavery in a Nation, insomuch that Popery and Slavery have been thought insepa-rable: not to derogate from the merit of the Roman Catholick Persuasion, which has been the Darling of so many Monarchs upon that account; I shall make bold to say that other Religions, and particularly the Lutheran, has succeeded as effectually in this Design as ever Popery did. 'Tis confest indeed that Popery would certainly introduce Slavery, but 'tis denied that the last cannot come in without the assistance of the former; and whoever takes the pains to visit the Protestant Countries abroad, who have lost their Liberty even since they changed their Religion for a better, will be convinced that it is not Popery as such, but the Doctrine of a blind Obedi-ence in what Religion soever it be found, that is the destruction of the Lib-erty, and consequently of all the Happiness of any Nation. Nay, I am Per-suaded that many are satisfied the late King James's Attempts to bring in Popery was the principal thing which rescued our Liberties from being en-tirely swallowed up; there seeming in his Reign, through the Interest and Dishonesty of some, the Dissoluteness, Laziness, and Ignorance of others, to have been (in many mens Opinions) a general tendency towards Slavery, which would scarcely have been vigorously enough opposed, had he left the business of Religion untouched; and if once introduced, it had been maintained more effectually than in the days of Popery; I say more effectually, because the dependence which the Romish Clergy and Monks have on the Church of Rome, causes often a clashing of Interests, and derogates from that intire Obedience the Subjects owe to the Prince, which is preached up by that Church, as often as the Sovereign acts according to their direction, and down again whenever he displeases them; whereof we have had frequent Examples in this Kingdom of England, where there have been Bishops and Abbots in the days of Popery, as zealous Assertors of the Liberties of the People, as any Lay-men could be, whether out of a true Principle, or not, I will not determine; but Occasions have been taken by them to raise Tumults and Wars, and in the Scuffle the Liberties of the People (of which both King and Church-men strove who should be the Masters) have escaped untouched: but in Denmark, as well as other Protestant Countries of the North, through the entire and sole dependence of the Clergy upon the Prince, without the interfering of the Authority of any Spiritual Superior, such as that of the Pope among the Romanists: through their Principles and Doctrine, which are those of unlimited Obedience; through the Authority they have with the Common People, etc. slavery seems to be more absolutely established than it is in France; as in effect it is more practised; for that King's Subjects are better treated; there is a Name of a Parliament at Paris, and other great Towns, though they meet for no other end, but to verify the King's Edicts; there is a formal Demand made of a Benevolence, or *Don Gratuit* in some Provinces, which probably they have not the power to deny; there is an encouragement of Trade, Manufactures, Learning, etc. all tending to the good of the People. Besides, we see by experience, that that King often has great quarrels with the Court of Rome, which when so ever his power is reduced to a lower ebb, that his Clergy are not over-awed by it, may produce such Divisions and Disturbances as possibly some Sparks of the People's Liberty may again proceed from the collision of two such hard Rocks: but in the Countries I have Spoken of, there is no hope of any Such resource; all is swallowed up in the King; Temporals and Spirituals, Soul, Body, Estate, and Conscience; the Army and the Priests are two sure Cards: the Prince that has one of them on his side, can hardly fail; but he that has both depending on him, need fear nothing from his own Subjects, let him use them never so ill.

Much has been spoken and written by several Authors of the rigor of the Turkish Government, let us consider some particulars of it by way of comparison.

The Turks are the Conquerors of the Christians in the Countries they have over-run, and have a sort of barbarous Right to use them ill; yet they never persecute them upon account of Conscience; they suffer them for the most part to inhabit and cultivate their own Lands without disturbance, paying only a Caratch yearly for Tribute; which as I have been informed by a Minister of his Imperial Majesty's, amounted in Hungary, Sclavonia, Servia, and Bosnia, only to about ten Dollars for an ordinary Family in time of Peace, and during a War nothing. It is true, the Propriety of all Lands in Turkey is in the Grand Signior; but whether it be not better to be only a Farmer at an easie Rent, than to have the Name of a Proprietor without a comfortable Subsistence, and in effect to be Master of Nothing, I leave the Reader to judge.

The forcing away Children from the poor Christian Parents, is accounted a great hardship, though it be for the worldly Profit and Advancement of those Children; bating the point of Religion, it is a far less Mischief to deprive Parents of their Sons and Daughters, in order to maintain them well, than to leave a heavy Charge upon their Hands, after having taken away the possibility of Nourishing and Educating them.

The Sun, Soil, Climate, and Situation, with other Natural Advantages of the Grand Signior's Dominions, as to Profit and Pleasure, are infinitely beyond those of other Northern Countries that we are acquainted with. In Turkey the Harbours are always open, except some few places in the Black Sea; whereas here they are frozen up three or four Months in the Year. There the Fruits, Flesh, Corn and Herbs, have double the Virtue and Nourishment they have here; the Wine there is good and plentiful, and the very Water wholesome and pleasant; here the first is scarce, and the last very bad. In a word, in some Christian Countries of Europe, there seems to be most of the Mischiefs of a Turkish Government in an infinitely worse Climate: Besides, we are to consider, that the Turks themselves, who are Lords and Masters, live well and pleasantly, and it is their conquered Slaves whom they use in the manner above-mentioned.

If it be enquired, Whether Matters are like to last at the same rate they are now at in Denmark? Though nothing be more fallacious than a Judgment made of the future, I shall not omit speaking a few words in answer.

Many reasons might persuade one to think, that the Government upon the bottom it stands cannot last long. As in the first place, that natural Love of Liberty, which resided formerly in the Northern Nations more eminently than in other Parts of the World. What can be expected less from the Descendants of the ancient Goths and Vandals, who propagated and establish'd Liberty in so many other Countries, than to shake a heavy Yoak off themselves, which their Forefathers were not able to bear? especially since this Yoak is so extraordinary grievous, that the Chains which the Neighbouring Countries wear, are but Ornamental ones, if compared with theirs.

Secondly, The freshness and newness of this Alteration of their Condition. It being no more than thirty two years since it happened; and many remaining yet alive, who remember the days of Liberty, and in their private Discourses with their Friends and Children make Comparison between the past and present times, and condole with them the loss of so great a Blessing; it might seem that the Opinion of the present Government's not being sufficiently rooted, nor having gained Authority by length of time to settle, should encourage those that find themselves grieved, to think of Methods tending to a Change.

Thirdly, The Neighbourhood of the Swedes, who have still their Eye upon Denmark, and long to be sole Monarchs of the North, and Masters of the Baltick-Sea. Now the Burden being so great as it is, one would think the Natives, in hopes of Ease, would rather wish for, than defend their Country from an Invader; because they have little or no Property to lose, and imagine there is scarce a possibility of changing for the worse.

Fourthly, The numerousness of the Royal Family. There being four Princes, it will be rare if Concord be maintained among them all, especially since the younger are like to be but meanly provided for: so that frequent Occasions may be taken from Quarrels and Disputes (which possibly in future times may arise among them) of doing something in favour of Liberty.

These Reasons might cause one to make a Judgment, that the Danish Government could not long subsist as it is. But on the other hand, there are no less weighty ones which would induce to believe the contrary: For, first, the ancient Love of Liberty seems to be quite extinct in the North; and in its place to have succeeded the conveniencies of a dull Obedience. A miserable Life which jogs on at the same heavy rate, has a mixture of Melancholy Ease with it, which is preferred before those sudden Accidents, and brisk Traverses of Fortune which Commotions would occasion; especially by a People naturally of an unactive Body and heavy Spirit, depressed by their Misfortunes, which are now group up with them, and become their familiar Companions.

In the second place, the Newness of the Alteration of the Government seems to have little or no influence at present upon the People: for the King has taken such care by reducing Ancient and Rich Families to a low Estate, by raising new ones, by making all the People poor in Spirit, as well as Purse; that thirty two years has had an effect conducing to his purpose, as much as three hundred could have done: Insomuch that I verily believe, the Danes do now really love Servitude; and like the Cappadocians of old, could not make use of Liberty if it were offered them; but would throw it away if they had it, and resume their Chains. Possibly they would wish them less weighty, but Chains they could not live without. If there be one or two among so many thousands who are of contrary Sentiments, they dare not so much as mutter them to their own Children, nor would be heard with patience if they did.

Thirdly, The Unity of Religion, and the Opinions, together with the Authority of the Priests, seems to have cut away the root of Sedition, from whence Alterations might proceed.

Fourthly, A standing Army composed for the most part of Foreigners, who have no value for the Natives, nor any concern for their welfare. The Court seems to have had this in its eye, when it raised and maintained such an Army, but in process of time the Army is become the People; that is to say, the only thing worth the King's Care and Affection; and the People nothing, so that no Designs, tending to a Revolution, are to be feared from them.

Fifthly, The Swedes treat their own Subjects at such a rate as gives the Danes but little Prospect of benefit by a Change; and besides, there is such a fixed hatred between these two Nations, by reason of the Injuries they have so often given and received, that it is thought impossible that the Danes, who have been for the most part the Aggressors, as well as the sufferers, can ever forgive them. Many judicious Persons do think however, that the Swede would find means to overcome these Difficulties, did not the Discontents he has rais'd at home, make War dangerous to him, and the interest of almost all the other Princes of Europe concur in the Preservation of the Danes, under the Domination of their own King, by obstructing any further Accession of Power and Territories to the Swedes. And this is certainly such a Bar as cannot be leaped over, so that little of Alteration seems to be expected in Denmark from hence.

Lastly, Those Jealousies which use to reign in the Families of Princes, are not so common nor fatal in Germany as elsewhere: The King of Denmark is a German Prince himself, and 'tis likely will find such Means of preferring his younger Sons, as may content them, either by breeding them up to the War (which is the most ordinary way) or by assigning them Appanages in convenient Places not liable to dispute; besides, it is no rare thing in Germany to see Princes satisfied with very moderate Revenues. So that the commonness of the thing takes away the Discontent which might arise in high-born Spirits, by reason of the lowness of their Fortunes; and if any Wars be in Europe, thither they all run to get Bread, and Reputation. What else should we do for a Stock of Generals in such Havock as the present Wars make of them? therefore nothing of Intestine Commotions seems to be reasonably expected from hence, that shall alter the Form of Government; and from all these Reasons it may be concluded, That the present State is fix'd and durable, and that the People with great difficulty may perhaps change their Masters, but never their Condition.

FINIS.

Francogallia,
Or an Account of
the Ancient Free State
of France

Franco-Gallia:

OR, AN

ACCOUNT

OF THE

Ancient Free State

OF

FRANCE,

AND

Most other Parts of EUROPE,
before the Loss of their Liberties.
Written Originally in Latin *by the Famous Civilian*
FRANCIS HOTOMAN,
In the Year 1574.
And Translated into English *by*
the Author of the Account of DENMARK.

The SECOND EDITION, with Additions, and
a *New Preface* by the Translator.

LONDON:
Printed for *Edward Valentine,* at
the Queen's Head against St. *Dunstan's*
Church, *Fleet Street,* 1721.

THE PREFACE TO THE READER[1]

The following Treatise was composed by that most Learned and Judicious Civilian FRANCIS HOTOMAN, a grave, sincere, and unexceptionable Author, even in the opinion of his Adversaries. This Book gives an Account of the Antient Free State of above three Parts in four of all *Europe;* and has of a long time appeared to me so convincing and instructive in those Important Points he handles, that I could not be satisfied whilst it remained unknown, in a manner, to *Englishmen;* who, of all People living, have greatest Reason to be thoroughly instructed in what it contains; as having, on the one hand, the most to lose; and, on the Other, the least sense of their Right to it. Therefore a sincere Desire of Instructing the only Possessors of True Liberty in the World, what Right they have to that Liberty, of how great a Value it is, what Misery follows the Loss of it, and how easily, if Care be taken in time, it may be preserved, has induced me to Translate and send Abroad this small Treatise. And if it either opens the Eyes, or confirms the Honourable Resolutions of any of my Worthy Countrymen, I have gained a Glorious End; and done that in my study, which I would have promoted any other way, if I had been called to it. I hope to dye with the comfort of believing, that Old *England* will

[1.] This preface was included only in the 1711 Timothy Goodwin edition and is largely duplicated in the "Translator's Preface." See p. 173.

continue to be a free Country, and know itself to be such; that my Friends, relations, and Children, with their Posterity, will inherit their share of this inestimable Blessing, and that I have contributed my part to it.

I have often wish'd, in regard to my Author, that he had omitted his Nineteenth chapter, wherein he discovers a great Aversion to Female-Governments; having nothing to say in Excuse of him, but being a Lawyer and a *Frenchman,* he was Vindicating the Constitution of his Country: Certain it is (how little favourable soever such Governments have proved to *France*) other Nations have never flourish'd more, in Good Laws, Wealth and Conquests, than under the Administration of Women: There are not brighter Characters in Antiquity, than of *Semiramis, Thalestris, Thomiris, Zenobia,* and many Others. I am sure our Island in particular has never been able to boast of so much Felicity as under the Dominion of Queens; never been more enriched by Commerce, improved by Just Laws, adorned with more excellent Examples of Virtue, or more free from all those Struggles between Prerogative and Liberty, which have stained the Characters of our Otherwise most Glorious Kings. But Providence by yet more extraordinary Dispensations, has endeared them to us, by choosing them to be its Instruments of pulling down or bridling the proudest Empires, which threatened Universal Ruin. Our Ancestors under *Boadicia* made noble Effort for Liberty, which shook the Old *Roman* Dominion amongst us. Queen *Elizabeth* freed us from the double Tyranny of New *Rome* and *Spain:* And the Destruction of the present Grand Oppressor of *Europe,* seems reserved by Heaven to Reward the Piety and Virtue of our Excellent Queen.

The Bookseller to the Reader[2]

The following Translation of the Famous Hotoman's *Franco-Gallia* was written in the Year 1705, and first publish'd in the Year 1711. The Author was then at a great Distance from London, and the Publisher of his Work,

[2.] This section was not included in the 1711 Timothy Goodwin edition but is in the 1721 and 1738 editions.

for Reasons needless to repeat, did not think fit to print the Prefatory Discourse sent along with the Original. But this Piece being seasonable at all
Times for the Perusal of Englishmen, and more particularly at this Time,
I wou'd no longer keep back from the Publick, what I more than conjecture will be acceptable to all true Lovers of their Country.

THE TRANSLATOR'S PREFACE [3]

Many Books and Papers have been publish'd since the late Revolution, tending to justify the Proceedings of the People of England at that happy juncture; by setting in a true Light our just Rights and Liberties, together with the solid Foundations of our Constitution: Which, in truth, is not ours only, but that of almost all Europe besides; so wisely restor'd and establish'd (if not introduced) by the *Goths* and *Franks*, whose Descendants we are.

These Books have as constantly had some things, called Answers, written to them, by Persons of different Sentiments; who certainly either never seriously consider'd, that they were thereby endeavouring to destroy their own Happiness, and overthrow her Majesty's Title to the Crown: or (if they knew what they did) presumed upon the Lenity of that Government they decry'd; which (were there no better Reason) ought to have recommended it to their Approbation, since it could patiently bear with such, as were doing all they could to undermine it.

Not to mention the Railing, Virulency, or personal false Reflections in many of those Answers, (which were[4] always the Signs of a weak Cause,

[3.] The Translator's Preface was not included in the 1711 Timothy Goodwin edition. The preface forms the basis of the independent text later known as the *Principles of a Real Whig*.

[4.] The 1775 edition of the *Principles* has "are."

or a feeble Champion) some of them asserted the Divine Right of an Hereditary Monarch, and the Impiety of Resistance upon any Terms whatever, notwithstanding any Authorities to the contrary.

Others (and those the more judicious) deny'd positively, that sufficient Authorities could be produced to prove, that a free People have a just Power to defend themselves, by opposing their Prince, who endeavours to oppress and enslave them: And alledged, that whatever was said or done tending that way, proceeded from a Spirit of Rebellion, and Antimonarchical Principles.

To confute, or convince this last Sort of Arguers (the first not being worthy to have Notice taken of them) I set about translating the *Francogallia* of that most Learned and Judicious Civilian, Francis Hotoman; a Grave, Sincere and Unexceptionable Author, even in the Opinion of his Adversaries. This Book gives an Account of the Ancient Free State of above Three Parts in Four of Europe; and has of a long time appeared to me so convincing and instructive in those important Points he handles, that I could not be idle whilst it remain'd unknown, in a manner, to Englishmen: who, of all People living, have the greatest Reason and Need to be thoroughly instructed in what it contains; as having, on the one hand, the most to lose, and on the other, the least Sense of their Right, to that, which hitherto they seem (at least in a great measure) to have preserv'd.

It will be obvious to every Reader, that I have taken no great Pains to write elegantly. What I endeavour at, is as plain a Stile as possible, which on this Occasion I take to be the best: For since the Instruction of Mankind ought to be the principal Drift of all Writers (of History especially); whoever writes to the Capacity of most Readers, in my Opinion most fully answers the End.

I am not ignorant, how tiresome and difficult a Piece of Work it is to translate, nor how little valued in the World. My Experience has convinced me, that 'tis more troublesome and teazing than to write and invent at once. The Idiom of the Language out of which one translates, runs so in the Head, that 'tis next to impossible not to fall frequently into it. And the more bald and incorrect the Stile of the Original is, the more shall that of the Translation be so too. Many of the Quotations in this Book are drawn from Priests, Monks, Friars, and Civil Lawyers, who minded more, in those barbarous Ages, the Substance than the Stile of their Writings: And I hope those Considerations may atone for several Faults, which might be found in my Share of this Work.

But I desire not to be misunderstood, as if (whilst I am craving Favour for my self) I were making any Apology for such a Number of mercenary Scribblers, Animadverters, and Translators, as pester us in this Age; who generally spoil the good Books which fall into their Hands, and hinder others from obliging the Publick, who otherwise would do it to greater Advantage.

I take this Author to be one of those few, that has had the good Luck to escape them; and I make use of this Occasion to declare, that the chief Motive which induces me to send abroad this small Treatise, is a sincere desire of instructing the only Possessors of true Liberty in the World, what Right and Title they have to that Liberty; of what a great Value it is; what Misery follows the Loss of it; how easily, if Care be taken in time, it may be preserv'd: And if this either opens the Eyes, or confirms the honourable Resolutions of any of my worthy Countrymen, I have gained a glorious End; and done that in my Study, which I should have promoted any other way, had I been called to it. I hope to die with the Comfort of believing, that Old England will continue to be a free Country, and know itself to be such; that my Friends, Relations and Children, with their Posterity, will inherit their Share of this inestimable Blessing, and that I have contributed my Part to it.

But there is one very great Discouragement under which both I, and all other Writers and Translators of Books tending to the acquiring or preserving the publick Liberty, do lie; and that is, the heavy Calumny thrown upon us, that we are all *Commonwealth's-Men:* Which (in the ordinary Meaning of the Word) amounts to Haters of Kingly Government; not without broad, malicious Insinuations, that we are no great Friends of the present.

Indeed were the Laity of our Nation (as too many of our Clergy unhappily are) to be guided by the Sense of one of our Universities, solemnly and publickly declared by the burning of Twenty seven Propositions (some of them deserving that Censure, but others being the very Foundation of all our Civil Rights); I, and many like me, would appear to be very much in the wrong.[5] But since the Revolution in Eighty-eight, that we stand upon another and a better Bottom, though no other than our own old one, 'tis time that our Notions should be suited to our Constitution. And truly, as Matters stand, I have often wondered, either how so many of our Gentlemen, educated under such Prejudices, should retain any Sense at all of Liberty, for the hardest Lesson is to unlearn; or how an Education so diametrically opposite to our Bill of Rights, should be so long encouraged.[6]

Methinks a Civil Test might be contrived, and prove very convenient to distinguish those that own the Revolution Principles, from such as Tooth and Nail oppose them; and at the same time do fatally propagate Doctrines, which lay too heavy a Load upon Christianity it self, and make us prove our own Executioners.

[7]The Names of Whig and Tory will, I am afraid, last as long among us, as those of Guelf and Ghibelline did in Italy. I am sorry for it: but to some they become necessary for Distinction Sake; not so much for the Principles formerly adapted to each Name, as for particular and worse Reasons. For there has been such chopping and changing both of Names and Principles, that we scarce know who is who. I think it therefore necessary, in order to appear in my own Colours, to make a publick Profession of my Political Faith; not doubting but it may agree in several Particulars with that of many worthy Persons, who are as undeservedly aspers'd as I am.

My Notion of a Whig, I mean of a real Whig (for the Nominal are worse than any Sort of Men) is, That he is one who is exactly for keeping up to the Strictness of the true old Gothick Constitution, under the Three Estates of King (or Queen) Lords and Commons; the Legislature being seated in all Three together, the Executive entrusted with the first, but accountable to the whole Body of the People, in Case of Male Administration.

[5.] Molesworth refers here to *The judgment and decree of the University of Oxford past in their convocation July 21, 1683, against certain pernicious books and damnable doctrines destructive to the sacred persons of princes, their state and government, and of all humane society rendred into English, and published by command* (Oxford: Printed at the Theater, 1683).

6. Note in margin: "St. Chrysostom."

[7.] The 1726 extract reproduced in Ker starts here (p. 191).

A true Whig is of Opinion, that the Executive Power has as just a Title to the Allegiance and Obedience of the Subject, according to the Rules of known Laws enacted by the Legislative, as the Subject has to Protection, Liberty and Property: And so on the contrary.

A true Whig is not afraid of the Name of a *Commonwealthsman,* because so many foolish People, who know not what it means, run it down: The Anarchy and Confusion which these Nations fell into near Sixty Years ago, and which was falsely called a Commonwealth, frightening them out of the true Construction of the Word. But Queen Elizabeth, and many other of our best Princes, were not scrupulous of calling our Government a Commonwealth, even in their solemn Speeches to Parliament. And indeed if it be not one, I cannot tell by what Name properly to call it: For where in the very Frame of the Constitution, the Good of the Whole is taken care of by the Whole (as 'tis in our Case) the having a King or Queen at the Head of it, alters not the Case; and the softening of it by calling it a Limited Monarchy, seems a Kind of Contradiction in Terms, invented to please some weak and doubting Persons.

And because some of our Princes in this last Age, did their utmost Endeavour to destroy this Union and Harmony of the Three Estates, and to be arbitrary or independent, they ought to be looked upon as the Aggressors upon our Constitution.

This drove the other Two Estates (for the Sake of the publick Preservation) into the fatal Necessity of providing for themselves; and when once the Wheel was set a running, 'twas not in the Power of Man to stop it just where it ought to have stopp'd. This is so ordinary in all violent Motions, whether mechanick or political, that no body can wonder at it.

But no wise Men approved of the ill Effects of those violent Motions either way, could they have help'd them. Yet it must be owned they have (as often as used, through an extraordinary Piece of good Fortune) brought us back to our old Constitution again, which else had been lost; for there are numberless Instances in History of a Downfall from a State of Liberty to a Tyranny, but very few of a Recovery of Liberty from Tyranny, if this last have had any Length of Time to fix it self and take Root.

Let all such, who either through Interest or Ignorance are Adorers of absolute Monarchs, say what they please; an English Whig can never be so unjust to his Country, and to right Reason, as not to be of Opinion, that in all Civil Commotions, which side soever is the wrongful Aggressor, is accountable for all the evil Consequences: And through the Course of his reading (though my Lord Clarendon's Books be thrown into the Heap) he finds it very difficult to observe, that ever the People of England took up Arms against their Prince, but when constrain'd to it by a necessary Care of their Liberties and true Constitution.[8]

'Tis certainly as much a Treason and Rebellion against this Constitution, and the known Laws, in a Prince to endeavour to break through them, as 'tis in the People to rise against him, whilst he keeps within their Bounds, and does his Duty. Our Constitution is a Government of Laws, not of Persons. Allegiance and Protection are Obligations that cannot subsist separately; when one fails, the other falls of Course. The true Etymology of the word Loyalty (which has been so strangely wrested in the late Reigns) is an entire Obedience to the Prince in all his Commands according to Law; that is, to the Laws themselves, to which we owe both an active and passive Obedience.

By the old and true Maxim, *that the King can do no Wrong,* nobody is so foolish as to conclude, that he has not Strength to murder, to offer Violence to Women, or Power enough to dispossess a Man wrongfully of his Estate, or that whatever he does (how wicked soever) is just: but the Meaning is, he has no lawful Power to do such Things; and our Constitution considers no Power as irresistible, but what is lawful.

And since Religion is become a great and universal Concern, and drawn into our Government, as it affects every single Man's Conscience; though in my private Opinion, they ought not to be mingled, nor to have any thing to do with each other; (I do not speak of our Church Polity, which is a Part of our State, and dependent upon it) some account must be given of that Matter.

Whiggism is not circumscrib'd and confin'd to any one or two of the

---

[8.] Edward Hyde, Lord Clarendon's High Church *History of the rebellion,* partially composed in the early 1670s, was first published as *The history of the rebellion and civil wars in England, begun in the year 1641. With the precedent Passages, and Actions, that contributed thereunto, and the happy End, and Conclusion thereof by the King's blessed Restoration, and Return upon the 29th of May, in the Year 1660* (Oxford, 1702–4).

Religions now profess'd in the World, but diffuses it self among all. We have known Jews, Turks, nay, some Papists, (which I own to be a great Rarity) very great Lovers of the Constitution and Liberty; and were there rational Grounds to expect, that any Numbers of them could be so, I should be against using Severities and Distinctions upon Account of Religion. For a Papist is not dangerous, nor ought to be ill us'd by any body, because he prays to Saints, believes Purgatory, or the real Presence in the Eucharist, and pays Divine Worship to an Image or Picture (which are the common Topicks of our Writers of Controversy against the Papists); but because Popery sets up a foreign Jurisdiction paramount to our Laws. So that a real Papist can neither be a true Governor of a Protestant Country, nor a true Subject, and besides, is the most Priest-Ridden Creature in the World: and (when uppermost) can bear with no body that differs from him in Opinion; little considering, that whosoever is against Liberty of Mind, is, in effect, against Liberty of Body too. And therefore all Penal Acts of Parliament for Opinions purely religious, which have no Influence on the State, are so many Encroachments upon Liberty, whilst those which restrain Vice and Injustice are against Licentiousness.

I profess my self to have always been a Member of the Church of England and am for supporting it in all its Honours, Privileges and Revenues: but as a Christian and a Whig, I must have Charity for those that differ from me in religious Opinions, whether Pagans, Turks, Jews, Papists, Quakers, Socinians, Presbyterians, or others. I look upon Bigotry to have always been the very Bane of human Society, and the Offspring of Interest and Ignorance, which has occasion'd most of the great Mischiefs that have afflicted Mankind. We ought no more to expect to be all of one Opinion, as to the Worship of the Deity, than to be all of one Colour or Stature. To stretch or narrow any Man's Conscience to the Standard of our own, is no less a Piece of Cruelty than that of Procrustes the Tyrant of Attica, who used to fit his Guests to the Length of his own Iron Bedsted, either by cutting them shorter, or racking them longer. What just Reason can I have to be angry with, to endeavour to curb the natural Liberty, or to retrench the Civil Advantages of an honest Man (who follows the golden Rule, of *doing to others, as he would have others do to him,* and is willing and able to serve the Publick) only because he thinks his Way to

Heaven surer or shorter than mine? No body can tell which of us is mistaken, till the Day of Judgment, or whether any of us be so (for there may be different Ways to the same End, and I am not for circumscribing God Almighty's Mercy). This I am sure of, one shall meet with the same Positiveness in Opinion, in some of the Priests of all these Sects; The same Want of Charity, engrossing Heaven by way of Monopoly to their own Corporation, and managing it by a joint Stock, exclusive of all others (as pernicious in Divinity as in trade, and perhaps more). The same Pretences to Miracles, Martyrs, Inspirations, Merits, Mortifications, Revelations, Austerity, Antiquity, etc. (as all Persons conversant with History, or that travel, know to be true) and this *cui bono?*[9] I think it the Honour of the Reformed Part of the Christian Profession, and the Church of England in particular, that it pretends to fewer of these unusual and extraordinary Things, than any other Religion we know of in the World; being convinced, that these are not the distinguishing Marks of the Truth of any Religion (I mean, the assuming obstinate Pretences to them are not); and it were not amiss, if we farther enlarg'd our Charity, when we can do it with Safety, or Advantage to the State.

Let us but consider, how hard and how impolitick it is to condemn all People, but such as think of the Divinity just as we do. May not the Tables of Persecution be turn'd upon us? A Mahometan in Turkey is in the right, and I (if I carry my own Religion thither) am in the Wrong. They will have it so. If the Mahometan comes with me to Christendom, I am in the right, and he in the wrong; and hate each other heartily for differing in Speculations, which ought to have no Influence on Moral Honesty. Nay, the Mahometan is the more charitable of the two, and does not push his Zeal so far; for the Christians have been more cruel and severe in this Point than all the World besides. Surely Reprizals may be made upon us; as Calvin burnt Servetus at Geneva, Queen Mary burnt Cranmer at London. I am sorry I cannot readily find a more exact Parallel. The Sword cuts with both Edges. Why, I pray you, may we not all be Fellow-Citizens of the World? And provided it be not the Principle of one or more Religions to extirpate all others, and to turn Persecutors when they get Power (for

[9.] "To whose benefit" or "to whose profit."

such are not to be endured) I say, why should we offer to hinder any Man from doing with his own Soul what he thinks fitting? Why should we not make use of his Body, Estate, and Understanding, for the publick Good? Let a Man's Life, Substance, and Liberty be under the Protection of the Laws; and I dare answer for him (whilst his Stake is among us) he will never be in a different Interest, nor willing to quit this Protection, or to exchange it for Poverty, Slavery, and Misery.

The thriving of any one single Person by honest Means, is the thriving of the Commonwealth wherein he resides. And in what Place soever of the World such Encouragement is given, as that in it one may securely and peaceably enjoy Property and Liberty both of Mind and Body; 'tis impossible but that Place must flourish in Riches and in People, which are the truest Riches of any Country.

But as, on the one hand, a true Whig thinks that all Opinions purely spiritual and notional ought to be indulg'd; so on the other, he is for severely punishing all Immoralities, Breach of Laws, Violence and Injustice. A Minister's Tythes are as much his Right, as any Layman's Estate can be his; and no Pretence of Religion or Conscience can warrant the subtracting of them, whilst the Law is in being which makes them payable: For a Whig is far from the Opinion, that they are due by any other Title. It would make a Man's Ears tingle, to hear the Divine Right insisted upon for any human Institutions; and to find God Almighty brought in as a Principal there, where there is no Necessity for it. To affirm, that Monarchy, Episcopacy, Synods, Tythes, the Hereditary Succession to the Crown, *etc.* are *Jure Divino;*[10] is to cram them down a Man's Throat; and tell him in plain Terms, that he must submit to any of them under all Inconveniencies, whether the Laws of his Country are for it or against it. Every Whig owns Submission to Government to be an Ordinance of God. Submit your selves to every Ordinance of Man, for the Lord's Sake, says the Apostle. Where (by the way) pray take notice, he calls them Ordinances of Man; and gives you the true Notion, how far any thing can be said to be *Jure Divino:* which is far short of what your high-flown Assertors of the *Jus Divinum* would carry it, and proves as strongly for a Republican

[10.] "By divine right."

Government as a Monarchical; though in truth it affects neither, where the very Ends of Government are destroyed.

A right Whig looks upon frequent Parliaments as such a fundamental Part of the Constitution, that even no Parliament can part with this Right. High Whiggism is for Annual Parliaments, and Low Whiggism for Triennial, with annual Meetings. I leave it to every Man's Judgment, which of these would be the truest Representative; would soonest ease the House of that Number of Members that have Offices and Employments, or take Pensions from the Court; is least liable to Corruption; would prevent exorbitant Expence, and soonest destroy the pernicious Practice of drinking and bribing for Elections, or is most conformable to ancient Custom. The Law that lately pass'd with so much Struggle for Triennial Parliaments shall content me, till the Legislative shall think fit to make them Annual.

But methinks (and this I write with great Submission and Deference) that (since the passing that Act) it seems inconsistent with the Reason of the thing, and preposterous, for the first Parliament after any Prince's Accession to the Crown, to give the publick Revenue arising by Taxes, for a longer time than that Parliament's own Duration. I cannot see why the Members of the first Parliament should (as the Case now stands) engross to themselves all the Power of giving, as well as all the Merit and Rewards due to such a Gift: and why succeeding Parliaments should not, in their turn, have it in their Power to oblige the Prince, or to streighten him, if they saw Occasion; and pare his Nails, if they were convinced he made ill Use of such a Revenue. I am sure we have had Instances of this Kind; and a wise Body of Senators ought always to provide against the worst that might happen. The Honey-Moon of Government is a dangerous Season; the Rights and Liberties of the People run a greater Risk at that time, through their own Representatives Compliments and Compliances, than they are ever likely to do during that Reign: and 'tis safer to break this Practice, when we have the Prospect of a good and gracious Prince upon the Throne, than when we have an inflexible Person, who thinks every Offer an Affront, which comes not up to the Height of what his Predecessor had, without considering whether it were well or ill done at first.

The Revenues of our Kings, for many Ages, arose out of their Crown-

Lands; Taxes on the Subject were raised only for publick Exigencies. But since we have turn'd the Stream, and been so free of Revenues for Life, arising from Impositions and Taxes, we have given Occasion to our Princes to dispose of their Crown-Lands; and depend for Maintenance of their Families on such a Sort of Income, as is thought unjust and ungodly in most Parts of the World, but in Christendom: for many of the arbitrary Eastern Monarchs think so, and will not eat the Produce of such a Revenue. Now since Matters are brought to this pass, 'tis plain that our Princes must subsist suitable to their high State and Condition, in the best manner we are able to provide for them. And whilst the Calling and Duration of Parliaments was precarious, it might indeed be an Act of Imprudence, though not of Injustice, for any one Parliament to settle such a Sort of Revenue for Life on the Prince: But at present, when all the World knows the utmost Extent of a Parliament's possible Duration, it seems disagreeable to Reason, and an Encroachment upon the Right of succeeding Parliaments (for the future) for any one Parliament to do that which another cannot undo, or has not Power to do in its turn.

An Old Whig is for chusing such Sort of Representatives to serve in Parliament, as have Estates in the Kingdom; and those not fleeting ones, which may be sent beyond Sea by Bills of Exchange by every Pacquet-Boat, but fix'd and permanent. To which end, every Merchant, Banker, or other money'd Man, who is ambitious of serving his Country as a Senator, should have also a competent, visible Land Estate, as a Pledge to his Electors that he intends to abide by them, and has the same Interest with theirs in the publick Taxes, Gains and Losses. I have heard and weigh'd the Arguments of those who, in Opposition to this, urged the Unfitness of such, whose Lands were engaged in Debts and Mortgages, to serve in Parliament, in comparison with the mony'd Man who had no Land: But those Arguments never convinced me.

No Man can be a sincere Lover of Liberty, that is not for increasing and communicating that Blessing to all People; and therefore the giving or restoring it not only to our Brethren of Scotland and Ireland, but even to France it self (were it in our Power) is one of the principal Articles of Whiggism. The Ease and Advantage which would be gain'd by uniting our own Three Kingdoms upon equal Terms (for upon unequal it would be no Union) is so visible, that if we had not the Example of those Masters of the World, the Romans, before our Eyes, one would wonder that our own Experience (in the Instance of uniting Wales to England) should not convince us, that although both Sides would incredibly gain by it, yet the rich and opulent Country, to which such an Addition is made, would be the greater Gainer. 'Tis so much more desirable and secure to govern by Love and common Interest, than by Force; to expect Comfort and Assistance, in Times of Danger, from our next Neighbours, than to find them at such a time a heavy Clog upon the Wheels of our Government, and be in dread lest they should take that Occasion to shake off an uneasy Yoak: or to have as much need of entertaining a standing Army against our Brethren, as against our known and inveterate Enemies; that certainly whoever can oppose so publick and apparent Good, must be esteem'd either ignorant to a strange Degree, or to have other Designs in View, which he would willingly have brought to Light.

I look upon her Majesty's asserting the Liberties and Privileges of the Free Cities in Germany, an Action which will shine in History as bright (at least) as her giving away her first Fruits and Tenths: To the Merit of which last, some have assumingly enough ascribed all the Successes she has hitherto been blessed with; as if one Set of Men were the peculiar Care of Providence and all others (even Kings and Princes) were no otherwise fit to be considered by God Almighty, or Posterity, than according to their Kindness to them. But it has been generally represented so, where Priests are the Historians. From the first Kings in the World down to these Days, many Instances might be given of very wicked Princes, who have been extravagantly commended; and many excellent ones, whose Memories lie overwhelmed with Loads of Curses and Calumny, just as they proved Favourers or Discountenancers of High-Church, without regard to their other Virtues or Vices: for High-Church is to be found in all Religions and Sects, from the Pagan down to the Presbyterian; and is equally detrimental in every one of them.

A Genuine Whig is for promoting a general Naturalization, upon the firm Belief, that whoever comes to be incorporated into us, feels his Share of all our Advantages and Disadvantages, and consequently can have no Interest but that of the Publick; to which he will always be a Support to the best of his Power, by his Person, Substance and Advice. And if it be a Truth (which few will make a Doubt of) that we are not one third Part peopled (though we are better so in Proportion than any other Part of Europe, Holland excepted) and that our Stock of Men decreases daily through our Wars, Plantations, and Sea-Voyages; that the ordinary Course of Propagation (even in Times of continued Peace and Health) could not in many Ages supply us with the Numbers we want; that the Security of Civil and Religious Liberty, and of Property, which through God's great Mercy is firmly establish'd among us, will invite new Comers as fast as we can entertain them; that most of the rest of the World groans under the Weight of Tyranny, which will cause all that have Substance, and a Sense of Honour and Liberty, to fly to Places of Shelter; which consequently would thoroughly people us with useful and profitable Hands in a few Years. What should hinder us from an Act of General Naturalization? Especially when we consider, that no private Acts of that Kind are refused; but the Expence is so great, that few attempt to procure them, and the Benefit which the Publick receives thereby is inconsiderable.

Experience has shown us the Folly and Falsity of those plausible Insinuations, that such a Naturalization would take the Bread out of Englishmen's Mouths. We are convinced, that the greater Number of Workmen of one Trade there is in any Town, the more does that Town thrive; the greater will be the Demand of the Manufacture, and the Vent to foreign Parts, and the quicker Circulation of the Coin. The Consumption of the Produce both of Land and Industry increases visibly in Towns full of People; nay, the more shall every particular industrious Person thrive in such a Place; though indeed Drones and Idlers will not find their Account, who would fain support their own and their Families superfluous Expenses at their Neighbour's Cost; who make one or two Day's Labour provide for four Days Extravagancies. And this is the common Calamity of most of our Corporation Towns, whose Inhabitants do all they can to discourage Plenty, Industry and Population; and will not admit of Strangers but upon too hard Terms, through the false Notion, that they themselves, their Children and Apprentices, have the only Right to squander their Town's Revenue, and to get, at their own Rates, all that is to be gotten within their Precincts, or in the Neighbourhood. And therefore such Towns (through the Mischief arising by Combinations and By-Laws) are at best at a Stand; very few in a thriving Condition (and those are where the By-Laws are least restrictive) but most throughout England fall to visible Decay, whilst new Villages not incorporated, or more liberal of their Privileges, grow up in their stead; till, in Process of Time, the first Sort will become almost as desolate as Old Sarum, and will as well deserve to lose their Right of sending Representatives to Parliament. For certainly a Waste or a Desert has no Right to be represented, nor by our original Constitution was ever intended to be: yet I would by no means have those Deputies lost to the Commons, but transferr'd to wiser, more industrious, and better peopled Places, worthy (through their Numbers and Wealth) of being represented.

A Whig is against the raising or keeping up a Standing Army in Time of Peace: but with this Distinction, that if at any time an Army (though even in Time of Peace) should be necessary to the Support of this very Maxim, a Whig is not for being too hasty to destroy that which is to be the Defender of his Liberty. I desire to be well understood. Suppose then, that Persons, whose known Principle and Practice it has been (during the Attempts for arbitrary Government) to plead for and promote such an Army in Time of Peace, as would be subservient to the Will of a Tyrant, and contribute towards the enslaving the Nation; should, under a legal Government (yet before the Ferment of the People was appeas'd) cry down a Standing Army in Time of Peace: I should shrewdly suspect, that the Principles of such Persons are not changed, but that either they like not the Hands that Army is in, or the Cause which it espouses; and look upon it as an Obstruction to another Sort of Army, which they should like even in Time of Peace. I say then, that although the Maxim in general be certainly true, yet a Whig (without the just Imputation of having deserted his Principles) may be for the keeping up such a Standing Army even in Time of Peace, till the Nation have recover'd its Wits again, and chuses Representatives who are against Tyranny in any Hands whatsoever; till the Enemies of our Liberties want the Power of raising another Army of quite different Sentiments: for till that time, a Whiggish Army is the Guardian of our Liberties, and secures to us the Power of disbanding its self, and prevents the raising of another of a different Kidney. As soon as this is done effectually, by my Consent, no such thing as a mercenary Soldier should subsist in England. And therefore;

The arming and training of all the Freeholders of England, as it is our undoubted ancient Constitution, and consequently our Right; so it is the Opinion of most Whigs, that it ought to be put in Practice. This would put us out of all Fear of foreign Invasions, or disappoint any such when attempted: This would soon take away the Necessity of maintaining Standing Armies of Mercenaries in Time of Peace: This would render us a hundred times more formidable to our Neighbours than we are; and secure effectually our Liberties against any King that should have a mind to invade them at home, which perhaps was the Reason some of our late Kings were so averse to it: And whereas, as the Case now stands, Ten Thousand disciplin'd Soldiers (once landed) might march without considerable Opposition from one End of England to the other; were our Militia well regulated, and Fire-Arms substituted in the Place of Bills, Bows, and Arrows (the Weapons in Use when our training Laws were in their Vigour, and for which our Laws are yet in Force) we need not fear a Hundred Thousand Enemies, were it possible to land so many among us. At every Mile's End, at every River and Pass, the Enemy would meet with fresh Armies, consisting of Men as well skill'd in military Discipline as themselves; and more resolv'd to fight, because they do it for Property: And the farther such an Enemy advanced into the Country, the stronger and more resolved he would find us; as Hannibal did the Romans, when he encamped under the Walls of Rome, even after such a Defeat as that at Cannae. And why? Because they were all train'd Soldiers, they were all Freemen that fought *pro aris & focis:*[11] and scorn'd to trust the Preservation of their Lives and Fortunes to Mercenaries or Slaves, though never so able-body'd: They thought Weapons became not the Hands of such as had nothing to lose, and upon that Account were unfit Defenders of their Masters Properties; so that they never tried the Experiment but in the utmost Extremity.

That this is not only practicable but easy, the modern Examples of the

[11.] Literally translated as "for our altars and hearths," but more commonly as "for God and country."

Swissers and Swedes is an undeniable Indication. Englishmen have as much Courage, as great Strength of Body, and Capacity of Mind, as any People in the Universe: And if our late Monarchs had the enervating their free Subjects in View, that they might give a Reputation to Mercenaries, who depended only on the Prince for their Pay (as 'tis plain they had) I know no Reason why their Example should be followed in the Days of Liberty, when there is no such Prospect. The Preservation of the Game is but a very slender Pretence for omitting it. I hope no wise Man will put a Hare or a Partridge in Balance with the Safety and Liberties of Englishmen; though after all, 'tis well known to Sportsmen, that Dogs, Snares, Nets, and such silent Methods as are daily put in Practice, destroy the Game ten times more than shooting with Guns.

If the restoring us to our Old Constitution in this Instance were ever necessary, 'tis more eminently so at this time, when our next Neighbours of Scotland are by Law armed just in the manner we desire to be, and the Union between both Kingdoms not perfected. For the Militia, upon the Foot it now stands, will be of little Use to us: 'tis generally compos'd of Servants, and those not always the same, consequently not well train'd; rather such as wink with both Eyes at their own firing a Musket, and scarce know how to keep it clean, or to charge it aright. It consists of People whose Reputation (especially the Officers) has been industriously diminished, and their Persons, as well as their Employment, rendered contemptible on purpose to enhance the Value of those that serve for Pay; insomuch that few Gentlemen of Quality will now a-days debase themselves so much, as to accept of a Company, or a Regiment in the Militia. But for all this, I can never be persuaded that a Red Coat, and Three Pence a Day, infuses more Courage into the poor Swaggering Idler, than the having a Wife and Children, and an Estate to fight for, with good wholesome Fare in his Kitchen, would into a Free-born Subject, provided the Freeman were as well armed and trained as the Mercenary.

I would not have the Officers and Soldiers of our most Brave and Honest Army to mistake me. I am not arguing against them; for I am convinced, as long as there is Work to do abroad, 'tis they (and not our home dwelling Freeholders) are most proper for it. Our War must now be an Offensive War; and what I am pleading for, concerns only the bare Defensive Part. Most of our present Generals and Officers are fill'd with the true Sprit of Liberty (a most rare thing) which demonstrates the Felicity of her Majesty's Reign, and her standing upon a true Bottom, beyond any other Instance that can be given; insomuch, that considering how great and happy we have been under the Government of Queens, I have sometimes doubted, whether an Anti-*Salick Law* would be to our Disadvantage.

Most of these Officers do expect, nay (so true do I take them to be to their Country's Interest) do wish, whenever it shall please God to send us such a Peace as may be relied upon both at home and abroad, to return to the State of peaceable Citizens again; but 'tis fit they should do so, with such ample Rewards for their Blood and Labours, as shall entirely satisfy them. And when they, or the Survivors of them, shall return full of Honour and Scars home to their Relations, after the Fatigues of so glorious a Service to their Country are ended; 'tis their Country's Duty to make them easy, without laying a Necessity upon them of striving for the Continuance of an Army to avoid starving. The Romans used to content them by a Distribution of their Enemies Lands; and I think their Example so good in every thing, that we could hardly propose a better. Oliver Cromwell did the like in Ireland, to which we owe that Kingdom's being a Protestant Kingdom at this Day, and its continuing subject to the Crown of England; but if it be too late to think of this Method now, some other must be found out by the Wisdom of Parliament, which shall fully answer the End.

These Officers and Soldiers thus settled and reduced to a Civil State, would, in a great measure, compose that invincible Militia I am now forecasting; and by reason of their Skill in military Affairs, would deserve the principal Posts and Commands in their respective Counties: With this advantageous Change of their Condition, that whereas formerly they fought for their Country only as Soldiers of Fortune, now they should defend it as wise and valiant Citizens, as Proprietors of the Estates they fight for; and this will gain them the entire Trust and Confidence of all the good People of England, who, whenever they come to know their own Minds, do heartily hate Slavery. The Manner and Times of assembling, with several other necessary Regulations, are only proper for the Legislative to fix and determine.

A right Whig lays no Stress upon the Illegitimacy of the pretended Prince of Wales; he goes upon another Principle than they, who carry the Right of Succession so far, as (upon that Score), to undo all Mankind. He thinks no Prince fit to govern, whose Principle it must be to ruin the Constitution, as soon as he can acquire unjust Power to do so. He judges it Nonsense for one to be the Head of a Church, or Defender of a Faith, who thinks himself bound in Duty to overthrow it. He never endeavours to justify his taking the Oaths to this Government, or to quiet his Conscience, by supposing the young Gentleman at St. Germains unlawfully begotten; since, 'tis certain, that according to our Law he cannot be looked upon as such. He cannot satisfy himself with any of the foolish Distinctions trump'd up of late Years to reconcile base Interest with a Show of Religion; but deals upon the Square, and plainly owns to the World, that he is not influenc'd by any particular Spleen: but that the Exercise of an Arbitrary, Illegal Power in the Nation, so as to undermine the Constitution, would incapacitate either King James, King William, or any other, from being his King, whenever the Publick has a Power to hinder it.

As a necessary Consequence of this Opinion, a Whig must be against punishing the Iniquity of the Fathers upon the Children, as we do (not only to the Third and Fourth Generation, but) for ever: since our gracious God has declared, that he will no more pursue such severe Methods in his Justice, but that the Soul that sinneth it shall die. 'Tis very unreasonable, that frail Man, who has so often need of Mercy, should pretend to exercise higher Severities upon his Fellow-Creatures, than that Fountain of Justice on his most wicked revolting Slaves. To corrupt the Blood of a whole Family, and send all the Offspring a begging after the Father's Head is taken off, seems a strange Piece of Severity, fit to be redressed in Parliament; especially when we come to consider, for what Crime this has been commonly done. When Subjects take Arms against their Prince, if their Attempt succeeds, 'tis a Revolution; if not, 'tis call'd a Rebellion: 'tis seldom consider'd, whether the first Motives be just or unjust. Now is it not enough, in such Cases, for the prevailing Party to hang or behead the Offenders, if they can catch them, without extending the Punishment to innocent Persons for all Generations to come?

The Sense of this made the late Bill of Treasons (though it reach'd not so far as many would have had it) a Favourite of the Old Whigs; they thought it a very desirable one whenever it could be compass'd, and perhaps if not at that very Juncture, would not have been obtained all: 'twas necessary for Two different Sorts of People to unite in this, in order for a Majority, whose Weight should be sufficient to enforce it. And I think some Whigs were very unjustly reproach'd by their Brethren, as if by voting for this Bill, they wilfully exposed the late King's Person to the wicked Designs of his Enemies.

Lastly, The supporting of Parliamentary Credit, promoting of all publick Buildings and Highways, the making all Rivers Navigable that are capable of it, employing the Poor, suppressing Idlers, restraining Monopolies upon Trade, maintaining the liberty of the Press, the just paying and encouraging of all in the publick Service, especially that best and usefullest Sort of People the Seamen: These (joined to a firm Opinion, that we ought not to hearken to any Terms of Peace with the French King, till it be quite out of his Power to hurt us, but rather to dye in Defence of our own and the Liberties of Europe) are all of them Articles of my Whiggish Belief, and I hope none of them are heterodox. And if all these together amount to a Commonwealthsman, I shall never be asham'd of the Name, though given with a Design of fixing a Reproach upon me, and such as think as I do.[12]

Many People complain of the Poverty of the Nation, and the Weight of the Taxes. Some do this without any ill Design, but others hope thereby to become popular; and at the same time to enforce a Peace with France, before that Kingdom be reduced to too low a Pitch: fearing, lest that King should be disabled to accomplish their Scheme of bringing in the Pretender, and assisting him.

Now although 'tis acknowledg'd, that the Taxes lye very heavy, and Money grows scarce; yet let the Importance of our War be considered, together with the Obstinacy, Perfidy, and Strength of our Enemy, can we possibly carry on such a diffusive War without Money in Proportion?

[12.] Both Ker's extract and the 1775 edition of *The Principles of a Real Whig* end here.

Are the Queen's Subjects more burden'd to maintain the publick Liberty, than the French King's are to confirm their own Slavery? Not so much by three Parts in four, God be prais'd: Besides, no true Englishman will grudge to pay Taxes whilst he has a Penny in his Purse, as long as he sees the Publick Money well laid out for the great Ends for which 'tis given. And to the Honour of the Queen and her Ministers it may be justly said, That since England was a Nation, never was the publick Money more frugally managed, or more fitly apply'd. This is a further Mortification to those Gentlemen, who have Designs in View which they dare not own: For whatever may be, the plausible and specious Reasons they give in publick, when they exclaim against the Ministry; the hidden and true one is, that through the present prudent Administration, their so hopefully-laid Project is in Danger of being blown quite up; and they begin to despair that they shall bring in King James the Third by the Means of Queen Anne, as I verily believe they once had the Vanity to imagine.

INDEX OF THE CHAPTERS

A SHORT EXTRACT OF THE LIFE OF FRANCIS HOTOMAN,

Taken out of Monsieur Bayle's Historical Dictionary *and other Authors.*

Francis Hotoman (one of the most learned Lawyers of that Age) was Born at Paris the 23rd of August, 1524. His Family was an Ancient and Noble one, originally of Breslaw, the Capital of Silesia. Lambert Hotoman, his Grandfather, bore Arms in the Service of *Lewis* the 11th of France, and married a rich Heiress at Paris, by whom he had 18 Children; the Eldest of which (John Hotoman) had so plentiful an Estate, that he laid down the Ransom-Money for King Francis the First, taken at the Battle of Pavia: *Summo galliae bono, summâ cum suâ laude,*[13] says Neveletus.

Peter Hotoman his 18th Child, and Master of the Waters and Forests[14] of France (afterwards a Counsellor in the Parliament of Paris) was Father to Francis, the Author of this Book. He sent his Son, at 15 Years of Age,

[13.] "For the greatest benefit of France, with its highest thanks." The source is Neveletus's *Life of Hotman* cited in Note 3 to Remark [A] in Pierre Bayle's entry on Hotman. Monsieur Bayle, *An Historical and Critical Dictionary,* translated into English, . . . (London: Harper, Brown, et al., 1710), pp. 1716–21.

[14.] Note in margin: "Maistre des Eaux & Forrests," i.e., Master of Forests and Waters.

to Orleans to study the Common Law; which he did with so great Applause, that at Three Years End he merited the Degree of Doctor. His Father designing to surrender to him his Place of Counsellor of Parliament, sent for him home: But the young Gentleman was soon tired with the Chicane of the Bar, and plung'd himself deep in the Studies of Humanity and the Roman Laws;[15] for which he had a wonderful Inclination. He happen'd to be a frequent Spectator of the Protestants Sufferings, who, about that Time, had their Tongues cut out, were otherwise tormented, and burnt for their Religion. This made him curious to dive into those Opinions, which inspired so much Constancy, Resignation and Contempt of Death; which brought him by degrees to a liking of them, so that he turn'd Protestant. And this put him in Disgrace with his Father, who thereupon disinherited him; which forced him at last to quit France, and to retire to Lausanne in Swisserland by Calvin's and Beza's Advice; where his great Merit and Piety promoted him to the Humanity-Professor's Chair, which he accepted of for a Livelihood, having no Subsistence from his Father. There he married a young French Lady, who had fled her Country upon the Score of Religion: He afterwards remov'd to Strasburg, where he also had a Professor's Chair. The Fame of his great Worth was so blown about, that he was invited by all the great Princes to their several Countries, particularly by the Landgrave of Hesse, the Duke of Prussia, and the King of Navarre; and he actually went to this last about the Beginning of the Troubles. Twice he was sent as Ambassador from the Princes of the Blood of France, and the Queen-Mother, to demand Assistance of the Emperor Ferdinand: The Speech that he made at the Diet of Frankfort is still extant. Afterwards he returned to Strasburg; but Jean de Monluc, the Bishop of Valence, over-persuaded him to accept of the Professorship of Civil Law at Valence; of which he acquitted himself so well, that he very much heighten'd the Reputation of that University. Here he received two Invitations from Margaret Duchess of Berry, and Sister to Henry the Second of France, and accepted a Professor's Chair at Bourges; but continued in it no longer than five Months, by reason of the intervening Troubles. Afterwards he returned to it, and was there at the time of

15. Note in margin: "Les belles lettres."

the great Parisian Massacre, having much-a-do to escape with his Life; but having once got out of France (with a firm Resolution never to return thither again) he took Sanctuary in the House of Calvin at Geneva, and publish'd Books against the Persecution, so full of Spirit and good Reasoning, that the Heads of the contrary Party made him great Offers in case he would forbear Writing against them; but he refused them all, and said, The Truth should never be betray'd or forsaken by him. Neveletus says, "That his Reply to those that would have tempted him, was this: *Nunquam sibi propugnatam causam quae iniqua esset: Nunquam quae jure & legibus niteretur desertam praemiorum spe vel metu periculi.*"[16] He afterwards went to Basel in Swisserland, and from thence (being driven away by the Plague) to Mountbelliard, where he buried his Wife. He returned then to Basel (after having refused a Professor's Chair at Leyden) and there he died of a Dropsy in the 65th Year of his Age, the 12th of February, 1590. He writ a great many learned Books, which were all of them in great Esteem; and among them an excellent Book *de Consolatione.* His *Francogallia* was his own Favourite; though blamed by several others, who were of the contrary Opinion: Yet even these who wrote against him do unanimously agree, that he had a World of Learning, and a profound Erudition. He had a thorough Knowledge of the Civil Law, which he managed with all the Eloquence imaginable; and was, without dispute, one of the ablest Civilians that France had ever produced: This is Thuanus and Barthius's Testimony of him. Mr. Bayle indeed passes his Censure of this Work in the Text of his Dictionary, in these Words: *"Sa Francogallia dont il faisoit grand etat est celuy de tous ses ecrits que l'on aprouve le moins:*[17] —and in his Commentary adds, *C'est un Ouvrage recommendable du costè de l'Erudition; mais tres indigne d'un jurisconsulte Francois, si l'on en croit mesme plusieurs Protestants."*[18] I would not do any Injury to so great a Man as Monsieur

[16.] This passage is taken from Bayle's entry Remark [E]. Translation: "That he never had defended an unjust cause, and never had deserted a just and honorable one, either for hope of rewards or fear of danger." Bayle, *An Historical and Critical Dictionary.*

[17.] From the main text of Bayle's entry: "Of all his writings, his *Francogallia,* which he some much valued, is least approved." Bayle, *An Historical and Critical Dictionary.*

[18.] From Remark [E]: "It is a commendable work in point of learning, but very

Bayle; but every one that is acquainted with his Character, knows that he is more a Friend to Tyranny and *Tyrants,* than seems to be consistent with so free a Spirit. He has been extremely ill used, which sowres him to such a degree, that it even perverts his Judgment in some measure; and he seems resolved to be against Monsieur Jurieu, and that Party, in every thing, right or wrong. Whoever reads his Works, may trace throughout all Parts of them this Disposition of Mind, and see what sticks most at his Heart. So that he not only loses no Occasion, but often forces one where it seems improper and unreasonable, to vent his Resentments upon his Enemies; who surely did themselves a great deal more wrong in making him so, than they did him. 'Tis too true, that they did all they could to starve him; and this great Man was forced to write in haste for Bread; which has been the Cause that some of his Works are shorter than he designed them; and consequently, that the World is deprived of so much Benefit, as otherwise it might have reap'd from his prodigious Learning, and Force of Judgment. One may see by the first Volume of his Dictionary, which goes through but two Letters of the Alphabet, that he forecasted to make that Work three times as large as it is, could he have waited for the Printer's Money so long as was requisite to the finishing it according to his first Design. Thus much I thought fit to say, in order to abate the Edge of what he seems to speak hardly of the *Francogallia;* though in several other Places he makes my Author amends: And one may without scruple believe him, when he commends a Man, whose Opinion he condemns. For this is the Character he gives of this Work: "*Cest au fond un bel Ouvrage, bien ecrit, & bien rempli d'erudition: Et d'autant plus incommode au partie contraire que l'Auteur se contente de citer des faits.*"[19] Can any thing in the World be a greater Commendation of a Work of this Nature, than to say it contains only pure Matter of Fact? Now if this be so, Monsieur Bayle would do well to tell us what he means by those Words, *Tres indigne*

---

unworthy of a French civilian, if we believe even many Protestants concerning it." Bayle, *An Historical and Critical Dictionary.*

[19.] Cited from Bayle, Remark [I]: "That book of Hotman is at the bottom a fine piece, well written. And full of learning, and so much more vexatious to the contrary party, because the author contents himself to cite matters of fact." Bayle, *An Historical and Critical Dictionary.*

d'un jurisconsulte Francois. Whether a French Civilian be debarred telling of Truth (when that Truth exposes Tyranny) more than a Civilian of any other Nation? This agrees, in some measure, with Monsieur Teissier's Judgment of the *Francogallia*, and shews, that Monsieur Bayle, and Monsieur Teissier and Bongars, were *Bons Francois* in one and the same Sense. "*Son Livre intitulè, Francogallia, luy attira AVEC RAISON* (and this he puts in great Letters) *les blame des bons Francois*.[20] For (says he) therein he endeavours to prove, That France, the most flourishing Kingdom in Christendom, is not successive, like the Estates of particular Persons; but that anciently the *Kings* came to the Crown by the Choice and Suffrages of the Nobility and People; insomuch, that as in former Times the Power and Authority of Electing their *Kings* belonged to the Estates of the Kingdom, so likewise did the Right of Deposing their Princes from their Government. And hereupon he quotes the Examples of Philip de Valois, of King John, *Charles* the Fifth, and *Charles* the Sixth, and *Lewis* the Eleventh: But what he principally insists on, is to show, That as from Times Immemorial, the French judg'd Women incapable of Governing; so likewise ought they to be debarred from all Administration of the Publick Affairs." This is Mr. Bayle's Quotation of Teissier, by which it appears how far Hotman ought to be blamed by all true Frenchmen, *AVEC RAISON.* But provided that Hotman proves irrefragably all that he says (as not only Monsieur Bayle himself, but every body else that writes of him allows) I think it will be a hard matter to persuade a disinterest'd Person, or any other but a *bon Francois,* (which, in good English, is a Lover of his Chains) that here is any just Reason shewn why Hotman should be blam'd.

Monsieur Teissier, although very much prejudiced against him, was (as one may see by the Tenor of the above Quotation, and his leaving it thus uncommented on) in his Heart convinc'd of the Truth of it; but no *bon Francois* dares own so much. He was a little too careless when he wrote against Hotman, mistaking one of his Books for another; viz. his Commentary *ad titulum institutionum de Actionibus,* for his little Book *de gradi-*

[20.] Cited from Bayle, Remark [D]: "His book intituled *Francogallia,* drew upon him, WITH REASON, the censure of true French men." Bayle, *An Historical and Critical Dictionary.*

bus cognationis; both extremely esteemed by all learned Men, especially the first: Of which Monsieur Bayle gives this Testimony: *"La beauté du Stile, & la connoissance des antiquités Romaines eclatoient dans cet Ouvrage, & le firent fort estimer."*[21] Thuanus, that celebrated disinterest'd Historian, gives this Character in general of his Writings. "He composed (says he) several Works very profitable towards the explaining of the Civil Law, Antiquity, and all Sorts of fine Literature; which have been collected and publish'd by James Lectius, a famous Lawyer, after they had been review'd and corrected by the Author. Barthius says, that he excelled in the Knowledge of the Civil Law, and of all genteel Learning.[22] *'Ceux la mesmes qui ont ecrits contre luy* (says Neveletus) *tombent d'accord quil avoit beaucoup de lecture & une profonde Erudition.'"*[23] The Author of the *Monitoriale adversus Italogalliam,* which some take to be Hotoman himself, has this Passage relating to the *Francogallia: "Quomodo potest aliquis ei succensere qui est tantum relator & narrator facti? Francogallista enim tantum narrationi & relationi simplici vacat, quod si aliena dicta delerentur, charta remaneret alba."*[24] It was objected to him, that he unawares furnish'd the Duke of Guise and the League at Paris with Arguments to make good their Attempts against their *Kings.* This cannot be deny'd; but at the same time it cannot be imputed to Hotoman as any Crime: Texts of Scripture themselves have been made use of for different Purposes, according to the Passion or the Interests of Parties. Arguments do not lose their native Force for being wrong apply'd: If the Three Estates of France had such a fundamental Power lodg'd in them; who can help it, if the Writers for the League made use of Hotoman's Arguments to support a wrong Cause? And this may suffice to remove this Imputation from his Memory. He was a Man of a very

[21.] Remark [B]: "The beauty of the style, and the knowledge of the Roman antiquities, that shined in that piece, gave him a great reputation." Bayle, *An Historical and Critical Dictionary.*

22. Note in margin: "Belles literature."

[23.] "Even those that wrote against him concurred with each other that he was well read and had a deep learning."

[24.] Remark [I]: "How can anybody be in a passion with a person who is only a relater of a fact? For the writer of that book doth nothing but relate, and if his quotations from other writers were taken away nothing would be left but clean paper." Bayle, *An Historical and Critical Dictionary.*

handsome Person and Shape, tall and comely; his Eyes were blewish, his Nose long, and his Countenance venerable: He joined a most exemplary Piety and Probity to an eminent Degree of Knowledge and Learning. No Day pass'd over his Head, wherein he employ'd not several Hours in the Exercise of Prayer, and reading of the Scriptures. He would never permit his Picture to be drawn, though much intreated by his Friends; however (when he was at his last Gasp, and could not hinder it) they got a Painter to his Bed's-side, who took his Likeness as well as 'twas possible at such a time. Basilius Amerbachius assisted him during his last Sickness, and James Grinaeus made his Funeral-Sermon. He left two Sons behind him, John and Daniel; besides a great Reputation, and Desire of him, not only among his Friends and Acquaintance, but all the Men of Learning and Probity all over Europe.

Explication of the Roman Names
mention'd by Hotoman

Aedui,	People of Chalons and Nevers,
Agrippina, Colonia,	Cologn.
Alsaciones,	People of Alsace.
Ambiani,	People of Amiens.
Aquisgranum	Aix la Chapelle
Aquitani,	People of Guienne and Gascogn.
Armorica,	Bretagne and Normandy.
Arremi,	People of Auvergne and Bourbonnois.
Artebates,	People of Artois.
Attuarii,	People of Aire in Gascogn.
Augustodunum	Autun.
Aureliani,	People of Orleans.
Bibracte,	Bavray, in the Diocese of Rheims.
Bigargium,	Bigorre forté.
Bituriges,	People of Bourges.
Caninefates,	People on the Sea-Coast, between the Elb and the Rhine.
Carisiacum,	Crecy.
Carnutes,	People of Chartres and Orleans.
Ceutones,	People of Tarentaise in Savoy.
Ceutrones,	People of Liege.
Condrusii,	People of the Condros in Germany.
Dusiacum,	non liquet [Not evident].[25]
Eburones,	People of the Diocese of Liege.
Gorduni,	People about Ghent and Courtray.
Grudii,	People of Lovain.
Hetrusci,	People of Tuscany.

[25.] "Not evident" is a translation of *non liquet*. In other words, Hotman cannot identify the modern place-name.

Laudunum,	Laon.
Lentiates,	People about Lens.
Leuci,	People of Metz, Toul and Verdun.
Levaci,	People of Hainault.
Lexovium,	Lisieux.
Lingones,	People of Langres.
Lugdunum,	Lyons.
Lutetia,	Paris.
Marsua,	non liquet [Not evident].
Massilia,	Marseilles.
Nervii,	People of Hainault and Cambray.
Nitiobriges,	People of Agenois.
Novemopulonia,	Gascony.
Noviomagum,	Nimeguen.
Pannonia,	Hungary.
Pleumosii,	People of Tournay and Lisle.
Rhaetia,	Swisserland.
Rhemi,	People of Rheims.
Senones,	People of Sens and Auxerre.
Sequana,	the River Seine.
Sequani,	People of Franche Comté.
Suessiones,	People of Soissons.
Tolbiacum,	non liquet [Not evident].
Toxandri,	People of Zealand.
Trecassini,	People of Tricasses in Champagne.
Treviri,	People of Triers, and Part of Luxemburg.
Ulbanesses,	non liquet [Not evident].
Veneti,	People of Vannes.
Vesontini,	People of Besançon,
Witmarium,	non liquet [Not evident].

THE AUTHOR'S PREFACE

To the most Illustrious and Potent Prince FREDERICK, Count Palatine of the Rhine, Duke of Bavaria, *etc.* First Elector of the Roman Empire, His most Gracious Lord, Francis Hotoman, wishes all Health and Prosperity.

'Tis an old Saying, of which Teucer the Son of Telamon is the supposed Author, and which has been approved of these many Ages, "A Man's Country is, where-ever he lives at Ease."[26] For to bear even Banishment it self with an unconcern'd Temper of Mind like other Misfortunes and Inconveniences, and to despise the Injuries of an ungrateful Country, which uses one more like a Stepmother than a true Mother, seems to be the Indication of a great Soul. But I am of a quite different Opinion: For if it be a great Crime, and almost an Impiety not to live under and suffer patiently the Humours and harsh Usage of our Natural Parents; 'tis sure a much greater, not to endure those of our COUNTRY, which wise Men have unanimously preferr'd to their Parents. 'Tis indeed the Property of a wary self-interested Man, to measure his Kindness for his Country by his own particular Advantages: But such a sort of Carelessness and Indifferency seems a Part of that Barbarity which was attributed to the Cynicks and

[26.] Note in margin: "Patria est ubicunq: est bene." GS *Franc.* identify it as Cicero, *Tusculan Disputations,* bk. 5, 37 (Loeb 532–33).

Epicureans; whence that detestable Saying proceeded; "When I am dead, let the whole World be a Fire." Which is not unlike the Old Tyrannical Axiom; "Let my Friends perish, so my Enemies fall along with them."[27] But in gentle Dispositions, there is a certain inbred Love of their Country, which they can no more divest themselves of, than of Humanity it self. Such a Love as Homer describes in Ulysses, who preferred Ithaca, though no better than a Bird's Nest fix'd to a craggy Rock in the Sea, to all the Delights of the Kingdom which Calypso offer'd him.[28] *Nescio quâ natale Solum dulcedine cunctos Ducit, & immemores non sinit esse sui:*[29] Was very truly said by the Ancient Poet; When we think of that Air we first suck'd in, that Earth we first trod on, those Relations, Neighbours and Acquaintance to whose Conversation we have been accustomed.

But a Man may sometimes say, My Country is grown mad or foolish, (as Plato said of his) sometimes that it rages and cruelly tears out its own Bowels. We are to take care in the first Place, that we do not ascribe other Folks Faults to our innocent Country. There have been many cruel *Tyrants* in Rome and in other Places; these not only tormented innocent good Men, but even the best deserving Citizens, with all manner of Severities: Does it therefore follow, that the Madness of these *Tyrants* must be imputed to their Country? The Cruelty of the Emperor Macrinus is particularly memorable; who as *Julius Capitolinus* writes, was nicknamed *Macellinus*, because his House was stained with the Blood of Men, as a Shambles is with that of Beasts.[30] Many such others are mention'd by Historians, who for the like Cruelty (as the same *Capitolinus* tells us) were stil'd, one *Cyclops*, another *Busiris*, a 3rd *Sciron*, a 4th *Tryphon*, a 5th *Gyges*. These were firmly persuaded, that Kingdoms and Empires could not be secur'd without Cruelty: Would it be therefore reasonable, that good Patriots should lay aside all Care and Solicitude for their Country? Certainly they ought rather to succour her, when like a miserable op-

[27.] GS *Franc.* (p. 136) identify this as a quote within Suetonius, *Nero* (Loeb 2:154).

[28.] Homer, *Odyssey*, bk. 5.

[29.] "By what sweet charm I know not the native land draws all men nor allows them to forget." Ovid, *Ex Ponto.* I.3. 35–36 (Loeb 283).

[30.] The account is in *Scriptores Historiae Augustae*, s.v. "Macrinus" (Loeb 2:76).

pressed Mother, she implores her Children's Help, and to seek all proper Remedies for the Mischiefs that afflict her.

But how fortunate are those Countries that have good and mild Princes! how happy are those Subjects, who, through the Benignity of their Rulers may quietly grow old on their Paternal Seats, in the sweet Society of their Wives and Children! For very often it happens, that the Remedies which are made use of prove worse than the Evils themselves.

'Tis now, most Illustrious Prince, about Sixteen Years since God Almighty has committed to your Rule and Government a considerable Part of *Germany* situate on the Rhine. During which time, 'tis scarce conceivable what a general Tranquillity, what a Calm (as in a smooth Sea) has reigned in the whole Palatinate; how peaceable and quiet all things have continued: How piously and religiously they have been governed: Go on most Gracious Prince in the same Meekness of Spirit, which I to the utmost of my Power must always extol. Proceed in the same Course of gentle and peaceable Virtue; *Macte Virtute;*[31] not in the Sense which Seneca tells us the Romans used this Exclamation in, to salute their Generals when they return'd all stain'd with Gore Blood from the Field of Battle, who were rather true Macellinus's: But do you proceed in that Moderation of Mind, Clemency, Piety, Justice, Affability, which have occasion'd the Tranquillity of your Territories. And because the present Condition of your *Germany* is such as we see it, Men now-a-days run away from Countries infested with Plunderers and Oppressors, to take Sanctuary in those that are quiet and peaceable; as Mariners, who undertake a Voyage, forecast to avoid Streights, *etc.* and Rocky Seas, and chuse to sail a calm and open Course.

There was indeed a Time, when young Gentlemen, desirous of Improvement, flock'd from all Parts to the Schools and Academies of our *Francogallia,* as to the publick Marts of good Literature. Now they dread them as Men do Seas infested with Pyrates, and detest their Tyrannous Barbarity. The Remembrance of this wounds me to the very Soul; when I consider my unfortunate miserable Country has been for almost twelve Years, burning in the Flames of Civil War. But much more am I griev'd,

[31.] Translation: "Increase in excellence."

when I reflect that so many have not only been idle Spectators of these dreadful Fires (as Nero was of flaming Rome) but have endeavour'd by their wicked Speeches and Libels to blow the Bellows, whilst few or none have contributed their Assistance towards the extinguishing them.

I am not ignorant how mean and inconsiderable a Man I am; nevertheless as in a general Conflagration every Man's Help is acceptable, who is able to fling on but a Bucket of Water, so I hope the Endeavours of any Person that offers at a Remedy will be well taken by every Lover of his Country. Being very intent for several Months past on the Thoughts of these great Calamities, I have perused all the old French and German Historians that treat of our *Francogallia,* and collected out of their Works a true State of our *Commonwealth;* in the Condition (wherein they agree) it flourished for above a Thousand Years. And indeed the great Wisdom of our Ancestors in the first framing of our Constitution, is almost incredible; so that I no longer doubted, that the most certain Remedy for so great Evils must be deduced from their Maxims.

For as I more attentively enquired into the Source of these Calamities, it seemed to me, that even as human Bodies decay and perish, either by some outward Violence, or some inward Corruption of Humours, or lastly, through Old Age: so *Commonwealths* are brought to their Period, sometimes by Foreign Force, sometimes by Civil Dissentions, at other Times by being worn out and neglected. Now though the Misfortunes that have befallen our *Commonwealth* are commonly attributed to our Civil Dissentions, I found, upon Enquiry, these are not so properly to be called the Cause as the Beginning of our Mischiefs. And Polybius, that grave judicious Historian, teaches us, in the first place, to distinguish the Beginning from the Cause of any Accident.[32] Now I affirm the Cause to have been that great Blow which our Constitution received about 100 Years ago from that Prince,[33] who ('tis manifest) first of all broke in upon the noble and solid Institutions of our Ancestors. And as our natural Bodies when put out of joint by Violence, can never be recover'd but by replacing and restoring every Member to its true Position; so neither can we reasonably

[32.] GS *Franc.* identify the passage from Polybius as *Histories,* bk. 6, chap. 5.
33. Note in margin: "Lewis the XI."

hope our *Commonwealth* should be restor'd to Health, till through Divine Assistance it shall be put into its true and natural State again.

And because your Highness has always approv'd your self a true Friend to our Country; I thought it my Duty to inscribe, or, as it were, to consecrate this Abstract of our History to your Patronage. That being guarded by so powerful a Protection, it might with greater Authority and Safety come abroad in the World. Farewell, most Illustrious Prince; May the great God Almighty for ever bless and prosper your most noble Family.

Your Highness's most Obedient, Francis Hotoman.
12 Kal. Sep. 1574.

CHAPTER I

The State of *Gaul*, before it was reduced into a Province by the Romans

My Design being to give an Account of the Laws and Ordinances of our *Francogallia,* as far as it may tend to the Service of our *Commonwealth,* in its present Circumstances; I think it proper, in the first place, to set forth the State of *Gaul,* before it was reduced into the Form of a Province by the Romans: For what *Caesar, Polybius, Strabo, Ammianus,* and other Writers have told us concerning the Origin, Antiquity & Valour of that People, the Nature and Situation of their Country, and their private Customs, is sufficiently known to all Men, though but indifferently learned.

We are therefore to understand, that the State of *Gaul* was such at that time, that neither was the whole under the Government of a single Person: Nor were the particular *Commonwealths*[34] under the Dominion of the Populace, or the Nobles only; but all *Gaul* was so divided into *Commonwealths,* that the most Part were govern'd by the Advice of the Nobles; and these were called Free; the rest had *Kings:* But every one of them

---

[34.] Comment in margin added by Molesworth (not in Hotman's original): "*Civitas,* a Commonwealth."

agreed in this *Institute,* that at a certain Time of the Year a *publick Council* of the whole Nation should be held; in which *Council,* whatever seem'd to relate to the whole Body of the *Commonwealth,* was appointed and established. *Cornelius Tacitus,* in his 3d Book, reckons Sixty-four *Civitates;* by which is meant (as *Caesar* explains it) so many Regions or Districts; in each of which, not only the same Language, Manners and Laws, but also the same Magistrates were made use of. Such, in many Places of his History, he principally mentions the Cities of the Aedui, the *Rhemi* and *Arverni* to have been. And therefore *Dumnorix* the Aeduan, when *Caesar* sent to have him slain, "began to resist, and to defend himself, and to implore the Assistance of his Fellow Citizens; often crying out, That he was a Freeman, and Member of a Free *Commonwealth*," lib. 5. cap. 3.[35] To the like purpose *Strabo* writes in his Fourth Book "Most of their *Commonwealths* (says he) were govern'd by the Advice of the Nobles: but every Year they anciently chose a Magistrate; as also the People chose a General to manage their Wars."[36] The like *Caesar,* lib. 6. cap. 4.[37] writes in these Words: "Those *Commonwealths* which are esteem'd to be under the best Administration, have made a Law, that if any Man chance to hear a Rumour or Report abroad among the Bordering People, which concerned the *Commonwealth,* he ought to inform the Magistrates of it, and communicate it to no body else. The Magistrates conceal what they think proper, and acquaint the Multitude with the rest: For of Matters relating to the Community, it was not permitted to any Person to talk or discourse, but in Council." Now concerning this Common Council of the whole Nation, we shall quote these few Passages out of *Caesar.* "They demanded (says he) lib. 1. cap. 12.[38] a General Council of all *Gallia* to be summon'd; and that this might be done by *Caesar*'s Consent." Also, lib. 7. cap. 12.[39] "a Council of all *Gallia* was summon'd to meet at *Bibracte;* and there was a vast Con-

[35.] GS *Franc.* identify the reference as Caesar, *Bellum Gallicum,* bk. 5, chap. 7 (Loeb 242).

[36.] GS *Franc.* identify the Greek reproduced in the margin as a citation from Strabo, *Geography,* bk. 4, 4.3 (Loeb 2:242).

[37.] GS *Franc.* (p. 148) identify it as Caesar, *Bellum Gallicum,* bk. 6, chap. 21; in fact, it is bk. 6, chap. 20 (Loeb 344).

[38.] GS *Franc.* identify it as *Bellum Gallicum,* bk. 1, chap. 31 (Loeb 44).

[39.] GS *Franc.* identify it as *Bellum Gallicum,* bk. 7, chap. 63 (Loeb 468).

course from all Parts to that Town." And lib. 6. cap. 1.[40] "*Caesar* having summon'd the Council of *Gaul* to meet early in the Spring, as he had before determin'd: Finding that the *Senones, Carnutes* and *Treviri* came not when all the rest came, he adjourned the Council to Paris." And, lib. 7. cap. 6.[41] speaking of Vercingetorix, "He promis'd himself, that he should be able by his Diligence to unite such *Commonwealths* to him as dissented from the rest of the Cities of *Gaul,* and to form a General Council of all *Gallia;* the Power of which, the whole World should not be able to withstand."

Now concerning the *Kings* which ruled over certain Cities in *Gallia,* the same Author makes mention of them in very many Places: out of which this is particularly worthy our Observation; That it was the Romans' Custom to caress all those *Reguli* whom they found proper for their turns: That is, such as were busy Men, apt to embroil Affairs, and to sow Dissentions or Animosities between the several *Commonwealths.* These they joined with in Friendship and Society, and by most honourable publick Decrees called them their Friends and Confederates: And many of these *Kings* purchased at a great Expence this Verbal Honour from the Chief Men of Rome. Now the *Gauls* called such, *Reges,* or rather *Reguli,* which were chosen, not for a certain Term, (as the Magistrates of the Free Cities were) but for their Lives; though their Territories were never so small and inconsiderable: And these, when Customs came to be changed by Time, were afterwards called by the Names of *Dukes, Earls,* and *Marquisses.*

Of the *Commonwealths* or *Cities,* some were much more potent than others; and upon these the lesser *Commonwealths* depended; these they put themselves under for Protection: Such weak Cities *Caesar* sometimes calls the Tributaries and Subjects of the former; but, for the most part he says, they were in Confederacy with them. *Livius* writes, lib. 5. "that when *Tarquinius Priscus* reigned in Rome, the *Bituriges* had the principal Authority among the *Celtae,* and gave a King to them." When *Caesar* first enter'd *Gaul,* A.U.C.[42] 695. he found it "divided into Two Factions; the *Aedui* were at the Head of the one, the *Arverni* of the other, who many

[40.] GS *Franc.* identify it as *Bellum Gallicum,* bk. 6, chap. 3 (Loeb 318).
[41.] GS *Franc.* identify it as *Bellum Gallicum,* bk. 7, chap. 29 (Loeb 72).
[42.] "After the founding of Rome."

Years contended for the Superiority": [43] But that which greatly increas'd this Contention, was, Because the *Bituriges,* who were next Neighbours to the *Arverni,* were yet in *fide & imperio;* that is, Subjects and Allies to the *Aedui.* On the other hand, the *Sequani* (though Borderers on the *Aedui*) were under the Protection of the *Arverni,* lib. 1. cap. 12. lib. 6. cap. 4.[44] The Romans finding such-like Dissentions to be for their Interest; that is, proper Opportunities to enlarge their own Power, did all they could to foment them: And therefore made a League with the *Aedui,* whom (with a great many Compliments) they styled *Brothers and Friends of the People of Rome.* Under the Protection and League of the *Aedui,* I find to have been first the *Senones,* with whom some time before the *Parisians* had join'd their *Commonwealth* in League and Amity. Next, the *Bellouaci,* who had nevertheless a great City of their own, abounding in Numbers of People, and were of principal Authority and Repute among the *Belgae,* lib. 2. cap. 4. and lib. 7. cap. 7.[45] *Caesar* reckons the *Centrones, Grudii, Laevaci, Pleumosii, Gordunni,* under the Dominion of the *Nervii,* lib. 5. cap. 11. He names the *Eburones* and *Condrusii* as Clients of the *Treviri,* lib. 4. cap. 2. And of the *Commonwealth* of the *Veneti* (these are in *Armorica* or *Britanny*) he writes, that their Domination extended over all those Maritime Regions; and that almost all that frequented those Seas were their Tributaries, lib. 3. cap. 2. But the Power of the *Arverni* was so great, that it not only equall'd that of the *Aedui,* but a little before *Caesar's* Arrival, had got most of their Clients and Dependents from them, lib. 6. cap. 4. lib. 7. cap. 10. Whereupon, as *Strabo* writes in his 4th Book, they made War against *Caesar* with Four hundred thousand Men under the Conduct of their General *Vercingetorix.* These were very averse to Kingly Government; So that *Celtillus,* Father to *Vercingetorix,* a Man of great Power and Reputation (reckon'd the first Man in all *Gaul*) was put to Death, by Order of his *Commonwealth,* for aspiring to the *Kingdom.* The *Sequani,* on the other hand, had a King, one *Catamantales,* to whom the *Romans* gave the Title of their *Friend* and *Ally,* lib. 1. cap. 2. Also the *Suessiones,* who

[43.] GS *Franc.* identify it as Caesar, *Bellum Gallicum,* bk. 1, chap. 31 (Loeb 46).
[44.] Ibid., bk. 1, chap. 31 (Loeb 46) and bk. 6, chaps. 11–12 (Loeb 332).
[45.] Ibid., bk. 2, chap. 14 (Loeb 108) and bk. 7, chap. 59 (Loeb 464).

were Masters of most large and fertile Territories, with 12 great Cities, and could muster Fifty thousand fighting Men, had a little before that time *Divitiacus*, the most potent Prince of all *Gallia* for their King; he had not only the Command of the greatest Part of *Belgae*, but even of *Britanny*. At *Caesar*'s Arrival they had one *Galba* for their King, lib. 2. cap. 1. In *Aquitania*, the Grandfather of one *Piso* an *Aquitanian*, reigned, and was called Friend by the People of Rome, lib. 4. cap. 3. The *Senones*, a People of great Strength and Authority among the *Gauls*, had for some time *Moritasgus* their King; whole Ancestors had also been *Kings* in the same Place, lib. 5. cap. 13. The *Nitiobriges*, or *Agenois*, had *Olovico* for their King; and he also had the "Appellation given him of Friend by the Senate" of Rome, lib. 7. cap. 6.

But concerning all these Kingdoms, one thing is remarkable, and must not lightly be past by; which is That they *were not hereditary*, but *conferr'd* by the People upon such as had the Reputation of being just Men. Secondly, That they had no *arbitrary* or *unlimited Authority*, but, were bound and *circumscribed* by *Laws;* so that they were no less accountable to, and subject to the Power of the People, than the People was to theirs; insomuch that those *Kingdoms* seem'd nothing else but *Magistracies for Life.* For *Caesar* makes mention of several private Men, whose Ancestors had formerly been such *Kings;* "among these he reckons *Casticus*, the Son of *Catamantales*, whose Father had been King of the *Sequani* many Years, lib. 1. cap. 2. and *Piso* the *Aquitanian*, lib. 4. cap. 3. also *Tasgetius*, whose Ancestors had been *Kings* among the *Carnutes*," lib. 5. cap. 8.

Now concerning the Extent of their *Power* and *Jurisdiction*, he brings in *Ambiorix*, King of the *Eburones*, giving an account of it, lib. 5. cap 8. "The Constitution of our Government is such (says he) that the People have no less Power and Authority over me than I have over the People. *Non minus habet in me juris multitudo, quam ipse in multitudinem.*"[46] Which Form of Government, *Plato*, *Aristotle*, *Polybius* and *Cicero* have for this Reason determined to be the *best* and most *Excellent:* "Because (says Plato) should Kingly Government be left without a Bridle, when it has attained

---

[46.] As GS *Franc.* point out, the Latin fragment is a version from Caesar, *Bellum Gallicum*, bk. 5, chap. 27 (Loeb 268).

to supreme Power, as if it stood upon a slippery Place, it easily falls into Tyranny: And therefore it ought to be restrained as with a Curb, by the Authority of the Nobles; and such chosen Men as the People have empower'd to that End and Purpose."[47]

[47.] As GS *Franc.* (p. 154, n. 37) point out, this is not a passage from Plato.

CHAPTER II

Probable Conjectures concerning the ancient Language of the Gauls

In this Place it seems proper to handle a Question much disputed and canvass'd by Learned Men; viz. What was the Language of the *Gauls* in those old Times? For as to what belongs to their Religion, Laws, and the Customs of the People, *Caesar,* as I said before, has at large given us an account. In the first place we ought to take notice, that *Caesar,* in the Beginning of his Commentaries, where he divides the *Gauls* into Three Nations, the *Belgae,* the *Aquitanae,* and the *Celtae,* tells us they all differ'd, not only in their Customs, but in their Language: Which also *Strabo* confirms, lib. 4. where he says they were not of one Language, but a little differing in their Languages. And the same thing *Ammianus Marcellinus* testifies in his 15th Book. But what many Learned Men (especially of our own Country) have maintained, viz. That the *Gauls* commonly used the *Greek* Tongue, may be refuted by this single Instance which *Caesar* takes notice of, lib. 5. cap. 12. That when Q. *Cicero* was besieged in his Camp, he dispatched Letters written in the *Greek* Language, "Lest (if they were intercepted) his Designs should be discover'd by the *Gauls.*" But to this some object, what *Strabo* writes, lib. 4. viz. "That all Sorts of good Literature (and especially that of the *Greek* Language) flourish'd at Marseilles to such a degree, that the *Gauls,* by the Example of the *Massilians,* were mightily delighted with the *Greek* Tongue, insomuch that they began to write their very Bargains and Contracts in it." Now to this there is a short and ready reply: For, in the first place, if the *Gauls* learnt *Greek* by the Example of the *Massilians,* 'tis plain, 'twas none of their Mother-tongue. Secondly, *Strabo* in the same place clearly shows us, that the Fashion of writing their Contracts in *Greek* began but in his Time, when all *Gallia* was in Subjection to the Romans. Besides, he speaks precisely only of those *Gauls* who were Borderers and next Neighbours to the *Massilians;* of whom he says, that not only many of their private Men, but even their Cities (by publick Decrees, and proposing great Rewards) invited several Learned Men of *Massilia* to instruct their Youth.

It remains that we should clear that place in *Caesar,* where he tells us "the *Gauls* used Greek letters in their publick and private Reckonings" (*"Graecis literis usos fuisse."*)[48] But let us see whether the word *Graecis* in that place ought not to be left out, not only as *unnecessary* but *surreptitious.*[49] Since it was sufficient to express *Caesar*'s Meaning to have said, that the *Gauls* made no use of Letters or Writing in the Learning of the Druids, but in all other Matters, and in publick and private Accounts, they did make use of Writing: For *uti litteris,* "to use Letters," is a frequent Expression for "Writing" among Latin Authors. Besides, it had been a Contradiction to say the *Gauls* were unskill'd in the *Greek* Tongue, as *Caesar* had averr'd a little before; and afterwards to say, that they wrote all their publick and private Accounts in *Greek.* As to what many suppose, that the words *literis Graecis* in that place, are not to be taken for Writing *Greek,* but only for the Characters of the Letters; I can less approve of this Explanation than the former; because though many ancient Writers (as we just now said) frequently used the Expression, *Uti litteris* for *Scribere;* yet I never observ'd, that any of them ever used it to signify the Forms and Fashions of the Characters. Neither does it make at all for their Opinion, what *Caesar* says in the First Book of his Commentaries, viz. That there

---

[48.] GS *Franc.* identify it as *Bellum Gallicum,* bk. 6, chap. 14 (Loeb 338).
[49.] "Superfluous."

were found in the Helvetian Camp, Tablets, *literis Graecis conscriptas;* as if the same Person, who had learnt to make use of the *Greek* Forms of Characters, might not as easily have learnt the *Greek* Language; or as if there might not be among the *Helvetii,* Priests or Gentlemen's Sons, who might then have learnt *Greek,* as our's now learn Latin; *Greek* being at that Time a Language in Vogue and Esteem. The very Neighbourhood of the School of *Massilia* is sufficient to confute that Opinion: And therefore *Caesar,* when he speaks of his own Letter to *Cicero,* tells us, he sent that Letter written in *Greek* Characters, lest (in case it were intercepted) his Designs should be discover'd by the Enemy. *Justinus,* lib. 20. says, there was a Decree of the Senate made, that no Carthaginian, after that Time, should study the *Greek* Language or Writing, lest he should be able to speak or write to the Enemy without an Interpreter. *Tacitus,* in his Book *de moribus Germanorum,* tells us, "that several Tombs and Monuments were yet to be seen in the Confines of *Germany* and Swisserland with *Greek* Inscriptions on them."[50] *Livius,* lib. 9. says, "The Roman Boys formerly studied the Tuscan Language, as now they do the *Greek.*" And in his 28th Book, "Hannibal erected an Altar, and dedicated it with a large Inscription of all his Atchievements, in the *Greek* and Punick Tongues." *Item* Lib. 40. "Both Altars and Inscriptions on them in the *Greek* and Latin Tongues." Lastly, I cannot imagine, that *Caesar* would have expressed himself, (if he had meant, as these would have him) *Graecis literis scribere* [writing Greek letters]; but rather, *Graecarum literarum forma,* [the form of Greek Letters] as we see in *Tacitus, Annals* Lib. 11. "*Novas literarum formas addidit . . . :* He added new Characters of Letters: Having found, that the *Greek* Literature was not begun and perfected at once." And again, "*Et formae literis latinis quae veterrimis Graecorum, etc.*"[51]

Now lest any body should wonder, how the Word *Graecis* crept into *Caesar*'s Text, I will instance you the like Mischance in Pliny, *Natural History* lib. 7. cap. 57. where 'tis thus written, "*Gentium consensus tacitus primum omnium conspiravit ut IONUM literis uterentur.*" And afterwards, "*Sequens gentium consensus in tonsoribus fuit.*" And again, "*Tertius consensus*

[50.] Tacitus, *Germania*, chap. 3 (Loeb 268).
[51.] "The forms of Latin script were the most ancient letters of the Greeks."

est in Horarum observatione."[52] Now who is there that sees not plainly the Word IONUM ought to be left Out, as well because 'tis apparently unnecessary, (for Pliny had no farther Design than to let us know, that Men first of all consented in the Writing and Form of their Letters) as because 'tis false, that the *Ionian* Letters were the first invented; as Pliny himself in his foregoing Chapter, and *Tacitus*, lib. 11. have told us. I have observed however two Places (*Gregorius Turonensis*, lib. 5. and *Aimoinus*, lib. 3. cap. 41.) wherein 'tis intimated, that the *Gauls* used the Forms of the *Greek* Letters: For where they speak of King *Chilperick*, "He added (say they) some Letters to our Letters; and those were, ω, ψ, ξ, φ; and sent Epistles to the several Schools in his Kingdom, that the Boys should be so taught." *Aimoinus* mentions only three Letters, χ, Θ, Φ. But we must understand, that these were *Franks*, not *Gauls;* or rather *Franco-gauls*, who made use of their own native Language, the German Tongue; not that ancient Language of the *Gauls*, which had grown out of use under the Roman Government: Besides, if the *Francogalli* had made use of the *Greek* Letters, how came they at first to except these, when they made use of all the rest? But we have said enough, and too much of this Matter. As for their Opinion who believe that the *Gauls* spoke the German Language, *Caesar* confutes it in that single place, wherein he tells us, "that *Ariovistus*, by Reason of his long Conversation in *Gallia*, spoke the *Gallick* Tongue."[53]

Now for two Reasons their Opinion seems to me to be most probable, who write, that the *Ancient Gauls* had a peculiar Language of their own, not much differing from the British: First, because *Caesar* tells us it was the Custom for those *Gauls* who had a mind to be thoroughly instructed in the Learning of the Druyds, to pass over into Britain; and since the Druyds made no use of Books, 'tis agreeable to Reason, that they taught in the same Language which was used in *Gallia*. Secondly, because *Tacitus* in his Life of *Agricola*, writes, that the Language of the *Gauls* and *Britains*

[52.] As GS *Franc.* translate: "At first the tacit agreement of all the people conspired to have them use the letters of the Ionians"; "The next agreement of the people concerned the manner of wearing their hair"; "the third agreement was the matter of their reckoning time." They identify the source as Pliny, *Natural History*, bk. 8, 27; bk. 7, 59–60.

[53.] GS *Franc.* identify this as *Bellum Gallicum*, bk. 1, chap. 47 (Loeb 78).

differ'd but very little: neither does that Conjecture of *Beatus Rhenanus* seem unlikely to me, who believes the Language which is now made use of in *Basse Bretayne* [*Britones Britonantes*] to be the Remains of our ancient Tongue. His Reasons for this Opinion may be better learn'd from his own Commentaries, than told in this Place. The Language which we at present make use of, may easily be known to be a Compound of the several Tongues of divers Nations: And (to speak plainly and briefly) may be divided into four Parts. One half of it we have from the Romans, as every one that understands Latin ever so little, may observe: For besides, that the *Gauls* being subject to the Romans, would naturally fall into their Customs and Language, 'tis manifest that the Romans were very industrious to propagate their Tongue, and to make it universal, and (as it were) venerable among all Nations. And to that End settled Publick Schools up and down, at *Autan, Besancon, Lyons, etc.* as *Valerius Maximus, Tacitus,* and *Ausonius* tell us. The other half of it may be subdivided thus. One third of it we hold from the Ancient *Gauls,* another from the *Franks,* and the last from the *Greek* Language: For it has been demonstrated long since by many Authors, that we find innumerable *Frank* (that is, German) Words (as we shall hereafter prove) in our daily Speech. And several learned Men have shewn us, that many *Greek* Words are adapted to our common Use, which we do not owe to the Learning and Schools of the *Druyds*, (who I believe spoke no *Greek*); but to the Schools and Conversation of the *Massilians,* whom we formerly mentioned.

The State of *Gaul*, after it was reduced into the Form of a *Province* by the *Romans*

'Tis very well known to all learned Men, that *Gaul*, after having been often attempted with various Success, during a ten Years War, and many Battles, was at last totally subdued by *Caesar*, and reduced into the Form of a Province. It was the Misfortune of this most valiant and warlike People, to submit at length to the *Great Beast*, as it is called in Scripture, with which however they so strove for Empire for eight hundred Years, (as *Josephus* informs us) that no Wars with any other Nation, so much terrified Rome. And Plutarch in his Lives of Marcellus and Camillus; *Appian* in his 2nd Book of the Civil Wars; *Livius*, lib. 8. & 10. have recorded, that the Romans were so afraid of the *Gauls*, that they made a Law, whereby all the Dispensations (formerly granted to Priests and old Men, from serving in their Armies) were made void, in Case of any Tumult or Danger arising from the *Gauls:* which *Cicero* takes notice of in his *2nd Philippick, Caesar* himself in his 6th Book, and after him *Tacitus*, lib. *de moribus Germanorum,* do testify, That there was a time wherein the *Gauls* excell'd the *Ger-*

mans in Valour, and carried the War into their Territories, settling Colonies (by reason of their great Multitudes of People) beyond the Rhine.

Now *Tacitus* in his Life of *Agricola,* attributes the Loss of this their so remarkable Valour, to the Loss of their *Liberty;* "Gallos in bellis floruisse accepimus, mox segnities [segnitia] cum otio intravit, amissa Virtute pariter ac Libertate."[54] And I hope the Reader will excuse me, if the Love of my Country makes me add that remarkable Testimony of the Valour of the *Gauls,* mentioned by *Justin,* lib. 24. "The *Gauls* (says he) finding their Multitudes to increase so fast, that their Lands could not afford them sufficient Sustenance, sent out Three hundred thousand Souls to seek for new Habitations. Part of these seated themselves in Italy; who both took and burnt the City of Rome. Another part penetrated as far as the Shores of *Dalmatia,* destroying infinite Numbers of the *Barbarians,* and settled themselves at last in *Pannonia.* A hardy bold and warlike Nation; who ventured next after *Hercules,* (to whom the like Attempt gave a Reputation of extraordinary Valour, and a Title to Immortality) to cross those almost inaccessible Rocks of the Alps, and Places scarce passable by Reason of the Cold: Where after having totally subdued the *Pannonians* they waged War with the bordering Provinces for many Years. And afterwards being encouraged by their Success, subdivided their Parties; when some took their Way to *Graecia,* some to *Macedonia,* destroying all before them with Fire and Sword. And so great was the Terror of the Name of the *Gauls,* that several *Kings* (not in the least threatened by them) of their own accord, purchased their Peace with large Sums of Money." And in the following Book, he says, "So great was the Fruitfulness of the *Gauls* at that time, that like a Swarm they fill'd all Asia. So that none of the Eastern *Kings* either ventured to make War without a mercenary Army of *Gauls,* or fled for Refuge to other than the *Gauls,* when they were driven out of their Kingdoms." And thus much may suffice concerning their warlike Praise and Fortitude, which (as *Tacitus* tells us) was quite gone, as soon as they lost their *Liberty.* Yet some Cities, or *Commonwealths,* (as *Plinius,*

[54.] GS *Franc.* (p. 172) identify this as *Agricola,* chap. 11. "We accept the fact, that the Gauls distinguished themselves in warfare; but after a time indolence was the consequence of leisure, for they lost their manliness with their liberty" (Loeb translation, 188). Note that Hotman's Latin has *segnitia;* Molesworth's has *segnities.*

lib. 4. cap. 11. tells us) were permitted to continue free, after the Romans had reduced *Gallia* to the Form of a Province. Such were the *Nervii, Ulbanesses, Suessiones* and *Leuci*. Also some of the Confederates: and among these he reckons the *Lingones, Rhemi, Carnutes* and *Aedui*.

But we may easily learn from these Words of *Critognatus* the *Arvernian*, mentioned by *Caesar*, lib. 7. what the Condition was of those *Commonwealths*, which had the Misfortune to be reduced into the Form of a Province. "If (says he) you are ignorant after what manner far distant Nations are used by the Romans, you have no more to do, but to look at our neighbouring *Gallia*, now reduced into the Form of a Province: Which having its Laws and Customs chang'd, and being subjected to the Power of the Axes, is oppress'd with perpetual *Slavery*."

We are to understand, there were three kinds of Servitude, or *Slavery*. First, *To have a Garrison of Soldiers imposed upon them, to keep them in Awe;* yet such Provinces as seemed peaceable and quiet, had no great Armies maintained in them. For *Josephus* writes in his 2nd Book of the *History of the Jews*, "That in the Emperor Titus's time, the Romans had but 1200 Soldiers in Garrison in all *Gaul*, although (says he) they had fought with the Romans for their *Liberty*, almost 800 Years, and had near as many Cities, as the Romans had Garrison-Soldiers." A Second Sort of Servitude was, when any Province was made Tributary, and compelled to pay Taxes; and to that End were forced to endure a Number of Tax-gatherers, that is, *Harpies* and *Leeches*, which suck'd out the very Blood of the *Provincials*.[55] *Eutropius* tells us, in his 6th Book, That *Caesar*, as soon as he had subdued *Gaul*, impos'd a Tax upon it, by the Name of a Tribute, which amounted to *H. S. Quadringenties*:[56] which is about a Million of our Crowns. A Third Sort of Servitude was, when the Provinces were not permitted to be govern'd by their *own Laws;* but had Magistrates and Judges, with full Power and Authority (*cum imperio & securibus*) over Life and Estate, sent them by the People of Rome. This Threefold *Slavery* not only our *Gallia*, but all the other Provinces, took most bitterly to heart; and therefore in *Tiberius's* Reign, not long after *Caesar's* Conquest, *Taci-*

[55.] GS *Franc.* identify this as a citation of Suetonius, *Caesar* 25 (Loeb 1:32).
[56.] Forty million *sesterces*.

tus tells us, That the Cities of *Gaul* rebell'd, because of the Continuance of Taxes, the Extortions of Usurers, and Insolence of the Soldiery.[57] And afterwards in *Nero's* Reign, *Suetonius* writes, "That the *Gauls* being weary of his Tyranny, revolted. The World (says he) having for near 13 Years, endured such a Sort of Prince, at last shook him off: The *Gauls* beginning the Defection." Now all *Gallia* was divided by the Romans into 16 Provinces, viz. *Viennensis, Narbonensis prima, Narbonensis secunda, Aquitania prima, Aquitania secunda, Novempopulana, Alpes maritime, Belgica prima, Belgica secunda, Germania prima, Germania secunda, Lugdunensis prima, Lugdunensis secunda, Lugdunensis tertia, Maxima Sequanorunt, & Alpes Graecae,* as *Antoninus* in his *Itinerary,* and *Sextus Rufus,* give an Account of them. But *Ammianus Marcellinus* treats of them more particularly, lib. 15.

But to return to what we were speaking of: 'Tis not to be imagined, how grievously, and with what Indignation, the *Gauls* bore the Insolencies and Plunderings of the Romans; nor how frequently they revolted upon that Account: and because they were not strong enough of themselves to shake off the Roman Tyranny, 'twas a common Custom with them, to hire German Auxiliaries. These were the first Beginnings of the Colonies of the *Franks:* For those *Germans,* whether they were beaten by the Romans, or (which is more likely) were bought off by them, began by little and little, to settle themselves in the Borders of *Gallia.* This gave occasion to *Suetonius,* in his Life of *Augustus,* to say, "He drove the *Germans* beyond the River Elb; but the *Suevi* and *Sicambri* (submitting themselves), he transplanted into *Gallia,* where he assign'd them Lands near the River *Rhine.*" Also in his Life of *Tiberius,* "He brought (says he) forty thousand of those that had surrendered themselves in the German War, over into *Gallia,* and allotted them Settlements upon the Banks of the *Rhine.*" Neither must we omit what *Flavius Vopiscus* records, concerning the Reign of *Probus* the Emperor; in whose time almost all *Gallia,* that is, sixty Cities, revolted from the Romans; and with common Consent, took up Arms for the Recovery of their *Liberty:* "Having done these things (says he) he march'd with a vast Army into *Gaul,* which after *Posthumus's* Death was all in Commotion, and when *Aurelianus* was kill'd, was in a Manner

---

[57.] GS *Franc.* identify this as *Annals* 3, 40 (Loeb 586).

possessed by the *Germans;* there he gain'd so many Victories, that he recover'd from the Barbarians sixty of the most noble Cities of *Gallia:* And
whereas, they had overspread all *Gallia* without Controul, he slew near
four hundred thousand of those that had seated themselves within the
Roman Territories, and transplanted the Remainders of them beyond the
Rivers Neckar, and Elb. But how cruel and inhuman the Domination of
the Romans was in *Gallia:* How intolerable their Exactions were: What
horrible and wicked Lives they led; and with how great Inveteracy and
Bitterness they were hated upon that Account by the *Gauls,* (especially by
the Christians) may best be learn'd from the Works of *Salvianus,* Bishop
of Marseilles, which treat of Providence: Therefore 'tis incredible to tell,
what Multitudes of *Germans* pour'd themselves into *Gallia;* the *Gauls* not
only not hindering, but even favouring and calling them in. *Latinus Paca-
tus,* in his Speech to *Theodosius,* has this Passage; "From whence should I
begin my Discourse, but from thy Mischiefs, O *Gallia!* who may'st justly
challenge a Superiority in Sufferings, above all the Nations of the Earth,
that have been vexed with this Plague?"[58] Now 'tis most plain both from
Sidonius Apollinaris, and especially from the above-mentioned *Salvianus,*
in many Places of his Writings, that our *Franks* were a Part of those German Nations, who thus entered into *Gallia.*

[58.] GS *Franc.* (p. 180) identify this as from *Latini Pacati Depanii panegyricus
Theodosio Augusto dictus.*

CHAPTER IV

Of the Original of the *Franks;* who having possessed themselves of *Gallia,* changed its Name into that of *Francia,* or *Francogallia*

The Order of our Discourse requires, that we should now enquire into the Original of the *Franks,* and trace them from their first Habitations, or (as it were) their very Cradles: In which Disquisition 'tis very much to be admired, that no mention has been made of them by *Ptolomy, Strabo,* or even by *Tacitus* himself, who of all Writers was most accurate in describing the Names and Situations of all the German Nations: and 'tis plain, the *Franks* were a German People, who possessed most parts of Europe for many Years, with great Reputation; of which we will quote but a few Instances out of many.

First, *Johannes Nauclerus* says thus, "*Charles* the Great was call'd King of the *Franks;* which is as much as to say, *King* of *Germany* and *France.* Now 'tis demonstrable, that at that time all *Gallia Transalpina,* and all *Germany* from the *Pyrenaean* Mountains, as far as *Hungary,* was called *Francia:* This last was called Eastern France, the former Western France";[59] and in this all true Historians agree.

Eguinarthus, in his *Life of Charlemain*, says, "The Banks of the River Sala, which divides the *Turingi* from the *Sorabi*, were afterwards inhabited by those called the *Eastern Franks*."[60] *Otto Frising. Chron. 5. cap. 4.* speaking of King *Dagobert's* Reign, "The Bounds of the *Franks* Dominions reach'd now (says he) from Spain, as far as Hungary, being two most noble Dukedoms, Aquitania and Bavaria"; but much more at large, lib. 6. cap. 17. And after him *Godfrey of Viterbo*, in his *Chronic. part.* 17. sub Anno 881. "Arnulphus (says he) ruled all Eastern Francia, which is now called the Teutonick Kingdom, or *Germany;* that is to say, Bavaria, Suabia, Saxonia, Turingia, Frisia, and Lotharingia: but *Odo* was King of *Western* France." Again, *sub Anno* 913. "It is apparent by the Authority of many Writers, that the Kingdom of *Germany*, which the Emperor Frederick at present holds, is part of the Kingdom of the *Franks;* for there (on both Sides the Rhine) the first *Franks* were seated; which as far as to the Limits of Bavaria, is now called Eastern France: But Western France is that Kingdom which lies on both Sides the Rivers Seine and Loire." And again he says, "In the time of *Charles* the Great, King of the *Franks*, all *Gallia*, that is, *Celtica, Belgica*, and *Lugdunensis*, and all *Germany* which reaches from the Rhine as far as Dalmatia, made but one Kingdom; which was called *Francia*." Almost all which Quotations have been taken out of *Otto*, as I said before. 'Tis to be noted, that *Rhegino* writes thus, in *Chron. anni* 577,[61] "After the Death of King *Pipin*, *Lewis* his Son (who had been present at his Father's Decease; and celebrated his Funerals) kept his Residence at Francfort, the principal Seat of the Eastern Kingdom." *Luitprandus Ticinensis* says, lib. 1. cap. 6. "It was order'd that *Wido* should have for his Share, that which Men call the *Roman France*, and *Berengarius* should have Italy." And a little after, "When he had march'd through the Territories of the Burgundians, he purposed to enter Roman France, *etc.*" Now it was call'd Roman France, first, because the *Franks* had possessed themselves of that *Gallia*, which was under the Roman Obedience. Secondly,

[59.] GS *Franc.* identify this as Nauclerus, *Chronica* (1579), p. 683.
[60.] GS *Franc.* (p. 182) identify this as from Einhard, *Chronicon*, A.D. 887.
[61.] The original has 576.

because the Roman Language prevail'd in that Country, as we formerly told you: Whence arose the Saying, *Loqui Romanum*, of such as used not the German or *Frank*, but the Latin Tongue. *Otto Frisingius, chron.* 4. *cap. penult.* says, "It seems to me, that those *Franks* who dwell in *Gallia*, borrowed the Language, which they make use of to this Day, from the Romans; for the others who stay'd about the Rhine, and in *Germany* use the Teutonick Tongue." And in Imitation of him, *Godfridus*, part. 17. cap. 1. "The *Franks* (says he) seem to me to have learn'd the Language which they make use of to this Day, from the Romans, who formerly dwelt in those parts." From all these 'tis apparent, that the Reputation and Power of the *Franks* was extraordinary great; as 'twas fitting for such as were Masters of a great Part of Europe.

Moreover we find, that those *Germans* which were transplanted by Emperor Frederick II into the Kingdoms of Naples and Sicily, and establish'd there as a presidiary Colony, were called *Franks, Petrus de Vineis, lib. epist.* 6. *cap.* 25.[62] "Following (says he) the Law and Custom of the *Franks*, in this Instance, that the Eldest Brother to the Exclusion of all the Younger succeeds, even in the Camp it self." *Imp. Freder. 2. Neapolitan constitutions.* lib. 2. tit. 32. speaking of those *Franks*, "who upon Occasion trusted the Fortune of their Lives, and of all their Estates, to the Event of a Duel, or single Combat." And again, "The aforesaid manner of Proof which all who observe the Rites of the *Franks* made use of." Also lib. 2. tit. 33. "which Law, our Will is, shall in all Causes be common both to the *Franks* and *Longobards.*"

Matters being thus plain, 'tis strange that *Gregory* Bishop of Tours (who writ concerning the Original of the *Franks* 800 Years ago) should say, in the first Part of his *History*, That although he had made diligent Enquiry about the Rise and Beginning of the *Franks*, he could find nothing certain: notwithstanding he had seen an ancient Book of a certain Historian of theirs, called, *Sulpitius Alexander;* who affirms nothing, either of their first Habitations, or the Beginnings of their Domination.

But we have found out that these People originally came from that

[62.] Note in margin, not found in the original: "These are only broken pieces of sentences, to prove, that the Germans (establish'd in Naples and Sicily) were called, and actually were Franks."

Country which lies between the Rhine and the Elb, and is bounded on the West by the Sea, almost in the same Tract where the greater and the lesser *Chauci* dwelt. "A People (says *Tacitus*) the most noble among all the *Germans,* who founded their Greatness and maintained it by Justice."[63] These were next Neighbours to the *Batavians;* for 'tis agreed on all Hands, that the *Franks* had their first Seats near the Sea-shore, in very marshy Grounds; and were the most skilful People in Navigation, and Sea-fights, known at that time: Whereof we have the following Testimonies. First, in *Claudian,* who congratulating Stilicon's Victory, writes thus; "*Ut jam trans fluvium non indignante* Chayco *Pascat* Belga *pecus, mediumque ingressa per* Albin Gallica Francorum *montes armenta pererrent.*"[64] In which Place he makes use of a Poetical License, and calls those People *Chayci,* which the Geographers call *Chauci.* Now that they were seated near the Sea, that Panegyrical Oration made to Constantine the Great, is a Testimony: "Quid loquor rursus, *etc.* What should I speak more of those remote Nations of the *Franks,* transplanted not from Places which the Romans of old invaded; but plucked from their very original Habitations, and their farthest Barbarous Shores, to be planted in the waste Places of *Gallia;* where with their Husbandry, they may help the Roman Empire in time of Peace; and with their Bodies, supply its Armies in time of War." And in another Panegyrick, by *Eumenius* the Rhetorician, we find this Passage, "*Aut haec ipsa, etc.* Or this Country, which was once overspread with the Fierceness of the *Franks,* more than if the Waters of their Rivers, or their Sea, had covered it; but now ceases to be barbarous, and is civilized." To the same Purpose is *Procopius's* Testimony, in his first Book of the *Gothick War;* For where he describes the place where the Rhine falls into the Ocean; "In these Parts (says he) there are great Marshes, where of old the *Germans* dwelt; a barbarous People, and at that time of small Reputation, which now are called *Franks.*" And *Zonarus,* in the 3rd Tome of his *Annals,* quotes this very Passage of *Procopius.* Also *Flavius Vopiscus,* in his *Life of Probus,* tells us, "That the *Franks* were discomfited by Probus in

[63.] GS *Franc.* identify this as Tacitus, *Germania* (Loeb 312).
[64.] GS *Franc.* (p. 191) translate as: "Beyond the river Beligian cattle feed; / gone are the Chayci who resisted them. / The Gallic herds that pass across the Elbe / Roam onwards over the mountains of the Franks."

their inaccessible Marshes. *Testes sunt Franci inviis strati paludibus.*"[65] Also *Sidonius Apollinaris* says thus; "*Francorum & penitissimas paludes, Intrares venerantibus Sicambris.*"[66]

Now what we have said concerning the Neighbourhood of the *Franks* to the Chauci, may be plainly proved by comparing of Places, and the Descriptions of their particular Seats. Those of the *Chauci* are described by Pliny, lib. 16. cap. 1. Those of the *Franks* by the Rhetorician Panegyrist, above mentioned: For *Pliny* says thus, "We have seen in the Northern parts the Nations of the *Chauci*, called *Majores & Minores*, where twice every 24 Hours the Ocean is forcibly driven in a great way over the Land, through a vast Passage which is there, making it a perpetual Controversy of Nature; and a Doubt, whether it ought to be reckon'd part of the Land or of the Sea."

The Panegyrist speaks in these Terms, "*Quanquam illa Regio, etc.* When thy noble Expeditions, O *Caesar*, have proceeded so far, as to clear and conquer that Country, which the Rhine runs through, with his cunning Meanders or Windings, [*Meatibus callidis,* for so it must be read, and not *Scaldis,* as in some Copies], and embraces in his Arms a Region, which I can scarce call Land; 'tis so soak'd with Water, that not only the Marshy part of it gives way, but even that which seems more firm, shakes when trod upon, and trembles at a Distance under the Weight of the Foot."

We think therefore we have made it plain from what Seats the Nation of the *Franks* first came into *Gallia;* that is to say, from that marshy Country which lies upon the Ocean, between the Rivers Elb and Rhine: which may be further confirm'd by this Argument. That the *Franks* were very well skill'd in maritime affairs, and sail'd far and near all about those Coasts: For so says *Eutropius*, lib. 9. where he gives a short History of the Emperor Galenus. "After this time, when Carausius had in charge to scour the Sea coasts of Belgia and Armorica, then infested by the *Franks* and Saxons, *etc.*" The very same thing *Paulus Orosius* mentions, lib. 7. Also what the Panegyrist, before cited, says in a certain Place, has reference to

[65.] GS *Franc.* translate this as "The mutilated Frankish corpses were scattered about amongst their inaccessible marshes."

[66.] GS *Franc.* translate this as "Enter, if you dare, the innermost Frankish marshes revered by the Sicambri."

this. "The *Franks* (says he) are cruel above all others; the tide of whose warlike Fury surmounting that of their very Ocean it self, carried them to the Sea coasts of Spain, which they very much infested with their Depredations." And therefore the Emperor *Justinian*, when he explains to the General Governor of Affrick the duty of his Office, makes mention of those *Franks* which were seated in a certain part of *Gallia*, bordering upon Spain.

But we find a very memorable Passage; which highly sets forth the great Glory of their warlike Achievements, in another place of that Panegyrick; viz. That a small Body of *Franks*, which *Probus* the Emperor had overcome and carried captive into Pontus, seiz'd on some Ships, wandered all about the Sea-coasts of *Graecia* and Asia, invaded Sicily, took *Syracusa*, and afterwards laden with Booty, return'd into the Ocean through the Streights of Gibraltar. "*Recursabat in animos sub Divo Probo & paucorum ex Francis Captivorum incredibilis audacia, & indigna foelicitas: qui à Ponto usque correptis navibus, Graeciam Asiamque populari, nec impunè plerisque Lybiae littoribus appulsi, ipsas postremò navalibus quondam victoriis nobiles ceperant Syracusas: & immenso itinere permensi, Oceanum, qua terras rupit intraverant: atque ita eventu temeritatis ostenderant, nihil esse clausum piraticae desperationi quò navigiis pateret accessus.*"[67]

And, as farther Arguments of what I have been proving, may be added all those Places in several Authors, which inform us that the Habitations of the *Franks* were Bordering upon the *Batavians*. The same Rhetorician, in his Speeches to Maximianus and Constantine, says, "Many thousand *Franks*, who had crossed the Rhine, and invaded *Batavia*, with other Countries on this Side, were slain, driven out, or carried away captive."

Besides there is a notable Instance in *Corn. Tacitus*, lib. 20. where speak-

[67.] The preceding passage rather summarizes the Latin extract: "How in the reign of the divine Probus a small band of captive Franks, with incredible daring and a good fortune they scarcely deserved, sailed from Pontus in vessels they had surreptitiously acquired as far as Greece and Asia, plundering as they went, and voyaged along much of the coast of Libya, though not without some loss. Finally, after several naval victories, they even took the noble city of Syracuse, and, having sailed on for a vast distance, entered the great ocean where it surges between the continents. By that foolhardy deed they showed that no place on earth where ships might sail was safe from the curse of piracy." See GS *Franc.* p. 195.

ing of the Neighbourhood of *Frisia* and *Batavia* to each other, he mixes the *Caninefates* among them, whose Custom in Electing their *Kings* was (as I shall hereafter shew) the very same with that of the *Franks*. "Ambassadors (says he) were sent to the *Caninefates,* to persuade them to enter into the Confederacy: That People inhabit one part of the Island, equal as to their Descent, Laws and Valour, to the *Batavians;* but inferior in Number." And again "Brinnio being set upon a Shield (according to the Custom of the Country) and hoisted up on Men's Shoulders, was chosen their Commander." Which Words will prove of no small Authority for us, when we come hereafter to that Part of the Controversy.

The Case being so; I cannot forbear wondering at the Opinion of the Learned *Andreas Turnebus,* who despising the Authority of so many grave and ancient Writers, says that he thinks the *Franks* were originally of Scandinavia: because in Ptolomy he finds the *Phirassi* seated in that Peninsula, which Word he will needs suppose to be corrupted; and that, instead of it, the Word *Franci* ought to be there: but brings no Reason for his Opinion more than his own mere guess, though this Opinion differs manifestly from all other ancient Authors.

As to all those who are pleas'd with Fables, and have deduced the Original of the *Franks* from the *Trojans,* and from one *Francion,* a Son of Priam, we can only say, that they furnish Materials for Poets rather than Historians: And among such, *William Bellay* deserves the first Place, who, though he was a Person of singular Learning and extraordinary Ingenuity; yet in his Book, which treats of the Antiquities of *Gallia* and France, seems rather to have design'd a Romance, like that of *Amadis,* than a true History of the *Francogallican* Affairs.[68]

[68.] The work referred to is Du Bellay, *Epitome de l'Antiquité des Gaules de France* (1556).

Of the Name of the *Franks*, and their sundry Excursions; and what time they first began to establish a Kingdom in *Gallia*

But I think it requisite that we should enquire a little more carefully into this Name of *Franks;* which, as we told you before, is not to be found in any of the ancient Descriptions of *Germany.* That I may no longer detain the Reader in Suspense, it must needs be, that either the Nation of the *Franks,* by which such mighty things were done, was at first very obscure and mean, (as we see in Switz, an ordinary Village); yet because the first beginning of the *Liberty* of those Countries proceeded from thence, gave the name of Switzers to all the rest of the Cantons: Or (which seems to me most probable) this Appellation had its Original from the Occasion; viz. When those that set up for the prime Leaders and Beginners, in recovering the publick liberty, called themselves *Franks;* by which name the *Germans* understood such as were *Free,* and under no Servitude; as the Writers of that Nation do unanimously hold: And therefore in ordinary Speech, by a *Frank* was meant a *Freeman*, by a *Franchise*, an *Asylum*, or place of refuge; and *Francisare* signified to restore to liberty and freedom.[69] The first Proof we shall give of this, is, what *Procopius* in his first Book of the *Gothick* Wars relates. The *Franks* (says he) were anciently by a general name call'd *Germans;* but after they exceeded their Limits, they obtain'd the name of *Franks:* Of the same Opinion I find *Gregory of Tours*, the *Abbot of Ursperg, Sigibertus* and *Ado of Vienne*, and *Godfrey of Viterbo* to have been; viz. That they had the Name of *Franks* from their freedom, and from their ferocity, (alluding to the sound of the words *Francos Feroces*,) because they refused to serve as Soldiers under *Valentinian* the Emperor, and to pay Tribute as other Nations did. A second Proof may be that of *Cornelius Tacitus*, who in his 20th Book, speaking of the *Caninefates*, whom we have formerly demonstrated to have been the very next Neighbours, if not the true *Franks* themselves, and of their Victory over the Romans, he has this expression: *Clara ea victoria, etc.* "That Victory (says he) was of great Reputation to them immediately after it, and of great Profit in the Sequel, for having by that Means got both Weapons and Ships into their Possession, which before they were in great want of; their Fame was spread over all *Germany* and *Gaul*, as being the first beginners of *Liberty; Libertatis Auctores celebrabantur.*" For the *Germans* thereupon sent Ambassadors, offering their Assistance. May the *Omen* prove lucky! and may the *Franks* truly and properly deserve that name; who after having shaken off that Yoke of *Slavery*, imposed upon them by *Tyrants*, have thought fit to preserve to themselves a commendable *liberty* even under the Domination of *Kings: For to obey a King is not servitude:* neither are all who are govern'd by *Kings*, presently for that Reason to be counted *Slaves*, but such as submit themselves to the un-bounded Will of a *Tyrant*, a Thief, and Executioner, as Sheep resign themselves to the Knife of the Butcher. Such as these deserve to be called by the vile names of *Servants* and *Slaves*.

Therefore the *Franks* had always *Kings*, even at that very time when they profess'd themselves the vindicators and assertors of the publick lib-

---

[69.] The phrases "publick liberty" and "liberty and freedom" are expansions of the Latin originals *libertatem, libertatis*.

erty: And when they constituted *Kings*, they never intended they should be *Tyrants* or *Executioners*, but *keepers* of their *Liberties*, *Protectors*, *Governors* and *Tutors*. Such, in short, as we shall describe hereafter when we come to give an Account of the *Francogallican* Government.

For, as to what a certain, foolish and ignorant Monk, called *John Turpin*, has wrote (in his Life, or rather Romance of *Charlemagn*) concerning the Original, of the Word *Frank*, viz. That whoever contributed Money towards the Building of *St. Denis's Church*, should be called *Francus*, that is, a Freeman; is not worthy of being remembered, no more than all the rest of his trifling Works, stuff'd full of old Wives Tales, and mere Impertinencies.

But this may be truly affirm'd, that this name of *Franks*, or (as *Corn. Tacitus* interprets it) Authors of *Liberty*, was an Omen so lucky and fortunate to them, that through it they gain'd almost innumerable Victories. For after the *Franks* had quitted their ancient Seats upon that glorious Design, they deliver'd not only *Germany*, their common country, but also France from the Tyranny and Oppression of the Romans; and at last (crossing the Alps) even a great part of Italy it self.

The first mention made of this illustrious name, we find in *Trebellius Pollio's* Life of the *Emperor Gallienus*, about the 260th Year after Christ. His Words are these: "*Cum, etc.* Whilst Gallienus spent his time in nothing but Gluttony and shameful Practices, and govern'd the Commonwealth after so ridiculous a manner, that it was like Boy's play, when they set up *Kings* in jest among themselves; the *Gauls*, who naturally hate luxurious Princes, elected Posthumus for their Emperor, who at that time was *Gallienus's* Lieutenant in *Gaul* with imperial Authority, Gallienus thereupon commenced a War with Posthumus; and Posthumus being assisted by many Auxiliaries, both of the *Celtae* and the *Franks*, took the Field along with Victorinus."[70] By which Words we may plainly perceive, that the *Gauls* crav'd the Assistance of the *Franks;* that is, of these Authors or Beginners of *Liberty*, to enable them to shake off the *Tyrant Gallienus's* Yoke: Which same thing *Zonaras* hints at in his Life of *Gallienus*, when

---

[70.] GS *Franc.* identify this as *Scriptores Historiae Augustae*, s.v. "Gallieni" (Loeb 3:22 and 3:30).

he says, "He fought against the *Franks*."[71] We find another mention made of the same People in *Flavius Vopiscus's Life of Aurelian*, in these Words: "At Metz the Tribune of the 6th Legion discomfited the *Franks*, who had made Incursions, and overspread all *Gallia;* he slew 700, and sold 300 Captives for *Slaves*." For you must not expect that our *Franks*, any more than other Nations in their Wars, were constantly victorious, and crown'd with Success. On the contrary, we read that Constantine, afterwards call'd the Great, took Prisoners two of their *Kings*, and exposed them to the Wild Beasts at the publick shews. Which Story both Eutropius in his 9th Book, and the Rhetorician in that *Panegyrick* so often quoted, make mention of.

And because the same Rhetorician in another place speaks of those Wars in the Confines of the *Batavi*, which we have shewn not to be far distant from the *Franks*, I will set down his Words at Length. "*Multa Francorum millia, etc.* He slew, drove out, and took Prisoners many thousand *Franks*, who had invaded *Batavia*, and other Territories on this side the Rhine." And in another Place says, "He clear'd the Country of the *Batavians*, which had before been possess'd by several Nations and *Kings* of the *Franks;* and not satisfied with only overcoming them, he transplanted them into the Roman Territories, and forced them to lay aside their Fierceness as well as their Weapons."[72] From which place we are given to understand, not obscurely, that Constantine, (being constrain'd to do so by the *Franks*) granted them Lands within the Bounds of the Roman Empire. *Ammianus*, lib. 15. writes, that the *Franks*, during the Civil Wars between Constantine and Licinius, sided with Constantine, and fought very valiantly for him. And in other places of the same Book he records, that during the Reign of Constantine, the Son of Constantine, great numbers of *Franks* were at that Court in high favour and authority, with *Caesar*. "Afterwards, says he, Malarichus on a sudden got power, having gained the *Franks;* whereof at that time great numbers flourish'd at Court." During the Reign of Julian, call'd the Apostate, the same *Franks*

[71.] GS *Franc.* (p. 208) identify the Greek passage as *Annal* xii, 24.
[72.] GS *Franc.* (p. 208) identify it as *Panegyricus Maximiano et Constantino* iv. The *Panegyric Latini* were a collection of twelve anonymous fourth-century Roman orations.

endeavour'd to restore the City of Cologne (which was grievously oppress'd by *Roman* Slavery) to its liberty: and forced it, after a long Siege, to surrender through Famine; as the same *Ammianus* tells us, lib. 12. And because one Band of those *Franks* fix'd their Habitations upon the Banks of the River Sala, they were thereupon called *Salii*; concerning whom he writes in the same Book, "Having prepar'd these things, he first of all march'd toward the *Franks*; I mean those *Franks* which were commonly called *Salii*, who had formerly with great boldness fix'd their Habitations within the Roman Territories, near a place called *Toxiandria.*" Again, in his 20th Book he makes mention of that Country possess'd by the *Franks* beyond the Rhine, and called "Francia." "Having on a sudden pass'd the Rhine, he entered the Country of those *Franks* called *Attuarii*, a turbulent sort of People, who at that time made great Havock on the Frontiers of *Gallia.*" And in his 30th Book, where he speaks of King *Macrianus*, with whom *Valentinian* the Emperor had lately made a Peace on the Banks of the Rhine, in the Territory of Metz, "He died, says he, in *Francia*, whilst he was utterly wasting with Fire and Sword all before him, being kill'd in an Ambush laid for him by that valiant King *Mellobaudes.*" Now of this *Mellobaudes*, King of the *Franks*, the same Author in his following Book gives this Character; "That he was brave and valiant, and upon the score of his Military Virtue constituted great Matter of the Household by the Emperor *Gratianus*, and Lieutenant-General (in conjunction with *Nannienus*) of that Army which was sent against the *Lentiates*, a People of *Germany.*" Afterwards, by virtue of a Treaty concluded between the *Franks* and the Emperor *Honorius*, they defended the Frontiers of the Roman *Gallia* against *Stilicon:* For *Orosius* tells us in his last Book, "That the Nations of the *Alani, Suevi* and *Vandali*, being (together with many others) encouraged by *Stilicon*; pass'd the Rhine, wasted the Territories of the *Franks*, and invaded *Gallia.*"

After the Emperor *Honorius's* time, we have very little in History extant concerning the *Frank's* Warlike Deeds. For to those Times must be apply'd what St. Ambrose writes in his Letter (the 29th) to Theodosius the Emperor: That the *Franks* both in Sicily and many other Places, had overthrown *Maximus* the Roman General. "He (says he, speaking of *Maximus*) was presently beaten by the *Franks* and Saxons in all places of the

Earth." But in the Reign of *Valentinian* the 3rd, that is, about the 450th Year of Christ, 'tis plain, by the consent of all Writers, that *Childeric*, the Son of *Meroveus*, King of the *Franks*, completed the Deliverance of *Gallia* from the Roman Tyranny, after a continued Struggle of more than 200 Years; and was the first that establish'd in *Gallia* a firm and certain Seat of Empire: For although some reckon *Pharamond* and *Clodio-crinitus* as the first *Kings* of the *Franks*, yet without doubt there were many before them, who (like them) had cross'd the Rhine, and made Irruptions into *Gallia:* but none had been able to settle any peaceable Dominion within the Limits of *Gallia.* Now *Meroveus*, who is commonly reckon'd the 3rd King; though he was indeed King of the *Franks*, yet he was a Stranger and a Foreigner, not created King in *Gallia*, not King of the *Francogalli;* that is to say, not elected by the joynt Suffrages of both Nations united: In short, all these were *Kings* of the *Franci*, and not of the *Francogalli*. But *Childeric*, the Son of *Meroveus*, was (as we said before) the first that was elected by the publick Council of the associated *Franks* and *Gauls;* and he was created King of *Francogallia* presently after his Father *Meroveus* had been kill'd in a Battle against *Attila*, during the Reign of *Valentinian* the Third, a dissolute and profligate Prince. At which time the *Angli* and *Scoti* took Possession of *Great Britain;* the *Burgundians* of *Burgundy, Savoy* and *Dauphine;* the Goths of *Aquitain;* the *Vandals* of *Africk* and *Italy,* nay of *Rome* it self; the *Hunni* under their Leader *Attila* wasted *Gallia* with Fire and Sword. This *Attila* having an Army of about Five hundred thousand Men, over-ran all *Gallia* as far as Toulouse. *Aetius* was at that time Governor of *Gallia*, who fearing the Power of *Attila*, made a League with the Goths, and by their assistance defeated *Attila* in a Battle; wherein, 'tis said, they slew no fewer than a Hundred and eighty thousand Men. But the Conqueror *Aetius* being suspected by Valentinian of aspiring to the Empire, was afterwards, by his Command, put to Death; and within a little while after, he himself was slain by Maximus before-mention'd.

During these Transactions, *Meroveus*, King of the *Franks*, taking his Opportunity, pass'd the Rhine, with a great Army; and joyning in Confederacy with many Cities, who assisted in the common Cause of the publick *Liberty,* possess'd himself at length of the innermost Cities belonging to the *Celtae*, between the Seine and the *Garonne*. He being dead, and both Nations (the *Gauls* and *Franks*) united into one *Commonwealth;* they unanimously elected *Childeric,* the Son of *Meroveus,* for their King, placing him upon a Shield according to ancient Custom; and carrying him upon their Shoulders thrice round the place of Assembly, with great Acclamations of Joy, and universal Congratulation, saluted him King of *Francogallia.* Of all which particulars, *Sidonius Apollinaris, Gregorius Turonensis, Otto Frising. Aimoinus,* and others are Witnesses; whose Testimonies we shall further produce, when we come to treat of the Manner of the Inauguration of the King.

The Words of the same *Otto,* in the last Chapter but one of his 4th Book concerning their taking possession of several Cities, are these. "The *Franks,* after having pass'd the Rhine, in the first place put to flight the Romans, who dwelt thereabouts; afterwards they took *Tournay* and *Cambray,* Cities of *Gallia;* and from thence gaining ground, by degrees they subdued *Rheims, Soissons, Orleans, Cologne* and *Triers.*" And thus much may briefly be said touching the first King of *Francogallia.* To which we shall only subjoin this Remark: [73] That although the *Francogallican* Kingdom has lasted from that time to this, almost One thousand two hundred Years; yet during so long a space, there are but three Families reckon'd to have possess'd the Throne, viz. the *Merovingians;* who beginning from Meroveus, continued it to their Posterity two hundred eighty three Years. The *Carolingians,* who drawing their Original from *Charles* the Great, enjoy'd it 337 Years: And lastly, the *Capetians,* who being descended from Hugh *Capet,* now rule the Kingdom, and have done so for Five hundred and eighty Years past.

73. Note in margin: "Hotoman's *Francogallia* was written Anno 1574."

CHAPTER VI

Whether the Kingdom of *Francogallia* was *hereditary* or *elective;* and the manner of making its *Kings*

But here arises a famous Question; the decision of which will most clearly show the Wisdom of our Ancestors. Whether the Kingdom of *Francogallia* were Hereditary, or conferr'd by the Choice and Suffrages of the People? That the German *Kings* were created by the Suffrages of the People, *Cornelius Tacitus*, in his Book *De moribus Germanorum*, proves plainly; and we have shown, that our *Franks* were a German People: *Reges ex nobilitate, Duces ex virtute sumunt;* "Then *Kings* (says he) they chuse from amongst those that are most eminent for their Nobility; their Generals out of those that are famous for their Valor." Which Institution, to this very day,[74] the *Germans, Danes, Swedes* and *Polanders* do retain. They elect their *Kings* in a Great Council of the Nation; the Sons of whom have this privilege (as *Tacitus* has recorded) to be preferred to other Candidates. I do not know whether any thing could ever have been devised more prudently, or more

---

74. Note in margin: "1574."

proper for the Conservation of a *Commonwealth,* than this Institution. For so Plutarch, in his Life of *Sylla,* plainly advises. "Even (says he) as expert Hunters not only endeavour to procure a Dog of a right good Breed, but a Dog that is known to be a right good Dog himself; or a Horse descended from a generous sire, but a tried good horse himself: even so, those that constitute a *commonwealth,* are much mistaken if they have more regard to *kindred,* than to the qualification of the Prince they are about to set over them."

And that this was the Wisdom of our Predecessors in constituting the *Francogallian kingdom,* we may learn, First, from the last will and Testament of the Emperor *Charlemagn,* publish'd by *Joannes Nauclerus* and *Henricus Mutius;* in which there is this clause, "And if any Son shall hereafter be born to any of these, my three Sons, whom the People shall be willing to Elect to succeed his Father in the Kingdom; My Will is, that his Uncles do consent and suffer the Son of their Brother to reign over that portion of the Kingdom which was formerly his father's." Secondly, What *Aimoinus,* lib. I. cap. 4 says, of *Pharamond,* commonly counted the first King of the *Franks,* in these Words. "The *Franks* electing for themselves a King, according to the custom of other Nations, raised up *Pharamond* to the Regal Throne." And again, lib. 4. "But the *Franks* took a certain Clerk or Priest called Daniel; and as soon as his Hair was grown, established him in the Kingdom, calling him *Chilperic.* And lib. *4* cap. *67.* King *Pipin* being dead, his two Sons, *Charles* and *Carlomannus* were elected kings by the consent of all the *Franks.* And in another place As soon as *Pipin* was dead, the *Franks* having appointed a solemn Convention, constituted both his Sons *Kings* over them, upon this foregoing condition, that they should divide the whole Kingdom equally between them." And again, after the Death of one of the Brothers "But *Charles,* after his Brother's Decease, was constituted King by the consent of all the *Franks.*" Also, towards the end of his History of *Charles* the Great, he says, "The Nobility of the *Franks* being solemnly assembled from all parts of the Kingdom; he, in their presence, called forth to him *Lewis* King of *Aquitain,* (the only one of *Heldegardis's* Sons then living) and by the advice and consent of them all, constituted him his Associate in the whole Kingdom, and Heir of the Imperial Dignity." Thus much out of *Aimoinus.*

Many Testimonies of the like nature we find in *Gregorius Turon.* whereof we shall cite only these few following, lib. 2. cap. 12. "The *Franks* (says he) having expelled *Childeric,* unanimously elected *Eudo* for their King." Also lib. 4. cap. 51 "Then the *Franks* (who once looked towards *Childebert* the Elder) sent an Embassy to *Sigebert,* inviting him to leave *Chilperic* and come to them, that they by their own Authority might make him King." And a little after, "The whole Army was drawn up before him; and having set him upon a Shield, they appointed him to be their King." And in another place, "*Sigebert* agreeing to the *Franks* proposals, was placed upon a Shield, according to the Custom of that Nation, and proclaimed King; and so got the Kingdom from his Brother *Chilperic.*" And presently after, "The *Burgundians* and *Austrasians* concluded a Peace with the *Franks,* and made *Clotharius* King over them in all the three Kingdoms,"[75] which particular the Abbot of Ursperg confirms. "The *Burgundians* (says he) and *Austrasians* having struck up a Peace with the *Franks,* advanced *Clotharius* to be King and sole Ruler of the whole Kingdom." And in another place "The *Franks* appointed one of his Brothers, called *Hilderic,* who was already King of the *Austrasians,* to be also their King."

To this matter belongs what *Luitprandus Ticenensis* writes, lib. 1. cap. 6. "And when he was about to enter into that *Francia* which is called Roman, (after having cross'd the Countries of the *Burgundians*) several Ambassadors of the *Franks* met him, acquainting him that they were returning Home again; because being tired with long expectation of his coming, and not able any longer to be without a King, they had unanimously Chosen *Odo* or *Wido,* though 'tis reported the *Franks* did not take *Wido* upon this occasion for their King, *etc.*"

But concerning this *Odo,* the Story is memorable which *Sigebert* relates from whence we may more clearly be inform'd of the manner of their rejecting their King's Son, and "setting up another in his stead." For (sub anno 890.) he says thus "But the *Franks* neglecting *Charles* the Son of *Lewis the Stammerer,* a Boy scarce ten years old; elected *Odo* for their King, who was Son of *Duke Robert,* slain by the Romans." Also *Otto Frising. Chronic.* lib. 6. cap. 10. "The *Western Franks* (says he) with the

[75.] GS *Franc.* could not identify this citation in Gregory of Tours.

consent of *Arnolphus*, chose for their King *Odo* a valiant Man, and Son of Robert." Also in the *Appendix* to *Gregory of Tours*, lib. 15. cap. 30. "After the Death of *Dagobert, Clodoveus* his Son obtain'd his Father's Kingdom, being at that time very young, and all his *Leudes* (that is, Subjects) raised him to the Throne, in Villa Masolano." Also *Sigebert.* in *chronic. anno* 987. "*Lewis* King of the *Franks* being dead, the *Franks* had a mind to transfer the Kingdom to *Charles* the Brother of *Lotharius;* but whilst he spent too much time, deliberating with his Council concerning that Affair, *Hugo* acquires the Kingdom of the *Franks etc.*" There are many Testimonies of the same Kind in Ado, viz. anno 686. "*Clodoveus* the King dying, the *Franks* elect *Clotarius* his Son for their King." And again, "*Clotarius* having reigned four Years, died; in whose stead the *Franks* elected *Theodorick* his Brother." Again, anno 669. "The *Franks* establish'd in the Kingdom a certain Clerk, called Daniel, having caused him to quit his Tonsure and Orders, and name him *Chilperic*." And again, "The *Franks* appoint, as King over them, *Theodoric* the Son of *Dagobert*." Also *Otto Frising.* chron. 6. cap. 13. "*Otto* (says he) King of the *Franks* being dead, *Charles* was created King by unanimous Consent." The *Appendix to Greg. Turon.* lib. 11. cap. 101. says thus, "When *Theodoric* was dead, the *Franks* elected *Clodoveus* his Son, who was very young, to be their King." And cap. 106. "But the *Franks* appoint one *Chilperick* to be their King." Also *Godfrey of Viterbo*, chron. part. 17. cap. 4. "But *Pipin* in being elected by the *Franks*, was declared King by Pope *Zacharias*, they having thrust their cowardly King *Hilderic* into a Monastery."

From these Proofs, and very many others like them, I think 'tis most plain, that the *Kings* of *Francogallia* were made such rather by the Suffrages and Favour of the People, than by any Hereditary Right. Of which a farther Argument may be the Forms and Ceremonies used by our Ancestors, at the Inauguration of their *Kings*. For we observe, the very same Custom was continued at the Election of our *Kings*, which we told you before out of *Cornelius Tacitus,* was formerly practised by the *Caninefates,* (the *Franks* own Country-men) viz. that they set their Elected King upon a Shield, and carried him on high on Men's Shoulders. So did we; for whoever was chosen by the Votes of the People, was set upon a Shield, and carried thrice round the place of publick Meeting for Election, or round about the Army on Men's Shoulders, all the People expressing their Joy by Acclamations, and clapping of Hands. *Greg. Turon.* lib. 2. where he makes mention of King *Clodoveus*'s Election, "But they (says he) as soon as they heard these things, applauding him both with their Hands and Tongues, and hoisting him on a Shield, appointed him to be their King." Also lib. 7. cap. 10. where he speaks of *Gondebaldus*, "And there (says he) placing their King upon a Shield, they lifted him up; but 'tis reported, that as they were carrying him round the third time, he fell down; so that he was scarcely kept from tumbling to the very Ground by those that stood about him." Of which Accident *Aimoinus*, lib. 3. cap. 6. gives us this Account, "They called forth *Gondebaldus*, and according to the Custom of the ancient *Franks*, proclaimed him their King, and hoisted him on a Shield; and as they were carrying him the third time round the whole Army, of a sudden they fell down with him, and could scarce get him up again from the Ground." The like says *Ado. Vien.* Aetat. 6. "*Sigebertus* consenting to the *Franks*, was placed upon a Shield, according to the Custom of that Nation, and proclaimed King": And peradventure from hence arose that Form among those Writers, who treat of the Creation of a King; *In Regem elevatus est.*[76]

But now we come to the third Part of this Controversy, in order to understand, how great the *Right and Power of the People was, both in making* and *continuing their Kings.* And I think it is plainly proved from all our Annals, that *the highest Power of abdicating their Kings,* was lodged in the People.[77] The very first that was created King, of *Francogallia*, is a remarkable Instance of this Power. For when the People had found him out to be a profligate lewd Person, wasting his time in Adulteries and Whoredoms they removed him from his Dignity by universal Consent, and constrain'd him to depart out of the Territories of France: and this was done, as our Annals testify, in the Year of Christ 469. Nay, even *Eudo*, whom they had placed in his stead, abusing his Power through excessive

[76.] "He is elevated to kingship."

[77.] These italicized passages would have had special resonance for British audiences in the 1700s given the ongoing debate about the fall of James II in 1688–89. The Latin text reads: "ordinum ac populi ius potestasque fuerit." Molesworth's translation silently drops the "ordinum" or "estates" qualification.

Pride and Cruelty, was with the like Severity turned out. Which Fact we find attested by *Gregory of Tours,* lib. 2. cap. 12. *Aimoinus,* lib. 1. cap. 7. *Godfrey of Viterbo,* part. 17. cap. 1. *Sigebertus,* sub annis 461 & 469. "*Childeric* (says *Gregorius*) being dissolved in Luxury, when he was King of the *Franks;* and beginning to deflower their Daughters, was by his Subjects cast out of the Throne with Indignation, whereupon he finding they had a Design to kill him, fled into *Thoringia.* But the *Abbot* of *Ursperg* says, "the People were unwilling to kill him but contented themselves with having turned him out, *because he was a dissolute Man,* and a Debaucher of his Subjects Daughters." *Sigebertus* says, "*Hilderick* behaving himself insolently and luxuriously, the *Franks* thrust him out of the Throne, and made *Aegidius* their King."

And this most glorious and famous Deed of our Ancestors, deserves the more diligently to be remark'd, for having been done at the very Beginning, and as it were, the Infancy of that Kingdom; as if it had been a Denunciation, and Declaration, that the *Kings* of *Francogallia* were made such, upon certain *known Terms and Conditions;* and *were not Tyrants* with *absolute unlimited* and *arbitrary Power.*

Their Successors also, keeping up the same Custom, in the Year of Christ 679, forced *Childeric,* their Eleventh King, to *Abdicate,* because he had behaved himself insolently and wickedly in his Government. And he having formerly caused a certain Nobleman, called *Bodilo,* to be tied to a Stake and whipp'd, without bringing him to a Tryal, was a few Days after slain by the same *Bodilo.* Our Authors are *Aimoinus,* lib. 4. cap. 44. *Trithemius,* anno 678. and *Sigebertus,* anno 667.

The Severity of our Ancestors appear'd in the same Manner a little while after, in the Instance of their 12th King *Theodoric;* who being a wicked and covetous Prince, "the *Franks* (says *Aimoinus*) rose up against him, and cast him out of the Kingdom, cutting off his Hair by force," lib. 4. cap. 44. *Ado,* Aetat. 6. anno 696. but *Sigebertus* sub anno 667. imputes a great many of his Crimes to *Ebroinus* his Favourite and chief General. "King *Theodorick* (says he) was deposed by the *Franks,* because of the Insolence of *Ebroinus,* and his Brother *Hilderick* was with unanimous Consent chosen King." And *Ado* says, "The *Franks* cast *Theodorick* out of the Kingdom, shaved *Ebroinus* in the Monastery of *Lexovium,* and afterwards raised *Childerick* to be King over them." Also the Appendix to *Greg.* of *Tours*, lib. 2. cap. 64. "The *Franks* rise up In Arms against *Theodorick*, cast him out of the Kingdom, and cut off his Hair: They shaved also *Ebroinus*."

The like Virtue our Ancestors exerted in the Case of *Chilperick* their 18th King, whom they "forced to abdicate the Kingdom," and made him a Monk, judging him unworthy to sit at the Helm of so great an Empire, "by reason of his Sloth."[78] Whereof *Aimoinus*, lib. 4. cap. 61. *Sigebertus* and *Trithemius*, anno 750. and *Godfrey*, Chronic, part. 17. cap. 4. are our Witnesses.

Again, a sixth Example of the like Severity is extant in *Charles the Gross*, their 25th King; who for the like Cowardise, and because he had granted away part of France to the *Normans*, *suffering his Kingdom to be dismembered*, was "rejected and turn'd out by the Nobility and Gentry of the Kingdom,"[79] as *Sigebertus* tells us anno 890. Which same thing *Godfridus* records, part. 17. But more at large *Otto Frising.* chron. 6. cap. 9. where he adds this memorable Passage, "This Man (says he) who next to *Charles* the Great, had been the King of greatest Power and Authority of all the *Kings* of the *Franks*, was in a short time reduced to so low a Condition, that he wanted Bread to eat; and miserably begg'd a small Allowance from *Arnolphus*, who was chosen King in his stead, and thankfully accepted of a poor Pension: From whence we may observe the uncertain and miserable State of all Human Greatness; that he who had govern'd all the Eastern and Western Kingdoms, together with the Roman Empire, should at last be brought down to such a Degree of Poverty, as to want even Bread." A Seventh Instance is *Odo* the 26th King, who after he had been elected King in the Room of *Charles* the Son of *Lewis* the Stammerer, was, in the 4th Year of his Reign, by the *Franks*, banish'd into Aquitain, and commanded to abide there; they replacing in his stead the same *Charles* the Son of *Lewis*. Which Fact is recorded by *Sigebertus*, sub anno 894. *Aimoinus* lib. 5. cap. 42. and *Godfridus* part. 17.

We must add to this Number *Charles* the 27th King, surnamed (be-

---

[78.] Note in margin: "Regno se abdicare coegerunt" and "propter inertiam." GS *Franc.* translate as "They obliged him to resign the throne." Molesworth prefers "abdicate" for contextual reasons.

79. Note in margin providing the Latin: "ab optimatibus Regni repudiatus."

cause of his Dulness[80]) *Charles* the *Simple:* Who having through his Folly suffer'd his Kingdom to run to Decay, and lost Lorrain (which he had before recover'd) was "taken and cast into Prison, and *Rodolphus* was chosen" in his place, as *Aimoinus,* lib. 5. cap. 42. and *Sigebertus,* anno 926. do testify.

80. Note in margin providing the Latin: "Propter stuporem ingenii."

CHAPTER VII

What Rule was observ'd concerning the Inheritance of the deceased King, when he left more Children than one

All that we have above said, tends to prove, that the Kingdom of *Franco-gallia* in old times, did not descend to the Children by Right of Inheritance (as a private Patrimony does); but was wont to be bestow'd by the Choice and publick Suffrages of the People: So that now there is the less Room left for the Question, — What Rule was observed in Relation to the Children of the deceased King, when he left more than one behind him. For since the Supreme Power not only of Creating, but also of dethroning their *Kings*, was lodged in the Convention of the People, and Publick Council of the Nation; it necessarily follows, that the ordering the Succession (whether they should give it entirely to one, or divide it) was likewise in the People. Although in this place another Question may arise, viz. supposing the People should reject the Son of their King, and elect a Stranger, whether any thing should be allowed to the first to maintain his Dignity? For the Solution, of which 'tis to be understood, that Lawyers[81]

[81.] Molesworth silently translates "Roman Law" as "lawyers."

reckon four Kinds of such Goods, as may be properly said to be under the King's Governance;[82] viz. the Goods of *Caesar,* the Goods of the Exchequer; the Goods of the Publick, and Private Goods. The Goods of *Caesar* are such as belong to the Patrimony of every Prince, not as he is King, but as he is *Ludovicus,* or *Lotharius,* or *Dagobertus.* Now this Patrimony is called by the Gallican Institutions, The King's Domain; which cannot be alien'd, but by the Consent of the publick Council of the Nation, as we shall make it appear hereafter, when we come to treat of the Authority of that Council. The Goods of the Exchequer are such as are given by the People, partly to defend the King's Dignity, and partly appropriated to the Uses and Exigencies of the *Commonwealth.* The Goods of the Publick (as the Lawyers call them) are such as inseparably belong to the Kingdom and *Commonwealth.* The private Goods are reckon'd to be such Estate, Goods and Fortune, as are esteemed to belong to every Father of a Family. Therefore upon the Death of any King, if the Kingdom be conferr'd on a Stranger, the Patrimonial Estate, as Lawyers call it, (being what was not in the King's Power to alienate) shall descend by Inheritance to his Children: But that which belongs to the Kingdom and *Commonwealth,* must necessarily go to him who is chosen King, because it is part of the Kingdom. Although it may be reasonable, that Dukedoms, Counties, and such like (by Consent of the publick Convention of the People) may be assigned to such Children for the Maintenance of their Quality; as *Otto Frising. Chron.* 5. cap. 9 and *Godfrey of Viterbo,* tell us, That *Dagobert* Son of *Lotharius* being made King, assigned certain Towns and Villages near the Loire, to his Brother *Heribert* for his Maintenance. Which *Aimoinus* confirms, lib. 4. cap. 17. and further adds, that he made a Bargain with him, to live as a private Person, and to expect no more of his Father's Kingdom. Also in his 61. chap. where he speaks of King *Pipin,* "He bestowed (says he) some Counties on his Brother *Grifon,* according to the Order of the Twelve Peers." And to this belongs what *Greg. Turon.* writes, lib. 7. cap. 32. "*Gondobaldus* sent two Ambassadors to the King with consecrated Rods in their Hands, (that no Violence might be offer'd them by

[82.] Note in margin providing the Latin: "In Regis ditione"; GS *Franc.* indicate the original text as "in principis imperio ac ditione" ("within the authority and at the disposal of the prince," GS *Franc.,* p. 247).

any body, according to the Rites of the *Franks*) who spoke these Words to the King, *Gondobaldus* says, he is a Son of King *Clotharius*, and has sent us to claim a due Portion of his Kingdom."

But to return to the Question, as far as it relates to the Succession of the Kingdom; I can find out no certain Rule or Law in *Francogallia* touching that Matter; because (as I said before) the Kingdom was not hereditary. 'Tis true, that in many *Noble Patrimonies* there was what we call *Fiefs, Feuda;* as *Otto Frising.* lib. 2. cap. 29. observes, "'Tis the Custom (says he) in Burgundy, which is also in most of the other Provinces of France, that the Authority of the Paternal Inheritance always falls to the Elder Brother, and his Children, whether Male or Female; the others looking on him as their Lord." And that the same was practised among the whole Nation of the *Franks, Petrus de Vineis,* lib. epist. 6. epist. 25. and in other places of his Writings, sets forth at large. But in the Succession of the Kingdom a different Rule was observ'd. For our Records do testify, that in old times the Kingdom of *Francogallia,* upon the Death of the King, was very often, not bestowed by the People on any one of his Sons, but divided into convenient Parcels, and a part assigned to each of them. Therefore when *Clodoveus* the 2nd King dyed, anno 515. who left four Sons, *Theodorick, Clodoveus, Childebert,* and *Clotharius,* we find the Kingdom was thus divided among them; *Theodorick* had the Kingdom of Metz for his Share, *Clodoveus* that of Orleans, *Clotharius* that of Soissons, and *Childebertus* that of Paris, as 'tis recorded by *Agathius,* lib. hist. 1. *Greg. Turon.* lib. 3. cap. 1. *Aimoinus* lib. 2. cap. 1. *Rhegino* sub anno 421.

Again, after the Death of *Clotharius* the 4th King, the Kingdom was divided among his four Sons. So that *Cherebertus* had that of Paris; *Guntranus,* Orleans: *Chilpericus, Soissons:* and *Sigebertus* that of Rheims, Greg. lib. 4. cap. 22. *Aimoinus* lib. 3. cap. 1. *Rhegino* sub anno 498.

On the other hand, *Otto Frising.* chron. 5. cap. 9. and *God. Viterb.* tell us, That about the Year 630, when *Lotharius* the 7th King died, *Dagobertus* his Son reigned singly in France, and assigned to his Brother *Heribert* some Cities and Villages on the River Loire, for his Maintenance. For from *Clodoveus's* Time till now, the Kingdom of the *Franks* was confusedly subdivided among the Sons, and the Sons of Sons, each of which reigned over the part allotted him. "The Extent of the Kingdom of the

Franks reaching now from Spain, as far as to Hungary: *Dagobert* being sole King of all the *Franks,* gave Laws to the Bavarians." So says *Godefridus,* not without good Grounds, as many wise Men have thought. For, as *Justin* tells us, lib. 21. "That Kingdom will be much more potent, which remains under the Domination of one Person, than when 'tis divided among many Brothers."

But after some Years, when the Kingdom of the *Franks* was excessively enlarged on all Sides, and King *Pipin* was dead, the General Council of the *Gauls* changed this Method again. Which serves to confirm what we said before; viz. That the whole Power, relating to that Matter, was lodged in that Council. For *Eguinarthus,* in his *Life of Charlemagn,* writes thus, "After King *Pipin*'s Death, the *Franks* having assembled themselves in a solemn general Convention, did there appoint both his Sons to be their *Kings,* upon this Condition, that they should equally divide the whole body of the Kingdom between them: And that *Charles* should reign over that part of it, which their Father *Pipin* enjoy'd; and *Carloman* over the other Part which their Uncle held." Also the *Abbot* of *Ursperg* says, "When *Pipin* was dead, his two Sons *Charles* and *Carloman,* by the Consent of all the *Franks,* were created *Kings,* upon Condition, that they should divide the whole body of the Kingdom equally between them." The same Method in dividing the Kingdom, was practised after the Death of *Charlemagn,* as 'tis manifest by his last Will and Testament, recorded by *Joannes Nauclerus,* and *Eguinarthus*'s History of his Life. Wherein we find almost all Europe so divided among his three Sons, that nothing was assigned either as a Portion or Dower, to his Daughters; but the marrying and providing for them was entirely trusted to the Care and Prudence of their Brothers. *Otto Frisingensis,* chron. 6. cap. 6. and *Rhegino* in chron. Anno 877. assure us, that the same Manner of dividing the Kingdom was practised in East France, after the Death of King *Lewis the Stammerer,* in 874. Again, some Years after, anno 880. after King *Lewis* the 23rd King's Death, the very same way of dividing the Kingdom was made use of; which however we are to observe, was "not in the Power and Arbitriment of the *Kings* themselves; but done by the Authority of the Publick Council," as we may easily collect from these Words of *Aimoinus,* lib. 5. cap. 40. "The Sons (says he) of *Lewis,* late King of the *Franks* met at Amiens, and divided their Fathers Kingdom between them, according to the Direction of their faithful Subjects."

From all which Arguments 'tis very plain, that anciently there was no certain Law or Right of *Francogallia* touching this Matter; but the whole Power of disposing of it was lodged in the Publick Council of the Nation. Indeed afterwards in the Reign of Philip the 3rd, (the 41st King) it was ordained, that certain Lordships might be set out and assigned to younger Brothers: But even of this Law there were various interpretations, and many Controversies arose concerning Daughters; so that we can deliver nothing for certain in this Affair; only thus much we may truly say, That if the Ancient Institution of our Ancestors ought to be our Rule, the Determination of this whole Matter must be left to the Publick General Council of the Nation: that according to the Number of Children, some particular Lordships or Territories, may (*by its Authority*) be assigned for their Maintenance.

Of the *Salick Law,* and what Right Women had in the *King*'s their Father's Inheritance

Because we have undertaken to give an Account of the Law and Right of Regal Inheritance, we must not omit making mention of the *Salick Law;* which is both daily discours'd of by our Countrymen, and in the memory of our Forefathers serv'd to appease a great and dangerous Contention, which arose touching the Succession to the Crown.[83] For when (Anno 1328.) *Charles* the Fair, Son of *Philip* the Fair, died, leaving his Wife with Child of a Daughter, (which some Months after was born) *Edward* King of England (Son of *Isabella,* the Daughter of *Philip* the fair, and Sister to *Charles* lately dead) claimed the Inheritance of his Grandfather's Kingdom as his Right. But *Philip* of Valois, Cousin-german by the Father's Side to the deceased King, standing up, alledged that there was an ancient Regal Law, called the *Salick Law,* by which all Women were ex-

[83.] Issues of female succession in the Hanoverian line (i.e., Sophia of Hanover) rendered this chapter (translated between 1705 and 1711) very sensitive for an Anglophone audience.

cluded from the Inheritance of the Crown. Now this Law both *Gaguinus* and other Writers of like stamp tell us, was written by *Pharamond;* and he calls it a most famous Law, even to his Time. For in his Life of Philip of Valois; "The *Salick Law* (says he) was a Bar to Edward's Title; which Law being first given by *Pharamond* to the *Franks,* has been religiously observed, even to those days. By that Law, only the Heirs Male of our *Kings* are capable of governing the Kingdom, and no Females can be admitted to that Dignity. The Words of that Law are these: *Nulla hereditatis portio de terra Salica ad mulierem venito;* 'Let no part of the Inheritance of Salick Land come to a Woman.' Now (says *Gaguinus*) the French Lawyers call Salick Land, such as belongs only to the King, and is different from the Allodial which concerns the Subjects; to whom, by that Law, is granted a free dominion of any thing, not excluding the Princely Authority." And to the same Purpose, not only almost all the *Francogallican* Historians, but even all the Lawyers and Pettifoggers have wrote to this Day, as *Paponius* testifies, *Arrest.* lib. 4. cap. 1. So that now the mistake has prevailed so far, as to have obtained the Force of a Law. To explain this, it must be remembered (which we formerly gave an account of) that the *Franks* had two Seats of their Empire, and two Kingdoms; One in France, which remains to this Day; The other beyond the Rhine, near the River Sala; from whence they were called *Salii,* and *Salici Franci* (joyning the two Names together) but for the most part briefly *Salici;* the Kingdom of these last, and even their very Name is in a Manner extinct. *Ammianus Marcellinus* makes mention in his History (as we told you before) of these *Salii,* and shews, that they are called the Eastern *Franks,* as the other were called the Western. Now as there were two Kingdoms of the *Franks,* so they had different Laws: those that belonged to the *Salii,* were called *Salick;* those that belonged to the *Francogalli,* were called French. *Eguinarthus* in his Life of *Charles* the Great says thus: "After he had assumed, the Imperial Title, finding that his Peoples Laws were in many Things deficient, (for the *Franks* have two Laws, very different from each other in many cases,) he thought of adding such as were wanting." The Author of the Preface to the *Salick Law* has this Passage. "The renowned Nation of the *Franks,* before it was converted to the Catholick Faith, enacted the *Salick Law* by the Great Men of the Nation, who at that Time were their Governors;

and from among a great many, four Persons were chosen; *Wisogast, Arbogast, Salogast,* and *Windogast;* who during three Conventions [*tres mallos*] carefully perusing all Causes from their Original, gave their Judgment and Decree of every one of them in this Manner, *etc."* *Sigebertus* in *Chron.* anni 422. & *Otto Frising.* lib. 4. cap. Penult. make use of almost the same Words. "From that time (say they) the Laws recommended to them by *Wisigastaldus* and *Salogastus,* began to be in Force. By this *Salogastus,* they tell us, that Law was invented, which from his Name is to this Day called the *Salick Law;* and the most noble of the *Franks,* called *Salici,* observe it at this time." Thus say the old Chronographers. By which we may refute the Error of such as derive the *Salick Law,* à Sale, that is, *Prudence;* or that it was called corruptly *Lex Salica,* instead of *Gallica;* than which nothing can be more absurd. But much greater Errors spring from the same Fountain: First, That People are so far imposed upon by those Authors, as to believe the *Salick Law* had reference to the Publick Right of the *Commonwealth* and the Government, also to the *Hereditary Succession* of the Kingdom. Now the very Records or Tables of this *Salick Law* were not many Years ago found and brought to light; from whose Inscription it appears, that they were first written and publish'd about *Pharamond's* time: Besides, that all the Heads and Articles, both of the *Salick* and French Laws, were Constitutions relating only to private Right between Man and Man, and meddled not with the publick Right of the Kingdom or *Commonwealth:* among the rest one Chapter, tit. 62. has this in it. "Of the Salick Land, no Part or Portion of Inheritance passes to a Female; but this falls to the Male Off-spring; that is, the Sons shall succeed to the Inheritance: But where a dispute shall arise (after a long Course of Time) among the Grandsons and great Grandsons, *de Alode terrae;*[84] let it be divided, *Non per stirpes sed per capita."*[85] The like Law, *Extat apud Ripuarios,* tit. 58. *Item apud Anglos,* tit. 7. Where they are so far from enacting any thing relating to the Inheritances of Kingdoms, that they do not so much as affect Feudal Successions, but only belong to Allodial; although a portion was assigned to Women out of those Allodial Lands. Which way

[84.] Note in margin: "*Allodium* is the contrary to *Feudum:* Gothick Words, for which 'tis difficult to find proper English." [*de Alode terrae:* concerning allodial land.]
[85.] "Not by the shoots but by the heads."

soever this matter may be, 'tis manifest in the first place, that although no Article, either of the *Frank* or *Salick Law* were extant, which debars Women from the Inheritance of the Crown; yet the Customs and Institutions of a Nation, preserv'd inviolate by universal consent, during so many Ages, obtain the Force of a written Law: For though *Childeric,* the third King, left two Daughters behind him at his Death, the Kingdom was given to his Brother *Lotharius* and his Daughters excluded. Again, after the Death of *Cherebert* the 5th King, who left three Daughters; the Succession devolv'd upon his Brother *Sigebert.* Also when *Gontrannus* King of Burgundy and Orleans died, the Kingdom was conferr'd on his Brother *Sigebert,* not on his Daughter *Clotilda.* Lastly, Philip of Valois's Advocates might with greater Caution, as well as efficacy, have argued for him out of the Feudal Law, by which all Inheritances of *Fiefs* descend to the Male Issue only, and not to the Female, who are not admitted to them. And when there happens a Want of Heirs Males in that Line or Branch wherein the *Fief* is lodged, then the *Feudum* or *Fief* returns back to the other Stock or Branch: which was the very Case at that Time. But such *Fiefs* as through a Depravation of the Law, are convey'd down to Women, cannot properly be called *Feuda,* but *Feudastra,* as in other of our Writings we have made it appear.

CHAPTER IX

Of the Right of Wearing a large Head of Hair peculiar to the Royal Family

It will not be amiss in this Place to give some Account of a Custom of our Ancestors, relating to the Hair worn by the Royal Family: For 'tis recorded, that our Forefathers had a particular Law concerning it; viz. That such as were chosen *Kings* by the People, or were of the Regal Family, should preserve their Hair, and wear it parted from the Forehead, on both Sides the Head, and anointed with sweet Oyl, as an Ornament and peculiar Mark of their being of the Royal Family; whilst all other Persons, how nobly born soever, had no right to wear a large Head of Hair; but were obliged to go with their Heads shorn or shaved, upon the Account (as 'tis probable) that they should be more ready and expedite in their continual military Exercises, as the Roman Histories tell us of *Julius Caesar,* and several others. *Aimoinus,* lib. 1. cap. 4. says "The *Franks* chusing for themselves a King, according to the Custom of other Nations, raised, *Pharamond* to the Throne, to whom succeeded his Son *Clodio-crinitus;* For at that time the *Kings* of the *Franks* wore large Heads of Hair." Also lib. 3. cap. 61. "*Gundoaldus* being brought up by his Mother after the regal manner, wore a long Head of Hair, according to the Custom of the ancient

Kings of the *Franks*." In like Manner *Agathius*, lib. de Bell. Goth. 1. where he speaks of *Clodoveus*, one of our *Kings*, who was taken in Battle by the Burgundians, (he calls him *Clodamirus*). "As soon (says he) as his Horse had thrown him, the Burgundians espying his large Head of Hair, which fell back over his Shoulders, presently knew him to be the Enemy's General; for 'tis not lawful for the *Kings* of the *Franks* to cut off their Hair, but even from their Childhood they remain untrimm'd, and always keep a large Head of Hair hanging low down upon their Backs." And we have many Instances that it was our Ancestor's Custom, whenever they either deprived any one of the Crown, or took away all Hopes of obtaining the Kingdom, to cut off his Head of Hair. *Aimoinus* in the same Place "He earnestly beholding him, commanded his Hair to be cut off, denying him to be his Son. Also Having caused his Hair to be cut off a second Time, he put him in Prison at Cologne; from whence making his Escape, he fled to *Narses*, and suffer'd his Hair to grow again, *etc.*" Which Story *Gregory of Tours,* lib. 6. cap. 24. likewise records. Also cap. 44. where he speaks of King *Theodorick.* "The *Franks* (says he,) rose up in Arms against him, and cast him out of the Kingdom, and cut off his Head of Hair by Force." But there is a very remarkable, or rather horrible Story related by *Gregory of Tours,* concerning *Crotilda,* the Queen Mother; who chose rather to have the Heads of her two Grandsons cut off than their Hair. 'Tis in his 3rd Book, cap. 18. "Our Mother (says the King to his Brother) has kept our Brother's Sons with her, and intends to advance them to the Throne; we must concert what Measures ought to be taken in this Affair; whether we shall order their Hair to be cut off, and so reduce them to the State of common Subjects; or whether we shall cause them to be put to Death, and afterwards divide the Kingdom between us: Then they sent *Archadius* with a Pair of Scissors in one Hand, and a naked Sword in t'other to the Queen; who approaching her, showed them both to her, and said, Your Sons, most Glorious Queen, have sent me to know your Pleasure, what Destiny you are pleased to allot to these two Youths; whether by suffering their Hair to be cut off, you will have them to live; or whether you had rather have both their Throats cut. Whereupon She chose rather to see them both kill'd, than to have their Hair cut off." I further observe, that it was the Fashion when our *Kings* went to single Combat, to have their long Hair tied up in a large knot atop of their Helmets like a Crest and that was their cognizance or mark in all their Fights. Therefore *Aimoinus*, lib. 4, cap. 18. where he speaks of the dreadful Combat between King *Dagobert* and *Bertoaldus*, Duke of the *Saxons:* "The King (says he) having his Hair, together with a Part of his Helmet, cut off with a Blow of a Sword on his Head, sent them by his Esquire to his Father, desiring him to hasten to his assistance."

Now when I consider what might be the Reasons of this Institution, I can find none but this: That since it had been the ancient Custom of the *Gauls* and *Franks* to wear their Hair long (as it was also of the *Sicambri*, and of most others in those Parts) our Ancestors thought fit to continue, and in process of time to appropriate this Ornament, and Mark of Distinction to the Regal Family. No Person, though but indifferently learned, needs any Proof that the *Gauls* wore their Hair long, especially when he calls to mind that of the Poet *Claudian*, ex lib. in *Ruffin.* 2. "*Inde truces flavo comitantur vertice* Galli, *Quos* Rhodanus *velox*, Araris *quos tardior ambit, Et quos nascentes explorat gurgite* Rhenus."[86] Now that the *Franks* did so too, whom we have shewn to be descended from the *Chauci* or *Chaiici*, that single Passage of the Poet Lucan is sufficient to confirm.

> *Et vos* crinigeros *bellis arcere* Chaycos
> *Oppositi, petitis* Romam, *etc.*[87]

Which being so, we may easily comprehend the Reason why Strangers, who were ill affected towards our Nation, contumeliously called our *Kings*, who wore so great a Head of Hair, *Reges setatos*, bristled *Kings;* and not only so, but (though Bristles and long Hair be common to Lyons, Horses and Swine, all which are therefore called *Setosi*, or *Setigeri*) they stretched the Contumely so far, as to say, they had Hog's Bristles. From whence arose that filthy Fiction and foul Name, τριχοραχάτον[88] of which *Georgius Cedrenus* writes thus in his History, Ἐλέγοντο δὲ οἱ ἐκ τοῦ γένους ἐκείνου καταγόμενοι κριστάτοι, ὃ ἑρμηνεύεται τριχοραχάτοι εἶχον γὰρ κατὰ

[86.] GS *Franc.*, p. 281, translate the passage as "Thence follow the hirsute Gauls, yellow-crowned, / whom the swift Rhone and the tardy Saone surround / while the Rhine seeks out their watery origins."

[87.] GS *Franc.* translate the passage as "On Rome's behalf you boldly sought to check the long-haired *Chayci* from their warlike course."

[88.] "Hairy crests."

τῆς ῥάχεως αὐτῶν τρίχας ἐκφυομένας, ὡς χοῖροι; that is, "They who were of the Kingly Race were called *Cristati,* which may be interpreted Bristle-back'd; because they had all along their Backbones Bristles growing out like Swine." Which Passage of Cedrenus, I believe, is corrupted, and instead of the Word ΚΡΙΣΆΤΟΙ, ought to be ΣΕΤΆΤΟΙ, or perhaps both. For as some Persons called them pleasantly *Christati,* by Reason of their large erected Bunch of Hair upon the Tops of their Helmets; so their ill-Willers called them upbraidingly *Setati,* or *Setigeri.* If *Cedrenus* had not been so very plain in this Passage, and the Appellation of *Cristati* be to be retained, I should rather have thought they might have been called τριχοχάρακτοι, as being remarkable for their large Heads of Hair.

CHAPTER X

The Form and Constitution of the *Francogallican* Government

These Things being thus briefly premised, we think it proper now to set forth in what Manner the Kingdom of *Francogallia* was constituted. And we have already made it plain, that the People reserv'd to themselves all the Power not only of Creating, but also of Abdicating their *Kings*. Which Form of Government 'tis manifest our Ancestors had, before they were brought under by the Romans. "So that the People (as *Caesar* tells us) had no less Authority and Power over their *Kings*, than the *Kings* had over the People. *Populus non minus in Regem, quam rex in populum imperii ac potestatis retinet.*" Although 'tis probable the *Franks* did not derive this Constitution of their *Commonwealth* from the *Gauls*; but from their Countrymen, the *Germans*; of whom *Tacitus*, lib. de mor. Germ. says, "*Regibus non est infinita aut libera Potestas.* Their *Kings* have not an Arbitrary or Unlimited Power." Now 'tis manifest that no Form of Government is more remote from Tyranny, than this: for not one of the three distinguishing Marks, or Characteristicks of Tyranny, which the old Philosophers make mention of can be found in the Form and Constitution of our Government. First, as to a forced Obedience; i.e., that a King should rule over a People against their Wills; we have shewn you already, that the Supreme Power, both of Electing and Abdicating their *Kings,* was in the People. Secondly, as to a Life-guard composed of Foreigners, (which they reckon the Second Mark of *Tyranny*); so far were our *Francogallican Kings* from making use of Mercenary Strangers for their Guards, that they had not so much as their own Countrymen and Citizens, for that Purpose; but placed their whole Trust and Confidence in the Love and Fidelity of their Subjects; which they thought a sufficient Guard.

As an Argument of this, we may observe what *Gregory of Tours* writes, lib. 7. cap. 18. and *Aimoinus,* lib. 3. cap. 63. "King *Gontrannus* being inform'd by an ordinary Fellow at Paris, that *Faraulphus* lay in Wait for him, presently began to secure his Person by Guards and Weapons; so that he went no whither (not even to the Holy Places) without being surrounded with armed Men and Soldiers." We have at present a very famous History extant of St. *Lewis,* written by that excellent Person *Joannes Jonvillaeus,* who lived very familiarly with that King for many Years; in which whole History there is not the least Mention made of Guards or Garrisons, but only of Porters or Door-keepers; which in his native Tongue, he calls Ushers.

Now as to the third Mark of Tyranny, which is when Matters are so carried, that what is done tends more to the Profit and Will of the Person governing, than to that of the governed, or the Good of the *Commonwealth;* we shall hereafter prove, that the Supreme Administration of the *Francogallican* Kingdom was lodged in the Publick Annual Council of the Nation, which in After-Ages was called the Convention of the Three Estates. For the Frame of this Government was the very same which the Ancient Philosophers, and among them Plato and Aristotle (whom Polybius imitates) judged to be the best and most excellent in the World, as being made up and constituted of a mixture and just temperament of the three Kinds of Government, viz. the Regal, Noble, and Popular. Which Form of a *Commonwealth, Cicero* (in his Books *de Republica*) prefers to all other whatsoever. For since a Kingly and a Popular Government do in their Natures differ widely from each other, it was necessary to add a third and middle State participating of both, viz. that of the Princes or Nobility; who, by reason of the Splendour and Antiquity of their Families, approach, in some degree, to the Kingly Dignity; and yet, being Subjects,

are upon that Account on the same foot and interest with the Commons.
Now of the Excellency of this Temperament in a *Commonwealth*, we have
a most remarkable Commendation in *Cicero*, taken by him out of *Plato's*
Books *de Republica;* which, because of its singular Elegancy, we shall here
insert at length. "Ut in fidibus (inquit) ac tibiis, atque cantu ipso, ac voci-
bus, tenendus est quidam concentus ex distinctis sonis, quem immutatum
ac discrepantem aures eruditae ferre non possunt; isque concentus ex dis-
simillimarum vocum moderatione concors tamen efficitur, & congruens;
Sic ex summis, & mediis, & infimis interjectis ordinibus, ut sonis, mode-
ratâ ratione civitas, consensu dissimillimorum concinit, & quae *harmonia*
à musicis dicitur in *cantu,* ea est in *Civitate concordia:* arctissimum-atque;
optimum in Republica vinculum incolumitatis, quae sine iustitiâ nullo
pacto esse potest." i.e., "As in Fiddles and Flutes, and even in Singing
and Voices, a certain Consort of distinct Sounds is to be observed; which
if it be alter'd, or not tunable, skilful Hearers cannot bear or endure: And
this Consort of very different Tones, is, through a just Proportion of the
Notes, rendered Concord, and very agreeable: Even so a *Commonwealth*,
judiciously proportioned, and composed of the first, the middlemost,
and the lowest of the States, (just as in Sounds) through the Consent of
People very unlike to each other, becomes agreeable: And what Musicians
in Singing call Harmony, that in a *Commonwealth* is Concord; the very
best and strongest Bond of Safety for a Government, which can never
fail of being accompanied with Justice." Our Ancestors therefore following this Method, of a just Mixture of all the three kinds, in the constituting their *Commonwealth,* most wisely ordained, that every Year on the
Calends of May, a Publick Council of the whole Nation should be held:
at which Council the great Affairs of the Republick should be transacted
by the common Consent and Advice of all the Estates. The Wisdom and
Advantage of which Institution, appears chiefly in these three things:
First, That in the Multitude of prudent Counsellors, the Weight and Excellency of Counsel shews it self more apparently, as Solomon and other
Wise Men have said. Secondly, *Because it is an essential part of liberty, that
the same persons, at whose cost and peril any thing is done, should have it done
likewise by their authority and advice; for* ('tis a common Saying) *what concerns all, ought to be approved by all.* Lastly, That such Ministers of State

as have great Power with the Prince, and are in high Employments, may be kept within the Bounds of their Duty, through the awe they stand in of this great Council, in which all the Demands and Grievances of the Subject are freely laid open. "For such Kingdoms as are ruled by the arbitrary Will and Pleasure of one Prince, may most justly (as Aristotle in his third Book of Politicks observes) be reckon'd Governments of Sheep,[89] and brute Beasts, without Wit or Judgment; not of Freemen, who are endued with Understanding, and the Light of Reason." The Case is thus That even as Sheep are not guided or tended by one of their own kind, nor Boys govern'd by one of themselves, but by something of more Excellency; even so a Multitude of Men ought not to be ruled and govern'd by one single person, who perhaps understands and sees less than several others among them; but by many select persons, who, in the Opinion of all Men, are both very prudent and eminent; and who act by united Counsels, and, as it were, by one Spirit, composed and made up of the Minds of many Wise Men.

Now whereas it may be objected, that most *Kings* have a constant Privy Council to advise them in the Administration of publick Affairs: We answer, That there is a great deal of Difference between a Counsellor of the King, and a Counsellor of the Kingdom. This last takes care of the safety and profit of the whole *Commonwealth;* the other serves the humour and studies the conveniences of one Man only; and besides, these King's Counsellors reside, for the most part, in one certain Place; or at least near the Person of the Prince, where they cannot be supposed to be thoroughly acquainted with the Condition of the more remote Cities or Provinces; and being debauched by the Luxury of a Court-life, are easily depraved, and acquire a lawless Appetite of Domineering; are wholly intent upon their own ambitious and covetous designs; so that at last they are no longer to be consider'd as Counsellors for the Good of the Kingdom and *Commonwealth*, but Flatterers of a single Person, and *Slaves* to their own and their Prince's Lusts.

Concerning this Matter, we have a most excellent Saying of the Emperor *Aurelian,* recorded by *Flavius Vopiscus.* "My Father used to tell me

[89.] The original has "cattle" rather than "sheep."

(says *Aurelian*) that the Emperor *Dioclesian,* whilst he was yet a private Man, frequently said, That nothing in the World was more difficult than to govern well. For, four or five Persons combine together, and unanimously agree to deceive the Emperor; they determine what shall be approved or disapprov'd. The Emperor, who, for the most part, is shut up in his Palace, knows nothing of the truth of affairs; he is compell'd to hear and see only with their Ears and Eyes; he makes Judges, such Persons as do not deserve to be made so; he removes from Offices in the *Commonwealth* such as he ought to keep in; in short, a good, provident and excellent Emperor is sold by such Counsellors." Now our Ancestors, in the constituting their Commonwealth, wisely avoiding these mischiefs (as Mariners would do dangerous Rocks) decreed that the Publick Affairs should be managed by the joynt Advice and Counsel of all the Estates of the Kingdom. To which Purpose the King, the Nobles, and the Representatives of the Commons out of the several Provinces, were obliged to meet at a certain time every year. And this very same institution we find to have been that of many other Nations. First in our Ancient *Gallia,* where the Administration of Publick Affairs was intrusted with the Common Council of the chosen Men in the whole Nation, as we have above demonstrated. But because we are now speaking of a Kingdom, I shall give Instances of them. 'Tis manifest, that in old Times the Council of the Amphyctions was instituted in Greece (as *Suidas* and others testify) by King *Amphyction,* Son of *Deucalion;* and therein it was ordained, that at a certain appointed time every year, Representatives chosen out of the Twelve *Commonwealths* of Greece should meet at *Thermopylae,* and deliberate concerning all the weighty Affairs of the Kingdom and *Commonwealth:* For which Reason, *Cicero* calls this the Common Council of *Graecia,* Pliny calls it the Publick Council.

We find the like Wisdom in the Constitution of the German Empire, wherein the Emperor represents the Monarchical State, the Princes represent the Aristocratical, and the Deputies of the Cities the Democratical; neither can any Matter of Moment appertaining to the whole German Republick be firm and ratified, but what is first agreed upon in that great Convention of the Three Estates. To this End was framed that ancient and famous Law of the Lacedemonians, which joyned the *Ephori* to their *Kings;* "Who, as Plato writes, were designed to be like Bridles to the

Kings, and the *Kings* were obliged to govern the Commonwealth by their Advice and Authority."[90] *Pliny*, lib. 6. cap. 22. makes mention of the like Practice in the Island of Taprobana, where the King had thirty Advisers appointed by the People; by whose Counsel he was to be guided in the Government of the *Commonwealth*; "For fear (says he) lest the King (in case he had an unlimited Power) should esteem his Subjects no otherwise than as his *Slaves* or his Cattle." Furthermore, we find the very same Form of Administration of the Kingdom of England, In *Polydore Virgil*'s History of *England*, lib. 11. where he has this passage in the Life of Henry the First, "Before this Time the *Kings* used to summon a publick Convention of the People in order to consult with them, but seldom: So that we may in some manner say, that the Institution derived its Original from Henry; which took such deep Root, that it has always continued ever since, and still does so; viz. That whatever related to the Well-governing or Conservation of the *Commonwealth*, ought to be debated and determined by the great Council. And that if either the King or the People should act any thing alone, it should be esteemed invalid, and as nothing, unless it were first approved and established by the Authority of that Council. And for fear this Council should be cumbred with the Opinions of an unskilful Multitude, (whose Custom it is to distinguish nothing justly) it was as first establish'd by a certain Law, what Sort of Persons, and what Numbers either of the Priests or of the People should be called to this Council, which, after a French Name, they commonly call A Parliament; which every King at the Beginning of his Reign uses to hold, and as often afterward as he pleases, or as Occasion requires." Thus far *Polydore Virgil*.

But among all the Laws and Customs of this Kind, there is none so remarkable as that of the Spaniards; who, when they elect a King in the *Common-Council* of *Arragon*, (in order to keep up a perpetual Remembrance of their Privileges) represent a Kind of Play, and introduce a certain Personage, whom they call by the Name of *The Law of Arragon*,[91] whom (by a publick Decree) they declare to be greater and more Powerful than their King; and afterwards they harangue the King (who is elected

---

[90.] GS *Franc.* identify this as from *Laws* III 692 (Loeb 219).
91. Note in margin: "La justicia di Arragon."

upon certain Terms and Conditions) in Words which (because of the remarkable Virtue and Fortitude of that Nation in repressing the unbridled
Will of their Prince,) we will here set down at length. "*Nos que valemos
tanto come vos, ii podemos mas que vos; vos elegimos Reii con estas ii estas con-
ditiones; intra vos ii nos un que manda mas que vos:* That is, We, who are of
as great Value as you, and can do more than you, do elect you to be our
King, upon such and such Conditions: Between you and us there is one
of greater Authority than you."[92]

Seeing then that the Case is so, and that *this has always been a constant
and universal Law of all Nations, that are governed by a Kingly, and not by a
Tyrannical Power.* 'Tis very plain, that this most valuable liberty of holding a Common-Council of the Nation, is not only a Part of the *People's
Right;* but that all Kings, who by Evil Arts do oppress or take away this
Sacred Right, ought to be esteemed Violaters of the Laws of Nations; and
being no better than Enemies of Humane Society, must be consider'd not
as *Kings,* but, as *Tyrants.*

But to return to the Matter in Hand. Our *Commonwealth* being constituted by the Laws of our Ancestors, upon the bottom above-mention'd,
and participating of all the three Kinds of Government; it was ordain'd,
that once every Year (and as much oftener as important Occasions should
make it necessary) a Solemn General Council should be held: which, for
that reason, was called a Parliament of the Three Estates. By that Word
was meant a Convention or Meeting of Men out of several Parts of the
Country to one Place, there to confer and deliberate concerning the Publick Welfare: And therefore all Conferences (though between Enemies)
in order to a Peace or Truce, are always in our Chronicles called by the
name of Parliaments. Now of this Council, the King sitting in his Golden
Tribunal, was chief; next to him were the Princes and Magistrates of
the Kingdom; in the third place were the Representatives: of the several
Towns and Provinces, commonly called the Deputies: For as soon as the
Day prefixed for this Assembly was come, the King was conducted to the
Parliament-House with a Sort of Pomp and Ceremony, more adapted
to popular Moderation, than to Regal Magnificence: which I shall not

[92.] GS *Franc.* (pp. 102, 307–8) identify the source for this quote as Zurita and
Lucius Marinaeus.

scruple to give a just account of out of our own Publick Records; it being a sort of Piety to be pleased with the Wisdom of our Ancestors; though in these most profligate Times, I doubt not but it would appear ridiculous to our flattering Courtiers. The King then was seated in a Wagon, and drawn by Oxen, which a Waggoner drove with his Goad to the Place of Assembly: But as soon as he was arrived at the Court, or rather indeed the Venerable Palace of the Republick, the Nobles conducted the King to the Golden Throne; and the rest took their Places (as we said before) according to their Degrees. This State, and in this Place, was what was called *Regia Majestas, Royal Majesty*. Of which we may even at this Day observe a signal Remain in the King's Broad Seal, commonly called the *Chancery* Seal. Wherein the King is not represented in a military Posture a Horseback, or in a Triumphant Manner drawn in his Chariot by Horses, but sitting in his Throne Robed and Crown'd, holding in his Right Hand the Royal Sceptre, in his Left the Sceptre of Justice, and presiding in his Solemn Council. And indeed, in that Place only it can be said that Royal Majesty does truly and properly reside, where the great Affairs of the *Commonwealth* are transacted; and not as the unskilful Vulgar use to profane the Word; and whether the King plays or dances, or prattles with his Women, always to stile him Your Majesty.

Of all these Matters, we shall give only a few Proofs, out of many which we could produce. First, out of *Eginarthus,* who was Chancellor to *Charles* the Great, and wrote his Life. These are his Words: "Wherever he went (speaking of *Charlemagn*) about the publick Affairs, he was drawn in a Waggon by a Pair of Oxen, which an ordinary Waggoner drove after his rustical Manner. Thus he went to the Courts of Justice, thus to the Place of the Publick Convention of his People, which every Year was celebrated for the Good of the Realm; and thus he used to return Home again." *Joannes Nauclerus* gives us an Account of the very same Thing, in almost the same Words, *Chron. Generat.* 26. So does the Author of the *Great Chronicle,* in the Beginning of his Life of *Charlemagn,* Fol. 77.[93] Neither ought this to seem so great a Wonder to any, who considers it was the Fashion in those Days for our *Kings* and Queens, and the Royal

[93.] This is a mistake for folio 177 of the *Grandes chroniques* (1514); see GS *Franc.* p. 324.

Family, to be drawn by Oxen; of which we have one instance in *Greg. Turon.* lib. 3. cap. 26. "*Deuteria*, (says he) Wife of King *Childebert*, seeing her Daughter by a former Husband grown to Woman's Estate, and fearing lest the King (being in Love with her) should lye with her, caused her to be put into a Sort of Litter with untamed Oxen, and thrown Headlong off a Bridge." *Aimoinus*, lib. 4. cap. 30. makes mention of the Golden Throne, where he speaks of King *Dagobert:* "He proclaimed, says he, *Generale P L A C I T U M in loco nuncupato Bigargio,* a Great Council in a Place named *Bigargium:* To which all the Great Men of France assembling with great Diligence on the Kalends of May, the King thus began his Speech to them, sitting on his Golden Throne." Also in his 41st Chapter, speaking of King *Clodoveus* Sitting in the midst of them, on his Golden Throne, he spoke in this Manner, *etc. Sigebertus* in *Chron.* Anni 662. "'Tis the Ancient Custom (says he) of the *Kings* of the *Franks*, every Kalends of May, to preside in a Convention of all the People, to salute and be saluted, to receive Homage, and give and take Presents." *Georgius Cedrenus* expresses this in almost the same Words.[94]

Now, concerning the Authority of the People, who were thus gather'd together at the Great Council, we have many Testimonies. *Aimoinus*, lib. 4. cap. 41. speaking of *Clodoveus* the Second; "Although (says that King in his Speech) the Care of our Earthly Principality obliges us to call you together *Francigenae cives*, and to consult you in Affairs relating to the Publick, *etc.*" Also in his 74th Chapter of the same Book "In the Beginning of the Year he went into Saxony, and there he held a General Convention every Year, as he used to do every Year in France also." Again, lib. 4. cap. 13. where he speaks of *Charles* the Great "When the Hunting near Aix la Chapelle was ended, as soon as he returned, he held a General Convention of his People, according to usual Custom, *etc.*" Cap. 116. "The Emperor having held Two Conventions, one at Nimeguen, the other at Compiegn, wherein he receiv'd the Annual Presents, *etc.*" Again, Cap. 117. "In the Month of August he came to Wormes, and holding there the General Convention according to constant Practice, he received the Yearly Gifts which were offer'd him, and gave Audience to several Am-

[94.] The original duplicates a passage in Greek.

bassadors, *etc.*" Again, Lib. 5. cap. 31. "The *General Placitum* was held on the Ides of June, in the Town *Dusiacum.*"

And this may suffice touching this solemn General Council, which both French and German Historians, through a deprav'd Custom of the Latin Tongue, called by different Names; sometimes *Curia*, sometimes *Conventus Generalis*, but for the most part *Placitum. Gregorius*, lib. 7. cap. 14. says thus: "Therefore when the Time of the *Placitum* approached, they were directed by King *Childebert, etc.*" *Aimoinus*, lib. 4. cap. 109. "In the middle of the Month he held the General Convention at *Thionville*, where there was a very great Appearance of the People of the *Franks;* and in this *Placitum*, the singular Compassion of the most Pious Emperor eminently show'd it self, *etc.*"

Now it was the Custom in that Council to send Presents from all Parts to the King; as may appear from many Places which might be quoted, wherein that Council is called *Conventus Generalis. Aimoinus*, lib. 4. cap. 64. speaking of King *Pipin*, "He compell'd them (says he) to promise they would obey all his Commands, and to send him every Year at the Time of the General Convention, Three Hundred Horses, as a Gift and Token of Respect. *Item*, cap. 85. Not forgetting the Perfidy of the Saxons, he held the General Convention beyond the Rhine, in the Town of *Kuffstein*, according to the usual Custom."

This Council was sometimes called by another Name, *Curia*, the Court; from whence proceeded the common Saying, when People went to the King's Hall or Palace, "We are going to Court"; because they seldom approach'd the King, but upon great Occasions, and when a Council was call'd. *Aimoinus*, lib 5. cap. 50. "*Charles*, (says he) the Son of the Danish King, sued (or prosecuted) several Noble-Men of Flanders very conveniently at this *Curia*, or Court." Item, cap. *Sequenti;* "Henry King of the Romans being dead, at that Great and General Court, *Curia*, held at Mentz. *etc.*" Also *Otto Frising. Lib. Frideric.* 1. cap. 40. "After these Things, the Prince enter'd Bavaria, and there celebrated a General Curia, Court, in the Month of February." Item, cap. 43. "*Conrad* King of the Romans, calling the Princes together at Frankfort, a City of East France, celebrated there a General Court."

CHAPTER XI

Of the *Sacred Authority* of the *Publick Council;* and what Affairs were wont to be transacted therein

We think it necessary in this Place to consider what Kind of Affairs were wont to be transacted in this general *Annual Council,* and to admire the great *Wisdom* of our Ancestors in *constituting our Republick.* We have (in short) observed that they are these that follow. First the Creating or Abdicating of their *Kings.* Next, the declaring of Peace or War. The making of all Publick Laws: The Conferring of all great Honours, Commands, or Offices belonging to the *Commonwealth:* The assigning of any part of the deceased *Kings* Patrimony to his Children, or giving Portions to his Daughters; which they usually called by a German name *Abannagium;* that is, *pars exclusoria,* a Part set out for younger Children. Lastly, all such Matters as in popular Speech are commonly call'd Affairs of State: Because it was not lawful to determine or debate of any thing relating to the *Commonwealth* but in the General Council of the States.

We have already produced sufficient Proofs of the Electing and Abdicating their *Kings,* as well from the last Will and Testament of *Charles* the

Great, as from several other Authors: To which we will add this one Passage more out of *Aimoinus,* lib. 5. cap. 17. where speaking of *Charles* the *Bald,* he says thus, "Having summon'd a General Council at *Carisiacum,*[95] he there first gave his Son *Charles arma virilia;* that is, he girt him with a Sword, or knighted him, and putting a Regal Crown upon his Head, assign'd *Neustria* to him, as he did Aquitain to *Pipin.*"

Now concerning the Administration of the Kingdom, *Aimoinus* gives us this remarkable Instance, Lib. 5. Cap. 35. speaking of *Charles* the Bald. "*Charles* (says he) being about taking a Journey to Rome, held a general *Placitum* on the Kalends of June at Compeign; and therein was ordained under particular Heads, after what Manner his Son *Lewis* should govern the Kingdom of France, in Conjunction with his Nobles, and the rest of the Faithful People of the Realm, till such time as he returned from Rome."

Also in the same Book, Cap. 42. speaking of *Charles* the Simple: "Whose Youth (says he) the principal Men of France judging (as it was indeed) very unfit for the Exercise of the Government of the Realm, they held a General Council touching these weighty Affairs; and the great Men of the *Franks,* Burgundians, and Aquitanians being assembled, elected *Odo* to be *Charles's* Tutor and Governor of the Kingdom."

Now concerning the Power of making Laws and Ordinances, that single Passage in *Gaguinus's* Life of St. *Lewis* is a sufficient Proof. "As soon (says he) as King *Lewis* arrived at Paris, he called a General Convention, and therein reformed the *Commonwealth;* making excellent Statutes relating to the Judges, and against the Venality of Offices, *etc.*" Concerning the conferring the great Honours and Employments upon Persons of approved Worth, *Aimoinus* lib. 5. cap. 36. gives us this instance; speaking of *Charles* the Bald, he tells us, "That whereas he began (before his Inauguration) to distribute the Governments and great Offices of the Realm according to his own liking; the Great Men summon'd a General Council, and sent Ambassadors to the King; neither would they admit him to be crown'd till he had made use of their Advice and Authority in disposing of those great Employments. The Nobles (says he) being very much dis-

---

95. Note in margin: "Crecy."

pleas'd, because the King conferr'd Honours without their Consent; for that Reason, agreed together against him, and summon'd a general Convention in the Town of *Witmar,* from whence they sent Ambassadors to *Lewis,* as *Lewis* likewise sent his Ambassadors to them, *etc."*

Also the Appendix to *Gregory of Tours,* lib. 2. cap. 54. "That same Year (says he) King *Clotharius, cum Proceribus & Leudibus,* i.e., with the Nobility and Free Subjects of Burgundy, met at Troyes, and when he earnestly solicited them to advance another Person to the same Place and Degree of Honour which *Warnhar* (lately deceased) had enjoy'd, they unanimously refused to do it; and said, they would by no Means have any Mayor of the Palace, earnestly desiring the King to excuse them": And thus they gained their Point with the King.

To this Head may be referr'd all the Contentions of such Princes, as were foreseen might be dangerous to the *Commonwealth.* These were debated in the General Council. For *Aimoinus,* lib. 4 cap. 1. where he speaks of *Clotharius,* Son of *Chilperic,* from whom Queen *Brunechild* demanded the Kingdom of *Austratia,* says thus: "*Clotharius* made answer, that she ought to call a Convention of the Nobles of the *Franks,* and there debate (by common consent) an Affair relating to the Community. That as for him, he would submit to their Judgment in all Things, and would not obstruct in any Measure whatever they should command." The same Thing is recorded in the Appendix to *Gregory of Tours,* lib. 2. "*Clotharius* (says he) made Answer to her, that he would refer the Difference between them, to the Determination of the Select *Franks,* and promis'd to fulfil whatsoever they should ordain." Also *Aimoinus* lib. 5. cap. 12. where he speaks of King *Lewis* the Pious, who was grievously tormented with the Contentions of his Sons, says thus, "When Autumn approached, they whose Sentiments differ'd from the Emperor's, were for having the General Convention held in some Town of France. *Item* cap. 13. He appointed the General Convention of his People to be held at Thionville. And after a little Time, summon'd his People to meet on the Feast of St. Martin, and used all his Endeavours to recall his Son *Pipin* who had absented himself; but he refused to come, *etc."* *Gaguinus* making Mention of this same Passage, says; "When the Conspirators found out they should not be able to dethrone the King, without the Consent of the Nobility in Convention, they labour'd by all Means to have the Great Council held within the Limits of France. But *Lewis* knowing for certain that those *Franks* were gained by his Enemies against him, refused it, and summon'd the Convention to meet at Mentz, and ordered that none should be admitted Armed to the Council: But his Sons, (who had conspired against their Father) lest they should want the Authority of a *Publick Convention*, assembled a Council at *Compeigne*, consisting of the Bishops and Nobility of the Kingdom. And *Lotharius* taking his Father out of Custody, brought him to *Compiegne*."

Again, *Aimoinus*, lib. 5. cap. 38. where he speaks of *Lewis* the *Stammerer*, who held a Council at *Marsua*, wherein he treated a Peace with his Cousin, says: "In that *Placitum*, or Parliament, these Articles which follow were agreed upon between them, *by and with the Consent of the faithful Subjects of the Realm.*"

To proceed, We find further, that it was the Custom (when any Prince, or Person of Extraordinary Quality was accused of any Crime) to summon him to appear before the Great Council, and there he was to stand his Trial. Thus in the Reign of King *Clotharius,* when Queen *Brunechild* stood accused, and was found guilty of many capital Crimes, the King made a Speech to the Estates of the Great Council of *Francogallia,* in these Words; which are recorded by *Aimoinus,* lib. 4. cap 1. "It belongs to you my most dear Fellow-Soldiers, and high Nobility of France, to appoint what Kind of Punishment ought to be inflicted on a Person guilty of such enormous Crimes, *etc.*" And *Ado* Aetat. 6. sub Anno 583. tells us, "The *Franks* passing Sentence upon her in the King's Presence, condemn'd her to be torn in pieces by wild Horses."

Now concerning the dividing of the Royal Patrimony and the Appanages, we have the same Person's Testimony, lib. 5. Cap. 94. where speaking of Charlemagn, he has these Words. "These Matters being ended, the King held a Convention of the Nobility and Gentry of the *Franks,* for the making and maintaining a firm Peace among his Sons, and dividing the Kingdom into Three Parts, that everyone of them might know what Part of it he ought to defend and govern, in case they survived him." Also in that Place where he speaks of the Partition made among the Children of *Lewis,* lib 5. cap. 40. he says thus. "They went to *Amiens,* and there they divided their Father's Kingdom among them, according to the Advice and Direction of their faithful Subjects." Further, cap 41. where he writes of *Carloman*, who held his Great Council then at Worms. "To this *Placitum* (says he) came *Hugo*, and preferred his Petition for that Part of the Kingdom, which his Brother *Lewis* (*in Locarium acceperat*) had rented of him, or received in Pawn."

We may further observe, from very many instances, that whenever the King had any expensive Design in Hand, such as the Building of Churches or Monasteries he took first the Advice of the Council of the Estates. For *Aimoinus*, lib. 4. cap. 41. where he speaks of *Clodeveus* the Second, tells us, that sitting on his Throne, he began his Oration to the General Council in these Words. "*Quamquam Franciginae cives, etc.* Although (says he) the Care I ought to take of my Kingdom, obliges me to take your Advice in all Matters relating to the Publick, *etc.*"

And thus much may suffice on this Point. From all which we think it appears plainly, that the whole Power of the Administration of the Kingdom was lodg'd in the Publick Council, which they called *Placitum;* because according to the Idiom of the Latin Tongue, that is properly termed *Placitum,* which after having been proposed and debated in a Council of many Persons, is at last agreed to, and resolved upon by them. And therefore *Cicero,* with others of the Ancients, were wont to call such-like Determinations, *Placita Philosophorum* a council of philosophers.

Since therefore the Matter is so, I hope the Opinion which we have formerly given in some of our other Books, will not be esteemed absurd; viz. That the common Form used by the King's Secretary in the last Clause of our Ordinances and Edicts, *Quia tale est P L A C I T U M nostrum,* arises from hence: For anciently those Laws were written in the Latin Tongue, (as is sufficiently proved by *Aimoinus,* the Capitulary of *Charles* the Great, and many other Records); but afterwards when the King's Secretaries or Clerks began to make use of the Vulgar Tongue, through Ignorance, or rather Malice, they translated it thus, "Car tel est nostre Plaisir: For such is our Will and Pleasure."

Now as to the Power of the People, we have this farther Argument extant in the same Capitulary of *Charles* the Great. "Let the People (says it) be consulted touching all the Heads of the new Laws, which are to be added to the former; and after they have all given their Consents, let them set their Hands and Seals to every Article." From which Words, 'tis apparent that the People of France were wont to be bound by such Laws only, as they had publickly agreed to in their Parliaments. Also *in fine Leg. Aleman* we find this Passage. "This is decreed by the King and his Nobles, and all the Christian People which compose the Kingdom of the *Merovingians*." Also *Aimoinus*, lib. 5 cap. 38. "In this *Placitum* the Laws which follow were agreed upon, to be observed between them, by the Consent of the faithful Subjects. An Agreement made between the Glorious Kings, *etc.* by the Advice and Consent of their faithful Commons, *etc.*"

Lastly, we cannot omit observing, that so great was the Reputation and Authority of this General Council, even among Strangers, that foreign Princes submitted to have their Controversies and Differences decided by it. The Appendix to *Greg. Turon.* lib. 2. cap. 37. Anno 12. of *Theodorick's* Reign, has this Passage in it. "When *Alsaciones*, [perhaps *Alsatia*] in which Country he had been brought up, and which was left him by his Father *Childebert*, fell nevertheless to *Theodebert*, according to the Custom in use among the Barbarians; the two *Kings* agreed that their Difference should be decided by the Judgment of the *Franks*, (in *Saloissa castro*) in their Camp near the River Sala."

CHAPTER XII

Of the Kingly Officers, commonly call'd
Mayors of the Palace

Before we treat farther of the uninterrupted Authority of the Publick Council, we think it not improper to say somewhat of those Regal great Officers, which, during the *Merovingian* Race were called (*Majores domus*) Masters or Mayors of the Palace. These having for some Time encroach'd upon the Kingly Power, finding at last a fit Opportunity, seiz'd upon it entirely as their own. Their Dignity near the Persons of our *Kings* seems to have been much the same with that of *Praefecti Pretorio*, or Generals of the Guards in the Time of the Roman Emperors, who were sometimes also stiled *Aulae Praefecti*. They were usually appointed in and by the same convention which chose the *Kings*, and were wont to be Chiefs or Heads of the Publick Council. And upon this Account we frequently meet with such-like Expressions as these among our Historians. "They elected such and such a Man to the Dignity of Mayor of the Palace. *Herchinold*, Mayor of the Palace, being dead, the *Franks* conferr'd that Dignity upon *Ebroinus*, and appointed him to be Mayor or in the King's Court. Also They chose *Hilderick* for their King, and *Wolfold* for Mayor of the Palace." Which Quotations of ours might indeed have been made as properly in our foregoing Chapter, where we proved that the greater Employments were not usually given by the *Kings,* but appointed by the Yearly General Council, and conferred upon Men of the greatest Fidelity and Probity.

But in this Magistracy, the same Thing happened, which Plutarch tells us (in his *Life of Lysander*) came to pass when *Agesilaus* was appointed by the Lacedemonians to be General of their Army, and *Lysander* to be Legate or Lieutenant-General: "Even as in Stage-Plays, (says he) the Actors who represent a Servant or Messenger, have better Parts, and are more regarded than him that wears the Crown and Scepter, who scarce speaks a Word in the whole Play: So the chief Authority and Command was lodg'd in *Lysander,* whilst with the King remained only a naked and empty Title." Just so it fell out in our *Francogallia;* Fair Opportunities of increasing the Power of these Mayors of the Palace, being offer'd by the Sloth and Negligence of our *Kings;* among whom we may reckon *Dagobert, Clodoveus, Clotharius, Childericus, Theodoricus, etc.* For the Author of the History of the *Franks,* often cited by *Venericus Vercellensis,* though without naming him, writes, That during the Reign of *Clotharius,* Father of *Dagobert,* the Kingdom of the *Franks* began to be administered and govern'd by some which were called *Provisores Regiae,* or *Majores Domus.* The same says *Godfrey Viterbo parte Chron.* 16. Whereupon, whilst those Mayors of the Palace executed all the important Affairs of the *Commonwealth,* and commanded all the Armies in Time of War; and the *Kings* (spending their Days in Sloth and Idleness) tarried at Home, content with the bare Title of a King; Matters at last were brought to such a pass, that during the Reign of *Childerick* the 18th King, *Pipin,* Mayor of the Palace, (who in the *King's* Name had waged great and long Wars, and had overcome and reduced the Saxons to Terms of Submission) finding a fit Occasion to assume the Regal Title which was offer'd him, did not let it slip: Especially seeing himself at the Head of a great and victorious Army, that espoused his interests. Of which we have the Testimony of many Authors. First *Otto Frising. Chron.* 5. cap. 12. and his Transcriber *Godfrey Viterbo* Part. 16. who write thus. "The *Kings* of France, before the Time of *Pipin* the Great, (formerly Mayor of the Palace) were in a Manner but Titular Princes, having very little to do with the Government of the Realm. *Sigebertus* says almost the same thing sub. Anno 662. "From this Time, (says he) the *Kings* of the *Franks* degenerating from their ancient Wisdom and Fortitude enjoy'd little more than the bare Name of King. They did indeed bear the Title according to Custom, as being of the ancient Regal Race; but neither acted nor disposed of any thing. The whole Administration and Power of the Kingdom, was lodg'd in the Hands of the Mayor of the Palace."

Yet in reading such-like Authorities, we ought to take this Observation along with us. That since *Pipin* and his Sons laboured (as 'tis probable they did) under a great Load of Envy, for having violently wrested the Royal Dignity from King *Childerick,* they made it their Business to find out and employ plausible ingenious Historians, who magnified the Cowardliness of *Childerick* and his Predecessors, upbraiding them with Sloath and Idleness, beyond what they deserv'd. And among such as these, we may reckon *Eguinarthus,* Chancellor to *Charles* the Great, and one that did him special Service of this Nature; who in the Beginning of his Book writes thus. "The Family of the *Merovingians,* out of which the *Franks* used to elect their *Kings,* is supposed to have lasted as long as to *Hilderic;* who by the Appointment of Pope *Stephen,* was deposed, shaven, and thrust into a Monastery. Now though it may be said to have ended in him, yet in truth, for a long Time before, it ceased to have any Value or Excellency, bating the bare empty Title of King. For both the Riches and Power of the Kingdom, were at the Disposition of the Prefects of the Palace, commonly called *Majores Domus;* with whom was also lodg'd the Authority of the Empire: Neither was there any Thing left remaining to the King, but only that contenting himself with the Title, he should sit on a Throne, wearing his Hair and Beard very long, and representing the Person of a Ruler; sometimes giving the first and last Audience to Ambassadors from Foreign Parts, and returning such Answers as were made for him, as if they proceeded immediately from himself. But besides the unprofitable Name of a King, and a precarious Allowance for his private Expences, (which the Mayor of the Palace was pleased out of Bounty to give him) he had nothing that he could call his own, except one Village of very small Revenue, where he had a little House, and a few Servants, barely sufficient for his necessary Occasions, *etc.*"

Sigebertus, sub Anno 662. taking *Eguinarthus* for his Pattern, inveighs against the former *Kings* in almost the same Contumelious Terms. "Whose Custom (says he) it was, indeed, to make an Appearance like a Prince, according to what had been usual to their Family; but neither to act, nor dispose of any thing, only to tarry at Home, and to Eat and Drink like Irrational Creatures." As if the like Sloth and Cowardise ought to be imputed to all the former *Kings,* among whom we nevertheless find many brave Men, such as *Clodoveus,* who not only defeated a great Army of *Germans,* which had made an Irruption into France, in a great Battle near *Tolbiacum;* but also drove the Remainder of the Romans out of the Confines of *Gallia.* What shall we say of *Childebert* and *Clotharius,* who rooted the Visigoths and Ostrogoths out of Provence and Aquitain, where they had seated themselves? In the Histories of all which Princes, there is no Mention made of any Mayor of the Palace, but cursorily, and by the By, as one of the King's Servants. This we may see in *Gregorius,* lib 5. cap. 18. where he speaks of *Gucilius.* Lib. 6. cap. 9. and cap. 45. Lib. 7. cap. 49. And we find this Employment to have been not only in the King's Palace, but also in the Queen's; For the same Gregorius, lib. 7. cap. 27. mentions one *Waddo* as Mayor of the Palace, in the Court of Queen *Riguntha:* And in very many other Places of their Histories, we find both Gregorius and *Aimoinus* making Mention of these Masters of the Court and the King's House.

Now the first beginning of the great Authority of these *Praefecti Regii,* was (as we told you before) during the Reign of King *Clotharius* the Second, about the Year of our Lord 588. that is, about 130 Years after the constituting the *Francogallican* Kingdom; which we may also learn from the before-mention'd Historian, so often quoted by *Venericus.*

Yet there are two other Historians, (though not of equal Credit) *Sigebertus* and *Trithemius,* who refer the Beginning of so great a Power in the Mayor of the Palace, to the Reign of *Clotair* the Third; whose *Magister Palatii* was one *Ebroinus,* a Man of extraordinary Wickedness and Cruelty: But however this may be, we find Historians calling them by several other Appellations; such as *Comites Domus Regiae, Praefecti Aulae, Comites Palatii, etc.*

CHAPTER XIII

Whether *Pipin* was created King by the Pope or by the Authority of the *Francogallican* Council

Having in the former Chapter given an Account, that after the Expulsion of *Childeric*, (a stupid Prince, in whom the Line of the *Merovingians* ended) *Pipin*, from being Mayor of the Palace, was created King; It will be worth our Enquiry, to know by whose Authority the Kingdom was conferr'd upon him. For Pope *Gelasius* says thus, Cap. 15. Quest. 6. "A Roman Pope, viz. *Zacharias*, deposed the King of the *Franks*, not so much because of his evil Actions, as because he was stupid, and unfit for the Exercise of so great a Trust; and in his Stead, substituted *Pipin*, Father of *Charles* the Emperor: Absolving all the *Franks* from their Oath of Allegiance to *Childeric*."

And there is scarce an Author who does not acquiesce in this Testimony of one Pope, concerning the Power of another: Thus *Ado, Lambertus, Rhegino, Sigebertus, Aimoinus, Landulphus*, nay, even *Venericus Vercellensis*, (in the Book which we formerly quoted) cites these Words out of the Epistle of Pope *Gregory* the 7th to *Herman* Bishop of Metz; viz. "A certain Pope of Rome deposed the King of the *Franks* from his Kingdom, not so much for his Wickedness, as his being unfit for so great a Power; and after having absolved all the *Franks* from the Oath of Fidelity they had sworn to him, placed *Pipin* in his Room. Which *Otto Frisingius*, lib. *Chron.* 5. cap. 23. and *Godfrey, Chron.* Part. 17. laying presently hold of, break out into this Exclamation. From this Action, the Popes of Rome derive an Authority of changing and deposing Princes, *etc.*"

But pray let us enquire whether the Truth of this Story, as to the Matter of Fact, be sufficiently proved and attested. For in the first Place, 'tis manifest, That not one of all that great Number of *Kings* of the *Franks*, which we have instanced to have been Elected or Abdicated, was either created or abdicated by the Pope's Authority. On the contrary, we have irrefragably prov'd, that the whole Right, both of *making* and *deposing* their *Kings*, was lodg'd in the yearly great Council of the Nation; so that it seems incredible the *Franks* should neglect or forgoe their Right, in this single Instance of *Pipin*. But to make few Words of this Matter, *Venericus Vercellensis* gives us the Testimony of an ancient Historian, who has written of all the *Francogallican* Affairs; whereby that whole Story of the Pope, is prov'd to be a Lye: And 'tis clearly demonstrated, that both *Childerick* was deposed, and *Pipin* chosen in his room, according to the usual Custom of the *Franks*, and the institutions of our Ancestors: That is to say, by a solemn General Council of the Nation; in whose Power only it was, to transact a Matter of so great weight and moment; as we have before made it appear. The Words of that Historian are these. "That by the Counsel, and with the Consent of all the *Franks*, (a Relation of this Affair being sent to the Apostolick See, and its Advice had) the most noble *Pipin* was advanced to the Throne of the Kingdom, By the Election of the whole Nation, the Homage of the Nobility, with the Consecration of the Bishops, *etc.*" From which Words, 'tis most apparent that *Pipin* was not appointed King by the Pope, but by the People themselves, and the States of the Realm. And *Venericus* explains this Matter out of the same Historian. "*Pipin*, Mayor of the Palace (says he) having all along had the Administration of the Regal Power in his Hands, was the first that was appointed and elected to be King, from being Mayor of the Palace; the Opinion of Pope Zachary being first known, because the Consent and Countenance of a Pope of Rome, was thought necessary in an Affair of this Nature. And presently after he tells us; The Pope finding that what the Ambassadors had deposed was just and profitable, agreed to it; and *Pipin* was made King by the unanimous Suffrages and Votes of the Nobility, *etc.*" To the very same Purpose writes *Ado* of Vienna, Aetat. 6. Sub Anno 727. "Ambassadors (says he) were sent to Pope Zacharias, to propose this Question to him; Whether or no the *Kings* of the *Franks*, who had scarce any Power in their Hands, but contented themselves with the bare Title, were fit to continue to be *Kings?* To which *Zacharias* return'd this Answer, That he thought the Person who governed the *Commonwealth*, ought rather to have also the Title of King: Whereupon the *Franks*, after the Return of the Ambassadors, cast out *Childeric,* who then had the Title of King; and by the Advice of the Ambassadors, and of Pope *Zacharias,* Elected *Pipin,* and made him King."

Besides the above Proofs, we have *Aimoinus*'s Testimony to the same purpose, lib. 4. cap. 61. where he concludes thus. "This Year *Pipin* got the Appellation of King of the *Franks,* and according to their ancient Customs was elevated to the Royal Throne in the City of Soissons, *etc.* Nay, even *Godfrey of Viterbo* himself, *Chron.* part. 17. cap. 4. *Pipin* (says he) was made King by Pope Zacharias, (ex electione Francorum) through the Election of the *Franks, Hilderic* their slothful King being, by the *Franks,* thrust into a Monastery."

In like Manner *Sigebertus,* sub Anno 752. The Authors of the *Miscellany History,* lib. 22. *Otto Frising.* lib. 5. cap. 21, 22, 23. And the Author of the Book intituled *Fasciculus temporum,* do all clearly agree in the Account given of this Transaction. From which we may easily gather, that although the *Franks* did consult the Pope before they created *Pipin* King, yet it cannot therefore be any Ways inferr'd from thence, that he was made King by the Pope's Authority; for 'tis one Thing to make a King, and another to give Advice touching the making him: 'Tis one Thing to have a Right of Creation, and another that of only giving Advice; nay; no Man has a Right of so much as giving Advice in Matters of this nature, but he whose Advice is first ask'd.

Lastly, no Man has more clearly explained this whole Matter than *Marsilius Patavinus;* who during the Reign of *Lewis* of Bavaria, writ a

Book *de translatione imperi*, in which, Cap. 6. he has these Words. "*Pipin*, a very valiant Man, and Son of *Charles Martel*, was (as we read) raised to the Dignity of being King of the *Franks*, by Pope *Zacharias*. But *Aimoinus* more truly informs us, in his *History* of the *Franks*, that *Pipin* was legally elected King by the *Franks* themselves, and by the Nobility of the Kingdom was placed in the Throne. At the same Time *Childeric*, a dissolute Prince, who contenting himself with the bare Title of a King, wasted both his Time and Body in Wantonness, was by them shaven for a Monk: So that *Zacharias* had no hand in the deposing him, but consented (as some say) to those that did. For such deposing of a King for just Causes, and electing of another, does not belong to any Bishop or Ecclesiastick, nor to any College of Clergymen; but to the whole Body of Citizens [*ad universitatem civium*] inhabiting that Region, and to the Nobles of it, or to the majority of them both." Therefore those Pretences of the Popes, to a Power of creating or abdicating *Kings*, are apparently false to every body. But besides this fabulous Device, which is a sufficient Instance of their wickedness and malice, I think it worth my while to add a remarkable Letter of Pope *Stephen*, adapted to the foregoing Fable; by which we may make a Judgment of the madness and folly of that old crafty Knave. This Letter is extant; in *Rhegino*, a Benedictine Monk, and Abbot of Prum, an irrefragable Testimony in an Affair of this Nature; 'tis in *Chron.* anni 753. "*Stephen* the Bishop, Servant of the Servants of God, *etc.* As no Man ought to boast of his Merits, so neither ought the wonderful Works of God which are wrought upon his Saints without their desert, to be buried in Silence, but published abroad as the Angel admonished *Tobias*. I being constrained through the Oppression of the holy Church, by that most wicked, blasphemous, and not worthy to be named Wretch, *Aistolphus*, to fly for Refuge to that excellent and faithful Votary of St. Peter, Lord *Pipin*, the most Christian King, took my Journey into France; where I fell into a mortal Distemper, and remained some time in the District of Paris, in the venerable Monastery of St. *Denis* the Martyr And being now past Hopes of Recovery, methought I was one Day at Prayers in the Church of the same blessed Martyr, in a Place under the Bells: And that I saw standing before the great Altar our Master *Peter*; and that great Master of the Gentiles, our Master *Paul;* whom I knew very well by their Vestments.

And a little after, I saw the blessed Lord *Denis,* a tall and slender Man, standing at the Right Hand of our Lord *Peter.* And then that good Pastor the Lord Peter said 'This good Brother of ours asks for Health.' Then reply'd the blessed Paul 'He shall be healed presently.' And thereupon approaching to our Lord *Denis,* he amicably put his Hand upon his Breast, and look'd back upon our Lord Peter, and Lord Peter with a chearful Countenance said to our Lord *Denis,* his Health shall be your particular Act of Favour. Then presently Lord *Denis* taking a Censer full of Incense, and holding a Branch of Palm-tree in his Hand, accompanied with a Presbyter and Deacon, who assisted him, came near to me, and said, Peace be with thee, Brother, be not afraid, thou shalt not die until thou return in Prosperity to thy own See. Rise and be healed, and dedicate this Altar to the Honour of God, and the Apostles St. *Peter* and St. *Paul,* whom thou seest standing before thee, with Masses of Thanksgiving. Whereupon I was presently made whole. And being about to accomplish that which I was commanded to do, they that were present said I was mad. So I related all that I had seen to them, to the King, and all his People, and how I had been cured; and I fulfilled all that I was bid to do. These things happen'd in the 753rd Year, from the Incarnation of our Lord on the Ides of August; at which Time being strengthened by the Power of *Christ,* between the Celebration of the Consecration of the above-mention'd Altar, and the Oblation of the Sacrifice, I anointed King *Pipin* and his two Sons, *Charles* and *Carloman, Kings* of the *Franks.* Moreover, I laid Hands upon, and blessed *Bertranda* the King's Wife, cloathed with her Royal Mantle, and the Grace of the Sevenfold Holy Spirit: And the Nobles of the *Franks* being sanctified by the Apostolical Benediction, and the Authority delivered by Christ to St. Peter, obliged themselves solemnly, and protested, That neither they, nor any of their Posterity, would at any Time hereafter, presume to constitute any Person, as King over them, but only such as were of the Race of King *Pipin.*"

CHAPTER XIV

Of the *Constable,* and *Peers* of France

Besides the great Office of Mayor of the Palace before spoken of, there was another which we must take Notice of; because it seems, in the Memory of our Forefathers, to have succeeded in Place of the former: And that was the Office of Count of the *Kings* Stable; called at first, *Comes stabuli;* and by Corruption at last, *Connestabuli.* Now all those who enjoy'd any extraordinary Honours or Employments in the King's Court, and assisted in the Administration of the *Commonwealth,* were commonly called *Comites,* Counts; which was likewise the Custom of the Ancients, as I have in some other of my Works demonstrated. So *Cicero,* in many Places, calls *Callisthenes, Comitem Alexandri magni* [count of Alexander the Great]. This *Comes stabuli* was in a manner the same with the *Magister Equitum* among the Romans, that is, General of the Horse; to whom were subject those Keepers of the Horses commonly called Querryes. *Greg. Turon.* lib. 5. cap. 39. says, "The Treasurer of *Clodoveus* being taken out of the City of Bourges, by *Cuppau,* Count of the Stable, was sent in Bonds to the Queen, *etc.*" And again, cap. 48. where he speaks of *Leudastes,* "She took him (says he) into Favour, rais'd him, and made him Keeper of the best Horses; which so filled him with Pride and Vanity, that he put in for the

Constableship; [*Comitatum Stabulorum*] and having got it, began to despise and undervalue every body." From these Quotations it appears, that
though the Custody of the Horses was a very honourable Employment,
yet 'twas much inferior to that of Constable. *Aimoinus*, lib. 3. cap. 43. gives
the same Account of this *Leudastes*. "Being grown very intimate with the
Queen, he was first made Keeper of the Horse; and afterwards obtaining
the Constableship above the rest of the Keepers, he was (after the Queen's
Death) made by King *Charibert*, Count of Tours." And cap. 70. "*Leudege-
filus*, Praefect of the King's Horses, whom they commonly call Constable,
being made General of that Expedition by the King, order'd the Engines
to be drawn down, *etc.*" Also lib. 4. cap. 95. where he speaks of *Charles*
the Great, "The same Year (says he) he sent *Burchard, Comitem Stabuli sui*,
which we corruptly call *Constabulum*, with a Fleet against Corsica." The
Appendix to *Gregory* calls him, *Comestabulum*, lib. 11. "*Brunechildis* (says
he) was brought out of the Village, *ab Erporre Comestabulo.*"

　　This being so, *Albertus Krantzius*, lib. Suet. 5. cap. 41. ventures to affirm,
that this Constable was the same with what the *Germans* call Mareschal.
"They named (says he) a Governor, one of the best Soldiers, who might
have the Power of Convocating the Assembly of the Kingdom, and of acting in all Matters like the Prince. Our Countrymen call him a Mareschal,
the French call him Constable, *etc.*" This seems the more probable, because
I do not remember any Mention to have been made in ancient Times, of a
Mareschal in our *Francogallia;* so that 'tis very likely to have been an Institution of our latter *Kings*, accommodated to the Custom of the *Germans*.

　　That this *Comitatus Stabulorum*, a Constableship, had its rise from the
Institution of the Roman Emperors, I do not at all question; although
it grew by Degrees among us from slender Beginnings, to the Height of
chief Governor of the Palace. In former times that Dignity was a Sort
of *Tribunatus Militaris. Ammianus*, lib. 26. has this Expression, where
he speaks of *Valentinian* the Emperor, "Having fixed his Stages, or Days
Journeys, he at last entered into Nicomedia; and about the Kalends of
March, appointed his Brother Valens to be Governor of his Stables, *cum
tribunatus dignitate*, with tribunitial Dignity." What Kind of Dignity that
was, we may find in the Code of *Justinian*, lib. 1. Cod. de *comitibus & tri-
bunis Schol*. Where 'tis reckoned as a great Honour for them to preside

over the Emperor's Banquets, when they might adore his Purple. Also in lib. 3. *Cod. Theodos. de annon. & tribut. perpensa,* 29. *Cod. Theod. de equorum Collatione,* & lib. 1. *Cod. Theod.* wherein we may find a Power allowed them, of exacting Contribution to a certain Value from the Provincials who were to furnish War-Horses for the Emperor's Service.

It now remains that we discourse a little of those Magistrates, which were commonly called Peers of France; whereof we can find no Records or Monuments, though our Endeavours have not been wanting. For among so great a Number of Books, as are called Chronicles and Annals of *Francogallia,* not one affords us any probable Account of this Institution. For what *Gaguinus,* and *Paulis Aemilius* (who was not so much an Historian of French Affairs, as of the Pope's) and other common Writers do affirm, to wit, That those Magistrates were instituted by *Pipin* or *Charlemagn,* appears plainly to be absurd; because not one of all the German Historians, who wrote during the Reigns of those *Kings* or for some time after, makes the least Mention of those Magistrates. *Aimoinus* himself who wrote a History of the Military achievements and institutions of the *Franks,* down to the Reign of *Lewis* the Pious, and the Appendix, which reaches as far as the Time of *Lewis* the Younger, being the 37th King, speak not one Word of these Peers in any Place of their Histories; so that till I am better inform'd,[96] I must concur in Opinion with *Gervase* of Tilbury, who (as *Gaguinus* says in the Book which he wrote to the Emperor *Otho* the IVth, *de otiis imperialibus*) affirms, That this Institution is first owing to King Arthur of Britain, who ruled some time in Part of France.

For I suppose the Original of that Institution to be this; that as in the Feudal Law such are called, *Pares curiae beneficiarii,* i.e., Equal Tenants by Homage of the Court, or *Clientes* ὁμότιμοι, Clients of like holding, or *Convassalli,* Fellow Vassals, who hold their Fiefs and Benefices from one and the same Lord and Patron; and upon that Account are bound to him in Fealty and Obedience: just so King Arthur having acquired a new Principality, selected twelve great Men, to whom he distributed the several Parts and Satrapies of his Kingdom, whose Assistance and Advice he made use

[96.] From this point until the end of the chapter, the passage was suppressed in subsequent sixteenth-century editions; see GS *Franc.,* pp. 377 and 531.

of in the Administration of the Government. For I cannot approve of their Judgment, who write, that they were called Peers, because they were *Pares Regi*, the King's Equals; since their Parity has no Relation to the Regal Dignity, but only to that Authority and Dignity they had agreed should be common among them. Their Names were these, the Dukes of Burgundy, Normandy, and Aquitain; the Counts of Flanders, Toulouse, and Champagne; the Archbishops of Rheims, Laon, and Langres; the Bishops of Beauvais, Noyon, and Chalons. And as the *Pares Curtis*, or *Curiae*, in the Feudal Law, can neither be created, but by the Consent of the Fraternity; nor abdicated, but by Tryal before their Colleagues; nor impeach'd before any other Court of Judicature; so these Peers were not bound by any Judgment or Sentence, but that of the Parliament, that is, of this imaginary Council; nor could be elected into the Society, or ejected out of it, but by their Fellows in *Collegio*.

Now although this Magistracy might owe its Original to a Foreign Prince; yet when he was driven out, the succeeding *Kings* finding it accommodated to their own Ends and Conveniences, ('tis most probable) continued and made use of it. The first Mention I find made of these Peers, was at the Inauguration of Philip the Fair, by whom also (as many affirm) the Six Ecclesiastical Peers were first created.

But *Budaeus*, an extraordinary Learned Man, calls these Peers by the Name of Patricians and is of opinion that they were instituted by one of our *Kings*, who was at the same time Emperor of *Germany;* because, *Justinian* says, those *Patres* were chosen by the Emperor, *quasi Reipub. patronos tutoresque*, as it were Patrons and Tutors of the *Commonwealth*. I do not reject this Opinion of that Learned Person; such a thing being very agreeable to the Dignity of these Peers. For in the times of the later Roman Emperors, we find the Patrician Dignity not to have been very unlike that of the Peers; because (as *Suidas* assures us), they were (partly) the Fathers of the Republick, and were of Council with the Emperor in all weighty Concerns, and made use of the same Ensigns of Authority with the Consuls; and had greater honour and power than the *Praefectus Praetorio*, though less than the Consul; as we may learn ex *Justiniani Novellis;* from *Sidon. Apollin. Claudian;* and *Cassiodorus* especially.

But when the Empire was transferr'd to the *Germans*, we do not believe this Honour was in use among them. Neither is it likely, that none of the German Historians should have made the least Mention of it, if any Patritians of that kind had been instituted by a German Emperor, who at the same Time was King of *Francogallia*.

Lastly, The same *Budaeus* tells us in that Place, though a little doubtingly, that the like dignity of Peers had been made use of in other neighbouring Nations; and that in the *Royal Commentaries*, Anno 1224, 'tis found written, that a certain Gentleman of Flanders, called *Joannes Nigellanus*, having a Controversy there, appeal'd from the Countess of Flanders to the Peers of France; having first taken his Oath that he could not expect a fair and equal Tryal before the Peers of Flanders. And when afterwards the Cause was by the Countess revoked to the Judgment of the Peers of Flanders, it was at Length for certain reasons decreed, that the Peers of France should take cognisance of it. What the reasons were of transferring that Tryal, *Budaeus* does not tell us; which one versed in the Feudal Laws should never have omitted. But 'tis time to return to our principal business.

Of the continued Authority and Power of the Sacred Council, during the Reign of the Carolingian Family

We have, as we suppose, sufficiently explain'd what was the Form and Constitution of our *Commonwealth*, and how great the Authority of the Publick Council was during the Reigns of the *Kings* of the *Merovingian* Family. We must now proceed to give an Account of it under the *Carolingian* Race. And as well all our own as the German Historians, give us Reason to believe that the very same Power and Authority of the Orders or States of the Kingdom, was kept entire. So that the last Resort and Disposal of all Things, was not lodged in *Pipin, Charles,* or *Lewis,* but in the Regal Majesty. The true and proper Seat of which was (as is above demonstrated) in the Annual general Council. Of this *Eguinarthus* gives us an Account, in that little Book we have already so much commended. Where, speaking of what happen'd after the Death of *Pipin,* he tells us, "that the *Franks* having solemnly assembled their general Convention, did therein constitute both *Pipin*'s Sons their *Kings,* upon this Condition, That they should equally divide the whole Body of the Kingdom between them; and that *Charles* should govern that Part of it which their Father *Pipin* had possess'd, and *Carlomannus* the other Part which their Uncle *Carlomannus* had enjoy'd, *etc.*" From whence 'tis easily inferr'd, that the States of the Kingdom still retain'd in themselves the same Power, which they had always hitherto been in Possession of (during near 300 Years) in the reigns of the *Merovingian Kings*. So that although the deceased King left Sons behind him, yet these came not to the Crown so much through any right of succession, as through the appointment and election of the States of the Realm. Now that all the other weighty affairs of the Nation used to be determined by the same General Council, *Aimoinus* is our witness, lib. 4. cap. 71. where he speaks of the War with the Saxons. "The King (says he) in the beginning of the Spring went to Nimeguen; and because he was to hold a General Convention of his People at a Place called *Paderburn*, he marched from thence with a great Army into Saxony. And again, cap. 77. Winter being over, he held a Publick Convention of his People in a Town called *Paderburn*, according to the yearly Custom. Also cap. 79. And meeting with his Wife in the City of *Wormes*, he resolved to hold there the General Council of his People." In all which Places he speaks of that *Charles*, who through his warlike achievements had acquired the Dominion of almost all Europe, and by the universal consent of Nations had obtained the surname of the Great: Yet for all that it was not in his Power to deprive the *Franks* of their ancient Right and *Liberty*. Nay, he never so much as endeavour'd to undertake the least matter of moment without the advice and authority of his people and nobles. And there is no doubt of it, after *Charles's* Death, *Lewis* his Son administered the Kingdom upon the same Terms and Conditions. For the Appendix to *Aimoinus*, lib. 5. cap. 10. tells us, that when *Charles* was dead, *Lewis* the Emperor, through a certain kind of Foreknowledge, summon'd the General Council of his People to meet at Doue, near the Loire. And again, cap. 38. where he makes mention of the Articles of Peace, concluded between King *Lewis* and his Cousin *Lewis*, "They summoned, says he, a *PLACITUM*, and in that *PLACITUM*, by the Advice and Consent of their faithful Subjects, they agreed to observe and keep the Articles which follow. In which *Placitum* it was also by common Consent found convenient, that both *Kings* should return with a Guard [*redirent cum scara*] *etc.*"

Also cap. 41. where he speaks of *Carloman* the Son of *Lewis* the Stammerer, "And so (says he) he departed from the Normans, and returned to Wormes, where he was on the Kalends of November to hold his *Placitum.*" Also in the following Chapter, where he speaks of *Charles* the Simple, "Whose Youth (says he) the great Men of France thinking unfit for the Administration of the Government, they held a Council concerning the State of the Nation."

But it would be an infinite Labour, and indeed a superfluous one, to quote all the Instances which might be given of this Matter: From what we have already produced, I think 'tis apparent to every Man, that till *Charles* the Simple's Reign, that is, for more than 550 Years, the Judgment and Determination of all the weighty Affairs of the *Commonwealth,* belonged to the great Assembly of the People, or (as we now call it) to the Convention of the Estates: And that this Institution of our Ancestors was esteemed sacred and inviolable during so many Ages. So that I cannot forbear admiring the Confidence of some Modern Authors, who have had the Face to publish in their Writings, That King *Pipin* was the first to whom the Institution of the Publick Council is owing. Since *Eguinarthus, Charles* the Great's own Chancellor, has most clearly proved, that it was the constant Practice of the whole *Merovingian* Line, to hold every Year the Publick Convention of the People on the Kalends of May; and that the *Kings* were carried to that Assembly in a Chariot or Waggon drawn by Oxen.

But to come to a Matter of greater Consequence, wherein the Prudence and Wisdom of our Ancestors does most clearly shew it self. Is it not apparent how great and manifest a Distinction they made between the King and the Kingdom? For thus the Case stands. The King is one principal Single Person; but the Kingdom is the whole Body of the Citizens and Subjects. "And Ulpian defines him to be a Traytor, who is stirred up with a Hostile Mind against the *Commonwealth,* or against the Prince. And in the *Saxon* Laws, Tit. 3. 'tis written, Whosoever shall contrive any thing against the Kingdom, or the King of the *Franks,* shall lose his Head. And again, The King has the same Relation to the Kingdom that a Father has to his Family; a Tutor to his Pupil; a Guardian to his Ward; a Pilot to his Ship, or a General to his Army." As therefore a Pupil is not appointed for the Sake of his Tutor, nor a Ship for the sake of the Pilot, nor an Army for the sake of a General, but on the contrary, all these are made such for the sake of those they have in charge: Even so a *People* is not designed for the sake of the King; but the King is sought out and instituted for the People's sake. For a *People* can subsist without a King, and be governed by its Nobility, or by it Self. But 'tis even impossible to conceive a Thought of a King without a People. Let us consider more Differences between them. A King as well as any private Person is a Mortal Man. A Kingdom is perpetual, and consider'd as immortal; as Civilians use to say, when they speak of Corporations, and aggregate Bodies. A King may be a Fool or Madman, like our *Charles* VI. who gave away his Kingdom to the English: Neither is there any Sort of Men more easily cast down from a Sound State of Mind, through the Blandishments of unlawful Pleasures and Luxury. But a Kingdom has within it self a perpetual and sure Principle of Safety in the Wisdom of its Senators, and of Persons well skill'd in Affairs. A King in one Battle, in one Day may be overcome, or taken Prisoner and carried away Captive by the Enemy; as it happen'd to St. *Lewis,* to King John, and to Francis the First. But a Kingdom though it has lost its King, remains entire; and immediately upon such a Misfortune a Convention is call'd, and proper Remedies are sought by the chief Men of the Nation against the present Mischiefs: Which we know has been done upon like Accidents. A King, either through Infirmities of Age, or Levity of Mind, may not only be misled by some covetous, rapacious or lustful Counsellor; may not only be seduced and depraved by debauch'd Youths of Quality, or of equal Age with himself; may be infatuated by a silly Wench, so far as to deliver and fling up the Reins of Government wholly into her Power. Few Persons, I suppose, are ignorant how many sad Examples we have of these Mischiefs: But a Kingdom is continually supplied with the Wisdom and Advice of the grave Persons that are in it. Solomon, the wisest of Mankind, was in his old Age seduced by Harlots; *Rehoboam,* by young Men; *Ninus,* by his own Mother *Semiramis; Ptolomaeus* surnamed *Auletes,* by Harpers and Pipers. Our Ancestors left to their *Kings* the Choice of their own Privy-Counsellors, who might advise them in the Management of their private Affairs; but such Senators as were to consult in common, and take care of the publick Administration, and instruct the King in the Government of his Kingdom, they reserved to the Designation of the Publick Convention.

In the Year 1356: after King *John* had been taken Prisoner by the English, and carried into England, a Publick Council of the Kingdom was held at Paris. And when some of the King's Privy-Counsellors appeared at that Convention, they were commanded to leave the Assembly; and it was openly declared, that the Deputies of the Publick Council would meet no more, if those Privy-Counsellors should hereafter presume to approach that Sanctuary of the Kingdom. Which Instance is recorded in the *Great Chronicle* writ in French, Vol. 2. *Sub rege Johanne*, fol. 169. Neither has there ever yet been any Age wherein this plain distinction between a King and a Kingdom, has not been observed. The King of the Lacedemonians (as *Xenophon* assures us) and the *Ephori*, renewed every Month a mutual Oath between each other; the King swore that he would govern according to the written Laws; and the *Ephori* swore that they would preserve the Royal Dignity, provided he kept his Oath. *Cicero*, in one of his Epistles to *Brutus*, writes: "Thou knowest that I was always of Opinion, that our Commonwealth ought not only to be delivered from a King, but even from *Kingship*. *Scis mihi semper placuisse non Rege solum, sed Regno liberari republicam.*" Also in his Third Book *de Legibus* "But because a Regal State in our *Commonwealth*, once indeed approved of, was abolish'd, not so much upon the account of the Faults of a Kingly Government, as of the *Kings* who governed; it may seem that only the Name of a King was then abolished, *etc.*"

CHAPTER XVI

Of the *Capetian* Race, and the Manner of its obtaining the Kingdom of *Francogallia*

It has been already shewn, that the Kingdom of *Francogallia* continued in Three Families only, during One Thousand Two Hundred Years. Whereof the first was called the *Merovingian* Family. The second, the *Carolingian*, from the Names of their Founders or Beginners. For although (as we have often told you) the Succession to the Kingdom was not conferred as a Hereditary Right, but according to the Appointment of the General Council; yet the *Franks* were so far willing to retain the Custom of their Progenitors the *Germans*, (who as *Tacitus* tells us, chuse their *Kings* for their Nobility, and their Generals for their Valour) that for the most Part they elected such *Kings* as were of the Blood Royal, and had been educated in a Regal Manner, whether they were the Children, or some other Degree of Kindred to the Royal Family.

But in the Year 987, after the Death of *Lewis* the Fifth, who was the 31st King of *Francogallia*, and the 12th of the *Carolingian* Line, there happened a Migration or Translation of the Royal Sceptre, and a Change of the

Kingdom. For when there remained no Person alive of the former Family but *Charles* Duke of Lorrain, Uncle to the deceased King, to whom the Succession to the Kingdom, by ancient Custom seem'd to be due; there arose up one Hugh *Capet*, Nephew to *Hauvida*, Sister to the Emperor *Otho* the First, and Son to *Hugh* Earl of Paris; a Man of great Reputation for Valour, who alledged, that he being present upon the place, and having deserved extraordinary well of his Country, ought to be preferr'd to a Stranger, who was absent. For there having happened some Controversies between the Empire of *Germany*, and the Kingdom of France; *Charles* upon occasion had shewn himself partial for the Empire against France, and upon that Score had lost the Affections of most of the French. Whereupon *Charles* having rais'd an Army, made an Irruption into France, and took several Cities by composition. *Capet* relying on the Friendship and Favour of the Francogallican Nobles, got together what Forces he could, and went to meet him at Laon, a Town in the Borders of Champagne; and not long after a bloody Battle was fought between them, wherein *Capet* was routed, and forced to fly into the innermost Parts of France; where he began again to raise Men in Order to renew the War. In the mean time *Charles* having dismiss'd his Army, kept himself quiet in the Town of Laon with his Wife; but in the Year following he was on a sudden surrounded by *Capet*, who besieged the Town with a great Army.

There was in the Place one *Anselmus*, Bishop of the City. *Capet* found Means to corrupt this Man by great Gifts and Promises, and to induce him to betray both the Town and the King into his Hands; which was accordingly done. And thus having obtained both the City and the Victory, he sent *Charles* and his Wife Prisoners to Orleans, where he set strict Guards over them. The King having been two Years in Prison, had two Sons born to him there, *Lewis* and *Charles;* but not long after they all died. So that *Capet* being now Master of the whole Kingdom of France without Dispute or Trouble, associated his Son Robert with him in the Throne, and took care to get him declared his Successor. Thus the Dignity and Memory of the *Carolingian* Family came to an End, the 237th Year after the first beginning of their Reign. And this History is recorded by *Sigebert* in *Chron.* Ann. 987. as well as the Appendix, lib. 5. cap. 45.

We must not omit making Mention of the cunning Device made use of by *Hugh Capet*, for establishing himself in his new Dominion: For whereas all the Magistracies and Honours of the Kingdom, such as Dukedoms, Earldoms, *etc.* had been hitherto from ancient Times conferr'd upon select and deserving Persons in the General Conventions of the People, and were held only during good behaviour; whereof (as the Lawyers express it) they were but Beneficiaries; *Hugh Capet*, in order to secure to himself the Affections of the Great Men, was the first that made those Honours perpetual, which formerly were but temporary; and ordained, that such as obtained them should have a hereditary Right in them, and might leave them to their Children and Posterity in like Manner as their other Estates. Of this, see *Franciscus Conanus* the Civilian, *Comment,* 2. Cap. 9. By which notorious Fact, 'tis plain, that a great Branch of the Publick Council's Authority was torn away; which however (to any Man who seriously considers the Circumstances of those Times) seems impossible to have been effected by him alone, without the Consent of that Great Council it self.

CHAPTER XVII

Of the uninterrupted Authority of the *Publick Council* during the *Capetian* Race

We may learn out of *Froissard, Monstrellet, Gaguinus, Commines, Gillius,* and all the other Historians who have written concerning these Times, that the Authority of the Publick Council was little or nothing less in the Time of the *Capetian* Family, than it had been during the two former Races. But because it would be too troublesome, and almost an infinite Labour to quote every instance of this nature, we shall only chuse some few of the most remarkable Examples out of a vast number which we might produce.

And the first shall be, what happened in the Year 1328. When *Charles* the Fair dying without issue Male, and leaving a Posthumous Daughter behind him; *Edward* King of England and Son to *Isabella,* Sister of *Charles,* claimed the Kingdom of France as belonging to him of Right. Now there could be no tryal of greater Importance, nor more illustrious, brought before the Publick Council, than a Controversy of this Kind.

And because it was decided there, and both *Kings* did submit themselves to the Judgment and Determination of the Council, 'tis an irrefragable Argument, that the Authority of the Council was greater than that of both *Kings.* This Fact is recorded not only by all our own Historians, but by *Polydore Virgil,* an English Writer, *Histor.* lib. 19. Moreover, that great Lawyer *Paponius, Arrestorum,* lib. 4. cap. 1. has left it on Record, (grounded, no doubt, upon sufficient Authorities), "That both *Kings* were present at that Council, when the Matter was almost brought to an open Rupture; by the Advice of the Nobles, a General Convention of the People and States was summon'd: and the Vote of the Majority was, that the Kinsman, by the Father's Side, ought to have the preference; and that the Custody of the Queen, then great with Child, should be given to Valois; to whom also the Kingdom was adjudged and decreed in case She brought forth a Daughter." Which History *Froissard,* Vol. 1. cap. 22. *Paponius Arrest.* lib. 4. cap. 1. Art. 2. and *Gaguinus* in *Philippo Valesio,* have published.

The Year 1356, furnishes us with another Example; at which Time King *John* was defeated by the English at Poitiers; taken Prisoner, and carried into England. "After so great a Calamity, the only hopes left were in the Authority of the Great Council; therefore immediately a Parliament was summon'd to meet at Paris. And although King *John*'s three Sons, *Charles, Lewis* and *John,* were at Hand, the eldest of which was of competent Age to govern; yet other Men were chosen, to wit, twelve approved Persons out of each Order of the States, to whom the Management of the Kingdom's Affairs was intrusted; and there it was decreed, that an Embassy should be sent into England to treat of Peace with the English." *Froissard,* Vol. 1. cap. 170. *Joannes Buchettus,* lib. 4. fol. 118. *Nich. Gillius* in *Chron. Regis Joannes,* are our Authors.

A third Instance we have Anno 1375, when the last Will and Testament of *Charles* the Fifth, surnamed the Wise, was produced: By which Will he had appointed his Wife's Brother, *Philip* Duke of Bourbon, to be Guardian to his Sons, and *Lewis* Duke of Anjou his own Brother, to be Administrator of the Kingdom till such Time as his Son *Charles* should come of Age. But notwithstanding this, a Great Council was held at Paris, wherein (after declaring the Testament to be void and null) it was decreed, that the Administration of the Kingdom should be committed to *Lewis,* the Boy's Uncle: "But upon this Condition, that he should be ruled and governed in that Administration, by the Advice of certain Persons named and approv'd by the Council." The Education and Tutelage of the Child was left to Bourbon; and at the same Time a Law was made, that the Heir of the Kingdom should be crown'd as soon as he should be full 14 Years old, and receive the Homage and Oath of Fidelity from his Subjects. *Froissard,* Vol. 2, cap. 60. *Buchett,* lib. 4. fol. 124. Chron. Brit. Cap.

A 4th Example we have in the Year 1392; at which Time the same *Charles* the Sixth was taken with a sudden Distraction or Madness, and was convey'd first to Mans, and afterwards to Paris; and there a General Council was held, wherein it was decreed by the Authority of the States, that the Administration of the Kingdom should be committed to the Dukes of Aquitain and Burgundy. *Froissard,* Vol. 4. cap. 44. is our Author.

5. Neither must we omit what *Paponius* (*Arrest.* lib. 5. tit. 10. Art. 4.) testifies to have been declared by the Parliament at Paris, within the compass of almost our own Memories, when Francis the First had a Mind to alienate Part of his Dominions; viz. "That all Alienations of that Kind made by any of his Predecessors, were void and null in themselves; upon this very Account, that they were done without the Authority of the Great Council, and of the Three Estates, as he calls them."

A 6th Example we have in the Year 1426, when *Philip* Duke of Burgundy, and *Hanfred* [Dux *Clocestriae*] were at mortal Enmity with each other, to the great detriment of the *Commonwealth;* and it was at last agreed between them to determine their Quarrel by single Combat: For in that Contention the Great Council interposed its Authority, and decreed that both should lay down their Arms, and submit to have their Controversies judicially tryed before the Council, rather than disputed with the Sword. Which History is related at large by *Paradinus,* in *Chron.* Burgund. lib. 3. Anno 1426.

A 7th Example happened in the Year 1484, when *Lewis* the Eleventh dying, and leaving his Son *Charles,* a Boy of 13 Years old; a Council was held at Tours, wherein it was decreed, "The Education of the Boy should be committed to *Anne,* the King's Sister"; but the Administration of the

Kingdom should be intrusted to certain Persons Elected and approved by that Council; notwithstanding *Lewis,* Duke of Orleans, the next Kinsman by the Father's Side, demanded it as his Right. A Testimony of which Transaction is extant in the Acts of that Council, printed at Paris; and in *Joannes Buchettus* 4th Book, folio 167.

CHAPTER XVIII

Of the Remarkable Authority of the Council against *Lewis* the Eleventh

The Power and Authority of the Council and the Estates assembled, appears by the foregoing Testimonies to have been very great, and indeed (as it were) Sacred. But because we are now giving Examples of this Power, we will not omit a signal Instance of the Authority of this Council, which interposed it self in the Memory of our Fathers against *Lewis* the Eleventh, who was reputed more crafty and cunning than any of the *Kings* that had ever been before him.

In the Year 1460, when this *Lewis* governed the Kingdom in such a Manner, that in many Cases the Duty of a good Prince, and a Lover of his Country, was wanting; the People began to desire the Assistance and Authority of the Great Council, that some Care might therein be taken of the Publick Welfare; and because it was suspected the King would not submit himself to it, the Great Men of the Kingdom (stirred up by the daily Complaints and Solicitations of the Commons), "resolv'd to gather Forces, and raise an Army; that (as *Philip* de *Commines* expresses it) they might provide for the Publick Good, and expose the King's wicked Administration of the *Commonwealth*." They therefore agreed to be ready prepared with a good Army, that in case the King should prove refractory, and refuse to follow good Advice, they might compel him by Force: For which Reason that War was said to have been undertaken for the Publick Good, and was commonly called the War *du bien public.* "*Commines, Gillius,* and *Lamarc,* have recorded the Names of those Great Men who were the principal Leaders, the Duke of *Bourbon,* the Duke of *Berry,* the King's Brother; the Counts of *Dunois, Nevers, Armagnac,* and *Albret,* and the Duke of *Charolois,* who was the Person most concerned in what related to the Government. Wherever they marched, they caused it to be proclaimed, that their Undertakings were only design'd for the Publick Good; they published Freedom from Taxes and Tributes, and lent Ambassadors with Letters to the Parliament at Paris, to the Ecclesiasticks, and to the Rector of the University, desiring them not to suspect or imagine those Forces were rais'd for the King's destruction, but only to reclaim him, and make him perform the Office of a Good King, as the present Necessities of the Publick required." These are *Gillius's* Words, lib. 4. fol. 152.

The Annals intituled the Chronicles of *Lewis* the Eleventh, printed at Paris by *Galliottus,* fol. 27. have these Words. "The first and chiefest of their demands was, That a Convention of the Three States should be held; because in all Ages it had been found to be the only proper Remedy for all Evils, and to have always had a force sufficient to heal such sort of mischiefs." Again, Pag. 28. "An Assembly was called on Purpose to hear the Ambassadors of the Great Men, and met on the 24th Day in the Townhouse at Paris; at which were present some Chosen Men of the University, of the Parliament, and of the Magistrates. The Answer given the Ambassadors, was, That what they demanded was most just; and accordingly a Council of the Three Estates was summon'd." These are the Words of that Historian. From whence the Old Saying of *Marcus Antonius* appears to be most true. "*Etsi omnes molestae semper seditiones sunt, justas tamen esse nonnullas, & prope necessarias: eas vero justissimas maximeque necessarias videri, cum populus Tyranni saevitia oppressus auxilium a legitimo Civium conventu implorat.* Although all Sorts of Seditions are troublesome, yet some of them are just, and in a manner necessary; but those are extraordinary just and necessary, which are occasion'd when the People oppress'd by the Cruelty of a *Tyrant,* implores the Assistance of a Lawful Convention."

Gaguinus, in his Life of *Lewis* the Eleventh, pag. 265. gives us *Charles*, the Duke of Burgundy's Answer to that King's Ambassadors. "*Charles* (says he) heard the Ambassadors patiently, but made Answer, That he knew no Method so proper to restore a firm Peace, at a Time when such great Animosities, and so many Disorders of the War were to be composed, as a Convention of the Three Estates. Which when the Ambassadors had by Special Messengers communicated to King *Lewis,* he hoping to gain his Point by Delays, summon'd the Great Council to meet at Tours, on the Kalends of April 1467; and at the appointed Time for the Convention, they came from all Parts of the Kingdom, *etc.*"

The same passage, and in almost the same Words, is recorded in the Book of *Annals,* fol. 64. and in the Great Chronicle, Vol. 4. fol. 242. where these very remarkable Words are further added. "In that Council it was appointed, that certain approved Men should be chosen out of each of the Estates, who should establish the *Commonwealth,* and take care that Right and Justice should be done. But *Gillius* in the Place abovemention'd says: After the Battle at Montlebery, many well-affected and prudent Men were elected to be Guardians of the Publick Good, according as it had been agreed upon between the King and the Nobles; among whom the Count of *Dunois* was the Principal, as having been the chief Promoter of that Rising." For it had grown into custom after the Wealth of the Ecclesiasticks was excessively increased, to divide the People into Three Orders or Classes, whereof the Ecclesiasticks made one; and when those Curators of the *Commonwealth* were chosen, twelve Persons were taken out of each Order. So that it was enabled in that Council, that 36 Guardians of the Republick should be created, with Power, by common consent, to redress all the Abuses of the Publick. Concerning which Thing, *Monstrellettus,* Vol. 4. fol. 150 writes thus: "In the first Place (says he) it was decreed, that for the re-establishing the State of the *Commonwealth,* and the easing the People of the Burthen of their Taxes, and to compensate their Losses, 36 Men should be elected, who should have Regal Authority, viz. 12 out of the Clergy, 12 out of the Knights, and 12 skilful in the Laws of the Land; to whom Power should be given of inspecting and enquiring into the Grievances and Mischiefs under which the Kingdom laboured, and to apply Remedies to all: And the King gave his Promise *in verbo Regis,* That whatsoever those 36 Men should appoint to be done, he would ratify and confirm."

Oliver de la Marck, a *Flemming,* in his History, cap. 35. writes the same thing, and mentions the same number of 36 Guardians or Curators of the *Commonwealth.* And he farther adds; "That because the King did not stand to his Promise, but violated his Faith, and the solemn Oath which he had publickly sworn, a most cruel War was kindled in *Francogallia,* which set it all in a Flame, and continued near 13 Years. Thus that King's Perjury was punish'd both by his own Infamy, and the People's Destruction."

Upon the whole Matter 'tis plain, that 'tis not yet a hundred Years compleat, since the *Liberties* of *Francogallia,* and the Authority of its annual General Council, flourished in full vigour, and exerted themselves against a King of ripe Years, and great Understanding; for he was above 40 Years old, and of such great Parts, as none of our *Kings* have equalled him. So that we may easily perceive that our *Commonwealth,* which at first was founded and established upon the Principles of *Liberty,* maintained it self in the same free and sacred State, (even by Force and Arms) against all the Power of *Tyrants* for more than Eleven hundred Years.

I cannot omit the great Commendation which that most noble Gentleman and accomplish'd Historian, *Philip de Commines,* gives of this Transaction; who in his 5th Book and 18th Chapter gives this Account of it, which we will transcribe Word for Word. "But to proceed: is there in all the World any King or Prince, who has a Right of imposing a Tax upon his People (though it were but to the Value of one Farthing) without their own Will and Consent? Unless he will make use of Violence, and a Tyrannical Power, he cannot. But some will say there may happen an Exigence, when the Great Council of the People cannot be waited for, the business admitting of no delay. I am sure, in the undertaking of a War, there is no need of such hast; one has sufficient leisure to think leisurely of that Matter. And this I dare affirm, that when *Kings* and Princes undertake a War with the consent of their Subjects, they are both much more powerful, and more formidable to their Enemies. It becomes a King of France least of any King in the World, to make use of such expressions as this. 'I have a Power of raising as great Taxes as I please on my Subjects'; for neither he, nor any other, has such a Power; and those Courtiers who use such Expressions, do their King no honour, nor increase his reputation with Foreign Nations; but on the contrary, create a fear and dread of him among all his Neighbours, who will not upon any Terms subject themselves to such a sort of Government. But if our King, or such as have a Mind to magnify his Power; would say thus; I have such obedient and loving Subjects, that they will deny me nothing in reason; or, there is no Prince that has a People more willing to forget the hardships they undergo; this indeed would be a Speech that would do him Honour, and give him reputation. But such Words as these do not become a King; I tax as much as I have a mind to; and I have a Power of taking it, which I intend to keep. *Charles* the Fifth never used such Expressions, neither indeed did I ever hear any of our *Kings* speak such a Word; but only some of their Ministers and Companions, who thought thereby they did their Masters service: But, in my opinion, they did them a great deal of injury, and spoke those words purely out of flattery, not considering what they said. And as a further Argument of the gentle Disposition of the French, let us but consider that Convention of the Three Estates held at *Tours,* Anno 1484. after the decease of our King *Lewis* the Eleventh: About that time the wholesome Institution of the Convention of the Three Estates began to be thought a dangerous Thing; and there were some inconsiderable fellows who said then, and often since, that it was High-Treason to make so much as mention of Convocating the States, because it tended to lessen and diminish the King's Authority; but it was they themselves who were guilty of High Treason against God, the King, and the Commonwealth. Neither do such-like Sayings turn to the Benefit of any Persons, but such as have got great Honours or Employments without any Merit of their own; and have learnt how to flatter and sooth, and talk impertinently; and who fear all great Assemblies, lest there they should appear in their proper Colours, and have all evil Actions condemned."

CHAPTER XIX

Of the Authority of the Assembly of the States concerning the most important Affairs of Religion[97]

We have hitherto demonstrated, that the Assembly of the States had a very great Power in all Matters of Importance relating to our Kingdom of France. Let us now consider, what its Authority has been, in things that concern Religion. Of this our Annals will inform us under the Year 1300 when Pope *Boniface* the Eighth sent Ambassadors to King *Philip* the Fair, demanding of him, whether he did not hold and repute himself to be subject to the Pope in all Things temporal as well as spiritual; and whether the Pope was not Lord over all the Kingdoms and States of Christendom. In Consequence of these Principles, he required of Philip to acknowledge him for his Sovereign Lord and Prince, and to confess that he held his Kingdom of France from the Pope's Liberality; or that if he refused to do this, he should be forthwith excommunicated, and declared a Heretick. After the King had given Audience to these Ambassadors, he summon'd the States

[97.] This chapter was not in the 1573 edition; in the 1576 edition it was chapter 18; in the 1586 edition it was chapter 22; see GS *Franc.*, pp. 428–40.

to meet at Paris, and in that Assembly the Pope's Letters were read, to the Purport following. "Boniface, universal Bishop, the Servant of the Servants of God, to *Philip* King of France, Fear God and keep his Commandments, it is our Pleasure thou shouldst know, that thou art our Subject, as well in things temporal as Spiritual, and that it belongs not to thee to bestow Prebends or collate Benefices, in any Manner whatsoever. If thou hast the Custody of any such that may be now vacant, thou must reserve the Profits of them for the Use of such as shall succeed therein: and if thou has already collated any of them, we decree by these Presents such Collation to be *ipso facto* void, and do revoke whatever may have been transacted relating there-unto; esteeming all those to be Fools and Madmen, who believe the contrary. From our Palace of the Lateran in the Month of December, and in the Sixth Year of our Pontificate." These Letters being read, and the Deputies of the States having severally delivered their Opinions about them, after the Affair was maturely deliberated, it was ordain'd; first, that the Pope's Letters should be burnt in the Presence of his Ambassadors, in the great Yard of the Palace: Then, that these Ambassadors with Mitres upon their Heads, and their Faces bedaub'd with Dirt, should be drawn in a Tumbrel by the common Hangman into the said Yard, and there be exposed to the Mockery and Maledictions of the People: finally, that Letters in the King's Name should be dispatched to the Pope, according to the Tenor following. "Philip by the Grace of God, King of France, to Boniface, who stiles himself universal Bishop, little or no greeting. Be it known to thy great Folly and extravagant Temerity, that in things temporal we have no Superior but God; and that the Disposal of the Vacancies of certain Churches and Prebends belong to us of Regal Right; that it is our due to receive the Profits of them, and our Intention to defend our selves by the Edge of the Sword, against all such, as would any way go about to disturb us in the Possession of the same; esteeming those to be Fools and Brainless, who think otherwise." For Witnesses of this History, we have the Author of the Chronicle of *Bretayne*, lib. 4. chap. 14.[98] and *Nicholas Gilles* in the *Annals of* France, to whom ought to be join'd *Papon*, in the first Book of his *Arrests*, tit. 5. art. 27.

[98.] Alain Bouchart, *Les Croniques annalles des pays d'Angleterre et Bretaigne* (Paris, 1531).

CHAPTER XX

Whether *Women* are not as much debarred (by the *Francogallican* Law) from the *Administration,* as from the *Inheritance* of the Kingdom

The present Dispute being about the Government of the Kingdom, and the chief Administration of Publick Affairs, we have thought fit not to omit this Question: Whether Women are not as much debarr'd from the Administration, as from the Inheritance of the Kingdom? And in the first Place we openly declare, that 'tis none of our intention to argue for or against the Roman Customs or Laws, or those of any other Nation, but only of the Institutions of this our own *Francogallia.* For as on the one Hand 'tis notorious to all the World, that by the Roman Institutions, Women were always under Guardianship, and excluded from intermeddling, either in publick or private Affairs, by Reason of the weakness of their Judgment: So on the other, Women (by ancient Custom) obtain the supreme Command in some Countries. "The Britains (says *Tacitus* in his *Life of Agricola*) make no distinction of Sexes in Government." Thus much being premised, and our Protestation being clearly and plainly proposed, we will now return to the Question. And as the Examples of some former Times seem to make for the Affirmative, wherein the Kingdom of *Francogallia* has been administered by Queens, especially by Widows and Queen-Mothers: So on the contrary, the reason of the Argument used in Disputations, is clearly against it. For she, who cannot be Queen in her own Right, can never have any Power of Governing in another's Right: But here a Woman cannot reign in her own Right, nor can the Inheritance of the Crown fall to her, or any of her Descendants; and if they be stiled Queens, 'tis only accidentally; as they are Wives to the *Kings* their Husbands. Which we have prov'd out of Records for twelve hundred Years together.

To this may be added (which we have likewise prov'd) that not only the sole Power of Creating and Abdicating their *Kings,* but also the Right of electing Guardians and Administrators of the *Commonwealth,* was lodged in the same Publick Council. Nay, and after the *Kings* were created, the supreme Power of the Administration was retained still by the same Council. And 'tis not yet full a hundred Years since 36 Guardians of the *Commonwealth* were constituted by the same Council, like so many *Ephori:* and this during the Reign of *Lewis* the Eleventh, as crafty and cunning as he was. If we seek for Authorities and Examples from our Ancestors, we may find several; there is a remarkable one in *Aimoinus,* lib. 4. cap. 1. where speaking of Queen *Brunechild,* Mother to young *Childebert;* "The Nobility of France (says he) understanding that *Brunechild* designed to keep the chief Management of the Kingdom in her own Hands; and having always hitherto, for so long a Time disdained to be subject to a Female Domination, did, *etc.*" And indeed it has so happened in the days of our Ancestors, that whenever Women got into their Hands the Procuration of the Kingdom, they have been always the occasion of wonderful Tragedies: Of which it will not be amiss to give some Examples. Queen *Crotildis,* Mother of the two *Kings, Childebert* and *Clotarius,* got once the Power into her Hands; and being extravagantly fond of the Sons of *Clodemer* (another of her Sons then dead) occasion'd a great deal of Contention, by her endeavouring to exclude her Sons, and promote these Grandsons to the Regal Dignity; and upon that Score she nourished their large Heads of Hair with the greatest Care and diligence imaginable, according to that ancient Custom of the *Kings* of the *Franks,* which we have before given an Account of. The two *Kings* (as soon as they understood it) presently sent one *Archadius,* who presenting her with a naked Sword and a Pair of Shears, gave her the Choice which of the two She had rather should be applied to the Boys Heads. But She (says *Gregory of Tours*) being enraged with Choler, especially when She beheld the naked Sword and the Scissors, answer'd with a great deal of Bitterness, "Since they cannot be advanced to the Kingdom, I had rather see them dead than shaven." And thereupon both her Grandsons were beheaded in her Presence. The same *Gregory,* lib. 3. cap. 18. subjoyns "This Queen, by her Liberalities and Gifts conferr'd upon Monasteries, got the Affections, *Plebis & vulgi,* of the common People and Mob: *Date frenos* (says Cato) *impotenti naturae, & indomito animali, & sperate ipsas modum licentiae facturas.* Give Bridles to their unruly Natures, and curb the untamed Animal; and then you may hope they shall set some Bounds to their Licentiousness." What an unbridled Animal and profligate Wretch was that Daughter of King *Theodorick,* by Birth an Italian; who being mad in Love with one of her Domesticks, and knowing him to have been kill'd by her Mother's Orders, feigned a thorough Reconciliation, and desir'd in Token of it to receive the Holy Sacrament of the Lord's Supper with her Mother; but privately mixing some Poyson in the Chalice, She at once gave the strangest Instance both of Impiety and Cruelty in thus murdering her own Mother. The Account given of it by *Gregory of Tours* is this: "They were (says he) of the Arrian Sect, and because it was their Custom that the Royal Family should communicate at the Altar out of one Chalice, and People of Inferior Quality out of another. (By the way, pray take notice of the Custom of Communicating in both kinds by the People.) She dropped Poyson into that Chalice out of which her Mother was to communicate; which as soon as she had tasted of it, kill'd her presently." *Fredegunda,* Queen-Mother, and Widow of *Chilperick* the First, got the Government into her Hands; She, in her Husband's Time, lived in Adultery with one *Lander;* and as soon as she found out that her Husband *Chilperick* had got Wind of it, she had him murdered, and presently seiz'd upon the administration of the Kingdom as Queen-Mother, and Guardian of her Son *Clotharius,* and kept possession of it for 13 years; in the first place she poyson'd her Son's Uncle *Childebert* together with his Wife; afterwards she stirred up the Hunns against his Sons, and raised a Civil War in the Republick. And lastly, She was the Firebrand of all those Commotions which wasted and burnt all *Francogallia,* during many Years, as *Aimoinus* tells us, [lib. 3. cap. 36. & lib. 8. cap. 29.].

There ruled once in France, *Brunechild,* Widow of King *Sigebert,* and Mother of *Childebert.* This Woman had for her Adulterer a certain Italian, called *Protadius,* whom She advanced to great Honours: She bred up her two Sons, *Theodebert* and *Theodorick,* in such a wicked and profligate Course of Life, that at last they became at mortal Enmity with each other: And after having had long Wars, fought a cruel single Combat. She kill'd with her own hands her Grandson *Meroveus,* the Son of *Theodebert:* She poysoned her Son *Theodorick.* What need we say more? *Date fraenos* (as Cato says) *impotenti naturae, & indomito animali; & sperate illas modum licentae facturas.*[99] She was the Occasion of the Death of Ten of the Royal Family: And when a certain Bishop reproved her, and exhorted her to amend her Life, She caused him to be thrown into the River. At last, a Great Council of the *Franks* being summoned, She was judged, and condemned, and drawn in pieces by wild Horses, being torn limb from limb. The Relators of this Story are, *Greg. Turonensis,* [lib. 5. cap. 39.] and [lib. 8. cap. 29.] And *Ado* [Aetat. 6.] *Otto Frising.* [*Chron.* 5. cap. 7.] *Godfridus Viterbiensis* [*Chron.* parte 16.] &. *Aimoinus* [lib. 4. cap. 1.]. Also the Appendix of *Gregory of Tours,* [lib. 11.1] whose Words are these: "Having convicted her of being the Occasion of the Death of Ten *Kings* of the *Franks;* to wit, of *Sigebert, Meroveus,* and his Father *Chilperick; Theodebert,* and his Son *Clothair; Meroveus,* the Son of *Clothair, Theodorick,* and his three Children, which had been newly killed, they order'd her to be placed upon a Camel, and to be tortured with divers sorts of Torments, and so to be carried about all the Army; afterwards to be tied by the Hair of the Head, one Leg and one Arm to a Wild Horses Tail; by which being kicked, and swiftly dragged about, She was torn Limb from Limb."

[99.] GS *Franc.* translate this as "If you loose the reins with women, as with an unruly nature and an untamed beast, you must expect uncontrolled actions."

Let us instance in some others: *Plectrudis* got the Government into her hands; a Widow not of the King, but of *Pipin*, who ruled the Kingdom whilst *Dagobert* the Second bore the empty Title of King. This *Plectrudis* having been divorced by her Husband *Pipin*, because of her many Adulteries and flagitious Course of Life; as soon as her Husband was dead, proved the Incendiary of many Seditions in France. She compell'd that gallant Man *Charles Martel*, Mayor of the Palace, to quit his Employment, and in his Place put one *Theobald*, a most vile and wicked Wretch; and at last She raised a most grievous Civil War among the *Franks*, who in divers Battles discomfited each other with most terrible Slaughters. Thus, says *Aimoinus*, [lib. 4. cap. 50. & cap. sequen.]. Also the Author of a Book called, The State of the Kingdom of France under *Dagobert* the Second, has these Words: "When the *Franks* were no longer able to bear the Fury and Madness of *Plectrude*, and saw no hopes of Redress from King *Dagobert*, they elected one *Daniel* for their King, (who formerly had been a Monk) and called him *Chilperick*." Which Story we have once before told you.

But let us proceed. The Queen-Mother of *Charles* the Bald, (whose Name was *Judith*) and Wife of *Lewis* the Pious, who had not only been King of *Francogallia*, but Emperor of Italy and Germany, got the Government into her Hands. This Woman stirred up a most terrible and fatal War between King *Lewis* and his Sons, (her Sons in Law) from whence arose so great a Conspiracy, that they constrained their Father to abdicate the Government, and give up the Power into their Hands, to the great Detriment of almost all Europe: The Rise of which Mischiefs, our Historians do unanimously attribute, for the most part, to Queen *Judith* in a particular Manner: The Authors of this History are the Abbot of Ursperg, *Michael Ritius* and *Otto Frising*. [*Chron.* 5. cap. 34.]. "*Lewis* (says this last) by Reason of the Evil Deeds of his Wife Judith, was driven out of his Kingdom. Also *Rhegino* [in *Chron.* ann. 1338.] *Lewis* (says he) was deprived of the Kingdom by his Subjects, and being reduced to the Condition of a private Man, was put into Prison, and the sole Government of the Kingdom, by the Election of the *Franks*, was conferr'd upon *Lotharius* his Son. And this Deprivation of *Lewis* was occasion'd principally through the many Whoredoms of his Wife *Judith*."

Some Ages after, Queen *Blanch*, a Spanish Woman, and Mother to St. *Lewis*, ruled the Land. As soon as She had seized the Helm of Government, the Nobility of France began to take up Arms under the Conduct of *Philip* Earl of *Bologn*, the King's Uncle, crying out (as that excellent Author *Joannes Jonvillaeus* writes) [cap. histor. 4.] "That it was not to be endured that so great a Kingdom should be governed by a Woman, and She a Stranger." Whereupon those Nobles rejecting *Blanch*, chose Earl Philip to be Administrator of the Kingdom: But *Blanch* persisting in her Purpose, sollicited Succors from all Parts, and at last determined to conclude a League with *Ferdinand* King of Spain: With *Philip* joyned the Duke of *Brittany*, and the Count de *Evreux* his Brother. These, on a sudden, seized on some Towns, and put good Garrisons into them. And thus a grievous War was begun in France, because the Administration of the Government had been seized by the Queen-Mother: It happened that the King went (about that Time) to *Estampes*, being sent thither by his Mother upon Account of the War: To that Place the Nobles from all Parts hastily got together, and began to surround the King; not with an Intention (as *Joinville* says) to do him any harm, but to withdraw him from the Power of his Mother: Which She hearing; with all Speed armed the People of Paris, and commanded them to march towards Estampes. Scarce were these Forces got as far as *Montlebery*, when the King (getting from the Nobles) joyned them, and returned along with them to Paris. As soon as *Philip* found that he was not provided with a sufficient Force of Domestick Troops, he sent for Succours to the Queen of *Cyprus*, (who at the same time had some Controversy depending in the Kingdom) She entering with a great Army into *Champagn*, plunder'd that Country far and near; *Blanch* however continues in her Resolution. This constrains the Nobility to call in the English Auxiliaries, who waste *Aquitain* and all the Maritime Regions; which Mischiefs arose through the Ambition and unbridled Lust of Rule of the Queen-Mother, as *Joinvillaeus* tells us at large, [cap. 7, 8, 9, 10].

And because many of our Countrymen have a far different Opinion of the Life and Manners of Queen *Blanch*, occasioned (as 'tis probable) by the Flattery of the Writers of those times; (For all Writers either through Fear of Punishment, or, by reason of the esteem which the *Kings* their

Sons have in the World, are cautious how they write of Queen-Mothers): I think it not amiss to relate what *Joinville* himself records [cap 76.] vis. That She had so great a Command over her Son, and had reduced him to that degree of timidity and lowness of Spirit, that She would very seldom suffer the King to converse with his Wife *Margaret,* (her Daughter-in-Law) whom She hated. And therefore whenever the King went a Journey, She ordered the Purveyors to mark out different Lodgings, that the Queen might lie separate from the King. So that the poor King was forced to place Waiters and Doorkeepers in Ambush whenever He went near his Queen; Ordering them, that when they heard his Mother *Blanch* approach the Lodgings, they should beat some Dogs, by whose Cry he might have warning to hide himself: And one day (says *Joinville*) when Queen *Margaret* was in Labour, and the King in Kindness was come to visit her, on a sudden Queen *Blanch* surprized him in her Lodgings: For although he had been warned by the howling of the Dogs, and had hid himself (wrapped up in the Curtains) behind the Bed; yet She found him out, and in the Presence of all the Company laid Hands on him, and drew him out of the Chamber: You have nothing to do here (said She) get out: The poor Queen, in the mean Time, being not able to bear the disgrace of such a Reproof, fell into a Swoon for grief; so that the Attendants were forced to call back the King to bring her to her self again, by whose return She was comforted and recovered. *Joinville* tells this Story [cap. hist. 76.] in almost these same Words.

Again, Some years after this, *Isabella,* Widow of *Charles* the 6th, (surnamed the Simple) got Possession of the Government: For before the Administration of the Publick Affairs could be taken care of by the Great Council, or committed by them to the Management of chosen and approved Men, many ambitious Courtiers had stirr'd up Contentions: Six Times these Controversies were renewed, and as often composed by agreement. At last *Isabella* being driven out of Paris, betook her self to Chartres: There, having taken into her Service a subtle Knave, one *Philip de Morvilliers,* She made up a Council of her own, with a President, and appointed this *Morvilliers* her Chancellor; by whose Advice She order'd a Broad-Seal, commonly called a Chancery-Seal, to be engraven; On which her own Image was cut, holding her Arms down by her Sides: and in her

Patents She made use of this Preamble. "*Isabella,* by the Grace of God, Queen of France; who, by reason of the King's Infirmity, has the Administration of the Government in her Hands, *etc.*"

But when the Affairs of the *Commonwealth* were reduced to that desperate estate, that all things went to rack and ruin, She was by the Publick Council banished to Tours, and committed to the Charge of Four Tutors, who had Orders to keep her lock'd up at home, and to watch her so narrowly, that She should be able to do nothing; not so much as to write a Letter without their Knowledge. A large Account of all this Transaction we have in *Monstrellet's* History. [Cap. 161. & Cap. 168].

CHAPTER XXI

Of the *Juridical Parliaments* in France

Under the *Capetian* Family there sprung up in *Francogallia* a Kind of Judicial Reign, [*Regnum Judiciale*] of which (by reason of the incredible Industry of the Builders up and Promoters of it, and their unconceivable Subtilty in all subsequent Ages), we think it necessary to say something. A Sort of Men now rule everywhere in France, which are called Lawyers by some, and Pleaders or Pettyfoggers by others: These Men, about 300 Years ago, managed their Business with so great Craft and Diligence, that they not only subjected to their Domination the Authority of the General Council, (which we spoke of before) but also all the Princes and Nobles, and even the Regal Majesty it self: So that in whatever Towns the Seats of this same Judicial Kingdom have been fix'd, very near the third part of the Citizens and Inhabitants have applied themselves to the Study and Discipline of this wrangling Trade, induced thereunto by the vast Profits and Rewards which attend it. Which every one may take Notice of, even in the City of Paris, the Capital of the Kingdom: For who can be three Days in that City without observing, that the third Part of the Citizens are taken up with the Practice of that litigious and Pettyfogging Trade? Insomuch, that the General Assembly of Lawyers in that City (which is called the Robed Parliament) is grown to so great a Height of Wealth and Dignity; that now it seems to be (what *Jugurtha* said of old of the Roman Senate) no longer an Assembly of Counsellors, but of *Kings*, and Governors of Provinces. Since whoever has the fortune to be a Member of it, how meanly born soever, in a few years time acquires immense and almost Regal Riches: For this reason many other Cities strove with Might and Main to have the like Privilege of Juridical Assemblies: So that now there are several of these famous Parliaments, to wit, those of *Paris, Toulouse, Rouen, Grenoble, Bourdeaux, Aix,* and *Dijon:* All which are fix'd and sedentary; besides an Eighth, which is ambulatory and moveable, and is called the Grand Council.

Within the Limits of these great Juridical Kingdoms there are others lesser, which we may call Provincial Governments, who do all they can to imitate the Grandeur and Magnificence of their Superiors; and these are called Presidial Courts: And so strong is the Force and Contagion of this Disease, that a very great Part of the French Nation spends its time and pains in Strife and Law-Suits, in promoting Contentions and Processes, just as of old, a great Number of the Egyptians were employ'd by their *Tyrants* in building Pyramids, and other such useless Structures.

Now the Word Parliament in the old Manner of Speech used by our Countrymen, "signifies a Debate, or discoursing together of many Persons, who come from several Parts, and assemble in a certain place, that they may communicate to one another Matters relating to the Publick." Thus in our ancient Chronicles, whenever Princes or their Ambassadors had a Meeting to treat of Peace or Truce, or other Warlike Agreements; the Assembly so appointed was always called a Parliament; and for the same Reason the Publick Council of the Estates was, in our old Language, called a Parliament. Which Assembly, being of great Authority, the *Kings* of the *Capetian* Race having a Mind to diminish that Authority by little and little, substituted in its Place a certain Number of Senators, and transferred the August Title of a Parliament to those Senators: And gave them these Privileges: First, That none of the King's Edicts should be of Force, and ratified, unless those Counsellors had been the Advisers and Approvers of them. Next, That no Magistracy or Employment in all France, whether Civil or Military, should be conferr'd on any Person, without his being inaugurated, and taking the Oaths in that Assembly. Then that there should be no *Liberty* of Appeal from their Judgment, but that all their Decrees should stand firm, and inviolable: In fine; whatever Power and Authority had anciently been lodged in the General Council of the Nation, during so many Years together, was at Length usurped by that Counterfeit Council, which the *Kings* took care to fill with such Persons as would be most subservient to their Ends.

Wherefore it will be worth our while, to enquire from what Beginnings it grew up to so great a Height and Power: First, a very magnificent Palace was built at Paris, by Order (as some say) of King *Lewis Hutin*, which in our Ancient Language signifies mutinous or turbulent. Others say, by Philip the fair, about the Year 1314. through the Industry and Care of *Enguerrant de Marigny* Count of *Longueville*, who was hanged some Years after on a Gallows at Paris, for embezzling the Publick Money. Whoever 'twas that built it, we may affirm, that our *Francogallican* Kings took the same Pains in building up this litigious Trade, that the Egyptian Monarchs are said to have done in employing their Subjects to build the Pyramids; among whom *Chemnis* is recorded to have gathered together 360,000 Men to raise one Pyramid. *Gaguinus,* in his History of King *Hutin's* Life, has this Passage, "This *Lewis* ordained, That the Court of Parliament should remain fixed and immoveable in the City of Paris, that Suitors and Clients might not be put to the Trouble of frequent Removals." Now what some affirm, that *Pipin* or *Charlemagn* were the Authors of this Institution, is very absurd, as we shall plainly make appear. For most of the Laws and Constitutions of *Charlemagn* are extant; in all which there is not the least Mention made of the Word Parliament, nor of that great fixed Senate; he only ordains, That in certain known Places his Judges should keep a Court, and assemble the People; which according to his usual Custom he calls a *Placitum,* or a *Mallum,* as [lib. 4. cap. 35. *Legis Franciae*] 'tis written, "He shall cause no more than three general *Placita* to be kept in one Year, unless by chance some Person is either accused, or seizes another Man's Property, or is summoned to be a Witness." There are many other Laws extant of that King's of the like Nature, by which we may observe the Paucity of Law-suits in his Days: And I am clearly of Opinion, that what I find several of our modern Authors have affirm'd is most true, vis. that the first Rise and Seeds of so many Law-suits, Calumnies and Contentions in this Kingdom, proceeded from Pope Clement the Fifth, who during the Reign of Philip the Fair, transferred the Seat of his Papacy to Avignon; at which time his Courtiers and Petty-Foggers, engaging into Acquaintance with our Countrymen, Introduced the Roman Arts of Wrangling into our Manners and Practice. But not to speak of such remote times. About the Year of our Lord 1230. reigned St. *Lewis,* as he is plainly called, whose Life *Johannes Jonvillaeus* (whom we have often mentioned) has written at large. Out of his Commentary we may easily learn, how few Contentions and Law-Suits were in those Days, since King *Lewis* either determined the Controversies himself in Person, or referred them to be determined by some of his Followers and Companions: And therefore [cap. 94.] he thus writes, "He was wont (says he) to command Lord *Nellius,* Lord *Soissons,* or my self, to inspect and manage the Appeals which were made to him. Afterwards he sent for us, and enquired into the State of the Case; and whether it were of such a Nature as could not be ended without his own Intervention. Oftentimes it happened, that after we had made our Report, he sent for the contending Parties, and heard the Cause impartially argued over again. Sometimes for his Diversion he would go to the Park of *Bois de Vincennes,* and sitting down upon a green sodd at the foot of an Oak Tree, would command us to sit by him; and there if anyone had Business, he would cause him to be called, and hear him patiently. He would often himself proclaim aloud, That if any one had Business or a Controversy with an Adversary, he might come near and set forth the Merits of his Cause; then if any Petitioner came, he would hear him attentively; and having thoroughly considered the Case, would pass Judgment according to Right and Justice. At other times he appointed *Peter Fountain* and *Godfrey Villet* to plead the Causes of the contending Parties. I have often (says he) seen that good King go out of Paris into one of his Gardens or Villa's without the Walls, dressed very plainly, and there order a Carpet to be spread before him on a Table; and, having caused Silence to be proclaimed, those which were at Variance with each other were introduced to plead their Causes, and then he presently did Justice without Delay." Thus far *Joinvillaeus.* By which we may guess at the small Number of Law-Suits and Complainants in those Days, and how careful our *Kings* were of preventing the Mischiefs that might arise from such as fomented Controversies.[100] {In the Capitular of *Charles* the Great this Law is extant, "Be it known unto all Persons both Nobility and People, by these our Patents, That we will sit one Day in every Week to hear Causes in Person."

We have the like Testimony in *William Buddaeus,* a very famous Man, and a Principal Ornament of our Kingdom of France. For in his Annotations on the *Pandects* (where he treats of this very Argument, and inveighs against this Kingdom of Brawlers and Petty-Foggers) he tells us, that he finds in the Regal Commentaries of Venerable Antiquity, (the free perusal of which his Quality did intitle him to) "That in the Reign of the same King *Lewis,* [Anno 1230.] several Controversies arose between the King and the Earl of Brittany; And that by Consent (as 'tis probable) of both Parties, a Camp-Court of Judicature was summoned to meet at *Enceniacum* [Enceny], wherein sat as Judges, not Lawyers, Civilians and Doctors, but Bishops, Earls, and Barons. And there the Earl of Brittany was cast, and it was ordered that the Inhabitants of his County should be absolved and freed from the Oath of Allegiance and Fidelity, which they had taken to him. Again, in the same King's Reign, [Anno 1259.] a Dispute having arisen about the County of Clermont between the King and the Earls of Poitou and Anjou, a Court of Judicature, composed of the like Persons, was appointed, wherein sat the Bishops and Abbots, the General of the Dominicans, the Constable, the Barons, and several Laicks. To this he subjoyns: Yet there were two Parliaments called each Year, at Christmas and at Candlemas, like as there are two *Scacaria* [exchequers] summoned in Normandy at Easter and at Michaelmas." Thus far *Budaeus;* to whom agrees what we find in an ancient Book concerning the Institution of Parliaments,} wherein this Article is quoted out of the Constitution of Philip the 4th, surnamed the Fair [ex Anno 1302.] "Moreover, for the Conveniency of our Subjects, and the expeditious determining of Causes, we propose to have it enacted, that two Parliaments shall be held every Year at Paris, and two *Scacaria* at Rouen: That the *Dies Trecenses* shall be held

[100.] GS *Franc.* (pp. 511, 533) establish that the passage enclosed in braces {} was suppressed in later editions.

twice a Year: and that a Parliament shall be held at Toulouse, as it used to be held in past times, if the People of the Land consent to it: Also, because many Causes of great Importance are debated in our Parliament, between great and notable Personages; We ordain and appoint, that two Prelates, and two other sufficient Persons, being Laymen of our Council; or at least one Prelate and one Laick, shall be continually present in our Parliaments, to hear and deliberate concerning the above-mentioned Causes." From which Words we may learn, First, how seldom the Courts of Judicature heard Causes in those Days. Next, how few Judges sat in those Parliaments. For as to the other Provinces and Governments of the Kingdom, we have (in the same Book) the Constitution of *Philip* the *Fair* in these words, [Anno 1302.] "Moreover, We ordain that our Seneschals and Bayliffs shall hold their Assizes in Circuit throughout their Counties and Bailwicks once every two Months at least."

Furthermore, *Budaeus* in the same Place, [Anno 1293.] writes, that Philip the Fair appointed, that three Sorts of People should sit in Parliament, viz. Prelates, Barons, and Clerks mixed with Laymen: "Since the Laicks (says he) are chosen promiscuously out of the Knights, and out of other Sorts of People. Also, that the Prelates and Barons should select fit Persons out of that third Estate, to exercise every Sort of Judicature; and at the same Time should chuse three Judges, who should be sent abroad into those Countries where the written Laws of the Land had their Course, that they might there judge and determine according to Law. And if any question of great importance were to be argued, they should take to their Assistance the most Learned Men they could get." In which place, *Budaeus* lamenting the Evil Customs of our Times; that is, this Kingdom of Lawyers now in vogue, breaks out with Juvenal into this Exclamation: "*Quondam hoc indigenae vivebant more!* So (says he) may I exclaim, that in Old times, when this Kingdom flourished, (as may appear by our Money coined of pure fine Gold) there was a plain and easy way of doing Justice; there were few Law-Suits, and those not of long Continuance, or indeed Eternal, as now they are; for then this Rabble-rout of pretended Interpreters of the Law had not invaded the Publick: neither was the Science of the Law stretched out to such an unlimited Extent; but Truth and Equity, and a prudent Judge, endued with Integrity and Innocence, was of more worth than Six hundred Volumes of Law-Books. But now to what a sad condition things are brought, every one sees, but no body dares speak out. [*Sed omnes dicere mussant.*]" Thus far honest *Budaeus;* a most inveterate Adversary of this Art of Chicanery, upon all occasions.

To return to our Purpose, of giving an Account upon what Foundations and Beginnings this Reign of Litigiousness was first raised. As *Cicero* writes, "that the Old High-Priests (by reason of the Multitude of Sacrifices) instituted three Assistants called *Viri Epulones,* although they themselves were appointed by Numa to offer Sacrifice at the *Ludi Epulares.*"[101] In like Manner, out of a very small number of Parliamentary Judges, (when Law-Suits and Litigiousness increased) swarm'd this incredible Multitude of Judges, and Spawn of Counsellors. And, in the first place, a great, sumptuous and magnificent Palace was built (as we told you before) either by the Command of *Lewis Hutin,* or of *Philip the Fair:* then (from a moderate Number of Judges) three Courts of Ten each, were erected a [*tres decuriae*] viz. Of the great Chamber of Accounts, or Inquests, and of Requests. Which Partition *Budaeus* speaks of in the above-quoted place, but more at large *Gaguinus* in his Life of King *Lewis Hutin.*

I must not omit one remarkable thing that ought for ever to be remembered, which both these Authors have transmitted to Posterity: viz. That this Meeting of the Court of Judicature was not perpetual and fixed, as 'tis now, but summonable by the King's Writs, which every Year were renewed by Proclamation about the beginning of November: "And that we may be certain (says *Gaguinus*) that the King was the Original and Author of this solemn Convention; the Royal Writs are issued every Year, whereby the Parliament is authorized to meet on the Feast-day of *St. Martin,* that is, on the 10th of November."

Now of the wonderful and speedy Increase of this Judicial Kingdom, we have this instance; That about a hundred Years after its beginning, that is, in the Year 1455, in the Reign of *Charles* the 7th, we find this Order made by him "From the Feast of Easter, till the End of the Parliament, the Presidents and Counsellors ought to meet in their respective Chambers at six a Clock every Morning: from the Feast of St. Martin forwards,

[101.] GS *Franc.* identify the source as *De Oratore* 3.19.73 (Loeb 2:58).

they may meet later." And a little after it says, "We judge it very necessary, that the Presidents and Counsellors of the Court should come to Parliament after Dinner, for the dispatch of Causes, and of Judgments." This was *Charles* the 7th's Order: But in *Charles* the Great's Reign, who ruled a Kingdom three Times as big, we find a very different Manner of rendering Justice; as we may easily understand by that Law of his; mention'd lib. 4. cap. 74. *Legis Franciae;* "Let a *Comes,* a Judge (says he) not hold a *Placitum,* (that is, not pass a Decree) but before Dinner, or Fasting."

Concerning the Word *Parliament,* and the Authority of that Name, we have this Argument; That when of old a Senate was instituted in *Dauphine* with supreme Authority, which was commonly called the *Council of Dauphine; Lewis* the 11th endeavouring to oblige the *Dauphinois,* who had well deserved from him, changed the Name of this Council into that of a Parliament, without adding any thing to the Privileges or Authority of it. Of which *Guidopappius* is our Witness. [Quest. 43 and again quest. 554].[102]

FINIS.

[102.] GS *Franc.* (p. 345) identify the source as Guy Pape, *Decisiones Gratiano-politanae* (1609), p. 27.

Some Considerations
for the Promoting of Agriculture
and Employing the Poor

SOME

CONSIDERATIONS

FOR THE

Promoting *of* Agriculture,

AND

EMPLOYING

THE

POOR.

DUBLIN:

Printed by GEORGE GRIERSON, at
the *Two Bibles* in *Essex-Street*, MDCCXXIII.

To The Gentlemen of the Honourable House of Commons of Ireland

Gentlemen,

Your Honourable House having under its Consideration the Heads of some Bills for the better providing for, and employing the Poor. And the Business of *Agriculture* being (next to that of the *Fishery*) one of the most easy and profitable Ways that can be thought of for that Purpose. The Writer of the following Sheets, cannot more properly Dedicate them than to You, who have lately given an eminent Instance of Your Wisdom and Love to Your Country, in Your just Censure and vigorous Resolutions against a Patent calculated to destroy Your Trade, rob You of Your Mony; and which calls You Slaves and Fools to Your Faces. I know not what good Thing may not be expected further from an Assembly which both understands and dares do its Duty. I am not so vain, as to think that all that I have here written is of Importance, but some Hints I have given in haste, which being improved by Gentlemen of greater Skill and Leisure, may be of Service to the Publick; the promoting of which, has always been the utmost Ambition of,

September 30th, 1723.
Your most humble Servant
R. L. V. M.

Some Considerations for the Promoting of Agriculture, Etc.

The dearth of Corn this last Winter, and the inconveniencies which arose from it, both in the misery of the common People, and the Exportation of our Mony for damaged Goods, (for so the most of it proved) shou'd set all heads a work to find out the *Causes* of this Mischief, in order to provide proper remedies for the future; which cannot well be effected if we mistake the *Causes* from whence our Evils proceed.

Some impute it to the *Covetousness and Cruelty of Landlords, who set hard Bargains to their Tenants:* Some to the *Restraints put by Landlords upon Plowing:* Others again to the *Mismanagement and little forecast of Tenants,* who sell off their Corn as soon as they can, after Harvest, and keep little or nothing in reserve for the latter end of the year, wherewith to supply the Markets; but snatch at the present Gain without regard to what may happen seven or eight Months after: and 'tis most certain that there is not in any part of *Europe* such an inequality in Markets as among us. We have always either a *Glut* or a *Dearth,* very often there are not ten days distance between the extremity of the one and the other: Such a want of *Policy* is there (in *Dublin* especially) in the most important affair of *Bread,* without a plenty of which the Poor must starve.

These are every one of them true in a great Measure; but we are to consider from whence they arise, and endeavour to prevent the *Source* and *Original* of them, for all these are the *Effects* rather than the *first Causes* of our Grievance.

I shall venture in one word to give my opinion, which is this, *That the whole Oeconomy of Agriculture is generally mistaken or neglected in this Kingdom.*

Either 'tis not understood, or 'tis thought below the consideration of the higher Ranks among us, and therefore not made the care of Parliaments as it ought to be, and as I hope it soon will be, if we be in earnest to employ and provide for the necessities of the Poor. 'Tis not putting them upon the Parish as they do in *England,* which will do our Business. We have Poor of several kinds, and must be differently treated; and besides, I hope we shall never imitate *England* in our provisions for the Poor, whatever we do in other matters; for altho' 'tis grown there so heavy a Tax (through the cheats in the Collection and Distribution) that in many places it exceeds eight Shillings in the Pound Rent,[1] yet I know no Country where the real Poor are worse taken Care of.

Agriculture is not only a Science, but the most useful one to Mankind: The Inventors of every part of it have been thought worthy of Divine honours. The Encouragers of it both by Practice and Precept, have been the greatest Men in the most flourishing Kingdoms and Common-wealths: The ablest *Statesmen, Philosophers* and *Poets,* have made it their principal Care, and given the best instructions concerning it, as knowing it to be that whereon the Life and well-being of the Community depends.

I have often wondred (when I consider how long it is since this Kingdom of *Ireland* has been united and annexed to the Crown of *England,* and the *English* customs, as to Habit, Language, and Religion, have been encouraged and enjoyn'd by Laws) how it comes to pass, that we should be so long a time, and so universally Ignorant of the *English* manner of manageing our Tillage and Lands as we now are; or if we formerly knew them, how we came to fall off from that Knowledge and the Practice of it to such a degree, that the *English* Tenants who pay double the Rent to

[1.] Assuming 20 shillings to the pound, the tax is 40 percent.

their Landlords for their Acres (which are much shorter then the *Irish* Acres) are able notwithstanding to supply us with Corn at a moderate Price, over and above the incident Charges of Freight, Porterage, *&c.* and the hazard of the Seas, whilst we are often Starving, though our Soil, if rightly managed, does not come behind the best in *Britain,* take one with another, and I have at last determined with my self, that this must needs be *thro' the difference in our Industry and Skill,* for we see that an *English* Farmer on a small Holding (sometimes not exceeding twenty Acres) shall live clean and comfortably, Cloath himself, Wife, Children, and Family decently; eat warm Victuals once every day, if not oftener; pay his Rent punctually; whilst the condition of the *Irish* Farmer on *a large Farm,* is the very reverse of all this. Whoever makes a step over into *Cheshire* shall be convinced of this truth as soon as he puts his foot a Shore.

I know nothing is more commonly said, than *Give your Tenant a good Bargain, Set him a long Lease, or a Lease of Lives, and you prevent these Mischiefs; He will Build, Plant, Improve, Live neatly, and surrender your Farm at the Expiration of his time in good Condition.* This may sometimes prove true, but I know by sad experience, that none of these encouragements are sufficient, unless your Tenant be both an understanding Man in the way of Husbandry, and a diligent honest Man; so that it seems necessary to enforce by Laws such a course of Husbandry, as shall constrain others of a contrary Disposition, to thrive and live Comfortably whether they will or no, and at the same time provide that the Landlord receive no Damage by the ill treatment of his Land. I have known some Tenants starve at half the Rent which others have grown rich upon!

But 'tis just People should be instructed, as well as compelled by Laws: At present every Tenant does with his Farm as he pleases (especially they who hold under old Leases) and that is what his Laziness, his Ignorance, or Dishonesty prompts him to, without regard to Covenants; rather setting his Landlord at defiance till the Lease be out, and in the mean time being unconcerned what may be the Event, even then relying, in case of a Suit of Law, upon what he calls a good Jury.

Some Man may say, shall I not manage the Land, which I pay Rent for, according as I think fit? I say, NO. Laws are often, and very wholsomly, prescribed for the Governance of private Property; as in the *Linnen* and

Woolen Manufacture, in the preserving of Beef, Butter, Hides, and Tallow, in the size and condition of Casks, and many other things. Why not for Corn and Land? which Import us as nearly at least, as any of those above mention'd?

If there be any Landlord so gripeing as to turn an old improving good Tenant out of his Farm, at the expiration of his Lease, let him suffer under the Obloquy of his Country, as such Landlords do in *Britain,* provided the Tenant give not the Cause to his Landlord for denying the continuance of his Holding.

For the Tenant must not imagine the Landlord wrongs him by demanding an encrease of Rent proportionable to the current rate of the product of his Farm. If every Barrel of Bread-Corn, Drink-Corn, or Horse-Corn, if Wine, Flesh, Fish and all other necessaries for Housekeeping, stands the Landlord in double now, to what it did thirty or forty Years ago, then the Landlord puts no hardship on his Tenant if he asks, double the old Rent, and if he gets it, 'tis plain the Landlord is not one farthing the Richer.

I have known many good old Tenants complain and cry out of their Landlords unjustly, and in a humour throw up their Farms, rather than comply with such a demand; when another able Tenant has taken it, perhaps at treble the old Rent, then have I seen the old Tenant repent his own oversight, and non-complyance, when it has been too late to remedy it: Tenants should also consider that our Mony is at least one thirteenth part worse now, than it was before the Revolution, when 'twas on the same foot as in *England:* By what steps it came to be otherwise I cannot at present recollect, but 'twas a fatal mistake in those who brought it about (if it were not the Bankers) and those who connived at it; and this Diminution of the value of our Coin, affects only (and very greatly too) all the Landlords in the Kingdom, nor wou'd it be to the disadvantage of the Tenant if set right again, as I could plainly prove if it were proper at this time.

The Tenants to prevent an encrease of Rent upon the determination of their Leases, which they pretend to think is an hardship, or injustice done them by the Landlords, either in mistaken Policy or Spite, fall into the present mischievous methods of ruining both: The Landlord's Land is spoil'd for eight or ten Years, and the Tenant generally misses his aim of renewing his Lease at undervalue; for the common method is this; the Tenant when he finds he cannot renew upon his own Terms, towards the latter end of his Lease, does all he can to destroy his Farm, by turning up all the green Sward of it, and Plowing it all (sometimes even the Meadows) by taking false Crops, Pill-Fallowing,[2] neglecting to Manure it, selling off all the Hay, Straw, and other Fulture of it, not giving it its due Seasons, suffering the Houses, Fences, and other Conveniencies or Ornaments of it to run to decay, without any sufficient Remedy to the Landlords, for all this Waste; the Terms of *Stiff, Staunch* and *Tenantable*, being to be explain'd by a Jury of Farmers, and the Damages given, seldom answering the bare Costs of Suit. These Practices have enforced most Landlords of late, either to endeavour to tye up their Tenants from plowing at all (they being desirous to see the green Side of their Land remain uppermost) or else to take their Estates into their own Hands and Management, and turn Husbandmen themselves, till they can bring their Land into good Heart again, by letting it run waste for four or five Years, or by a good and chargeable Husbandry; so as by Degrees to be fit to bear Corn with profit.

What Gentleman would be at the Expence and Pains of this, cou'd he hope to sett his Lands to honest or improving Tenants, and at so good a Rate as the Improvement of the Kingdom, and the present Price of Provisions bear, in proportion to what they were formerly held at.

I have mentioned some, and will proceed to other of the Practices of Tenants among us, in relation to their Farms; contrary to the Custom of *England,* and of other thriving Countries: The Remedies will appear afterwards more plainly.

In the first Place, He will not be satisfied, unless he has a long Lease of Lives of forty, fifty or sixty Years, that he may sell it; and 'tis rare to find a Tenant in *Ireland,* contented with a Farm of a moderate Size: He pretends he cannot maintain his Family with less than a hundred Acres, nay (if at any distance from Town) two or three hundred Acres. Now I say, that this (for a Plowing Farm) is more than any Man of a moderate Fortune

[2.] *Pill-Fallowing* is a vernacular term for a form of tillage.

and Stock can manage: His Contrivance therefore, is to bring in one or more Partners, or Cottagers, who shall pay him one third more per Acre than he pays by his Lease to his Landlord; he himself not having Mony or Stock to sett his Affairs a going for so large a Quantity of Land. These Partners or Cottagers being not only Beggars and Thieves, but generally Harbourers of all such, are the Destroyers of all Farms: They plow up three Parts of four of the Land, without regard to Seasons or Manuring. They sow false Crops, Pill-fallow, break Fences, cut down Quicksetts and other Trees, for Fireing, or to mend their Carrs,[3] spoil Copses, dig their Turf irregularly in Pits and Holes. These sell their Straw and Hay, which ought to make Fulture and be expended on their Farms; and indeed, seldom have convenient Folds to feed their Beasts, and to collect it in: And if both they and their Principal do not break before the Expiration of the Lease (which is commonly the Case) they sling up the Farm in a much worse Condition, than 'twas in when first taken.

The Remedy for this is, not to sett to any Tenant for too long a Term, nor more Land or a greater Farm than he and his own Family or Servants can manage and wield after a husbandly Manner, with his own Stock and Substance; without his Letting any part of it off to others; and to make it Penal if he does so. And to prescribe some Methods whereby the Landlord may easily recover such Penalties. In *England* you seldom or never hear of such a thing as a Sub-tenant or Tenant's Tenant: Every Man resides on his Farm, and manages it in Person. Whereas here you shall often see three or four Setts of Tenants, one under another, who all live by that Difference (as the Cant was in the *South-Sea*-Cheat)[4] and the last poor miserable Tenant must make what he can of the Farm, by all the evil Usage of it imaginable: Perhaps this poor Sub-tenant's Bargain is to pay double Rent of what the first Tenant is to pay by Lease to the Prime Landlord; and 'tis ten to one, that this Man breaks and runs away, but not till he has destroy'd the Farm, at least, his part of it.

There are a sort of People, and those not of inconsiderable Figure in the World, who have made it their Business to take long Leases of Farms in

[3.] *Quicksetts* (or *quick-sett hedges*) and *carrs:* vernacular words for hedge-setting and agricultural carts, respectively.
[4.] A reference to the South Sea Bubble financial crisis of 1720.

abundance, in several Counties and Provinces, on purpose to Lett them out again to Underlings; these Land-jobbers ought to be discouraged all manner of Ways. Some of them have made vast Estates this Way, I have heard of an Alderman of a considerable Corporation, not far from *Dublin,* who did so. The fleeting under Officers of the Revenue, try to encrease their Income by taking Leases in the Towns where they are employed, and then alienating those Leases for Mony, when they are removed (as they frequently are) to other Places.

In *England* 'tis taken for granted, that a Tenant who comes into a Farm of good Land, with the Grass side uppermost, at the usual Rent of Corn-Land in that Country, and obtains Liberty to break it up, or make his best of it by Plowing it, has a profit during the first four Years equal to the Value of the Inheritance of the Land. Few Landlords in this Kingdom are sensible of this, and therefore do not provide accordingly.

Nothing is more sure, than that twenty Acres rightly distributed and well husbanded, shall yield more profit to the Tenant (and do no harm to the Landlord) than a hundred Acres managed as in *Ireland,* by most of the Farmers there, with infinite Damage to Landlord and Tenant.

Another mischievous Practice of *Irish* Tenants is countenanc'd, by what they call *The Custom of the Country:* In some Parts one way, in other Countries different; the Tenant plows all he can, and sows it the last Year (no matter whether with due regard to the Seasons or not) and then pays only the sixth, eighth or tenth Sheaff for the standing of his Corn. These Customs ought to be abolished, since 'tis certain, that the Land is more damaged this last Year, by this usage of the Tenant, and his carrying off all his last Crop of Straw, than most Landlords are aware of.

The true Time of the Year for a Tenant to enter into his Farm, is about *Michaelmas,*[5] he generally enters to all the Fallows,[6] and pays his Predecessor a known Rate for making them, as he is obliged to do. He enters to all the Manure of the Fold.[7] And tho' by this Method he be a little out of Pocket, by paying his first half Years Rent beforehand, yet he finds his

---

[5.] *Michaelmas:* the season around the 29th of September—one of the quarter days for the payment of rent.
[6.] *Fallows:* ploughed, arable land.
[7.] *Manure of the fold:* enclosure for sheep or cattle.

Accompt in it at long running; it may be in his next Crop. Now in *Ireland*, the Tenant usually enters at *Lady-Day*[8] in *Lent*, or *May-Day*, and has the first Crop with the Straw and Fulture carryed quite off his Farm by *The Custom of the Country*, which impoverishes his Farm, and puts him behind hand extremely. The Remedy, is to order the Commencement of Farms on *Michaelmas-Day* or *Alhollantide*,[9] and to abolish these *Customs of the Country*.

To Sett a Farm to a Manufacturer, Tradesman or Shopkeeper, spoils both the Tradesman and ruins the Farm: For in a little Time, this Manufacturer not being able to mind two different sorts of Business, as they should be minded, is either obliged to quit his Trade and turn absolute Farmer, or else to Sett his Farm (or great part of it) to some neighbouring Farmer, who shall plough his Share for him by the Halves (he not keeping a Plough of his own) and thus he loses one half of his Straw, or sells his Corn growing; both which are a Destruction of his Farm. Now a Manufacturer or Tradesman in the *English* Country Towns, who designs to pursue his Trade, desires no more Land in the Neighbourhood, than will Summer and Winter him two or three Cows, and a Horse or two; for which he commonly pays a very extraordinary Rate.

The Alienation of Leases of Farms, nay even of Leases for Lives, notwithstanding all Covenants in the Leases to the contrary, is another ruinous Practice to the Landlord, who at first Setts his Land to an improving rich Tenant, as he thinks, and within a few Years, or Months, finds his Farm Stock-jobb'd[10] to an Unthrift or a Beggar, who has neither the Skill nor the Will to improve it. If some Clause in a Law cou'd be contrived effectually, to prevent such Alienations, other than to the Wife, Children, or Executors of the first Farmer; it would be of special Service to the Landlord and prevent Land-jobbing. And whereas, in *England*, no Tenant is permitted to sell Hay or Straw, but is obliged on severe Penalties to expend it all upon his Farm, and to make Fulture of it, the like Care ought to be taken to prevent *Irish* Tenants who are not Proprietors of Land, from

[8.] *Lady-Day:* a date fixed by agreement for the payment of rent.

[9.] *Alhollantide* or *Allhallantide:* a vernacularism for the festival of All Saints' Day or Halloween; also, the season of All Saints, essentially late autumn.

[10.] *Farm Stock-jobb'd:* traded without regard to value.

selling their Hay and Straw; and this would hinder the impoverishing of their Farms.

It were a point worthy of Consideration, Whether the forbidding the thatching of Houses with Straw, and instead thereof, to oblige the making use of *Sedg, Slate, Tile,* or *Shingles,* would not, at the same time contribute to the keeping of our Farms in good Plight by the Fulture, and to the Beauty and Conveniency of our Buildings.

The Plowing with Oxen alone, or with Oxen and strong Horses before them, as is the Custom in the best Parts of *England;* shou'd be encouraged in this Kingdom. For tho' an Ox be a slow Beast in the Plough, yet he is sure and even in his Draught, very Manageable and Intelligent, and makes the best Beef after he is past his Work: Whereas, a lame Titt or Garran[11] is good for nothing.

The Fulture which proceed from Oxen and black Cattle, is of the best Sort for Corn-Land; these eat the Straw, and preserves the Hay for Horses and Sheep in hard Winters. The Fulture having first passed thro' the Beasts Bellies, and being well digested when laid on the Land, heartens it extremely: But a thriving Farmer will not content himself with the Dung of his own Fold, but every Time he goes to the Market Town, and carries his Cart loaded with his Corn thither, will (rather than bring it back empty) fill it with good Manure fit for the Use of his Field.

With this Usage, all the Common-field Lands in *England* have continually born good Corn, ever since the *Saxons* time, and will do so till Dooms-day. The Methods there taken are these, every Parish has three large Common-fields for Corn belonging to it (besides the Common for Pasture) wherein every Free-holder has his Share; one six Acres, another four, another eight or ten, according to his Substance; not lying *Contiguous* in each Field, but perhaps in two or three Places, according to the Quality of the Land: Two of these Fields are continually under Corn, *Viz.* one for the Winter Corn, and the other for the Summer: And the third is Fallow, and is well manured for the following Winter Corn-Crop or Barley, and thus it goes round with the three Common-fields: Lands thus well and husbandly managed, will never run out of heart in enclosed

---

[11.] *Titts and garrans:* types of small horses.

Farms; the Tenant has still a better Opportunity of Improvement, and by good and frequent Manuring, may afford to take three Crops before a Fallow: Otherwise, two Crops and a Fallow is the usual way of Husbandry, and 'tis esteemed very good Land which will answer this way of Management: This Method ought to be enjoyned in this Kingdom, and then the Plough wou'd not be at all detrimental to the Estates of Landlords, consequently so many Farms wou'd not be turned to Grass, or taken into the Landlord's own hands; one of which, the Landlords are now enforced to do, unless they are content to lose half the Value of their Estates, by the ill husbandry of their Tenants.

If Gentlemen would so far understand their own Interests, as to be willing to serve upon petty Juries, when Titles to Land, and Damages for Trespasses or Waste, are under Consideration, they would not be so much abused by those meaner Ranks of Men, who generally attend to serve upon Juries, and find their Account by doing so.

The *English* Customs in the Make and Fashion of their Ploughs, Harrows, Plough-geer, Carts, Tumbrils, Wains[12] and Wagons in their broad Ridges, plowing with Oxen, Drains, Beast-houses, Hovels, Stand-racks,[13] Folds in their way of laying down Land to Grass, even folding of Sheep in Pens upon their Corn Lands, and forty other Things necessary to the good Management of our Farms, ought either to be encouraged or enforced by proper Laws: And why should not this be done in these Instances, as well as in those of prohibiting burning Corn in the Straw, Drawing by the Tayl,[14] or the enjoyning the *English* Habit and Language, *&c.* All which, the Wisdom of our Ancestors thought necessary? And if a severe Penalty were put upon all Breakers or Plowers up of Meares and Bounds, whereby the stealing of Land (so common at present in every Village wherein there happens to be many Proprietors) might be prevented, it would be of great Service to the Publick.

And to obviate the evil Consequences which may ensue, upon Farmers

[12.] *Harrow:* a rudimentary plow or sled; *tumbril:* a dung or lumber cart; *wain:* four-wheeled, oxen-drawn wagon.

[13.] *Hovel:* an open shed for cattle or grain; *stand-rack:* drying frame.

[14.] *Drawing by the tayl:* a seventeenth-century Irish practice, since outlawed, in which horses pulled a plough by the tail rather than by means of a harness.

selling, or otherwise disposing of their whole Haggards[15] of Corn, between *Harvest* and *Easter,* whereby the Country has often been in danger of a Famine, before new Corn came in again; may it not be thought adviseable, to erect common Store-houses or Granaries, at the Charges of the Publick, in Cities or great Towns? where a sufficient Store of Corn may be yearly taken in, at the Market Price, after *Harvest* to be sold out again in Time of scarcity, at a profit not exceeding —— *per Cent?* This would always prevent any extraordinary Dearth, and would be of some Gain to the Publick; the common Bakers may be obliged to take of all such Corn, at a Price somewhat lower than Market Rate, before new Corn were brought into the Magazines.

Anciently, all the Guilds and Fraternities of Trades (especially in the City of *London*) were obliged to maintain such publick Granaries for the Use of their Fraternities; and at present, the Cities of *Dantzick, Coningsbery,* and many others in the *East*-Sea, draw a very great Commerce and Profit to themselves; by this Practice these Cities have constantly such a Provision of Corn before hand, that they are able at any Time, to lade upon demand, a hundred great Ships with it; they furnish *Holland,* and all other parts of *Europe* when Corn happens to be scarce: They have three Years Provision beforehand, with convenient large Magazines erected, with all Conveniencies for the better Preservation, Airing, and Winnowing of the Corn weekly, with sworn Officers to attend them; and no Ship needs to tarry above three Days for its full Lading, the want of such Stores, prevents our Commerce for Corn, makes our Markets rise and fall so suddenly and unequally: We have either a Glutt or a Famine before we can look about us.

It would be a great Encouragement to the industrious Farmer, if the payment and gathering of Tythes[16] were put upon a more easy and equal foot in this Kingdom. All who have right to Tythes, should be obliged to sett every Farmer his own Tythe, who would take it at the Rates which may be prescribed. The common Practice is now, to put such an exorbitant Price upon a poor Farmer's Tythe, that although he can best afford it, yet

---

[15.] *Haggard:* a yard or enclosure for storing and thrashing grain.
[16.] *Tythe:* a tenth part of annual agricultural produce paid to the local churchman.

he is not able to pay what is demanded, then some Tythe-jobber[17] (commonly a litigious, worthless wrangling Fellow, a *Papist* and a Stranger) is encouraged to bid high, on purpose to raise the Market: And if the Farmer is constrained, by reason of the Exorbitancy of the Demand, to let this Fellow have the Bargain, this Tythe-jobber puts all the Hardships imaginable on the poor Farmer to make his Mony. The *Bishops Courts* are generally inclinable to be favourable to these Plagues of the Common-Wealth, because they help to inhance the Churches gains; nay, in case they have overstrained themselves, and taken to hard a Bargain, their good Intention is valued, and they are often forgiven one third Part by him that has set them a Work; otherwise they break, having first carryed off so much of the Hay and Straw (consequently of the Fulture) off the Farm, as helps very much to the impoverishing it. There are more just Complaints against such Tythe-jobbers in *Ireland,* ten times over, than there are in *Great Britain.*

Therefore an Act of Parliament to ascertain the Tythe of Hops, now in the Infancy of that great growing Improvement, Flax, Hemp, Turnip Fields, Grass Seeds and dyeing Roots, or Herbs of all Mines, Coals, Minerals, Commons to be taken in, *&c.* seems necessary towards the encouragement of them.

Gentlemen who take to Farm Lands, adjoyning to their Freeholds for the conveniency of themselves or their Tenants wou'd do well to consider whether their claiming and seizing upon any part or parcel of such Farm'd Lands for their own, and refusing to surrender at the expiration of their Leases be of Credit to them; really People will be afraid to accommodate this way, Gentlemen who act as if they thought themselves too great to be cop'd with, and no wise Man will be willing to sett his Land either to his equal or superior.

Farmers or their under Cottagers are very apt now a days to take in, and enclose all the broad High-ways on each side of the Paved Causeys[18] adjoyning to their Farms, to the great disease of Travellers, who otherwise might (in Summer time especially) avoid the rugged Pavement, which is

[17.] *Tythe-jobber:* a trader in tythes.
[18.] *Causey:* a mound or embankment used to retain water in a river or pond; a causeway.

sometimes so narrow, that scarce two Carts can pass by each other with safety.

A Breed of large working Horses, not Racers, ought to be encouraged instead of those Titts or Garrans, which are generally made use of among our Farmers; the neighbouring Gentlemen should keep Stallions, and permit the use of them gratis to their Tenants. There are a set of People called Carrmen, who hold not an Acre of Land, but keep these filthy half starved Titts, either by nightly Stealing their Neighbours Grass and Hay, or by what they can pick up in the Highways, or the bare Commons; these Fellows cut and destroy Quick-sett Hedges, and young Woods, for Wyths, Gads,[19] and other Implements for their Carrs, &c. and therefore ought to be suppressed.

I think it may easily be proved that Commons in general are a Grievance and Nusance to this Kingdom, and serve principally as Seminaries to Beggars, Idlers, and Thieves; so far are they from being a relief to the Poor, that they really make and encourage them: Gentlemen are inclosing them in *England* as fast as they can, and there hardly passes a Session of Parliament there, wherein two or three Acts for taking in particular large Commons, have not the Royal Assent. The primary intention of Commons was not for Beggars, but for the Farmers Cattle, whilst their Field Lands were under Corn: And it has upon Tryals at Law been determined in *England,* that no Man has a right to Herbage on a Common, but such in the Parish or Mannor as hold sufficient Land, there to Winter those Cattle which they graze on the Common in Summer; which Cattle must be *Levant* and *Couchant*[20] on the said Farm Lands; but this is a point which must be left to the Lawyers; as also, whether there can be any such thing as an unstinted Common; I have been assured there cannot, not even in Wilds and Mountains: A brave Fund for one Provision for the Poor might arise from hence.

One hindrance to the conveniency of Farmers (especially of late since the Revolution) is, that very many of the common Roads cross the Country, leading from Village to Village, to Mill, Church, Sea and Market,

[19.] *Wyths* and *gads:* faggots or sticks used for refurbishment of agricultural wagons.

[20.] *Levant* and *couchant:* literally, "rising up and lying down"; a phrase describing the right of common usage on unfenced land.

have been stopp'd up by Gentlemen for the conveniency of their own Estates and Improvements; these have taken the advantage of the unsettled state of late times, and of the fearfulness of *Popish* Tenants, who dare not contest with them, and have really spoiled that intercourse which is so necessary to be kept up between Neighbours for the benefit of the Publick.

I am sorry to find it remarked by *English* Gentlemen who come among us (and I fear too truly) that very many of our Gentlemen of *Ireland,* are constrained to manage their own Lands, and turn their own Husbandmen, that they may avoid the destruction of their Estates by bad Tenants: This forces them in a manner to employ most part of their time in these low Employments and mean Company, to frequent Fairs and Markets, to mind their own Ploughs, Sheep and Cattle; thus they lose the best opportunities of reading and improving their natural Parts, which if cultivated, do not come behind those of our neighbouring Nation; but their Conversation being for the most part with the ordinary rank of Men, they degenerate by degrees; the best Education of many of their Sons, reaching no higher, than to know how to make the most of a Piece of Land. How can the Business of Parliament, the Duty owing to ones Country, and the Value of Publick Liberty, be sufficiently understood, under such a cramp'd, and low Education, help'd by little or no reading? The Consequences of which, are that they grow narrow Spirited, covetous and ungenteel; they are more subject to the snares and temptations of little Employments for themselves or relations, Smiles, good Dinners, Threatnings, *&c.* and in short, their Morals and Principles grow so debas'd, that except it be some Gentlemen of the Gown,[21] and many of the Army (where, I know none that have excell'd them) 'tis a shame to see in so large and plentiful a Kingdom, how low the rate of generous and polite Learning runs among our Nobility and Gentry: 'Tis true, we are told we are Slaves, but it must be our Care not to deserve being so.

The Tythes, or other profits in lieu of Tythes, which are paid by the *Roman Catholicks* to their Parish Priests (over and above what they pay to the Protestant Parson, or his tything Man) are such drains to their Purses,

---

[21.] *Gentlemen of the Gown:* clergymen, priests.

that 'tis a wonder how they can subsist and pay Rent under such an additional burden. I should think it no ill Policy or Husbandry, if the Publick paid the yearly Salaries to the *Popish* Priests, as the *Dutch* do to their Protestant ones, and that the poor Lay *Roman Catholick* Tenants were eas'd of it: This Contribution wou'd amount to no great Sum on the Establishment; five or six great unnecessary Pensions suppress'd, wou'd answer it; and this wou'd be one principal means to engage the Priests (as the *Dutch* do theirs) in the true interest of the Government: This Method has the less to be objected to it, now the *Popish* Priests are registred; but to expect to have a numerous People, without allowing the Exercise of a Religion, is both Tyrannical and Impolitick: Care may be taken at the same time to keep out the Regulars, and the Secular Priests wou'd contribute their assistance towards the doing it.

Now as to *Agriculture,* I should humbly propose, that a School for Husbandry were erected in every County, wherein, an expert Master of the *English* methods, shou'd teach at a fix'd yearly Salary; and that *Tusser*'s old Book of Husbandry shou'd be taught to the Boys, instead of a Primer or Psalter; to read, to copy, and to get it by heart, to which end it might be re-printed and distributed; and let no body object, that 'tis *old English;* we are not teaching Words, but Things: I am sure, 'tis the very best *English* Book of good Husbandry[22] and Housewifry that ever was published, fitted for the use of mean Men and Farmers, and ordinary Families. In these Schools, I wou'd not have any precepts, difference or distinction of Religions taken notice of, and nothing taught, but only Husbandry and good Manners; and that the Children should daily serve GOD, according to their own Religions, this School not being the proper place to make Proselytes in: I doubt not but some such Method as this wou'd make Husband-men, and prevent the increase of the Poor.

In many parts of *Ireland,* more especially near the great City of *Dublin,* the Women and Wives of the poor small Farmers, and Labourers, are generally of little or no Service towards the maintenance of their Fami-

---

[22.] Thomas Tusser (1524–80) was the author of *One Hundreth Pointes of Good Husbandrie* (1557), reprinted in 1561, 1562, 1564, and 1570. He also wrote *Five Hundreth Pointes of Good Husbandrie* (1573), which achieved twenty-one editions, the last in 1848.

lies, not applying themselves to any useful Work, whereby to earn Wages; but if the poor Man fall sick, whose labour put Bread in their Mouths, or if he dye, the whole Family starves; this idle way of Life inclines them to thieving and harbouring of Thieves. In Harvest time, instead of helping to gather in the Corn, they refuse Wages, and find it more profitable to run about the Country, Gleaning or Leasing (as they call it) teaching their Children laziness and wickedness: And their way of Leasing among the very Reapers and Stacks of Corn, ought to be forbidden by a Law, upon penalty of being duck'd, or some other disgraceful corporal Punishment. 'Tis not to be imagined, what great damage this sort of Cattle do to the most industrious Farmers, who (when you find fault with them for permitting it) will shake their heads and answer you, that 'tis a grievance grown so common, 'tis in vain to attempt to remedy it, without the help of a Law; and that they yearly lose near a tenth of their Crop this way. I have seen near a hundred of these Leasers in a Corn-field at once, whilst the Corn has been a Reaping, and whilst the poor Farmer has been chasing them out of one corner of his Field, they have poured in as fast at another, and carried off all they cou'd lay their hands on, even out of the Sheaves and Stacks.

Now in *England*, the Women and Children will assist at Harvest work, and earn their groat and two pence[23] *per* day, and when they Glean, they are not permitted to begin, till the Corn is Carted out of the Field: But whilst People find their account much more in Stealing *impunè*, than in Working, they will never Work, let the Season of the year be never so rainy or doubtful.

I shou'd think it no sin, in bad Harvest Weather, to constrain and oblige People to Work on Holy-days, nay sometimes on Sunday's afternoon, for by the same reason that an Ox or an Ass might be helped out of a Ditch, by the strictest observers of the Sabbath, a Field of good Corn in imminent danger of spoiling, may be secured by us, who lay not so great stress upon the observation of Sundays: I am sure they are generally spent in sinful Employments: No one who can think well of a Book of Sports

---

[23.] *Groat and two pence:* an amount originally denoting one-eighth ounce of silver but in practical usage meaning a small amount of money.

for that day, can make any rational objection to this necessary and charitable Work.

The want of Barns and Folds, with conveniencies of Beast-houses, Stables, Hovels, and Stand-Racks; the want of proper Husbandry Geer, *viz.* Carts, right Ploughs and Harrows, well contriv'd Drains, broad Ridges, and twenty other things towards the Improvement of *Agriculture,* are but too visible in this Kingdom; the number and use of all which, will be learnt by reading *Tusser*'s Book of Husbandry; as also the several sorts of Manure, *viz.* Lime, Sea Sand, scourings of old Ditches and Ponds, Sea Weed, *&c.* according to the situation, and suited to the several different Soils: All this and much more may be met with in old *Tusser*'s Book, which therefore cannot be too often recommended.

The Acts of Parliament for encouraging Planting and preserving Trees, and obliging Tenants to the due performance of Covenants (which now they generally neglect) want therefore to be reinforced. This in process of time wou'd make this naked Kingdom full of Fruit Trees, and replenish it with necessary Timber Trees, which now it wants to a degree, not known elsewhere in *Europe.* We shall soon see an end of Tanning and Building, not so much as a Ship or a Boat will be upon the Stocks, if very speedy and effectual care be not taken in this most necessary point. We must not depend upon the Woods of *Norway,* which upon any Quarrel between Princes wou'd fail us, and (without that) will be quite consumed in one Generation, being already generally cut down, especially near the Sea side; but in the mean while, care ought to be taken of such Buildings as we have, and the Dilapidations and waste committed by Tenants on Farms, ought to be prevented and punished. There are Laws in *England* against Farm Houses being demolished, which oblige even the very Proprietors of Estates.

What if a Praemium were rais'd upon the several Counties, and given at Assizes time, in proportion, to the five best Husband-men in that County, for four or five Years to come? He that cou'd bring the best proof of Increase of Crop, Goodness of his Corn, Diligence in Manuring, *&c.* and all this, thro' his following the prescribed good Methods of Husbandry, shou'd be intitled to the best reward, and the other four in their Order; this to be determined by a Grand Jury of Gentlemen. I remember such a

Law for the three best pieces of Linnen Cloath, in each County; but this Law was enervated by the partiality of young Jury Men, who gave the Praemium to the three handsomest Girls, according to the interest they cou'd make with the Body of the County.

The keeping of our Corn and Hay so long abroad in Stacks, and in the Fields, is a great waste: As 'tis never practised in *England,* so it ought to be forbidden here; where one often sees, one fourth part, both of Corn and Hay, destroyed in the Fields before 'tis carried home.

All Farmers and Cottagers in places where firing is scarce, and cannot be had for Labour, ought to be obliged (or their Landlords for them) to lay in such a competent store yearly, about *Michaelmas,* of Coals, Turf, Wood or Furrs,[24] as shall serve them during six Months in Winter: And the Constable of each Parish ought to make a return about *Allhallan-tide,* to two Justices of Peace in the Neighbourhood, of all the Farmers and Cottagers in their several Parishes, who have neglected this; which Justices should be impowered to take effectual Measures for the Performance. This would prevent the cutting down of Trees and Hedges for Firing, the cutting or plucking of the Hawm[25] of our Corn Fields, and the gathering of the Cow Dung, which ought to be part of the Manure of those Fields; and several other Mischiefs arising from the want of Firing of that sort of People, who depend upon such kind of Trespasses, for all they shall burn in the Winter.

A Penalty might be put upon all menders of Carrs, and all makers of Gadds, With's and other Carr-tackle, with young Trees or Hedg-Inclosures: And to this Purpose, every Farmer might be oblig'd to sow a Proportion of Hempseed sufficient to furnish him with such Tackle: And those who hold no grazing Land, or not sufficient, should be hindred from keeping Carrs and Horses; the Trade of such being no other than down-right Thievery.

The Parish Cesses[26] are now made generally, and applotted either by the meanest sort of People, or by Persons interested: And the Mony given

[24.] *Furrs:* gorse; a type of spiny evergreen shrub with yellow flowers.
[25.] *Hawm:* stems or stalks of peas, beans, and corn; also straw.
[26.] *Cesses:* cess pools or pits; covered communal cistern for waste water and sewage.

at Quarter-Sessions and at King's-Bench, for High-ways, &c. is for the most part put into designing Mens Hands, who will bribe a Sub-sheriff to be put upon the Grand Jury, with the Prospect of being made an Overseer; whereby our High-ways (which if they be good, are a great Encouragement to the Farmer) become scarce passable in Winter: If Gentlemen for their own sakes, would take part of this Trouble on themselves, the Country would not be so much abused as it now generally is. The like caution might be taken, in regard to Church-Wardens, Overseers of the Poor, Sacrament-Money, and other Charities, that all should go the right Way, as they are intended: I doubt not but Gentlemen will understand what I mean. I look upon the frequency of Briefs to be a Grievance, and since the Methods of obtaining them is no secret, I esteem the Way of collecting the Monies for them (not as formerly, at the Church-doors, but in the Face of the whole Congregation, in some remarkable Part of the Divine-Service, when all the Parishioners are likeliest to be present) to be an Invention within my Memory, calculated to work, rather on the Modesty, than the Charity of the Congregation.

The Mischief of many Holy-days, not only of the *Popish* ones, but even of many of our Church Holy-days, is really greater than most People are sensible of. 'Tis proclaimed on Sunday from the Desk, that such and such a Day in the following Week is appointed to be kept holy. And what is the Effect of this? Why truly, to give Warning, that all those in the Parish, who have a mind to be idle, drunk or debauch'd, may take that Day, as the fittest Opportunity to put their wicked Designs in Execution. I appeal to all the Clergymen in *Ireland,* whether what I say, be not constantly and literally true. I wish all the Saints Days were let slip, with all my Heart, and that People might be left at liberty to keep open Shop, plow, sow, reap and follow their lawful Trades on those Days; they would serve God better, and their Country and private Families, than now they do. As for the more solemn Days, of *Christmas,* and a few others, they ought to be observed by Devotion, not Luxury. I once heard a Merchant of *Leghorn* arguing, why the *Dutch* must necessarily be richer than the *Italians,* who are the skilfullest Merchants, and best Accountants in the World. Can it be otherwise? (*said he*) the *Dutch* have about a hundred Days more in the Year to get Mony in, than we are permitted to have by our Religion;

and this overballances all other Advantages we have over them in Parts, Sobriety and Stock.

Great Indulgence ought to be shewn to Farmers, and all sorts of Poor, who are overburden'd with many Children; these should be eas'd in their Taxes, Parish Cesses and Offices: I mean such Children, as are the product of Matrimony; but if they be such, as are every where permitted, most shamefully to live under Hedges, in Ditches and Hutts, worse than Hogsties; from whence you shall often see creeping out like Vermin, whole swarms of Bastards; the Produce of Adultery and Incest, and whereof, there are more in the Neighbourhood of *Dublin,* than any other part of the World; a Race of People like *Gypsies,* which no Priest takes any care of; yet are the Seminaries of all Rebellions, dangerous in Plague Times, revengeful at all Times, in burning Barns and Houses of such as are not kind to them, and Harbourers of Robbers: I say, if they be such sort of People, the Magistrate is obliged to root them out, or send them home, if they have a home; but they are most commonly *Aborigines,* the Product of that very Ditch where you find them, who would be hard put to it, to tell you the Relation they have to each other, all the Rules of Affinity and Consanguinity being confounded. These should be shipped off to the wildest of our Plantations abroad, and left there to their chance in this World, and the Children of them should be placed for long Terms of Years with Rope-makers, Coblers, Smiths, Owners of Ships, and other hard working Trades.

And now, that I have made mention of Ships, and His Grace our Lord Lieutenant has recommended to our Care, some Provision for the Poor, let our Fishery (in God's Name) find Employment for many thousands of them, in the Seas round about this Island. I need not mention how many natural Advantages we enjoy beyond any part of *Europe,* proper for this great and most beneficial Trade, the very fountain of Riches, the encrease of Seamen, and the food of Land-men: And if this of our Fishery happens to be annexed to a certain Monopoly and Company of Men, who design nothing less than to put it in Practice; but like the Dog in the Manger, which neither eats Hay himself, nor suffers the working Horse to do it, let, I say, Application be made speedily, to set us at liberty, that no Monopolies may obstruct the right of Nature and Charity: If we have any Freedom, let some Use be made of it, and the Application of it be this way.

A Residency of our Protestant Clergy in their Parishes, wou'd soon make Protestant Congregations, and increase those that already are made, and no effectual care can be taken of the Poor, till the Parson bestows his pains upon the Parish, and shall rather endeavour to make Protestants, than his Parish a perfect Sinecure, as some have done: And truly in my Opinion, all Sinecures are publick Grievances: The no Labourer is worthy of no Hire. I do not wonder at the little Scruple that is made of defrauding such a Parson of his Tythes. Whereas, I look upon it as one of the most crying pieces of Injustice, to cheat a worthy residing Clergyman of what he is firmly intitled to, by the Laws of the Land: Not *jure divino;* unless he could prove the Jewish Law binds Protestants. I cannot bear with Patience, that any Man shou'd pretend to have a higher or better Title to his Estate, than I have to mine.

Let Gentlemen consider, whether it be equal, that a small Lease of Lives, worth barely forty Shillings *per Annum*, should make such a Freehold, as gives a Title to choose a Representative in Parliament; when a large and beneficial Lease for a Term of Years, sets the Lessee only upon the Foot of one of the *Nomine censi*[27] among the *Romans,* who had no Suffrage, nor any part in the Government of the Common-Wealth; to me it looks a little oddly.

By the little Care that is taken in the Connection of the foregoing Paragraphs, which are put down just as they came into the Writers Head, the Reader may easily perceive, that either the want of Leisure, or want of Health, or a too forward Zeal to publish something speedily, which might be of Service to the Country, has prevailed with the Author of these few Pages, beyond any Consideration of his Reputation.

[27.] *Nomine censi:* merely named on the census without privilege.

Selected Sources Cited in *Francogallia*

This bibliography identifies a selection of most of the less obvious sources Hotman used in his *Francogallia*. Molesworth was reasonably accurate in his reproduction of the citations from these works, but his translation, like the original text, does not commonly identify the works beyond a short title and a book or chapter. For many of these citations the sources are fairly obvious: the classical works of Aristotle, Plato, Cicero, Tacitus, Sallust, and others were staples for the reading public, even of the eighteenth century. Modern forms of names are used here: thus, for example, Molesworth's "Eguinarthus" is our "Einhard." Less obvious were a range of medieval and early modern references. This list offers a sense of the range of material cited. A full and precise bibliography can be found in Geisey and Salmon's (GS *Franc.*) edition of Hotman's work at pp. 545–61.

Ado of Vienne. Archbishop ca. 800–875.
Adonis Viennensis Archiepiscopi breviarium Chronicorum ab origine mundi ad sua usque tempora, etc., in St. Gregory Bishop of Tours. *Gregorii Turonici Historiae Francorum libri decem, etc.* (1561).

Aemilius, Paulus. Historian; fl. ca. 1455–1529.
P. Aemylii . . . De rebvs gestis Francorvm libri X, et Chronicon de iisdem regibvs, a Pharamundo vsqve ad Henricvm II. By I. Du Tillet (Paris: Apud A. Paruum, 1548).

Agathias. Historian; fl. ca. 536–94.
Agathyus de bello Gotthorum et aliis peregrinis historiis per Christophorum Persona . . . e Graeco in Latinum traductus (1531).

Aimon of Fleury. Abbot; ca. 950–1008.
Aimoni monachi qui antea annonii nomine editus est, Historiae Francorum lib. V.
(Paris, 1567).

Ambrose, Bishop; d. 397.
Epistolae (Milan, 1490).

Ausonius. Roman poet; 309–395.
Ausonii Peonii poetae disertissimi epigrammata. Edited by Julius Aemilius Fer-
rarius (per Ioannem de Cereto alias Tacuinum: Venetiis, die. xi. Augusti,
1494).

Beatus Rhenanus. Historian; 1485–1547.
Rerum Germanicarum libri tres (Basel, 1531).

Bouchart, Alain. Historian; ca. 1478–1530.
*Les chroniques annalles des pays d'angleterre et bretaigne: contenant les faictz et
gestes des roys et princes qui ont regne oudit pays et choses dignes de memoire . . .
depuis Brutus iusques au . . . Françoys II.* (Paris, 1531).

Bouchet, Jean [Joannes Buchettus]. Historian; 1476–1550.
*Les Annales d'Aquitaine: faicts et gestes en sommaire des Roys de France & d'Angle-
terre, et pais de Naples et de Milan* (Poitiers, 1557).

Budé, Guillaume. Historian; 1467–1540.
Annotationes in 24 Pandectarum libros (Lugduni, 1546).
De asse et partibus eius libri quinque (Paris, 1524).

Cassiodorus. Roman politician; ca. 485–575.
Magni Aurelii Cassiodori Variarum libri XII, item De anima liber unus (Augusta,
1533).

Cedrenus, Georgius. Historian; 11th century.
*Georgii Cedreni Annales, siue Historiae ab exordio mundi ad Isacium Comnenum
usque compendium* (Basel, 1566?).

Commines, Philippe de. Chronicler; 1447–1511.
*Les Mémoires De Messire Philippe De Commines, Chevalier, Seigneur d'argenton:
sur les principaux faicts & gestes de Louis onzieme & de Charles huictième, son
filz, Roy de France* (Lyon: de Tournes, 1559).

Connan, François [Franciscus Conanus]. Lawyer; 1508–51.
Commentariorum iuris civilis libri X (Paris, 1558).

Corpus Juris Canonici (Paris: Guillard, 1541–1550).

Du Bellay, Guillaume [William Belay]. 1491–1543.
Epitome de l'antiquite des Gaules et de France. Plus sont adioustées une oraison et deux epistres (Paris, 1556).

Einhard. French courtier; ca. 770–840.
Vita et gesta Karoli Magni (Cologne: I. Soter, 1521).

Eutropius. Historian; 4th century.
Breviarium historiae Romanae (Pictaves, 1553).

Frederick II, 1215–1250.
Placita principium seu constitutiones regni Neapolitani cum glossis (Lyon, 1534).

Froissart, Jean. Chronicler; ca. 1337–ca. 1405.
Chroniques (Lyon, 1559).

Gaguin, Robert. Historian; 1433–1501.
De Francorum regum gestis (Paris, 1528).
Rerum Gallicarum annales (Frankfort, 1577).

Gilles, Nicolas. Historian; d. 1503.
Chroniques et annales de France (Paris, 1551).

Godfrey of Viterbo. Chronicler; ca. 1120–ca. 1198.
Pantheon, siue, Vniuersitatis libri: qui chronici appellantur, XX, omnes omnium seculoru[m] & gentium, tam sacras quàm prophanas historias complectentes (Basel, 1559).

Chroniques de France (Paris, Jean Maurand for Antoine Vérard, 1493).

Gregory of Tours. French bishop; ca. 538–94.
Gregorii Turonici historiae Francorum libri decem . . . appendix item sive liber XI (Basel, 1568).

Hostiensis. Canonist; ca. 1200–1271.
Decretum D. Gratiani, vniuersi iuris canonici pontificias constitutiones, et canonicas breui compendio complectens (Venice, 1566).

Joinville, Jean. Historian; 1225–1317.
L'histoire & cronique du treschrestien roy S. Loys, IX. du nom, & XLIIII. Roy de France (Poitiers: De l'Imprimerie d'Enguilbert de Marnef, 1561).

Krantz, Albert. Theologian; ca. 1450–1517.
Chronica regnorum aquilonarium, Daniae, Suetiae, Norvagiae (Argent., apud Ioannem Schottum, 1548).

La Marche [Lamarc], Olivier de. Chronicler; 1425–1502.
Les mémoires (Lyon, 1562).

Landulphus Sagax. Chronicler; fl. 1000.
Historiae miscellae a Paulo Aquilegiensi diacono primum collectae, post etiam a Landulpho Sagaci (Basel, 1569).

Marinaeus, Lucius. Historian; d. 1533.
Cronica d'Aragon (Valencia, 1524).
Marinei opus de rebus Hispaniae memorabilibus (Compl., 1533).

Monstrelet, Enguerran de. Chronicler; ca. 1390–1453.
Le premier, second, tiers volume de enguerran de monstrellet (Paris, 1518).

Mutius, Henricus. Humanist; 16th century.
De Germanorum prima origine, moribus, institutis (Basel, 1539).

Nauclerus, Johannes. Chronicler; d. 1510.
Chronica res memorabiles saeculorum omnium et gentium (Cologne, 1544).

Orosius. Historian; 5th century.
Pauli Orosii . . . Historiarum libri septem (Cologne, 1542).

Otto of Freising. Chronicler; ca. 1114–58.
Ottonis Phrisingensis Episcopi, viri clarissimi, Rerum ab origine mundi ad ipsius usq[ue] tempora gestarum, libri octo (Argentorati, 1515).

Pape, Guy. Jurist; 15th century.
Decisiones Guid. Pape: decisiones parlamenti Dalphinalis Grationopolis (Lyon, 1541).

Papon, Jean. Lawyer; 1505–90.
Du recueil d'arrêts notables des cours souveraines de France (Lyon, 1569).

Paul the Deacon. Historian; ca. 720–99.
Pauli Diaconi Ecclesiae Aquilegiensis Historiographi percelebris De origine et gestis Regum Langobardoru[m] Libri VI (Paris, 1514).

Petrus de Vinea. Diplomat, lawyer; 1190–1246.
Epistolarum . . . libri sex (Basel, 1566).

Procopius. Historian; ca. 500–565.
De bello italico aduersus Gothos (Aquila, ca. 1485).

Ritius, Michael. Historian; fl. 1500.
Michaelis Ritii . . . De regibus Francorum: lib. III (Basel, 1534).

Salvian. Bishop of Marseilles; ca. 400–484.
D. Saluiani Massyliensis Episcopi, De uero iudicio et prouidentia Dei, ad S. Salonium Episcopu[m] Vienensem libri VIII (Basel, 1530).

Seyssel, Claude de. Historian; 1450–1520.
La grand monarchie de France (Paris, 1541).

Sidonius Apollinaris. Poet; ca. 423–80.
Epistolae et carmina (1542).

Sigebert [of Gembloux]. Benedictine monk; 1030–1112.
Chronicon (Paris, 1513).

Theodosian Code. 5th century.
Codicis Theodosiani Lib. XVI, quam emendatissimi, adjectis quas certis locis fecerat Aniani Interpretationibus. Novellarum Theodosii, Valentiniani, Martiani, Maioriani, Seueri, Libri V. Cum Aniani Interpretationibus. Haec omnia curante Jacobo Cuiacio (Lugduni, 1566).

Trithemius, Johannes. Theologian; 1462–1516.
Compendium, sive Breviarum primi volominis annalium, sive historiarum, de origine Regum & gentis Francorum (Cologne, 1539).

Turnebus, Adrianus. Scholar; 1512–65.
Adversariorum (Paris, 1565).

Turpin, John. Archbishop of Rheims; d. ca. 800.
Germanicarum rerum quatuor celebriores vetustioresque chronographi, earum descriptionem ab orbe condito vsque ad tempora Henrici IIII (Frankfurt, 1566).

Urspergensis [Buchard von Ursberg], Abbot; ca. 1177–1231.
Chronicon Abbatis Vrspergen. A Nino Rege Assyriorvm Magno (1515).

Virgil, Polydore. Historian; 1470–1555.
Polydori Vergilii Urbinatis Anglicae historiae libri vigintiseptem (Basel, 1570).

Zonaras, Joannes. Byzantine historian; 12th century.
Annales (Lutetia, 1567).
Compendium historiarum (Basel, 1557).

Zosimus. Historian; fl. ca. 490–510.
Zosimi comitis et exaduocati fisci Historiae nouae libri VI (Basel, 1576).

Zurita, Jeronimo. Historian; 1512–80.
Anales de la Corona de Aragón (Zaragoza, 1580).

LOEB CLASSICAL LIBRARY

Ammianus Marcellinus. *History.* Translated by J. C. Rolfe. 3 vols. Cambridge, Mass.: Harvard University Press, 1935.

Appian. *Roman History.* Translated by Horace White. 4 vols. Cambridge, Mass.: Harvard University Press, 1913.

Caesar. *Bellum Gallicum* [*The Gallic War*]. Translated by H. J. Edwards. Cambridge, Mass.: Harvard University Press, 1917.

Cicero. *Cicero* vol. 3. *On the Orator, Books 1–2.* Translated by E. W. Sutton and H. Rackham. Cambridge, Mass.: Harvard University Press, 1959.

———. *Cicero* vol. 4. *On the Orator, Book 3. On Fate. Stoic Paradoxes. Divisions of Oratory.* Translated by H. Rackham. Cambridge, Mass.: Harvard University Press, 1959.

———. *Cicero* vol. 18. *Tusculan Disputations.* Translated by J. E. King. Cambridge, Mass.: Harvard University Press, 1945.

Ovid. *Tristia. Ex Ponto.* Translated by A. L. Wheeler. Revised by G. P. Goold. Cambridge, Mass.: Harvard University Press, 1988.

Plato. *Laws 1–6.* Translated by R. G. Bury. Cambridge, Mass.: Harvard University Press, 1926.

———. *Laws 7–12.* Translated by R. G. Bury. Cambridge, Mass.: Harvard University Press, 1926.

Scriptores Historiae Augustae. Translated by David Magie. 3 vols. Cambridge, Mass.: Harvard University Press, 1922.

Suetonius. *Suetonius* vol. 1. *Lives of the Caesars I.* Edited and translated by J. C. Rolfe. Cambridge, Mass.: Harvard University Press, 1951.

Suetonius. *Suetonius* vol. 2. *Lives of the Caesars II.* Edited and translated by J. C. Rolfe. Cambridge, Mass.: Harvard University Press, 1951.

Tacitus. *Agricola. Germania. Dialogue on Oratory. Agricola:* translated by M. Hutton; revised by R. M. Ogilvie. *Germania:* translated by M. Hutton; revised by E. H. Warmington. *Dialogue on Oratory:* translated by W. Peterson; revised by M. Winterbottom. Cambridge, Mass.: Harvard University Press, 1970.

———. *Annals, Books 4–6, 11–12.* Translated by John Jackson. Cambridge, Mass.: Harvard University Press, 1937, 1951.

———. *Annals, Books 13–16.* Translated by John Jackson. Cambridge, Mass.: Harvard University Press, 1937, 1951.

———. *Histories, Books 4–5. Annals, Books 1–3.* Translated by Clifford H. Moore and John Jackson. Cambridge, Mass.: Harvard University Press, 1962.

Ordonnance pour les Rangs du Royaume de Danemarck

ORDONNANCE
Pour les RANGS du Royaume de DANEMARCK.

I.

*Les Enfans naturels des Rois.

II.

1. *Le Grand Chancelier.
2. *Le Grand Tresorier, dit Schatz-meister.
3. *Le Grand Connêtable de Norwegue.
4. *Le General Marêchal de Camp.
5. Le General Admiral.
6. Les Comtes qui sont Conseillers Privez.
7. Les Chevaliers de l'Elephant qui sont Conseillers Privez, ou qui tiennent même rang avec eux.
8. *Les autres Connêtables.
9. Le Vice-Chancelier.
10. *Le Vice-Tresorier.
11. Les Vice-Connêtables.
12. Les autres Conseillers Privez.

III.

1. *Le Grand Maistre de l'Artillerie.
2. *Le Grand Marêchal Lieutenant.
3. Le General Admiral Lieutenant.
4. Les Generaux de Cavalerie, & d'Infanterie.
5. Les Generaux Lieutenants de Cavalerie & d'Infanterie.

IV.

1. Les Comtes qui sont faits Comtes, ou naturalisez par le Roy.
2. Les Barons qui sont faits Barons, ou naturalisez par le Roy; & ensuite les Chevaliers de Dannebrug, ou Cordons Blancs.

V.

1. *Le Grand Marêchal de la Cour.
2. *Le Premier Secretaire Privé, & d'Etat.
3. Le Premier Gentilhomme de la Chambre.
4. Le Grand Maistre des Ecuries.
5. Le Grand Veneur.
6. *Le Grand Echanson.

VI.

1. Les Conseillers d'Etat.
2. Les Conseillers de la Justice.
3. Les Commandeurs des Dioceses, & le Tresorier.

VII.

1. Les Generaux Majors, les Admiraux, le General Commissaire de l'Armée, les Colonels des Gardes du Corps ou Trabans.
2. Les Brigadiers.
3. Le Marêchal de la Cour.

VIII.

1. Les Conseillers de la Chancellerie. Les Envoyez Extraordinaires du Roy, & le Maistre des Ceremonies.
2. Les Conseillers de la Chambre des Comptes, le Procureur General.

3. Les Conseillers de Guerre.

4. Les Conseillers de l'Admirauté.

5. Les Conseillers de Commerce.

IX.

1. Le Sur-Intendant de Seeland.

2. Le Confesseur du Roy.

3. Le Recteur de l'Academie, l'année qu'il est Recteur; le President de la Ville de Copenhague.

X.

1. Les Colonels des Regimens des Gardes à Cheval & à Pied, les Vice-Admiraux, les Colonels de l'Artillerie.

2. Les autres Colonels de Cavalerie ou d'Infanterie.

3. Les Lieutenans Colonels des Gardes du Corps ou Trabans, & après eux les Bailliffs.

XI.

1. Les Gentilshommes de la Chambre du Roy & de la Reine.

2. Le Maistre de l'Ecurie.

3. Le Veneur du Roy.

4. Le Secretaire de la Chambre du Roy.

5. Le Secretaire de la Milice.

6. Le Grand Payeur.

XII.

1. Les Assesseurs de la haute Justice; les Conseillers d'Assistance en Norwegue, & les Sur-Intendans des autres Provinces.

2. Les Juges Provinciaux.

XIII.

1. Les Generaux Auditeurs, les Maistres Generaux des Quartiers.

2. Les Lieutenans Colonels, Scout-by-nachts, & Majors des Gardes du Corps a Trabans.

XIV.

1. Les Assesseurs de la Chancelerie, & de la Justice de la Cour de Norwegue.
2. Les Assesseurs du Consistoire, les Bourgmeisters de Copenhague, & le Medecin du Roy.
3. Les Assesseurs de la Chambre des Comptes, & après eux les Commissaires des Provinces.
4. Les Assesseurs du College de Guerre.
5. Les Assesseurs du College de l'Admirauté.
6. Les Assesseurs du College du Commerce.

XV.

Les Maistres de Cuisine, les Gentilshommes de la Cour, les Generaux Adjutans, les Majors, les Capitaines des Gardes à Cheval, les Capitaines Commandeurs des Vaisseaux.

XVI.

1. Les Secretaires de la Chancelerie, & de la Justice.
2. Le Secretaire de la Chambre des Comptes.
3. Le Secretaire du College de Guerre.
4. Le Secretaire de l'Admirauté.
5. Le Secretaire du Commerce.

Il y a à observer que quand plusieurs charges sont nommées ensemble, & qu'elles ne sont pas distinguées de quelque numero à part, ils prendront le rang entre eux selon qu'ils sont premiers en charge.

Les Ministres du Roy qui possedent quelques charges qui ne sont pas nommées dans cette Ordonnance, retiendront le même rang qu'ils ont eu jusques icy; & ceux à qui le Roy a déja donné ou donnera le rang de Conseiller Privé, joüiront du même rang que s'ils l'étoient effectivement.

Ceux qui possedent effectivement quelques charges, auront le rang avant ceux qui en ont seulement le titre, & ne font point de fonction.

Ceux que le Roy dispense de ne plus exercer leurs charges, retiendront pourtant le même rang qu'ils avoient eu exerçant leurs charges; & si quelqu'un prend une autre charge de moindre rang que sa premiere n'étoit, il retiendra pourtant le rang de la premiere.

Les Femmes se regleront ainsi: Après les Comtesses suivront les Gouvernantes, & Demoiselles de la Chambre, & de la Cour, pendant qu'elles sont en service; après elles les Femmes de Conseillers Privez, & de ceux qui tiennent rang avec eux; ensuite les Baronesses & autres Femmes selon la condition de leurs maris, tant de leur vivant qu'après leur mort, pendant qu'elles demeurent veuves.

La Noblesse qui n'a point de charge, & les Capitaines de Cavalerie & d'Infanterie, & autres persones ecclesiastiques & seculiers, tiendront le pas entre eux comme ils ont fait auparavant.

Sur quoy tous auront à se regler sous peine de la perte de la faveur Royale. Et si contre toute esperance se trouve quelqu'un qui de sa propre authorité fasse quelque chose contre cette Ordonnance, il payera tout aussi-tôt qu'il sera convaincu d'un tel crime l'amende de mille Reichs-Thalers; & outre, sera poursuivi par le General Fiscal du Roy, comme violateur des Ordres Royaux.

Fait à Copenhague, le 31 Decembre 1680.

INDEX

Molesworth's spelling in *An Account of Denmark* is not always consistent (Brandenburgh, Brandenburg), and he sometimes uses archaic or idiosyncratic forms (*Iseland* for *Iceland*). While the text necessarily retains his original usage, the index generally uses modern conventions, with Molesworth's alternative spellings cross-referenced or added in square brackets where necessary for the sake of clarity.

This book is set in Adobe Caslon Pro, a modern adaptation by Carol Twombly of faces cut by William Caslon, London, in the 1730s. Caslon's types were based on seventeenth-century Dutch old-style designs and became very popular throughout Europe and the American colonies.

This book is printed on paper that is acid-free and meets the requirements of the American National Standard for Permanence of Paper for Printed Library Materials, z39.48-1992. ∞

Book design by Louise OFarrell
Gainesville, Florida
Typography by Tseng Information Systems, Inc.
Durham, North Carolina
Printed and bound by Worzalla Publishing Company
Stevens Point, Wisconsin